# SPEEDWAY

## IN THE THAMES VALLEY

# SPEEDWAY
## IN THE THAMES VALLEY

*Robert Bamford and Glynn Shailes*

TEMPUS

First published 2002

PUBLISHED IN THE UNITED KINGDOM BY:

Tempus Publishing Ltd
The Mill, Brimscombe Port
Stroud, Gloucestershire GL5 2QG

PUBLISHED IN THE UNITED STATES OF AMERICA BY:

Tempus Publishing Inc.
2A Cumberland Street
Charleston, SC 29401

Tempus books are available in France and Germany from the following addresses:

Tempus Publishing Group
21 Avenue de la République
37300 Joué-lès-Tours
FRANCE

Tempus Publishing Group
Gustav-Adolf-Straße 3
99084 Erfurt
GERMANY

British Library Cataloguing in Publication Data.
A catalogue record for this book is available from the British Library.

ISBN 0 7524 2408 4

Typesetting and origination by Tempus Publishing.
PRINTED AND BOUND IN GREAT BRITAIN.

# CONTENTS

Acknowledgements                                              6

Introduction                                                 7

1. Oxford                                                    9

2. Reading                                                 111

3. Swindon                                                 197

# ACKNOWLEDGEMENTS

There are numerous people to thank for their help in the production of this book, starting with the various photographers, whose wonderful images have enhanced the finished product no end, namely Les Aubrey, Neil Ferguson, the late Ralph Jackson, Terry Onslow, Mike Patrick, Bill Taylor, Alf Weedon and the late Wright Wood. There are possibly some pictures where the photographer is not known, and we would also like to acknowledge them too.

Grateful thanks are due to Roger Beaman, Colin Goddard, Jeff Hatswell, Roger Hulbert, Dick Jarvis, John Jarvis, Tony Lethbridge, Roger Lewis, Geoff Parker, John Sampford, Bryan Seery, George Sheridan, Dave Stallworthy, Ian Steel, Barry Stephenson, Steve Thorn and Barry Wallace, all of whom have contributed over the years with the checking of heat details and the loan of programmes when required.

Many thanks are also due to people who have supported and encouraged various speedway projects over the years, these include Dave Armstrong, Nick Barber, Eric Barnes, Mick Bird, Pat Bliss, Terry Cheney, Colin Clarke, Max Connor, Brian Cox, Jack Cupido, Billy Douglas, Nick Dyer, Dave Eaton, Keith Farman, Graham Fraser, John Gaisford, Jimmy Grant, Pete Hackett, Stephanie Hale, John Hall, Steve Harland, Les Hawkins, Yvonne Hawkins, Paul Hawthorne, Graham Haynes, Jim Henry, Bryan Horsnell, Ted Humphrey, Mike Hunter, Jeremy Jackson, Matt Jackson, Dave James, Alan Jones, Howard Jones, Roger Last, Keith Lawson, Mike Leach, Ian Lewis, Peter Lipscomb, Hywel Lloyd, Jimmy McIntyre, Charles McKay, Trevor Miles, Peter Morrish, Ian Moultray, Bob Norman, Colin Parker, Fred Paul, Adrian Pavey, Dave Payne, Martin Phillips, Robin Playsted, Andy Povey, Bob Rowe, Peter Shiston, John Smart, Peter Stone, Tim Sugar, Norrie Tait, Mark Tregale, Dave Wall, Eric Watson, Bob Wayte, Gary Weldon, Alan Whale and Dave Wright.

# INTRODUCTION

As an area, the Thames Valley is somewhat difficult to define, but in speedway terms, there have only ever been three main teams that can be considered for such a publication: Oxford, Reading and Swindon. The fourth contender, California, has been briefly included in the Reading section of this book.

All three tracks have given long and continuous service to speedway, and have enjoyed many highs and lows along the way. There has always been local rivalry between the three teams and their supporters, mainly on a friendly level but very occasionally boiling over as in all sports where the opposition is just up the road.

Oxford first opened at their Sandy Lane venue in 1939, so they have completed the most seasons of operation out of the three Thames Valley tracks. That initial burst of activity came to a close in 1941, but Oxford reopened their doors in 1949 and have run continously ever since, right up to the present day. The Cheetahs, as they have mainly been known throughout their existence, have enjoyed six league titles during that time, the latest being a glorious Elite League campaign in 2001.

Many of the sport's greatest riders have donned an Oxford race jacket; names like Simon Wigg, Hans Nielsen, Ronnie Genz, Arne Pander, Jack Geran, Eddie Reeves, Marvyn Cox, Martin Dugard, Gordon Kennett, Ron How and Gordon McGregor just trip off the tongue. As you can imagine, with over fifty years of shale-shifting in Oxford, hundreds of riders have represented the side, and this book could be filled listing them alone!

Moving on to Reading, the Racers originally opened for business in 1968 at the Greyhound Stadium in Tilehurst. Apart from missing the 1974 season while a new home was constructed at Smallmead, Reading have run all the way through to the end of 2001, and they are all set to embark on the season ahead. Indeed, the future looks bright, as there are plans afoot for the Racers to move into a brand new stadium in the not too distant future.

Reading have been one of the most successful clubs of all time, having been crowned League Champions on no fewer than five occasions during their thirty-three years of completed race action. The Racers have been well served by some real legends of the track over the years, including Anders Michanek, Per Jonsson, Jan Andersson, David Mullett, John Davis, Dave Jessup, Bobby Schwartz and Armando Castagna to name but a few.

Further down the M4, Swindon have operated at their Abbey Stadium home ever since 1949. Earlier attempts to run the sport in the town saw three years of activity at the Swindon Autodrome from 1928 to 1930, during the sport's initial boom period when tracks were opening all over Britain.

In terms of silverware, the Robns have been the least successful of the three Thames Valley teams, having won the league just three times, the last occasion being way back in 1967. Despite their inability to win trophies with any regularity, Swindon's circuit is widely regarded as one of the finest racing tracks in the country, and continues to serve up tremendous racing.

Many fine riders have represented the Robins over their fifty-three-year existence, including Martin Ashby, Bob Kilby, Barry Briggs, Bob Jones, Phil Crump, Jimmy Nilsen, Mike Broadbanks and George White. Indeed, since 1949, some 450 riders have worn the famous Robins bib in league matches alone!

Over the years, many speedway tracks have come and gone, but the three Thames Valley teams have survived through thick and thin, entertaining many true and loyal fans along the way. In these times of economic uncertainty, this continues to be a tremendous achievement, especially when you consider the fact that speedway has rarely enjoyed the media exposure of other popular sports like football, cricket or rugby.

Glynn and I have thoroughly enjoyed compiling this comprehensive and detailed volume, and we hope that it will sit nicely alongside those other informative Tempus publications covering speedway in Scotland, London and East Anglia.

Robert Bamford
February 2002

# 1

# OXFORD

## The Early Days

Speedway racing, or dirt-track racing as it was known in the early days, came to Oxford Stadium on Easter Saturday, 8 April 1939, when the Oxford Motor Cycle Speedway Club, under their hardworking secretary Ted Mander, moved their racing activities from their old grass circuit at Sandford-on-Thames. Much of the credit to establish speedway at the stadium is due to the aforementioned Mr Mander, who described the new track at the stadium as a short circuit rider's dream of a perfect track. The new circuit, very different from the old grass circuit at Sandford-on-Thames, was comprised of sandy soil, and was 370 yards in length. Following an inspection by Mr Laughborough, the secretary of the A.C.U., the Oxford club received the following compliment: 'There is no amateur club in England that has a place of such magnificence and you are to be congratulated upon securing it.' So, on that April evening in 1939, Oxford Speedway was born, and little did Ted Mander know that he and his club were starting something that, a few years in the post-war period apart, would grow in stature and still be going strong over sixty years later.

To Roy Duke goes the honour of winning the first-ever meeting, and throughout the summer of 1939, regular meetings were held on Saturday evenings. Riders usually practised on race days from 6.30 p.m. to 7.30 p.m., with racing starting at 8 o'clock, and the leading riders of the day flocked to Oxford. Not only were there individual meetings, but there was team racing as well. Although there was no league competition as such, the Oxford club had matches against Smallford, Wisbech, High Beech and Reading. To add further interest, composite teams would sometimes be selected from the competitors on show, the first of these being 'Buster Yeoman's Team' *v.* 'Geoff Godwin's Team' on 1 July. Despite the declaration of war, the club continued its regular Saturday race meetings, with the final of the 1939 Speedway Championship taking place on 29 October and won by Geoff Godwin. The following week saw the last meeting of the season, when a team skippered by Danny Lee met a team captained by Ron Clarke.

## The 1940s

Racing resumed on 28 April 1940, when Jim Boyd (who was to join Oxford thirteen years later) led his team against another captained by Geoff Godwin. Meetings were held until 9 June, when the Speedway Championship final was held, and won by Ron Clarke, who was to become the captain of Bradford in the post-war period. Although

# The Oxford Motor-Cycle Speedway Club

## (Affiliated to the South Midland Centre of the Auto Cycle Union).

# RULES

**Headquarters :**

**THE MAGDALEN ARMS HOTEL, IFFLEY ROAD, OXFORD.**

**'Phone : 3159.**

---

**Hon. Secretary :**

**TED MANDER, 6 BARRETT STREET, OSNEY, OXFORD.**

**'Phone : 3102.**

*Oxford M.C.S.C. rule book.*

the Second World War was not yet over, the Oxford club were back in action in 1941, but the season did not last long. Just two meetings were held, on 4 May and 1 June. It was on 1 June that secretary Ted Mander announced that racing at the stadium would be suspended for the duration of the war, and although peace was declared in 1945, it was not until 1949 that the roar of the speedway machine was again heard at Cowley Stadium.

The final track record for the old circuit was 74.4 seconds, set by Bill Kitchen, who was to become captain of the famous Wembley Lions in the post-war speedway boom. Bill was one of the many riders to appear at Oxford in the early days who went on to reach the very top in league racing when it became properly established in 1946. Speedway enjoyed the most successful period in its history in the immediate post-war period, with meetings attended by huge crowds. Indeed, it was reported in 1946 that a Wembley *v.* West Ham cup match attracted a crowd of some 85,000 people! Having seen racing successfully staged before the outbreak of hostilities, stadium owner Mr L.V. Calcutt wanted Oxford to be part of the new boom. He promptly applied to the A.C.U. and the Speedway Control Board for a licence and a place in the new speedway league, a Third Division having been formed in 1947. Sadly, Mr Calcutt's efforts at that time bore no fruit, and it was not possible to obtain the necessary licences for all the alterations to the stadium that were deemed necessary by officialdom before any further speedway racing could take place, so the idea was temporarily suspended.

In the autumn of 1948, Mr Calcutt tried again, and this time the Speedway Control Board accepted the plans submitted by the Oxford boss. It was a major step forward, but there was still the question of obtaining a building licence, and the plan to re-launch Oxford Speedway received a setback when in the first instance, the application for the necessary licence was turned down. Mr Calcutt was not a man to take such a setback without a fight, and due to great efforts on his part, the authorities had second thoughts and granted the necessary building licence, but not until the end of January 1949. Thus began the great seventy days, when the stadium was virtually transformed. Offices, a medical room, track shops and, most importantly, a track had to be constructed. 400 tons of earth also had to be moved in order to make proper spectator accommodation available, for the go-ahead management were hoping for at least 10,000 regular supporters to back their new venture.

Whilst the Oxford management, combined with their helpers and contractors worked around the clock to transform the stadium, there was another problem to overcome, namely the entry of Oxford into Third Division league speedway. Having achieved so much in such a short space of time, Mr Calcutt was not going to see Oxford as simply a non-league side. His persistence eventually paid off and Oxford were accepted into the National League Division Three, with the first home league match going ahead on Thursday 21 April 1949, when the Oxford Cheetahs were born. The name Cheetahs came from the Oxford public themselves, as a result of a competition held by local newspaper, the *Oxford Mail*, to find a suitable name for the new team. Over 500 entries were received, with Cheetahs emerging as the clear winner. Colours for the Cheetahs it was agreed, would be dark blue with a yellow sash. Plans moved forward towards the opening day, when Her Grace, the Duchess of Marlborough, and

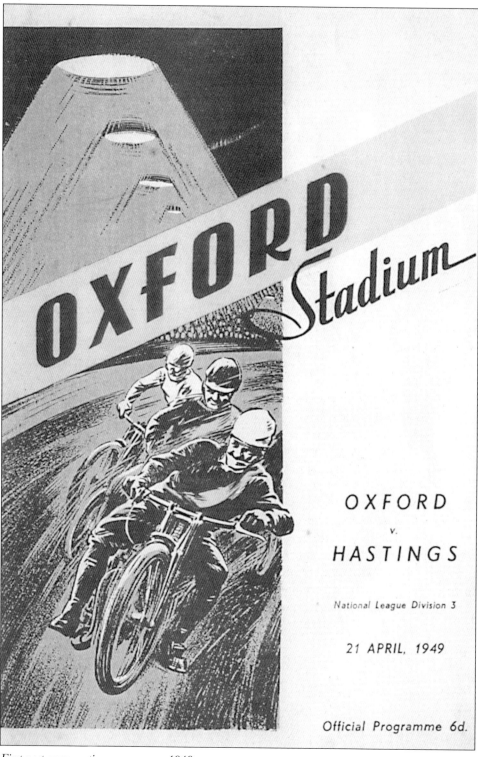

*First post-war meeting programme, 1949.*

Ron Johnson, the captain of New Cross Speedway, would declare the track open. But before that, the new Cheetahs would, in fact, be in action as a team, since their first match, a league encounter, was to be held at Exeter on Monday 18 April 1949.

So it was at Exeter that Ron Bear, who had joined Oxford as speedway manager, and Alf Elliott, who like the new manager had come from Poole, paraded the Oxford Cheetahs for the first time. Alf Elliott had played a master role in laying the re-vamped track at Cowley and was also the proud skipper of the new Oxford side. It was small wonder that Oxford, who had never ridden as a team before, were beaten by high flying Exeter (24-60), with Bert Croucher and Dennis Gray heading the Oxford scorechart, yielding 9 and 7 points respectively. Three days later, the Cheetahs were ready to perform on their own track, before their own supporters and just under 4,000 enthusiasts turned up to cheer their team in a league match against Hastings. Rain did its best to spoil Oxford's opening, but the gods smiled on the new Cheetahs and the inclement conditions cleared in time for the ceremonies to proceed. Ron Johnson, who was due to perform the official opening with the Duchess of Marlborough, was sadly unavailable, and his place was taken by the West Ham captain Aub Lawson. There was to be no fairytale ending to a memorable evening for the Oxford management, their team and the supporters, since the Cheetahs lost their opening fixture to the visiting 'Saxons' by 10 points (37-47).

The 1949 season was one of success and disappointment. The success was the support for the sport of speedway racing, which saw the Oxford public respond in magnificent fashion, with crowds increasing throughout the year. Meanwhile, the obvious disappointment was the fact that the Cheetahs finished as wooden spoonists in the league table. The failure of the team to click as a unit was understandable. It was summed up by their speedway manager, Mr Henry Chandler, in this way: 'The Cheetahs were born into league speedway racing, almost before it was possible to do any preliminary teamwork at all. We looked around and got together whatever riders were available, and many of them did not quite make the grade'. Mr Chandler's words were true, of course, as it took the Oxford management some time to get a settled side together. Injuries to Bert Croucher, who was a great success, and the absence of the inspiring Dennis Gray, due to RAF duties, certainly did not help the Cheetahs' cause. Both Bert and Dennis, who came on loan from Southampton and Wimbledon respectively, held their team places on merit throughout the season, while Alf Viccary, who came on loan from Harringay, also held a regular team spot. Alf was not quite as successful as either Dennis or Bert, but he had his moments during the season, which included a fine 12 point tally against Liverpool. Alf was, in fact, the one rider in the Cheetahs line-up with a 100 per cent record of league appearances.

There were also off-track problems to contend with, as manager Ron Bear left the club in July, however, Henry Chandler was available to take over, and went on to do a fine job in charge of the Cheetahs' fortunes. As the season progressed, riders came and went. Alf Elliott, the first Oxford captain, who had played an outstanding off-track role in laying the circuit, lost form and retired in late July. Meanwhile, Bob Aldridge, Maurice Hutchins and Bill Downton, all of whom had ridden in the early matches, soon disappeared from the Oxford scene. Jim Wright arrived from Cradley Heath in May, and Bill

Kemp was another Heathen to join the Oxford camp in June, while New Zealander Frank Boyle was another June arrival. All three became regulars in the Cheetahs team, but showed their best form only in flashes, although Frank Boyle became a great favourite with his whole-hearted efforts. Jim Coy, on loan from Wimbledon, and Australian Bill Reynolds were other riders given opportunities, but neither were the answer to Oxford's need for team-strengthening and it was not until mid-August that Oxford signed a rider who could answer their need for heat-leaders. The rider concerned was a tubby little New Zealander named Bob McFarlane, who arrived via Southampton on 18 August and celebrated with 10 points against Exeter. Unfortunately, the Cheetahs lost the match by a single point, but Bob's arrival had coincided with an injury to Bert Croucher, so it was a few weeks before Oxford could field a side that contained their three best riders – Bob McFarlane, Bert Croucher and Dennis Gray.

On 8 September, in a league match against Leicester, the Cheetahs raced to a fine win by 48 points to 36. Bert Croucher, who had taken over the captaincy from Alf Elliott, was still absent, but Bob McFarlane was in cracking form and recorded maximum points. In the same match, Dennis Gray racked up 11 points, as well as establishing a new track record of 68.8 seconds. In a mammoth league campaign consisting of 48 matches, Oxford won 11, lost 36 and drew just once. There is no doubt that of their 11 victories, the one that gave both supporters and riders the greatest satisfaction was the win over visiting Yarmouth on 14 July. Yarmouth were riding high in the league table at the time and came to Cowley confident of success, but it was Oxford, with Croucher, Viccary, Kemp and Boyle riding with great tenacity, who emerged as the winners by 43 points to 41. It was only the third league success of the year for Oxford, but it was a victory to savour. Despite gaining the unwanted wooden spoon, speedway in Oxford was firmly established as crowd levels continued to increase. Les Calcutt, the Oxford promoter, was determined to put the team problems of the season behind him and plan for the future. Writing in the final programme of the season, a challenge match against Walthamstow, Mr Calcutt stated: 'We intend to carry out a strengthening up process, by adding to the existing team, new riders of proven calibre during the closed season, and look forward to the 1950 Cheetahs being a truly formidable force in league racing.'

## The 1950s

1950 was a very special season in the history of Oxford, as the side completed their second year as members of the old Third Division. Having finished bottom

*Pat Clarke.*

*Frank Boyle.*

of the league table the previous year, promoter Les Calcutt was determined to build a Championship-winning side, of whom the Oxford public could be proud. He was not afraid to dip into the coffers to secure good riders and during the winter break he had been busy in the transfer market. Experienced lower division heat-leader Harry Saunders came from Tamworth, while Bill Osborne, another rider of considerable experience, joined via Walthamstow. Buster Brown, a highly promising junior, came from Wembley, but the bargain of the season was the £250 spent on the Rayleigh captain, Pat Clarke. In those bygone days, Pat was to become the 'King of Cowley', and it was he who headed the Oxford challenge for Third Division honours. Eric Irons from Cradley, who had been retired for a year, signed on after pre-season trials, and with Bob McFarlane, Frank Boyle, Bill Kemp, Ernie Rawlins and Jim Wright from the 1949 team, the Cheetahs had a squad of riders that were second-to-none. However, the injury bug hit Oxford even before the season started. Harry Saunders, who had been made captain, looped the loop in practice on the concrete starting gate and suffered back injuries, while in the opening fixture of the season Bill Osborne broke a leg. Both riders were out of the saddle for many weeks, but Oxford, with great strength in depth, somehow continued to take on and beat all-comers.

Not only was Pat Clarke leading the Cowley challenge both home and away, but the two Kiwis, Bob McFarlane and Frank Boyle, were enjoying a tremendous season. Eric Irons was also proving to be a fine signing and a good point-scorer. The Cheetahs' team riding was superb with the Pat Clarke/Frank Boyle pairing particularly thrilling the Cowley public as they raced to 5-1 after 5-1 maximum heat successes. Harry Saunders returned to the saddle in June and quickly found his best form, but more bad luck hit Oxford at Exeter in late July when Frank Boyle badly broke an ankle in a track crash. By then, however, Bill Osborne was fit to return, which was some compensation for the loss of the popular ginger-haired New Zealander. To further strengthen the side for the run in at the end of the 1950 campaign, Mr Calcutt signed Brian Wilson from Tamworth, but the lad who had been the Tammies number one rider never settled at Cowley and was something of a failure.

Leicester came to Cowley on 24 August and upset the Cheetahs' title plans a little by winning, but Oxford managed overcome the setback and went on to Third Division League Championship success. It is strange to relate that at no time in their Championship season were the Cheetahs able to field their strongest side. But it made no difference, since they had strength in depth and with the magnificent Pat Clarke leading the way, the boys in dark blue with a yellow sash raced to league glory. They also enjoyed late season success in the Autumn Cup, defeating Swindon and Poole in the three-team competition. However, the seal on a fine Oxford season was really set at Walthamstow on 23 October, when Pat Clarke again showed his class by winning the Third Division Riders' Championship, before the London club's highest-paid gate of 23,000 people. Those now far off days of 1950 were truly special, when the crowds at Cowley were tremendous. Indeed, it was estimated that some 6,000 spectators turned up for a pre-season practice! The atmosphere was always electric, and it was common place for Cheetahs supporters to be in their favourite spot soon after six o'clock because if they weren't, someone else had bagged it!

The 1951 season had seen the Oxford Cheetahs promoted to the Second Division of Speedway's National League, and initially they made quite an impact in the higher sphere of racing. They certainly caused a major surprise when they captured the Kemsley Shield at their first attempt, but make no mistake, they were worthy winners. Unfortunately, before the league programme began in earnest, the Cheetahs suffered a real body blow. Pat Clarke, who had carried all before him the previous season, was injured in a National Trophy match at Exeter and was out of action for the rest of the season with a badly broken leg. The loss of Pat Clarke, just as the Second Division campaign was about to begin, undoubtedly upset the balance of the Cheetahs side, and Oxford could never recover the great form they'd shown in the Kemsley Shield competition. To add to their team problems, Cyril Quick, the former Poole skipper who had been signed at the start of the season, just couldn't master the Cowley circuit, and was on his way to Yarmouth before the league fixtures got underway. Just why Quick was such a failure at Oxford was a mystery, since as a visitor in past seasons, he'd always appeared thoroughly at home and scored well.

In an effort to strengthen the side, the Oxford management signed three new riders. Herbie King came via Newcastle, while the experienced Roger Wise arrived on loan from Bristol, and former Aldershot skipper Doug Ible made a brief and unsuccessful stint, lasting only five matches. King was in and out of the line-up, and only against Glasgow on 30 August, when he scored 10 points, did he reveal any worthwhile form. Roger Wise fared slightly better, beginning with 8 points against Hanley on 31 May, but generally was no more than a reliable reserve in the team, and it was heat-leaders that the side desperately wanted. Despite their team problems, it was a good season for Bill Osborne, Bill Kemp and Ernie Rawlins. Osborne, now fully recovered from the broken leg, which had caused him to miss the greater part of the 1950 season, was a tower of strength. His average increased to 7.5 points a match and he was a real force around Oxford, where he recorded a string of double-figure scores. For both Bill Kemp and Ernie Rawlins, the season was one of success. Both had been back-up boys in the 1950 Championship-winning side, but both came good in 1951, taking the higher grade of racing in their stride.

The mighty Jack Young appeared at Cowley on 12 July, in a World Championship qualifying round, which he won with an untroubled 15-point maximum. No Oxford fan who witnessed Jack's superb riding was surprised when, later in the year, he became

World Champion after winning a three-man run-off at Wembley. On 2 August, the Cheetahs raced against Motherwell in a league match and were worthy winners by 53 points to 31. Skipper Harry Saunders was in great form, and in Heat 14, he lined up against the Motherwell riders Gordon McGregor and Keith Gurtner, with partner Bob McFarlane, hopeful of completing his maximum. In a great race, it was Gurtner who emerged the winner over Harry, but the surprise for the Oxford fans came when it was announced that Keith had beaten Pat Clarke's track record of 66.2 seconds, which had stood since 3 August 1950. Keith's time was 66 seconds and he'd achieved a new track record in the final heat of the match!

In the Second Division table, Oxford finished in twelfth position out of the sixteen teams, which all things considered, was a good effort. They recorded 12 wins, 2 draws, and tasted defeat on 16 occasions, and were left wondering how different things might have been if Pat Clarke had been fit, and had Bob McFarlane, Frank Boyle and Eric Irons shown their 1950 form. Frank Boyle in particular, was only a shadow of the rider who rode so well in 1950, and appeared not to have fully recovered from his ankle injury. On the Oxford terraces, however, things really buzzed and Thursday evenings couldn't come around quickly enough. The Oxford Supporters' Club was booming, meeting every Sunday night at 'The Cape of Good Hope' for billiards, darts or just a drink and a speedway chat.

The 1952 season promised much for the fans of Oxford Cheetahs in Division Two racing. They'd made a good start in the higher grade the previous season, and with a season's experience under their belts, things looked very hopeful down Cowley way. Pat Clarke had fully recovered from the broken leg that sidelined him for the whole of the 1951 league programme. But any hopes the Cheetahs had of tracking their star rider were dashed before the season started, when Pat expressed a desire for top league racing and was transferred to First Division West Ham. The Cheetahs management took this disappointment in their stride, and never being afraid to open the Cowley coffers, went into the transfer market and signed the vastly experienced Jim Boyd from Walthamstow, following the closure of the London track. Jim had been a successful performer in Second Division racing, and had ridden regularly at Oxford in pre-war meetings. He was just the man to replace Pat Clarke effectively. All the other tried and trusted favourites were back, namely Bill Osborne, Bill Kemp and Ernie Rawlins, along with the ever-reliable duo of Harry

*Jim Gregory.*

Saunders and Frank Boyle. Unfortunately, Bob McFarlane did not return, preferring to remain in his native New Zealand, where it was reported he was rhubarb farming. However, Ron Wilson, a useful rider who wanted a change from Leicester was signed, giving Oxford an all-round solid look.

Things certainly looked good on Easter Monday, when Oxford visited Poole, newly promoted from Division Three, for a league match and secured a creditable draw, with Bill Osborne scoring 11 points and new boy Jim Boyd notching 8. Sadly, the Cheetahs' early promise was not to be maintained and in a matter of weeks, injuries and an unprecedented period of form loss hit the team. It wasn't long before Oxford were struggling badly. The chequebook came out again and Jim Gregory was brought in from First Division Wimbledon, where he had been having a tough time. Whilst Jim's signing was a welcome boost, his team-mates just couldn't get their act together, and away from home, the Cheetahs took a fair few hidings. Ernie Rawlins was injured and missed practically the whole season, while both Bill Kemp and Herbie King were also missing from vital matches due to niggling injuries. Although Jim Boyd managed to steer clear from injury, his form was somewhat patchy. With no suitable riders available, Oxford gave opportunities to promising newcomers, but it was no surprise when the Cheetahs finished bottom of the league with just 24 points from their 44 matches. They won only 11 of their 22 home matches, losing 10, and drawing just once. Away from Cowley, they lost 21 matches and again only drew once – the aforementioned Easter Monday clash at Poole. It was a season that promised much and achieved nothing, with the only bright spot being the signing of Jim Gregory, who often took on the opposition single-handed. Jim's fine riding endeared him to a fifteen-year-old schoolboy, who was later to play a major role in the Cheetahs' success of the 1980s – his name was, of course, Bernard Crapper! There was great sadness during the 1952 campaign, when Oxford promoter Mr L.V. Calcutt passed away in August. No one had worked harder than Mr Calcutt to establish the sport of speedway in Oxford and he would be sorely missed.

The 1953 season saw Oxford under a new manager and in a new league. John Deeley, who was formerly associated with Walthamstow, joined the club as general manager, and after the disasters of the previous season, the Cheetahs joined the Southern League, which meant less travel and more local derbies. One thing was certain – after 1952, the only way Oxford could go was up and, as things turned out, the decision to opt for Southern League racing was a wise one. The Cheetahs retained most of their riders, except former skipper Harry Saunders, who had left under something of a cloud the previous year. Bob McFarlane returned from his rhubarb farm, while new signings saw Bill Codling join from Norwich, and former England international Ray Moore arrive via New Cross. It didn't take long for 'Bobby Mac' to find his scoring boots, but Codling struggled to come to terms with the Oxford track, while Moore was a great disappointment and didn't stay around for long. Despite the failure of the new signings, Oxford slowly, but surely, began to get things together. The fighting spirit, so often missing in 1952, returned and the natural response from the Oxford public saw things buzzing again at Cowley.

Jim Boyd and Jim Gregory led the Oxford attack during the season, and good backing was forthcoming from Bob McFarlane. At home, after a slightly indifferent start, the wins started to come, but try as they might the Cheetahs couldn't break their duck away from Cowley. Mind you, they came pretty close on a number of occasions. They lost by 3 points at Rayleigh, which was a fine effort, and they had two terrific meetings at Plymouth, losing by 4 points on one occasion and 6 on the second. The Cheetahs were proving to be attractive visitors, but lacked a third heat-leader; however, this was a situation that was to be put right as the season drew to its close. To strengthen the side in the meantime, Benny King was drafted in from Wolverhampton, and thanks to the 'Penny on the Bike' fund, organized by the Supporters' Club, money was made available to purchase one of Oxford's favourite sons, Frank Johnson. Frank had joined Cardiff in 1951, following the Cheetahs' promotion to the Second Division, but the closure of the Welsh track saw this Cowley-born thrill merchant return home, his presence certainly providing many thrills (and a few repairs to the safety fence) at Oxford.

The Coronation Best Pairs Tournament held at Oxford on 9 July, saw home success with Jim Gregory and Bill Osborne winning. Unfortunately, the overall result was already settled before the Cheetahs pair took to the track, since Oxford was staging the final round in the competition, which had already been won by the Exeter pairing. No matter, it was a home success to cheer. The following week, Oxford welcomed back former favourites Pat Clarke and Ernie Rawlins for an Oxford Past and Present *v.* New Zealand match. The powerful Kiwis, who included Ronnie Moore, Barry Briggs and Geoff Mardon in their line-up, also had home riders Bob McFarlane and Frank Boyle at reserve and won 62-46. Pat Clarke scored 11 points, and Jim Boyd top scored with 14 points for the Cheetahs Select. Meanwhile, Ronnie Moore raced to a superb 18-point maximum for New Zealand in what was a tremendous meeting.

Following the closure of Liverpool in August, Oxford finally signed the heat-leader they were missing, when Peter Robinson joined the ranks at Cowley. Peter had been a leading scorer in the Second Division for both Plymouth and Liverpool, and his signing was a feather in the cap for John Deeley. Actually, Peter was a local boy, who had ridden at Cowley in pre-war meetings and his arrival gave the Cheetahs a really strong looking side.

Oxford finished in sixth position in the

*Bob Baker.*

Southern League, but the great thing about the season was that all the old Cowley enthusiasm and team spirit had been re-kindled. There's no doubt that had Peter Robinson been available from the off, then the Cheetahs would have been challenging for honours, but at least they had re-established themselves and things were now on the up and up. The 1954 season saw the Oxford Cheetahs in the Second Division of the National League, due to the merger of the previous season's Second Division with the Southern League. Bristol dropped down from the First Division and in the early planning stages, the new league set-up boasted no fewer than sixteen teams. However, this happy situation didn't last very long, as Yarmouth never actually got going. Then Glasgow finished after a couple of Northern Shield matches, while Wolverhampton closed before their league campaign started. These were dark days for speedway, yet at Oxford things looked bright and support was actually on the increase.

On the team front Jim Boyd, after top scoring for the club in 1953, announced his retirement from the sport, as did Bill Kemp and Benny King, while Frank Boyle returned to his native New Zealand. Manager John Deeley looked around for replacements, and one of his first signings was Ronnie Genz, who had assisted Yarmouth in 1953. This was to prove one of the best-ever signings made by Oxford, for 'Genno' was to give great service to the Cheetahs for many seasons and proved to be the most loyal of club servants. To back the youth and enthusiasm of Ronnie Genz, Deeley looked for experience and from West Ham came Fred 'Kid' Curtis. Also incoming via Swindon was Bob Wells, who'd had considerable experience with Wembley before joining the Robins in 1952. So with these three newcomers to back the scoring efforts of Jim Gregory and Peter Robinson, plus old favourites Bill Osborne, Bob McFarlane and Frank Johnson, things were humming at Oxford when the Southern Shield competition opened the season.

The Cheetahs' start in the Southern Shield was not particularly good, so with Yarmouth a definite non-starter, the experienced Bob Baker was signed in order to add further strength to the side. Plymouth withdrew from the league in early July, and the closure of the Devon track resulted in another Oxford signing. New Zealander Bill Thatcher duly arrived at Cowley on 22 July for the match against Southampton, and just missed scoring a maximum on his debut. Sadly, the arrival of Bill Thatcher coincided with a couple of unfortunate happenings for Oxford. Bill Osborne broke a leg at Leicester in a freak accident, and Jim Gregory lost form and asked to be left out of the team. This was a real blow for Oxford, since Osborne was proving a reliable second string, and Gregory had scored well in the Southern Shield competition, including a very fine maximum at Swindon. So, for the Cheetahs' home match against Swindon on 29 July, the popular Jim Gregory was in the second half of the programme. It was a memorable match, firstly because the Cheetahs won, but also for the second-half performance of Dennis Newton. Newton had made a sensational start at Swindon in 1951, but had suffered a badly broken thigh, which sidelined him for most of that year. He came back in 1952, and was dubbed 'The Golden Boy', but was injured again and his form deserted him. Dennis, who had begun to rebuild his career, had signed for Wembley in 1953, but was still struggling to find his form.

Newton was subsequently loaned to Oxford in 1954, and in the match against his former club, Swindon, he'd come in as a late replacement for Bob McFarlane but failed to score. However, in the second half, he won both the Cumnor Scratch Race and the Botley Scratch Race in fast times, beating Jim Gregory, Bob Wells and the Swindon reserves Ray Harris and Gordon Leigh. It was the start of a comeback for Dennis, who went on to become a useful scorer, but the match really signalled the end of Jim Gregory's career as a Cheetah, and it wasn't long before Jim retired from active speedway racing. Oxford continued to do reasonably well in the league campaign. Peter Robinson had a good season and top scored with 172 points, while Ronnie Genz had a great time in his first year at Oxford, scoring 149 points. The Cheetahs finished mid-way in the final league table, winning 10 matches and losing 10. All in all, it was a fine season for Oxford, with the old team spirit successfully re-kindled by John Deeley, and, most importantly, increased support through the turnstiles.

The 1955 season saw the Cheetahs still as members of the Second Division of the National League, together with ten other teams and some interesting changes in race format, namely the introduction of the tactical substitute rule, and the fact that league matches were contested over sixteen heats. The idea of two reserves was scrapped, and teams now lined up with seven riders (six main team-men and one reserve), with the main team-men having five programmed rides and the reserve taking two. Sadly, it wasn't long before the Second Division was reduced by two tracks to just nine. The newly formed Weymouth promotion, under Mr Bill Dutton (formerly of Exeter, Cardiff and Swindon fame) didn't last beyond May, and a month later, the famous Bristol Bulldogs, who were crowned Second Division Champions the previous year, also closed their doors to speedway. Despite this, things still looked good at Oxford, with the team building and team spirit cultivated by manager John Deeley much in evidence as the Cheetahs boasted a really good top six in their line-up. Reg Trott, on loan from First Division Wimbledon, was added to the side and a further loan deal with Wembley was negotiated in order to retain the services of Dennis Newton. The Courtnell brothers, Terry and Maury, also made their Cowley debut. Maury was the original 'Teddy Boy', with the gear and the haircut to match. He was beginning his speedway career, but Terry had enjoyed previous experience with both Yarmouth and West Ham.

There were also some departures from Cowley. The popular New Zealander Bob McFarlane went home to New Zealand, while Bill Osborne, who was still recovering from injuries, decided to retire. Meanwhile, the harum-scarum Frank Johnson moved on (again), this time to the ill-fated Weymouth venture, and was later identified with Bristol, until their closure, prior to moving on to Belle Vue. Peter Robinson, now in his third term in the blue and yellow of Oxford, led the Cheetahs for the 1955 campaign. He was not quite the all-conquering heat-leader of 1954, but he was still a very reliable team-man. Robinson had, in fact, been a top-class heat-leader in the lower leagues since 1947, having served Southampton, Plymouth, Liverpool and the Cheetahs with distinction. Ronnie Genz, the outstanding signing of 1954, enjoyed a fine season with 249 league points. This was a much steadier 'Genno' than the previous year, and the points flowed as a result, much to the delight of the Oxford public. The big, and indeed welcome, surprise throughout the season for the Cheetahs was the form of Bob Baker. This former bricklayer, who'd been a leading light with Third Division

*Howdy Byford.*

Hull in 1949, and then with Second Division Yarmouth, really came into his own and enjoyed his best season in the sport, actually topping the Oxford scorechart with 261 league points.

Another rider to enjoy a good season was cheery Bill Thatcher, who'd come to Cowley via Plymouth the previous season. The Kiwi was a model of consistent scoring, and ended the year with over 200 points to his credit. The two loanees, Reg Trott and Dennis Newton, were enjoying themselves and hitting some useful scores, and, indeed, had the fast-starting Trott been available right from day one, the Cheetahs could well have made a very determined challenge to Poole at the top of the Second Division. It was in the reserve berth that the Cheetahs were weak – Fred Curtis and Bob Wells were, regrettably, over the hill, while Maury Courtnell lacked the necessary experience. The man who could have made a difference was Terry Courtnell, but he was a mere shadow of the rider who'd looked so promising with Yarmouth in 1953. Oxford finished in fourth position in the league, winning 15 of their matches, drawing once and losing 16 times. They had a real night to remember on 5 May, when they beat high-flying Rayleigh 63-33 in a league match, which was definitely their best performance of the year. On the individual front, it was disappointing when Ronnie Genz suffered injury and was unable to contest the First Division qualifying round of the World Championship. He was the Cheetahs' sole qualifier, but Oxford supporters had reason to feel very happy, when Dennis Newton finished a creditable fourth in the Midland Riders' Championship at Leicester, a meeting which was won by the Hunters' home star Ken McKinlay.

After building a good solid-looking side during the 1955 season, Oxford supporters eagerly looked forward to 1956, convinced that the Cheetahs would enjoy a very good year and make a real challenge for Second Division honours. Sadly, things just didn't work out, and right from the off the Cheetahs were struggling. The closure of First Division West Ham saw the return to Cowley of Pat Clarke but, unfortunately, it was not the Pat of old. The Hammers' demise also saw Oxford sign one of the greatest charac-ters the sport has known in Howdy Byford, and whilst the 'Champ' created plenty of interest for the Cowley supporters, he personally found that Second Division racing was every bit as tough and competitive as its First Division counterpart. The biggest disappointment was the failure of Bob Baker, who had been the Cheetahs' top scorer in 1955, and had enjoyed his best-ever season in speedway. Baker just could not get going and it came as no surprise when he announced his retirement early in the season. Unfortunately, Bob was not the only one to quit the sport early, as the popular Bill Thatcher was another man to call it a day. Reg Trott, such a success during 1955, did not return, having been transferred to Norwich by his parent club, Wimbledon.

The merry month of May saw a managerial change when John Deeley resigned and was replaced by Ted Flanagan. It didn't take Ted long to open the Oxford coffers and make a signing, when he persuaded Coventry to part with Tommy Miller, a former international rider, who earlier in his career had been regarded as one of the greatest riders Scotland had produced. Sadly, it followed a pattern of bad luck that seemed to dog the Cheetahs with some signings, for the change of track did nothing for the somewhat temperamental Miller, who disappointed greatly. In 7 matches, he totalled just 35 points and it wasn't long before he was lost to the sport. But it wasn't all gloom at Oxford, for whilst the older lads were disappearing from the scene, two of the younger element in the side were doing well. Ronnie Genz really came into his own and was head and shoulders above the rest of the side, scoring 279 points in 24 matches. Ronnie was followed by Dennis Newton, who plundered 151 points. Both Ronnie and Dennis qualified for the Midland Riders' Championship final (Howdy Byford also qualified as reserve), but neither had any luck and both finished way down the field, with Ken McKinlay of Leicester retaining his title.

The Cheetahs took some hammerings on their travels, due in the main to their inability to track a settled side, and an injury to Pat Clarke in July was just about the last straw. There were seven teams in the league and each raced their opponents four times during the course of the season (twice at home and twice away). The Cheetahs never succeeded in winning on an opponent's track and on 7 occasions away from Cowley, the home side managed to top 60 points. The Cheetahs' best performance on an opponent's track was in fact at the home of their old rivals Swindon, where they managed to score 41 points to the Robins' 55. This was a highly creditable result when you consider that Swindon emerged as the 1956 champions, and were a pretty tough nut to crack at Blunsdon. In all, Oxford raced 24 league matches, winning only 6, while drawing once and losing on 17 occasions. As they had done in 1952, Oxford collected the wooden spoon, by virtue of having an inferior points average to Leicester, who also finished with just thirteen league points. So, it was a season of great disappointment down Cowley way, yet support and enthusiasm from the terraces was still there, and despite some poor results, the Oxford riders still had plenty of encouragement from the loyal Cheetahs fans. An interesting note about the 1956 season was the date on which it officially closed, since Wimbledon staged the Christmas Vase on Boxing Day, which was won by Swindon's Bob Roger. Bob had shown his undoubted class to Cowley patrons earlier in the year, when winning the Kings of Oxford Trophy on

*Ronnie Genz.*

13 September.

The 1957 season was the start of a very bleak period in the history of speedway, with three of the sport's most well-known clubs failing to open their doors. First Division tracks Wembley, Bradford and Poole closed for one reason or another, with the result that there was an amalgamation of the First and Second Division to form an eleven-team National League. As if this wasn't enough in itself, a dark cloud hung over Oxford for some time, with the promoting company in serious trouble. Happily for everyone at Cowley, local businessman Dickie Worth came to the rescue by forming a new company to take over the fortunes of Oxford, and it was all systems go for the Cheetahs. After finishing in the basement position the previous year, Oxford supporters looked forward optimistically to 1957, since the only way the Cheetahs could go was up! With four former First Division sides in the new league, there had to be some equalization of team strengths and Oxford looked forward to receiving some top-class riders to strengthen their squad. Peter Robinson, Pat Clarke and Tommy Miller had all retired, and the Cheetahs suffered another body blow, when the promising Terry Courtnell lost his life in a motor accident whilst in South Africa.

To replace them came Jack Biggs, a vastly experienced Australian international rider, who had ridden with great success for Poole during 1956. Poole had been promoted to speedway's First Division during that year and Biggs had been top man for the Pirates. Fellow Aussie Ray Cresp was another signing, who came via Wembley. 1956 had been his first season in British speedway and he'd shown considerable promise. From Leicester came another rider to the Cowley camp with great experience, Gordon McGregor. Gordon had scored 240 points for the Hunters during 1956, and had been their second-highest point-scorer. So, with Ronnie Genz, Dennis Newton, Howdy Byford and the useful-looking Ray Bowers, Oxford had a strong-looking line-up, on paper at least. Unfortunately, and not for the first time at Oxford, things didn't work out on the track. New signings Biggs and McGregor never really displayed the form they'd shown in 1956, and were decidedly patchy. Cresp made good progress, but he was not a heat-leader and it was the popular Ronnie Genz who frequently led the Cheetahs' scoring.

Dennis Newton and Howdy Byford often struggled and it must have been very galling for the Oxford promotion to see local boy Ernie Lessiter scoring so well down the road at Swindon. Ernie had begun his speedway career at Oxford in 1950, but had been allowed to try his luck elsewhere. After a spell at Ringwood in the Southern Area League, Ernie had joined Weymouth in 1955, and upon the closure of the Dorset side, he had joined the Robins. Now he was a member of a very fine side at Blunsdon and was being described, quite rightly, as the best reserve in the league. How the Cheetahs could have done with him to add some backbone to their scoring efforts. Later on in the season, Maury McDermott joined the Oxford camp, and Frank Johnson returned, but neither was a success. The Cheetahs won 6 home matches, with one of their best efforts being a 50-46 win over Belle Vue, who were to finish the season as runners-up to Swindon, who went on to repeat their Second Division success of 1956, by becoming National League Champions. Away from Oxford, the Cheetahs had a surprising, but nevertheless, deserved success at Wimbledon, winning 49-46. That went some way to making up for the 34-62 mauling that the Dons had previously dished out to the Cheetahs at Cowley!

Ronnie Genz was the top Cheetah during the season, scoring 171 league points. He was definitely the man to beat around Oxford. Jack Biggs was next best with 158 points, whilst Gordon McGregor was third in the pecking order with 144 points. Ray Cresp was the only other Cheetah to top 100 points (he actually notched 104 points), which was a good effort in his second season of British speedway. The Cheetahs finished in ninth position in the league table, which meant that they'd improved on their 1956 position by a couple of places. They had been described by the speedway press as being a 'team without a star', which wasn't quite true, for Ronnie Genz was a very capable rider. What the Cheetahs desperately needed was someone to back 'Genno's' efforts consistently. All in all though, it wasn't a bad season with plenty of good racing to cheer the fans.

When the 1958 season dawned, the speedway press described the Oxford team as 'the mixture as before' (referring to the 1957 team). They turned out to be right, since the Cheetahs were ninth in an eleven-team National League in 1957, and in 1958 they finished eighth in a ten-team league, so it really was a case of no change at Cowley. But let's start at the beginning of the year. As far as the league was concerned, Bradford, who had taken over from Birmingham following their closure the previous season, were non-starters, while Rayleigh moved lock, stock and barrel to Poole, where they had, in fact, staged a couple of 'home' meetings during 1957. With Poole returning to the league, Jack Biggs moved back to the scene of his former triumphs in 1956, while Ray Cresp went to Ipswich, so the Cheetahs needed replacements. These came in the form of Eric Boothroyd and Arthur Wright, both formerly of Bradford, and Reg Duval, who arrived via Coventry. Unfortunately, Howdy Byford suffered a fractured skull before the league campaign got underway and with top man Ronnie Genz troubled with a serious eye infection for most of the season, further replacements became an urgent necessity.

Kiwi Charlie New was in dispute with Coventry, where he had been a top scorer, and thankfully he joined the Oxford camp, giving them an acceptable replacement for the departed Biggs. However, the team still lacked a top-class heat-leader with the high-scoring Ronnie Genz often absent. The Cheetahs' management therefore made overtures for the South African ace Doug Davies and the Swedish international Dan

*Gordon McGregor.*

Forsberg, who had ridden briefly, but with some success, for Birmingham in 1957. Sadly, despite all the publicity and razzmatazz, neither signing materialized, and Oxford had to keep going with the riders they had. Eric Boothroyd had filled a heat-leader berth at Birmingham/Bradford in 1957, but yet again it was a case of an established rider losing form when he arrived at Cowley, as Eric struggled to find form in the Cheetahs colours. The same could be said of Reg Duval, who had scored 121 league points for Coventry the previous year. At Oxford, his tally for league matches was 85, just two points less than Boothroyd, who netted just 87!

However, there were some things to keep Cowley fans happy. Gordon McGregor enjoyed a much better season, being far more consistent, and he frequently headed the Cheetahs' scoring. Charlie New gave him excellent backing, while Arthur Wright also had a good season, scoring 122 league points. Despite his eye trouble, Ronnie Genz weighed in with over a 100 points. Unfortunately for the Cheetahs though, no other rider managed to top three figures. Things might have been better on the team front if Dennis Newton had ridden to his true potential, but he was another rider to struggle and it was no surprise to anyone when he upped and left after a row with the management. The Cheetahs had but a single away success during the 1958 campaign, at Ipswich, where they won 51-45, but the Witches were unbelievably poor and most teams won there. Ipswich, in fact, only won once and drew once during the whole season! At home, Oxford managed 4 wins and 2 draws, their best victory being a 54-42 success against those Witches from Ipswich. The 48-48 draw with eventual champions Wimbledon was a fine effort, but Leicester, Norwich and Swindon all took league points from the Cheetahs' lair during the campaign. The Cheetahs did, however, get some publicity for pulling off what can only be described as the stunt of the season, when, with guest riders permitted for the top riders, they succeeded in using Barry Briggs (top point-scorer in the league with Wimbledon) as a guest for Howdy Byford!

The 1959 season will always have special memories for Oxford fans. The Cheetahs didn't accomplish anything special in their quest to climb the league table, but what made the year so special for everyone was the signing of the Danish Champion Arne Pander. There was no doubt that manager Ted Flanagan took a mighty gamble when he signed Arne, because in those days, the Danes were really untried in British speedway. However, right from the off, Pander showed that he was of heat-leader class, and my, how he thrilled the Cowley public. At long last, the Cheetahs had a rider who could take on and beat the world-class riders who featured in National League speedway. Among the top stars of the day were, of course, Peter Craven (at Belle Vue), Ken McKinlay (Leicester), Ove Fundin (Norwich), Brian Crutcher (Southampton), Ronnie Moore (Wimbledon) and Oxford now had a rider of equal calibre in Arne Pander.

There were the usual team changes before the season commenced, which saw Eric Boothroyd move to Leicester, while Charlie New was a non-starter, preferring to remain in his native New Zealand. Ronnie Genz was not immediately available, having undergone an operation to the eye injury that troubled him throughout most of 1958. Happily, Howdy Byford had recovered from injury and returned to the side and the 'Champ' was made team captain for the year. Ken Adams moved in from Poole, with Reg Duval moving in the opposite direction to Dorset. The rest of the early Cheetahs side was made up with Gordon McGregor, Roy Bowers, Arthur Wright, plus the up-and-coming Colin Gooddy. There was an early change, though, when Arthur Wright disappeared from the Cowley scene having struggled to find form, but Nick Nicholls arrived from Coventry and was a more than adequate replacement. On the league front, the National League was now down to nine teams, with Ipswich pulling out after their disastrous 1958 campaign. The National Reserve League was introduced to give more interest in the second half of meetings, but its introduction was stormy, mainly because of the self-made muddle over the league match format compared with that of the Britannia Shield. The Reserve League was a good idea in principle, but the idea bit the dust, with a number of

*Ken Adams.*

27

matches not being run.

The Britannia Shield wasn't a very successful competition for the Cheetahs, where they surprisingly competed in the Northern section. Out of 6 matches ridden, Oxford won 2 (against Leicester and Belle Vue) and lost 4, while they went out of the National Trophy to Southampton by 104 points to 112. In the National League, Oxford won 7 matches and lost 9, the big problem being that the Cheetahs relied far too heavily on Arne Pander. Arne rode in all 16 league matches for a total score of 174 points, plus five bonus for an average of 11.20. This was a tremendous effort when one considers that he was riding on British tracks for the first time! Home victories over Belle Vue, Coventry, Leicester, Norwich, Southampton and Swindon cheered the Cowley supporters, but Poole sneaked a one-point victory, and powerful Wimbledon gave the Cheetahs a heavy home defeat (34-56).

Away from Cowley, Oxford gave a fine performance at Belle Vue to win by 2 points, with Gordon McGregor scoring a maximum. The Cheetahs were desperately unlucky at Swindon, where they lost by a single point, despite a quite brilliant 15-point maximum from the 'Great Dane' Arne Pander. The side were also unlucky at Leicester, where they went down by just 2 points. There was to be no further away success for the Cheetahs and they lost heavily at Southampton (34-74), which was their worst performance of the season. They were also hammered at Wimbledon (38-70), who were to take the National League title by 9 clear points from their closest challengers, Leicester. Oxford finished the season in seventh position (from nine teams), which wasn't much of an improvement to their 1958 performance. After the immaculate Arne Pander, Oxford's best was Gordon McGregor, who yielded 153 points, but they were the only ones to top a century of points. Ronnie Genz was next in line, with 94 points, while Colin Gooddy made great progress to notch a creditable 61 points. In the incomplete National Reserve League, Oxford finished in sixth position having ridden 12 matches.

## The 1960s

The 1960 season heralded a welcome upsurge in speedway's fortunes, with the formation of a brand new ten-team Provincial League. At last, there was welcome news, with tracks opening rather than closing, and there was further good news when it was announced that New Cross would be re-opening and joining the National League. Ipswich returned, after a season's absence, with the Poole promotion moving to Suffolk, while a new promoting company took over at Poole and entered a team in the newly formed Provincial League. Oxford were now members of a National League that comprised ten teams and everyone down at Cowley looked forward to a enjoyable season. And that is just what it turned out to be, with the Cheetahs making a real challenge for league honours, and if they had had a little more strength at the lower end of the side, then they could easily have knocked Wimbledon off their perch at the top. With Arne Pander back for his second year at Oxford, things looked bright when Charlie New indicated he wanted to return to Cowley. Unfortunately, he had a last-minute change of heart and stayed at home, which became the second disappointment for Oxford in their quest for team strength. The first had been the failure to land the fast-starting Peter Moore, who had spent the later part of 1959 on loan to Norwich. The Oxford management had agreed a transfer fee with Moore's parent club, Wimbledon; however, with Ipswich returning to the National League, the rider was keen to return to a scene of his former triumphs, and subsequently lined up with the new Witches.

The Cheetahs started the 1960 season with much the same side as the previous season, with the exception of Nick Nicholls, who returned to Coventry. However, there was to be a marked contrast to the year before, and the most important factor was the return to form of Ronnie Genz. After two years of suffering with persistent eye trouble, it was a real treat to see 'Genno' showing all his old form, and with Gordon McGregor maintaining remarkable consistency in his scoring, the Cheetahs finally had two riders able to give Arne Pander the backing he so richly deserved. A couple of months after the start of the season, in June, the Cheetahs' management pulled off a smart piece of business, which was to give them extra strength in depth, and provide further support for their top three. It came in the form of an exchange deal, with the promising Colin Gooddy going to Ipswich, and the experienced Jack Biggs returning to Cowley. Jack had not had a very happy time at Ipswich, and was unable to settle, but his return to Cowley proved to be a real tonic for him and he soon re-captured his form, giving the Cheetahs a really impressive top four. A further new face for the 1960 season was Danny Dunton, who was with Belle Vue in 1959. Danny, of course, would return in later years to promote the fortunes of Oxford Speedway.

Eric Boothroyd returned after a short spell at Leicester, but unlike Jack Biggs, Boothroyd's return did not mean a rekindling of form and poor Eric struggled. Howdy Byford and Ken Adams were other riders to struggle, while it was Roy Bowers who was the best in the lower order, where the Cheetahs also gave opportunities to Dave Still, Cliff Cox and a young Bobby Dugard. At home, the Cheetahs enjoyed plenty of success with a number of good, close matches. Both Leicester and Norwich were beaten by 8 points, with Swindon and Southampton being defeated by 6, while Wimbledon and New Cross were seen off by just 2 points in real nail-biting matches. The best home victory was a 59-30 success over Coventry, with the next best being a 55-35 win over Ipswich.

*Colin Gooddy.*

Meanwhile, Belle Vue were the only club to take points from Cowley, when they won another tremendous match by 47 points to 43. Away from home, the Cheetahs enjoyed a decisive win at Ipswich (51-39), and a fine victory over Southampton, but the sweetest win of all was a 2-point success at Swindon on 1 October, with Arne Pander scoring a 12-point maximum, while Gordon McGregor weighed in with 11.

Nine days after the win at Swindon, and still with a hope of the League championship, the Cheetahs visited Wimbledon, only to go down fighting by 8 points (41-49). The worst away defeat was at Leicester, where Oxford lost 33-57, but they were desperately unlucky at Belle Vue, losing 43-47, an identical score to that at Cowley. All in all, it was a great season at Oxford, with the Cheetahs providing good value for money and always being attractive visitors on their travels. Third position in the league was a fine effort, with only Belle Vue and Champions Wimbledon finishing higher, with a mere four points between the Cheetahs and the Dons.

Oxford Cheetahs had every reason to be optimistic when the 1961 season dawned, after their successful time the year before. The National League was as before, with the same ten teams, and although there were one or two Provincial League clubs that fell by the wayside, the new set-up was prospering and eventually lined up with a very healthy eleven-team league. On the team front, Oxford had a few changes, with Eric Boothroyd and Ken Adams departing for the less demanding racing in the Provincial League, with Middlesbrough and Stoke respectively. Meanwhile, Reg Duval returned to Cowley following a year in the wilderness. With the same top four of Pander, Genz, McGregor and Biggs, who had successfully done the business in 1960, plus Dunton, Bowers and Byford, things were really humming at the beginning of the campaign. At the start things didn't go too badly and a storming league win over Coventry by 59 points to 19 suggested great things for the Cheetahs.

But, as so often happens, things didn't work out and the hand of fate was to deliver a crushing blow to Oxford in July, when Arne Pander suffered a fractured skull in a track accident at Coventry. This really knocked the Cheetahs sideways, and in truth, they never really recovered from it. Pander, since his arrival in 1959, had been the cornerstone of the Cheetahs team, having taken on and beaten the best in the league, while his mere presence had inspired confidence amongst his team-mates. They had come to rely on his regular double-figure scores and his absence was to have a demoralizing effect on the rest of the side. The popular Howdy Byford, who had really found the pace of the National League a trifle hot over the previous couple of years, left to join Provincial League side Exeter. There, he linked up with another former Cheetah in Roy Bowers, who had lost form completely and had been granted a transfer. As if the Oxford promotion didn't have enough problems, Jack Biggs, who in 1960 had supplied vital backing to the Cheetahs' heat-leader trio, underwent an operation, which affected both his form and fitness.

With the Provincial League offering valuable opportunities to young riders to make good and a stimulus to veteran riders who wanted one last fling, there really became a shortage of riders in the National League. The result of this was that team spots became too safe and in particular at Oxford, no rider at the lower end of the Cheetahs team was seriously challenged for his place, with the result that complacency set in. Despite the

*Arne Pander.*

problems, the Oxford promotion did try and do something constructive. Jim Tebby was signed from Wimbledon (he had, in fact, appeared for Oxford in 1956), but whilst he was young and promising, he needed to be in a team that could carry him for a spell whilst he learned the business. Indeed, had he been in the Cheetahs line-up the previous season, he could have been very useful, but in 1961, far too much was expected of him and he clearly wasn't the answer to Oxford's problems. Stylish Swede Bengt Brannefors had a short and unsuccessful time at Cowley. He was regarded as one of his country's up-and-coming riders, but was not of the Fundin or Knutsson class and was most disappointing.

After the injury to Arne Pander, it was left to Ronnie Genz to lead the Cheetahs' challenge and he continued to give sterling service to the Oxford cause. Often, however, the team gave the impression that they were just going through the motions and that view was definitely held by the Oxford promoters. Towards the end of the season, Dickie Worth, the Cheetahs' boss man, fed up with what he felt were some mediocre performances, threatened to put everyone in the squad (with the exception of Pander and Genz) on the transfer list. It put the final seal on a totally disappointing season. The Cheetahs won only 6 matches during the year, all at home, where they also drew once. Swindon and Wimbledon took points from Cowley, while away from home, Oxford had no success at all, their best effort being a 2-point defeat at Coventry. It was a troubled season for Oxford fans, who saw their side slide down the league table to finish one place above wooden spoonists Leicester.

The 1962 season followed an old familiar pattern that the Oxford supporters had often seen in the past, namely one of a weak team, and therefore poor results. It was also the year that saw handicap racing introduced, but the Cheetahs had no rider of the class to join the big five of Barry Briggs, Peter Craven, Ove Fundin, Bjorn Knutsson and Ronnie Moore. Had Arne Pander been fit and available, it is likely that the Dane would have made it a big six, but Arne was still recovering from his head injuries and missed the entire season. In the event, most of the Cheetahs squad rode off a 10-yard handicap or scratch. It was obvious from the start that without Pander, Oxford would struggle and he was never properly replaced. Sadly, New Cross, had folded after two seasons, while Leicester also closed and re-opened in the Provincial League, so the National League, at the start anyway, was down to just eight teams. The demise of Leicester brought Jack Geran and Alf Hagon to Cowley, but their form was patchy, again an old familiar occurrence when established riders came to Cowley. It seemed that only Ronnie Genz, now skipper of the Cheetahs, had any real enthusiasm for racing. Despite his threat of the previous year, promoter Dickie Worth didn't transfer the bulk of his side. It may have been better if he'd done so, because Jack Biggs spent most of the season in dispute with the bosses over one thing or another, and Gordon McGregor seemed to have lost his zest for speedway and was gloriously inconsistent.

To try and strengthen the team, Swedish international Per Tage Svensson was recruited and made a bright start with some early double-figure scores, but he flattered to deceive and after a few meetings his scores had diminished to just average. In mid-July, the National League lost another side when Ipswich closed down. This was another unfortunate happening for the Cheetahs, since they'd recorded an away win at Foxhall Heath, and at home they'd scored their biggest win of the year when beating the Witches 49-29. So, at a stroke, the Cheetahs lost 4 league points and promptly replaced unfortunate Ipswich at the bottom of the National League table. The closure of Ipswich saw Colin Gooddy return to Cowley and whilst 'Joe' (as he was affectionately known) tried hard, and his riding had a little bit of bite about it, he was not the answer

*Oxford 1962. From left to right, back row: Ted Flanagan (team manager), Jack Biggs, Gordon McGregor, John Bishop, Per Tage Svensson, Dickie Worth (promoter). Front row: Alf Hagon, Ronnie Genz (on machine), Jack Geran.*

to Oxford's problems. They desperately needed heat-leaders and Ipswich had only one in Peter Moore, and he linked up with the Cheetahs' near neighbours Swindon. What could have helped the Oxford cause was the allocation of the Witches' promising Swedish rider Leif Larsson, who was certainly not disgraced at Foxhall Heath, or even Ray Cresp, who'd ridden Cowley well a few seasons earlier. Surprisingly, Larsson returned home to Sweden, and never graced British speedway on a full-time basis again. Perhaps it was an indirect result of the promoters' pre-season conference decision to bar foreign riders, which in the event was hastily changed, but for some reason, one of Sweden's most up-and-coming riders was not re-allocated and he could have done Oxford a power of good.

Cresp, meanwhile, moved to Norwich, who were hardly aware of his presence, but he could have at least added to the competition for team places at Cowley. As had happened in the past, far too many team places were safe. The Cheetahs undoubtedly made a mistake in that direction by not giving more opportunities to John Bishop, a young novice who displayed a keenness often missing in some of his team-mates. An extended run for John would have paid dividends and, overall, he was a better prospect than the discontented Biggs or Reg Duval, who tried, unsuccessfully, to double-up with Provincial League Bradford. The teams raced each other twice home and away during the season, with Oxford winning only 4 home matches as a result of the Ipswich closure. Their best effort was a 47-31 victory over Coventry, and they did, in fact, complete a home double over the Bees. A 2-point triumph over Norwich and a 4-point victory over Swindon completed the 1962 Oxford successes. Away from home, Oxford lost all 12 matches, with their best effort being a 38-40 defeat at Swindon. Southampton soundly thrashed the Cheetahs twice, and generally Oxford were hard pushed to top a 30-point total on their travels. Towards the end of the season, manager Ted Flanagan departed and was replaced by Bert Hutchins. It was yet another unfortunate happening in a thoroughly disappointing season. It was small wonder that Oxford finished bottom of the league with a total of only 8 points.

Oxford fans looked forward to the 1963 season, believing that things could only improve after the disastrous year before. After all, they had been cheered by the news that Arne Pander would be back following a year's absence, having fully recovered from the bad injuries he received during 1961. There were the usual changes before the off, and neither of the moves of riders away from Cowley were a surprise. Jack Biggs departed for Coventry, while Gordon McGregor left to join Belle Vue. Added to this, Per Tage Svensson remained in Sweden and Reg Duval retired. In their places came Pander, of course, and from Southampton came established Australian international Chum Taylor. The Aussie had missed the 1962 season, and had returned in 1963 confident that he'd be lining up with the Saints; however, the Control Board considered Southampton too strong and the rider was posted to Oxford. It would be fair to say that Taylor didn't welcome the move, and made it clear that had he known of his move before the season began, he would have remained at home in Australia! A pre-season shock, which in the event was almost beyond belief, was the announcement that the Oxford management would consider offers for Ronnie Genz. Such a statement was total nonsense, since 'Genno' had been such a great servant to the club and over the years had proved to be the most consistent rider in the Oxford camp. Thankfully, common sense prevailed and Ronnie stayed at Cowley, linking with Pander, Geran, Gooddy, Hagon and Taylor, plus promising youngsters John Bishop and George Major to form a nicely balanced line-up.

The National League remained at seven sides, with the teams meeting each other twice. Handicap racing remained in place, with Pander given a 10-yard handicap like most of the main body of the team. The handicap rule, like most rules introduced, caused many problems over who started from where, with the result that match scores were often altered by officialdom due to riders starting from the wrong handicap. The Cheetahs were one of the sides to suffer, when, having beaten Belle Vue 40-38, the points scored by John Bishop were deducted as he had lined up at the gate, and not 10 yards back. The result was subsequently amended to a 34-38 defeat. This was a real nonsense of a situation when you consider the experience of John compared with Pander, Geran or Genz.

Happily, there was some evidence of increased enthusiasm from the team, but Oxford were to be badly hit by injuries. Chum Taylor broke a collar bone in a World Championship qualifying round at Poole, and was hardly back in action when he suffered a fractured ankle at Swindon. Alf Hagon was another rider to suffer a broken ankle, while Arne Pander sustained a broken thumb. As a result, it was no surprise that the Cheetahs were unable to move up from their basement position of 1962, and were only able to win six of their home matches, drawing one other. There were no successes at all on the road, but Oxford did provide spirited opposition at a number of tracks. The Cheetahs ran Coventry close in both matches at Brandon, losing by 2 points on the first occasion and 6 points in the second match. Not for the first time, Ronnie Genz was a tower of strength and he ended the season as the highest points plunderer in the side, with 172 in league matches. Jack Geran had a much better year, and Colin Gooddy came on in leaps and bounds, making good progress. Quite understandably, Pander was not back to his pre-injury form, but still topped the 100-point mark.

The 1964 season was the most troubled in the history of the sport, with the strong, thirteen-team Provincial League riding outside the jurisdiction of the Speedway Control Board. Things weren't so good in the National League though, with Southampton closing down, having been a victim of the developers. That left the league with a mere six teams, although that was subsequently increased to seven when West Ham re-opened. There were storm clouds over Oxford too, as promoter Dickie Worth's lease had ceased early in the year. The new season was only weeks away, when two new promoters, namely Cyril Melville and Rodney Rycroft, took over. New boys they may have been, but they came in with one basic sensible idea, namely that the Cheetahs would no longer be the chopping block for the rest of the league and their subsequent signings proved they meant business. Ron How, an established international heat-leader, was signed from Wimbledon, and Jimmy Gooch was also recruited via Norwich. Eddie Reeves, who had enjoyed limited experience in the Provincial League with New Cross the previous year, also joined the Cheetahs camp. With new eight-man teams, and fourteen-heat matches being the order of the day, at long last Oxford had a side strong in all departments: Arne Pander, Ronnie Genz, Jack Geran (captain), Colin Gooddy, Ron How, Jimmy Gooch, John Bishop and Eddie Reeves. Chum Taylor from

*Ron How.*

the 1963 outfit, had returned to Australia, although he was later to appear for Provincial League Poole, while George Major had a few meetings before the league campaign got under way, before he too opted for Provincial League action and linked with Cradley Heath.

Handicap racing, a thorny subject in pre-season wrangles, remained in National League racing, for part of the season anyway. In August Barry Briggs, who had joined Swindon following the closure of Southampton, threatened to retire if the scheme was not abolished. Leading A.C.U. Referee Cecil Telling backed 'Briggo' all the way, with the result that handicapping ceased for the latter part of the season, never to return, thank goodness. With a limited number of teams in the National League, the promoters opted for a one home, one away league format, which was a surprise. The league, therefore, did not start until June, with the Easter Challenge Cup, Britannia Shield and National Trophy matches filling the early season fixtures. There is no doubt that the Cheetahs, who had changed their race jackets from the familiar blue with yellow sash, to a cheetah's head on a blue background, were the team to beat. They were, in fact, unbeatable at home, and the most attractive visitors away, and it was strange after a number of mediocre seasons at Cowley to hear the cry from opponents that Oxford were too strong!

Yet, despite their success, support was not as forthcoming for the Cheetahs as their new promoters had hoped for. A hardcore of loyal fans existed, but looking at the season as a whole, the successful 1964 Cheetahs did not really enjoy the sort of support their efforts deserved. As expected, Ron How proved to be the number one man at Cowley, and he and Jimmy Gooch formed as good a pairing as the entire league possessed. Arne Pander showed all of his old form, while Jack Geran was a fine skipper. Ronnie Genz and Colin Gooddy were consistent, and the reserves, John Bishop and Eddie Reeves, showed plenty of spirit. Reeves, in particular, despite his lack of experience always battled for points, and his enthusiasm kept the top six on their toes. Despite their general success, the Cheetahs had to wait for their final league match to be sure of becoming Champions. Coventry were breathing down their necks, but in the end it was Oxford who lifted the Championship by a single point, winning 9 of their matches, and losing only 3. Indeed, it was Coventry who inflicted one of those defeats, beating the Cheetahs at Brandon by 51 points to 33. Oxford's other two defeats were suffered at Norwich and Belle Vue, by scores of 39-45 and 38-46 respectively. At home, Oxford never tasted defeat, with their best home success being a 54-30 victory over Wimbledon, and the closest they came to being beaten was when lowly Swindon managed 39 points at Cowley.

The Britannia Shield competition resulted in another Oxford triumph, with the Cheetahs winning by a solitary point, again from rivals Coventry. In all, Oxford won 8 matches, drew just once (at West Ham) and lost 3 times. To add to the happiness of Oxford fans in the remarkable season of 1964, Ron How, who had graced the individual World Final on seven occasions previously, again qualified for the big event in the speedway calendar. The meeting was held in Gothenburg, Sweden, where Ron scored 10 points and became the first Oxford rider ever to appear in the sport's premier event. It really was a season to cherish for the loyal Oxford fans, who had waited such a long time for their side to be successful, and in 1964 the Cheetahs were undoubtedly the team of the year.

The 1965 season heralded a new look to speedway, with an upsurge in the fortunes of the sport. Peace was declared after the problems that had prevailed in 1964 and a new eighteen-team British League was formed, following the amalgamation of the National League and the Provincial League. Norwich, of the old National League, fell to the developers, and Middlesbrough, formerly of the Provincial League, moved to Halifax, but everywhere else the sport was bubbling. The year also saw the formation of the B.S.P.A., who took over the day-to-day running of the sport. Despite the exciting happenings, it was, initially, another touch-and-go situation at Oxford. The 1964 management pulled out, and, yet again, the season had almost started before Danny Dunton and Ted Flanagan got the go-ahead to run the fortunes of Oxford. The amalgamation of the two leagues saw the introduction of rider control, a system introduced to ensure equalization of team strengths. The 1964 Cheetahs side was broken up, with long-serving Ronnie Genz moving to Poole, and Jack Geran going home to Exeter, together with Colin Gooddy. Nevertheless, Oxford still ended up with a strong heat-leader trio of Ron How, Arne Pander and Jimmy Gooch. John Bishop and Eddie Reeves also remained, and, in the beginning anyway, young and inexperienced riders were drafted into the side to make up the agreed seven-man teams. Incidentally, matches were now decided over thirteen heats, and each side raced each other once home and once away.

An interesting story around Oxford way in the early days of the season concerned tractor driver John Hook. It was claimed that Johnny was driving the tractor one week, and drafted into the Oxford side the next. In truth, that did actually happen, but John was not without some speedway experience, having had rides at Aldershot in their Southern League days and second-half outings at Belle Vue, Swindon and Cradley Heath during the 1960s. Remarkably, John won what was only his second race in the Cheetahs' league match against Poole on 22 April, but couldn't find form thereafter and lost his team place. He was one of many young riders introduced into the Oxford side at the lower end of the team. Other youngsters tried out included John Belcher, John

Leader, Bill Finch and Wayne Barry.

The season began with a good 5-point home win over Sheffield, but this was followed by a shock the week after, when Poole (with Ronnie Genz) won by 10 points. Despite this setback, the Cheetahs continued to be quite a formidable combination at home, and the arrival of Ken Vale was a real boost to the second-string department. The wide-riding style of Ken around the Oxford circuit was something that really got the pulses racing amongst the supporters and he soon became a great favourite. It looked as though Oxford had another winner when Glyn Chandler arrived and had a couple of useful meetings, but he lost form and soon disappeared from the Cowley scene. By June, the Cheetahs were climbing up the league table, and it was a good month with wins at Cradley Heath (42-36) and Glasgow (40-38). In addition to this, Jimmy Gooch won the World Championship qualifying round at Cowley, closely followed by another at Halifax two days later. Ron How was also successful, winning the World Championship qualifying round at Hackney on 19 June.

However, on 5 July, Oxford suffered a real body blow when Ron How suffered a shoulder injury in a Test Match against Russia. The injury required surgery over a long period of time, with the result that Ron was out for the season, and, ultimately, the injury caused his premature retirement from the sport. To try and restore the balance of the side, Oxford drafted in Stan Stevens and Jimmy Heard. Both were lads with some experience, but in no way was either of them an adequate replacement for Ron, and it was left to Jimmy Gooch and Arne Pander to provide the Cheetahs' main source of

*Oxford 1965. From left to right, back row: Ted Flanagan (team manager), Glyn Chandler, Ken Vale, Sid Knibbs, John Hook, Eddie Reeves, Jimmy Gooch, Danny Dunton (promoter). Front, on bike: Ron How.*

points. July ended with a 2-point British League win at Swindon, and a visit from the Polish touring side Gornik, with Oxford winning an interesting meeting 46-32. As the season drew to its close, there came more triumph and further injury problems. The exciting Ken Vale badly injured his back, but Jimmy Gooch, having scored 10 points at West Ham in the British Final, thus qualified for the World Final at Wembley on 18 September, where he scored 4 points. Arne Pander hit a purple patch, going through 6 successive league matches without defeat, and winning the Scottish Open Championship (with a 15-point maximum) at Edinburgh. The first British League Riders' Championship at Belle Vue on 16 October was won by Swindon's Barry Briggs, with that man Jimmy Gooch a fine runner-up.

Overall, it was a good season for the Cheetahs, who finished fourth in the league table, and one could not help thinking how different things might have been had Ron How and Ken Vale not been hurt. As it was, Oxford boasted three riders with averages in excess of 9 in British League matches, with Ron How achieving a brilliant 10.16 figure from his 18 meetings. Arne Pander scored 353 points for a 10.01 average, while Jimmy Gooch supplied fantastic support, recording 326 points for a 9.97 average. Individually, Gooch enjoyed his best-ever season, becoming Oxford's second World Finalist. After their successful debut season in the British League, things looked to be on the up-and-up for 1966 at Oxford, but it wasn't to be, with the Cheetahs dropping to fifteenth place in the final league table. The British League now boasted nineteen teams, welcoming King's Lynn to the fold, after their open licence season in 1965.

Oxford's problem was that they lacked a third heat-leader, and they had never properly replaced the high-scoring Ron How. Apart from Ron, Stan Stevens, Jimmy Heard and Ken Vale were all missing from the 1965 team. Replacements came in the shape of Des Lukehurst (allocated from Exeter) and Tony Clarke (via West Ham), while Maurice McDermott re-appeared on the Cowley scene. Unfortunately, none of them filled a heat-leader berth, and were terribly inconsistent in their scoring. Lukehurst, however, had two moments of triumph, scoring maximum points at Long Eaton in a Midland Cup fixture, and producing a classic last-heat ride in the home match against Wimbledon on 7 July, when he came from behind to join Pander for 5-1 and victory for the Cheetahs. Apart from that, Des was only a good second string, as his final average of 4.14 points showed.

Some things in speedway never change – in particular, the weather – and the Cheetahs' start to the 1966 campaign was blighted by the elements. The second match of the season (14 April) against Wolverhampton was snowed off and five days later, the away fixture against West Ham succumbed to Jupiter Pluvias, as did the home fixture against Hackney on 12 May. To add to their problems, Jimmy Gooch suffered a slipped disc, and John Bishop was absent for a spell with glandular fever. However, one thing cheered Cowley supporters, namely the form of the 'Great Dane' Arne Pander. Arne was back to his brilliant best, and double-figure scores just flowed from his wheels. The Cheetahs won their first home British League fixture on 21 April, against Belle Vue, and it was not until 28 July, when Poole forced a draw, that they dropped a home point. During that time, Pander registered double-figure scores in all 9 of their home league matches. Halifax visited Oxford the following week, with Arne having, for him, an off-

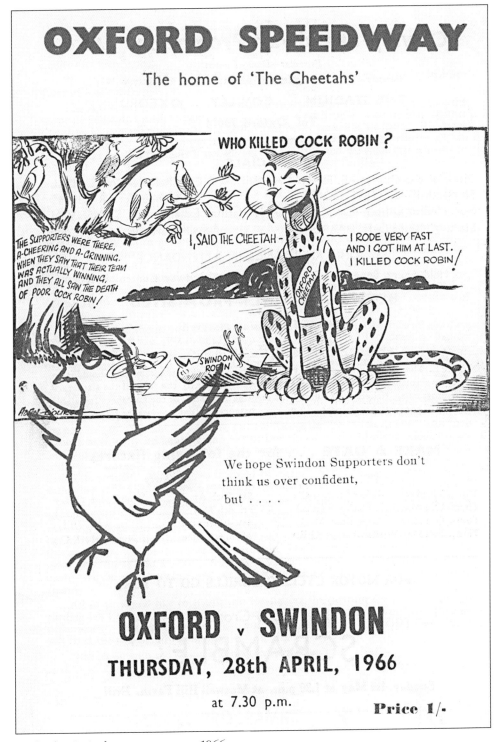

*Oxford v. Swindon programme, 1966.*

night with just 7 points, and bang went the Cheetahs' home record. Jimmy Gooch, upon his return from a back injury, gave Pander the backing he deserved and, in fact, as the season progressed, it was Jim who led the Oxford scoring. Eddie Reeves made good progress and his end of season average of just over 6 points looked good for the future, and John Bishop, whilst not coming on as fast as Reeves, still looked a useful prospect.

At home, Oxford were always good value, and it was only as the season drew to a close that their form slipped. The problem with the side was their lack of success away from Cowley, with a 3-point win at King's Lynn on 16 August being their sole success in the league. They did beat Long Eaton in a Midland Cup match (46-32), thanks to a Des Lukehurst maximum, but apart from these two successes, nothing came the Cheetahs' way on their opponent's tracks. At Cowley, 13 matches were won, with 2 draws and 3 defeats, which wasn't a bad record, but the 17 away defeats proved disastrous. Tony Clarke, from whom much was expected, did not prove himself at Cowley, and it was no surprise when he asked for a move at the end of the campaign. He was not the only one to request a transfer, and the club was rocked when Arne Pander indicated that he wanted away from Oxford. This was a real shock, but Pander, who'd enjoyed a fine season with a 9.51 British League average, claimed he was at loggerheads with the Cowley promoters and would be seeking pastures new in 1967.

As if this wasn't bad enough, the promoters indicated that the season had been poor financially, with crowds down on average. So 1966, which had produced so much thrilling racing at Cowley, ended on a note of uncertainty. As Robin Major, the *Oxford Mail* reporter put it, '1967 could be decisive at Oxford, one way or the other'. Happily, the 1967 season saw an upsurge in Oxford's crowds, with the Cowley turnstiles clicking away healthily to the joy of the promoters. Before the season began, there was the usual movement of riders, with the popular Jimmy Gooch and the promising John Bishop moving on to Newport, while Tony Clarke returned to West Ham. The good news was that Arne Pander decided that he wanted to stay. Newcomer Roy Trigg was allocated to Oxford from Hackney, while the Cheetahs also signed Leo McAuliffe upon his return to speedway. Another signing was a highly promising first-timer from New Zealand, who went by the name of Rick Timmo. So, with Des Lukehurst, Eddie Reeves and Maurice McDermott, the Cheetahs looked to have a well-balanced side, and one that was capable of challenging for league title honours.

At home, Oxford made a bright start, with wins against Belle Vue, Edinburgh and Cradley Heath, followed by a thrilling draw against Poole and a win against Exeter. Away from Cowley in the early weeks of the season, they took time to settle, and apart from a 2-point defeat at Hackney on 14 April, they were soundly beaten on their travels. However, the Cowley faithful believed it was only a question of time, as the potential was obviously there, but tragedy struck on the 11 May in a home match against near neighbours Swindon. From that moment on, the Cheetahs seemed destined to struggle near the foot of the league table. The tragedy occurred in heat seven, when popular Dane Arne Pander suffered a broken leg in a nasty-looking crash, which was to rule him out of action for the remainder of the season. There was no doubt it was a major blow for Oxford, as the speedy little Dane was riding with all his old fire and this was fully emphasized by his 9.57 average, attained from the 13 matches ridden prior to injury.

Eddie Reeves took over the captaincy of the Cheetahs following Arne's accident and promptly became the youngest skipper in the British League. Indeed, the youthful Eddie seemed to enjoy the extra responsibility and was always good for at least half-a-dozen points a match. The search to replace Pander saw the return to Cowley of the hard-riding Colin Gooddy, who had been a member of their 1964 National League title-winning side. Colin, who had moved to Exeter in the 1965 rider control allocations, welcomed a return to Oxford, and soon thrilled the Cowley faithful with a series of fighting displays. Despite the loss of Pander, and their inability to win away from Cowley (their sole success being a win over Cradley Heath in June by just a single point), there was much to cheer and interest the Oxford public in 1967. Rick Timmo was proving a most useful signing and showed his fighting qualities when forcing his way back into the side following a period of mid-season blues, which had seen him briefly forfeit his team place.

Roy Trigg took over the mantle of the Cheetahs' number one, as he averaged 9.38 points per match and won the qualifying rounds for the Midland Riders' Championship and the World Championship at Cowley with fine 15-point maximums. Des Lukehurst proved a reliable second string and was always good for half-a-dozen points, but the form of Maury McDermott was patchy, as was that of Leo McAuliffe, who never really raced to his true potential. The Cheetahs finished fourteenth out of a nineteen-team league, based almost entirely on a good home record. Only Wimbledon and Coventry took points away from Oxford, with the Bees winning a thriller by just a

*Oxford 1967. From left to right, back row: Arne Pander, Eddie Reeves, Danny Dunton (promoter), Des Lukehurst. Back row: John Bishop, Maury McDermott, Tony Clarke.*

single point on 20 July. Poole also gleaned a point from Cowley on 20 April, but all the same, 15 home wins was a fine effort. Away from home, there was only the one success at Cradley Heath, so there wasn't much for the supporters to cheer about on their travels. 1967 proved to be a season of fine close racing enjoyed by the improved Oxford crowds. However, it was a case of what might have been, had Arne Pander not been injured. Indeed, with Arne available, the Cheetahs could well have been British League Champions, an honour that went just down the road to local rivals Swindon.

Before the 1968 season began, there was the usual movement of riders, courtesy of the Rider Control Committee, which posted Roy Trigg to Cradley Heath after just one season at Cowley, while the steady Des Lukehurst found himself Hackney-bound. To replace them, John Bishop returned after a season at Newport, and Ronnie Genz came back after three years with Poole. At least the popular 'Genno' knew every inch of the Cowley circuit and was riding well, so Cowley fans knew that there was a ready-made replacement for the departed Trigg. The news that gladdened everyone was that Arne Pander was now fit, and with Colin Gooddy, Eddie Reeves, Leo McAuliffe and the promising Rick Timmo, the 1968 Cheetahs looked capable of making a real challenge for league honours. Promoters Danny Dunton and Dick Austen thought so too, with Mr Dunton predicting with confidence that his team would finish in the top three of the British League.

Sadly though, Oxford were to witness an old familiar pattern, with the injury bug striking with a vengeance before the tapes had even risen at Cowley. Again it struck the unfortunate Pander, who broke his collarbone in an open meeting at Wolverhampton a week before the Oxford opener. Fortunately, the plucky Dane made a swift recovery, but his absence caused the Cheetahs to make an indifferent start to the season. Swindon beat them in an opening challenge, and they had a home draw with King's

*Rick Timmo.*

Lynn in the Easter Egg Trophy, losing on aggregate. The match against West Ham fell victim to the weather, and their first home success came on 25 April, when they beat Belle Vue 43-35 in a league fixture.

Cradley Heath won 47-30 at Cowley on 2 May, but the following evening disaster struck yet again for Arne Pander, who crashed in a match at Hackney and fractured a shin bone, which was to rule him out of the side for at least three months. Pander's run of bad luck was almost unbelievable and the promoters were forced to look around for a replacement. No adequate replacement was available in the British League though, so Messrs Dunton and Austen turned their attention abroad, and after a month-long search came up with promising Danish youngster Godtfred Andreason. It was obvious that the newcomer would take time to settle, and everyone was prepared to be patient, but fortune refused to smile on the Cheetahs. In an away fixture at Newcastle, the unfortunate Andreason hit the Brough Park safety fence and was carried off with a broken leg. Despite the setbacks, the Cheetahs battled on and the month of May proved to be a turning point in the fortunes of Leo McAuliffe, who had achieved very little in the early matches. A large investment in new equipment began to pay dividends and it was a very different McAuliffe during the second half of the season.

By the time both Andreason and Pander were fit again, the Rider Control Committee, who had done precious little to help Oxford find a replacement when Pander was injured, ruled that the Cheetahs couldn't keep both Danes, so Arne finally broke his Cowley connections and went on loan to Poole. No sooner had this happened, than Andreason decided he was homesick and promptly upped and returned to Denmark! The last day of August saw the Cheetahs in a British League match at Cradley Heath, and there was more misfortune for Oxford, when lynchpin Ronnie Genz crashed, and was out for the rest of the season with a severe bout of concussion. Still the Cheetahs battled on, and September saw two good home British League wins over Exeter and King's Lynn, while October proved a good month, with the Cheetahs winning their final three home league matches, despite losing skipper Eddie Reeves with a blood infection.

With so many injury problems, it was hardly surprising that the Cheetahs finished in fifteenth position in the nineteen-strong British League. They still managed 16 home wins, with only Cradley Heath and Swindon taking league points from Cowley. Though on the road, Oxford had but one success, a fine 41-37 win over Wimbledon on 16 May. Ronnie Genz was Oxford's best until his unfortunate accident, while Eddie Reeves was steady and averaged nearly 8 points a match. Leo McAuliffe was a revelation in the post-May period, and a young novice called Mick Bell looked a fine prospect for the future. However, not for the first time were Oxford supporters left wondering just what might have been.

The 1969 season at Oxford was very much the same mixture as before, with the injury bug showing no sign of letting up. Despite this, the Cowley fans enjoyed some good racing, with Oxford continuing to ride very well at home. Problems started before the season really got underway, when Ronnie Genz attempted to make a comeback, but it was obvious that the brave 'Genno' wasn't going to make it. Meanwhile, Arne Pander was posted to Halifax, so at the start of the season, Oxford were down to just six riders. As a result, they had to use Swindon's Mike Broadbanks as a guest for their opening challenge match against Hackney on 27 March. It was obvious that this situation couldn't go on, and to bring the side up to strength Peter Jarman was signed from Wolverhampton. At least Oxford now had a full side, although there were no recognized top stars, but every rider was a potential 7-point man. Eddie Reeves was skipper again, supported by Colin Gooddy, Leo McAuliffe, Rick Timmo, Peter Jarman and John Bishop, with the highly promising Mick Bell, and other youngsters, Pete Saunders and Pete Seaton, waiting in the wings.

*Eddie Reeves.*

Misfortune, however, was just around the corner and struck again on 17 May, when Leo McAuliffe was badly injured in a track crash at Halifax, whilst competing in a World Championship qualifying round. Sadly, poor Leo, who was averaging over 7 points a match, was out for the remainder of the season. As in 1968, Oxford were left to find their own replacements, since Rider Control couldn't (or wouldn't) assist, which was hardly surprising as they had solved a problem at Newcastle by giving permission for the Diamonds to use a permanent guest rider! Oxford looked abroad again, and secured the services of a young rider from Sweden by the name of Conny Samuelsson. Conny had a fine reputation in the land of the lakes and was being described as the new Nygren or Fundin. Oxford promoter Danny Dunton was clearly on cloud nine, but unfortunately for both Danny and Oxford, Conny just couldn't come to terms with the Cowley circuit. With his confidence affected badly, Conny left for home after two months, never to return to British speedway.

Replacement riders were urgently needed, and they arrived in the form of George Major (a former Cheetah who was not enjoying the best of luck at Leicester) and David Crane (via King's Lynn). The move did George Major the world of good and in sixteen league matches, he averaged 5.27 points a match, and was riding exceptionally well as the season drew to a close. David Crane wasn't quite so successful, but still averaged around 4 points a match, which wasn't bad going. Eddie Reeves and Colin Gooddy proved to be the mainstays of the side, with consistent scoring. Eddie was rapidly becoming unbeatable at Cowley, while Colin Gooddy (or 'Joe' as he was known), was always battling away in the thick of things. Pete Jarman came good after an indifferent start and began to give Reeves and Gooddy vital backing, while a mid-season switch of machinery worked wonders for Rick Timmo, who began to make real progress.

Over at Reading in the Second Division, Mick Bell, who was on loan to the Berkshire club, was having the time of his life topping the Racers' scorechart with the utmost regularity and ending the season as their top point-scorer, with a 9.04 average from league and cup meetings. Mick was runner-up in the Second Division Riders' Championship, and when called upon to assist the Cheetahs in the top league, he scored many useful points. The Cheetahs' final position was again fifteenth in the British League, and once again they enjoyed a reasonably good home record, winning 13 matches, and losing 4 and drawing just once. There was, as usual, not much luck on opponents' tracks, but they came away with the league points from both West Ham and Wolverhampton. The worst away performance from Cowley was at Coventry, when on 12 April, the Bees ran riot and thrashed Oxford by 60 points to 18.

## The 1970s

The 1970 season dawned with good news for the Oxford Cheetahs. Firstly, Ronnie Genz, who had missed the 1969 season through injury, declared himself fit and prepared to make a comeback, and secondly, the management were able to persuade Swedish star Hasse Holmqvist to become an Oxford rider. In addition to this, Mick Bell, after a successful season on loan to Second Division Reading, became a full-time Cheetah, so along with Colin Gooddy, Eddie Reeves, Rick Timmo, Pete Jarman and George Major, the Oxford squad had a good look about it. Rider Control moved John Bishop, who had had a torrid time at Cowley during 1969, down the road to Swindon, while David Crane was allowed to seek pastures new. George Major had a poor start to the campaign and eventually left to link up with Second Division Doncaster.

The signing of Hasse Holmqvist was a real feather in the cap of promoter Danny Dunton, since it gave Oxford a proven heat-leader, capable of scoring points on any track. In addition, he was a real personality and an exciting rider to watch in action. Hasse had already proved his worth a few seasons earlier when, in 1967, he had signed for Wolverhampton and shown that he was capable of taking on and beating the best riders the British League had to offer. He had returned to Wolverhampton in 1968, but had failed to agree terms with them in 1969, preferring to remain in Sweden. The Cheetahs opened the season at Wimbledon on 26 March with high hopes, but found the Dons in a mean mood, and crashed to a 29-49 defeat. Nevertheless, Holmqvist showed his class with 12 points and if Mick Bell had not blown an engine, the result could have been much closer. The following day saw the season open at Cowley, with the Dons again supplying the opposition, and again they ran out winners, this time by 46 points to the Cheetahs' 35. Holmqvist quickly settled down to his new home track with a well-taken 10 points, and only machine problems prevented him from scoring a maximum. Ronnie Genz scored 6 points, but wisely (as at Wimbledon, where he'd scored 2 points) he took things steadily. However, the great news was that the popular 'Genno' was back and looked good too.

Rick Timmo was still awaiting the arrival of his machine and he missed the two opening matches, but he was back for the visit to Newcastle on Monday 30 March (riding the track spare) and the Cheetahs raced to their first league success of the season, winning 41-37. King's Lynn visited for the Easter Egg Trophy on 2 April, with Oxford recording a narrow 41-37 victory, but they lost 76-80 on aggregate after losing the second leg (35-43) at Saddlebow Road on 4 April. The home fixture against Belle Vue on 9 April fell victim to the weather, and the Cheetahs lost by 10 points at Glasgow the following day. Leicester came to Cowley on 16 April and the Cheetahs scored a resounding victory and followed this up with a 45-33 win over Wembley in a special challenge match to mark the 21st anniversary of post-war speedway at Oxford Stadium. This was followed by a home defeat by Cradley Heath and an away thrashing at Coventry, but the Cheetahs sprang a real surprise by journeying to Exeter on 11 May, and coming away with a 4-point victory.

A real night to remember, however, occurred on 18 June, when Swindon visited for a Midland Cup match. Pete Jarman was injured in heat four and out of the meeting, which had begun in tremendous style for Oxford, with Rick Timmo beating the one and only Barry Briggs, and breaking the season's track record of 66.4 seconds set by Hasse Holmqvist. Not to be outdone, Holmqvist equalled the new track record in heat three. Just for good measure, Colin Gooddy beat 'Briggo' in heat eleven, with the four-times World Champion gaining his revenge over 'Joe' in heat thirteen. The loss of Jarman cost the Cheetahs dear in the end though, and the Robins ran out winners by 4 points. At Swindon on 24 June, the Cheetahs lost the second leg 32-46, with Richard May (of Second Division Reading) guesting for the absent Jarman.

Perhaps the match most enjoyed by Oxford supporters came as the season drew to its close on 1 October, when Poole visited Cowley for a league fixture. The 1969 British League Champions had previously beaten the Cheetahs in the Knock Out Cup on 28 May by just 2 points. The match had been littered with controversy, and the final result had left the Cheetahs' management somewhat angry. However, this time there was to be no mistake with Oxford going on the rampage and winning by 22 points, with Ronnie Genz recording a maximum, while Holmqvist and Timmo each contributed a paid dozen. Oxford finished the campaign in thirteenth position, which spelt a slight improvement on the previous year. As in the past, they were good value at home, winning 14 matches and losing 4, but it was the same old story away from Cowley, and after their early wins at Newcastle and Exeter, there was no further away success for the Cheetahs. All in all, it was not a bad season, with Hasse Holmqvist a great success with 212 points (average 9.10) from 23 league fixtures, while Ronnie Genz made a successful comeback, and Colin Gooddy had his moments. The rest of the team were inclined to be patchy, being likely to score double figures one week and nothing the next.

The 1971 season was one of problems for Oxford, and from day one they struggled with what was a mediocre side. Promoter Danny Dunton's problems began when Hasse Holmqvist informed him that he would not be available until May, and even then he would still have to be free for his Swedish commitments. This, following the posting of Eddie Reeves to Hackney, Pete Jarman to Cradley Heath, and Mick Bell to Reading (who had replaced Newcastle in the British League) by the Rider Control Committee, really was the last straw for the Oxford boss. After working morning, noon and night to put a side together, Dunton finally decided to manage without Holmqvist's services. The Rider Control Committee had allocated replacements to Oxford in the shape of Norwegian Oyvind Berg, who arrived via Glasgow, while Ted Laessing joined from King's Lynn and Mike Gardner arrived from Cradley Heath. The hard-riding Berg was happy to join the Cheetahs camp, but both Laessing and Gardner said 'Thanks, but no thanks', and refused to come to Oxford. Rider Control did nothing to ease the

*Oyvind Berg.*

Cheetahs' problems, so Mr Dunton turned his attention to Ken McKinlay of West Ham. 'Hurriken' was rapidly approaching the veteran stage of his riding career and was initially posted to Wembley, but didn't fancy the move. Although he could not be described as a replacement for the absent Holmqvist, at least Ken was prepared to ride for Oxford, which was something.

As the first match approached, Oxford had just four riders on their books, namely Oyvind Berg, Colin Gooddy, Rick Timmo and Ronnie Genz. Ray Wilson of Leicester guested for the Cheetahs in their opening fixture against King's Lynn in the annual Easter Egg Cup, and Richard Greer from Mr Dunton's Second Division track (Peterborough) rode at reserve, with Pete Saunders filling the other reserve berth. To add to Oxford's problems, Oyvind Berg wasn't available for the match, so the Cheetahs used the rider replacement rule, and all things considered, it wasn't surprising that they lost by 4 points, with the ever-reliable Genz and Gooddy being joint top scorers with 11 points apiece from five starts. Ken McKinlay finally arrived at the Cheetahs camp, but they still went down by 2 points in their next home match, a challenge against Coventry. The following week saw the Cheetahs win their first British League match of the season (against Wimbledon) by a single point, with Oxford denying the visitors the use of rider replacement for the absent Cyril Maidment, on the grounds they had no number eight rider present!

Still, the Cheetahs did not have a proper seven-man side, with both Richard Geer (again) and Arthur Price from Second Division Boston filling in. This was a situation that really couldn't continue and subsequently Col Cottrell, who was having a tough time at Coventry, joined the Cheetahs, while from Newport came Norman Strachan. Neither signing could be regarded as the answer to Oxford's need for heat-leaders, but at least the Cheetahs now had seven riders and on 6 May in a Knock Out Cup match against Poole, they were able to finally track a side of their own. Oxford celebrated in fine style too, defeating the Pirates by 46 points to 32, with Ronnie Genz, Oyvind Berg and Colin Gooddy all recording double-figure scores. After some indifferent results, the Cheetahs scored a single-point victory over Exeter in the Knock Out Cup on 17 June, and the winning form returned for the visit of Wolverhampton on 1 July, when the Cheetahs recorded a fine 53-24 win. As the season progressed, Danny Dunton continued to canvass the Rider Control Committee for additional strength, and the news that Belle Vue's Tommy Roper was available prompted a request from Oxford for his services. Dunton had pursued Arthur Price as well, regularly making offers for the young Boston rider. By the end of July, Dunton had got his man with the signing of Roper, but lost out on Price, who was bound for King's Lynn.

Despite the plight of Oxford, the Rider Control Committee ordered the posting of Ronnie Genz to Newport upon Roper's arrival, so the Cheetahs' situation was largely unchanged. This was a truly unbelievable state of affairs. Roper made his Oxford debut on 5 August, and top scored with 12 points in the Cheetahs' 45-31 win over Halifax. The following week, however, Oxford raced against Exeter and Rick Timmo suffered injury in a heat six pile-up, and it was only prompt action by the track doctor that saved the young New Zealander's life. To add insult to injury, Exeter, with Bob Kilby scoring a fine 15 point maximum, took the league points, winning 41-37. By the end of August, to add to Oxford's problems, Col Cottrell retired and for the rest of the season Mr Dunton placed his faith in the up-and-coming youngsters from the Second Division. John Jackson form Crewe, Laurie Sims of Eastbourne and John Davis of Peterborough were drafted into the side as and when required, with Jackson looking particularly useful.

By mid-September, Rick Timmo was back and the month ended with Oxford picking up 4 valuable league points in a double-header against King's Lynn and Cradley Heath on 30 September, and the season ended with a fine home win (41-37) over Hackney. So, a disappointing and frustrating season finished with the Cheetahs dropping four places in the British League and finishing in seventeenth position. At home, they won 12 matches and lost 6, with a draw at Cradley Heath on 24 July being their sole away success. Oyvind Berg topped the Cheetahs' averages with a 7.52 figure, and Ken McKinlay also made the 7-point mark, whilst Gooddy, Timmo and Roper all hovered around 6 points per match.

It was all change in 1972, as Bob Dugard (from Eastbourne) joined Danny Dunton in a new company to run Oxford Speedway. Show business also came to Cowley with Acker Bilk becoming a director of the company, while Dave Lanning came on board to supervise the whole thing. The nickname of Cheetahs was dropped, and Oxford became known as the Rebels, with the confederate flag of the American Civil War being used as the side's body colour. There were also changes on the team front with Tommy Roper's departure, and the publicity-conscious management replaced him with Australian fireball Garry Middleton, who wanted away from Hackney. Middleton was a real personality, an all-action rider who had a habit of getting into all sorts of scrapes and often incurring the wrath of his fellow riders. Colin Gooddy, Ken McKinlay, the gutsy Oyvind Berg, Rick Timmo and Norman Strachan were back, and to complete the side, the management signed young Norwegian Svein Kaasa. Svein had been showing a great deal of promise in his homeland, and looked to be a fine prospect.

There was no doubt that Oxford was buzzing speedway-wise, and the fans eagerly looked forward to the opening meeting of the season on 25 March. It was not a dream debut for the new Rebels though, for they went down to a heavy defeat (19-59) at

Coventry in a British League encounter. The Rebels subsequently took to the track at Cowley for the opening fixture on the morning of 31 March, with Wimbledon being the visitors for a league fixture. Ken McKinlay was missing, having still not returned from a winter of racing in Australia, so Oxford utilized the rider replacement facility to cover for him, with Laurie Sims coming in as the number eight man. The meeting started in best possible way for the Rebels, with new skipper Garry Middleton defeating Ronnie Moore in a sensational opening heat. It went on to be a fine home start for the new Rebels, for in an exciting contest, they ran out the winners by 43 points to 35. Unfortunately, the good start didn't last, and the Rebels lost their next two home matches against King's Lynn and Coventry, while they also had no luck on their away trips to Wimbledon and Halifax. Wolverhampton visited Cowley on 20 April, and the Rebels' winning form returned with a narrow 41-37 victory, although Rick Timmo suffered a shoulder injury which sidelined him for a while.

After a reasonable start in the Cowley opener, Svein Kaasa had struggled and was released (he was later to link up with Glasgow), and the match against Wolverhampton saw him replaced with young Danish rider Preben Rosenkilde, formerly of Halifax. Rosenkilde looked all at sea in his early races, but showed plenty of promise and the following week lined up in the Midland Riders' Championship qualifying round, where he scored a creditable 5 points. Barry Briggs won the round with a 15-point maximum, with Rebels star Garry Middleton finishing as runner-up on 13 points. The month of May was a good one for the Rebels, with home wins over Hackney, Exeter and Halifax; however, Poole came to Cowley on 1 June and left with the league points. Bad luck hit the Rebels a week later in a challenge match against local rivals Reading, when the hard-riding Oyvind Berg crashed and hurt his shoulder and ribs, ruling him out of the side for a month.

Dave Lanning described the problems at Oxford in his programme editorial as a 'Midsummer Nightmare', which was very apt. Middleton was doing a good job, as was the popular Berg, while Rick Timmo was a useful second string, but McKinlay, Strachan and Rosenklide were struggling, and 'Joe' Gooddy was terribly inconsistent. The Rebels were in desperate need of strengthening as they were struggling to keep away from the cellar position in the British League. On 15 June, they were confident they had got their man when spectacular Swede Torbjorn Harrysson agreed terms with Oxford, but in the event he couldn't get released from his work. Hasse Holmqvist was contacted, but Swedish commitments meant it was no go, so another Swede, Gote Nordin, was sounded out, but he ended up helping out at Halifax. There were further problems for the Rebels when Sheffield visited Cowley on 22 June though. Garry Middleton withdrew from the meeting, complaining of being unfit to compete, with the result that the under-strength Oxford team went down to a 36-42 defeat.

Winning form returned on 29 June when the Rebels, with youngsters Roger Johns and Malcolm Ballard from Eastbourne in the side, walloped the visitors from Newport 51-27. Middleton recorded a 12-point maximum, and McKinlay (riding at reserve) was back to form with 11 points. A league success against Swindon was followed by defeats against Belle Vue and Leicester, and then came a creditable aggregate draw against Swindon in the Midland Cup. In the replay at Blunsdon, the Rebels raced to a marvel-

*Svein Kaasa.*

lous 39-39 draw, before winning the second leg at Cowley 41-36 (or so they thought) to become overall victors, but it was not to be. The match was full of controversy and ended with Swindon putting in an official protest over a starting malfunction in heat eleven. The result was amended by the Control Board to read Oxford 38 Swindon 40, which typified the sort of luck the Rebels were experiencing.

Reading came to Cowley for a league match on 14 September, and in a real nail-biter of a match, the Rebels held a 2-point lead going into heat eleven, but two Reading 5-1s in heats twelve and thirteen meant that the Racers left with the league points. So, the season drew to a close with the Rebels just avoiding the wooden spoon. It was a season of exciting racing, with Oxford at least high in the publicity stakes. Garry Middleton was their best rider with a superb 9.21 average from his 29 league matches, while Oyvind Berg always gave good support. If only they had been able to secure the services of a third heat-leader, Oxford could well have scaled the heights. Things were, however, looking up, with a marvellous array of young talent from Eastbourne and Peterborough frequenting the Oxford second halves. It may have been a disappointing season in terms of results, but the future was beginning to look very rosy indeed.

It was all change again in 1973, as Dave Lanning left after a year in the Oxford hot seat, while on the team front, there were the usual comings and goings. From the 1972 line-up, Colin Gooddy moved on to Cradley Heath, with Ken McKinlay and Norman Strachan moving to Second Division Scunthorpe and Long Eaton respectively. Sadly, the popular Oyvind Berg retired from British racing, while Garry Middleton decided he wanted away from Oxford. The Rebels welcomed Hasse Holmqvist back to Cowley, thanks to some sweet talking on the part of Danny Dunton, and another returnee was Eddie Reeves, who was back after a year at Hackney. Malcolm Ballard and Gordon Kennett became permanent Rebels, while Rick Timmo returned and was made skipper of the 1973 side. Some things, however, did not change and, not for the first time, the allocations made by the Rider Control Committee came to nothing. Dave Hemus wasn't interested in furthering his racing career at Oxford, and nothing was done to replace Middleton, who was determined to sit on the fence until he got a move. As a result, Oxford again began the season with guest riders, although the steady John Dews moved in from Wimbledon in place of Hemus.

The season was a month old before the Oxford team problems were settled, when Tony Lomas, who wanted a move from Coventry, came to Cowley, with Middleton going in the opposite direction to Brandon. To be fair, Tony didn't really want to ride for the Rebels, for he had his sights set on a move to Exeter, but on 12 April he made his home debut for Oxford wearing the number one race jacket. It was a nightmare debut too, as Tony's style wasn't suited to the Oxford track and he looked all at sea and most uncomfortable. Two days later, the Rebels journeyed to Halifax, where Tony was much happier on the wide sweeping bends of the Shay. The Rebels went down by 14 points, but Tony's 7-point return was well taken. A group of Oxford supporters certainly appreciated his efforts and organized a whip-round. They managed to collect £1.30, so that the Rebels latest signing could buy himself a pint (or two)!

News that Ivan Mauger was available from Belle Vue prompted an enquiry from Oxford, but despite a great deal of interest in the offer, Mauger moved to Exeter, so the team position remained the same at Cowley. On Good Friday morning, the Rebels entertained Reading in a challenge match, and lost by 8 points. Tony Lomas recorded a second place in his opening ride, but still couldn't come to terms with the Oxford track, and was actually replaced by Hasse Holmqvist in his final race. It was not until 17 May that Oxford picked up their first league victory of the season, a 44-34 victory over Leicester, thanks to a fine maximum from guest rider Terry Betts of King's Lynn. Constructive things were now happening on the team front, and finally in mid-May, the Rebels solved their team problems when Bob Kilby, the Exeter skipper, came to Cowley, with Tony Lomas moving to Exeter in return. Bob had been recovering from a leg injury, and the arrival of Ivan Mauger left him unsettled down in Devon, so a move that suited everyone finally came to pass. On 24 May, in a World Championship qualifying round at Oxford, Bob made his debut as a Rebel, and it was a sensational debut too, as 'Kilb' raced to a superb 14-point tally to win the meeting.

Oxford's joy in finally finding an established British League heat-leader was sadly destined to be short-lived. A track accident at Exeter had resulted in a badly torn cartilage for Bob and although he had bravely soldiered on, he was forced to pull out during a match versus Swindon on 7 June. On 20 June, 'Kilb' entered hospital for an operation, so it was back to guest riders for the unfortunate Rebels. Popular Norwegian Oyvind Berg was in Britain for the *Daily Mirror* International Tournament, and he returned to the Oxford side for a challenge match against Reading on 5 July. It was, however, to be a one-off appearance, as Oyvind wasn't interested in a permanent return to Cowley. A change in the team saw Eddie Reeves, who had been unable to find form at Oxford, leave for King's Lynn and a dispensation was obtained to use the promising John Davis of Peterborough for the remainder of the season.

Despite their problems, Oxford continued to serve up exciting speedway racing. Both Gordon Kennett and Malcolm Ballard had settled down to the cut and thrust of British League racing beautifully. Hasse Holmqvist was a tower of strength, while John Davis and Rick Timmo were steady. If only the Rebels had been able to track a settled side from the beginning of the year, they could well have challenged Reading for league honours. August saw 4 home wins out of 5, but the Rebels still couldn't beat Reading, who stole a 2-point win halfway through the month. Thankfully there was some good news though, when Bob Kilby returned to the saddle for a 45-33 win over Exeter a week later.

4 October saw a double-header against Cradley United and Reading, with the fixture versus the Racers being a challenge for the Twelfth Night Trophy. Hasse Holmqvist was absent, since he had to enter hospital for surgery on a knee injury, so Swindon's Norman Hunter deputized. The Rebels really went on the rampage to thrash Cradley 59-19, with John Davis romping to a fine maximum. In the second match, the Rebels still couldn't break the Reading bogey, losing 36-42, despite a fine 11 points from Bob Kilby. The season closed at Oxford on the evening of Sunday 7 October, with a rearranged league fixture against Wimbledon. The Rebels finished with a 47-30 success, helped no end by a superb 12-point maximum from Bob Kilby. That enabled the Cheetahs to finish the year in eleventh position, with Holmqvist and Kilby topping the averages on 7-plus figures, while Gordon Kennett, John Davis and Malcolm Ballard all

*Gordon Kennett.*

did exceptionally well to achieve averages in excess of 6.

The 1974 season dawned with the Oxford Rebels tracking a useful-looking team, which boasted a fine blend of youth and experience. From the 1973 line-up, Hasse Holmqvist was missing, and the sometimes controversial Malcolm Ballard was transferred to Poole, but Bob Kilby, John Dews, Gordon Kennett and Rick Timmo were all back. John Davis became a full-time Rebel, as did Richard Greer, who was transferred to Oxford from Peterborough. To replace Holmqvist, the Rebels' management obtained the services of Norwegian Ulf Lovaas, who had ridden for Cradley United towards the end of the previous season, and had shown a great deal of promise. Certainly there was much to interest Oxford fans, because the youth and enthusiasm of youngsters Gordon Kennett, John Davis, Richard Greer and Ulf Lovaas, was backed by the experience of Bob Kilby, John Dews and Rick Timmo. The opening fixture on 21 March, a Knock Out Cup match against Ipswich, provided some excellent racing, with the Rebels taking a narrow 40-37 victory. Bob Kilby, who had been made the 1974 skipper, led the scoring with 10 points, and Richard Greer had a fine match, also notching 10. Exeter were the visitors the following week in a Spring Gold Cup match, and the Rebels enjoyed more success, winning 49-29. The next day, however, they came down to earth with a bump, when on a visit to Newport, they were beaten 24-54, with only John Davis (10 points) making an impression on the tricky circuit.

Home victories throughout April against Newport (Spring Gold Cup), Wimbledon (British League) and Swindon in the Midland Cup, showed the Rebels were quite a force at Cowley, but away, they found success hard to come by. On 25 April, Belle Vue visited Oxford, and left with the league points, with Bob Kilby having a terrible time. 'Kilb' did not take long to put things right, as he romped to victory in a World Championship qualifying round at Oxford a week later. On 8 May, the Rebels visited Hull and gave their best performance away from Oxford to date, losing by just 2 points. Rick Timmo, who was having a tough time, asked to be rested from the side and for the match against Halifax on 16 May, Trevor Geer, a talented youngster from the Eastbourne stable, came into the side as a replacement. This match also saw the return of Peter Jarman (now a member of the Eastbourne side as well) filling in for the injured John Dews. It was a successful night for the Rebels too, as they secured a narrow 41-37 victory. Bob Kilby and Richard Greer led the scoring with 10 points apiece, but it was young Trevor Geer who was the match winner with a fine 8 points. Two days later, Oxford journeyed to Belle Vue and lost a real thriller of a meeting by just 6 points. Bob Kilby played a real captain's part, with a 14-point tally, while Ulf Lovaas also showed fine form, yielding a 9-point return.

Sheffield visited Oxford and left with the league points, thanks to Gordon Kennett having to compete in a World Championship qualifying round (ironically at Sheffield) which, in the event, was rained off! May ended with the Radio Oxford Best Pairs, which was won in fine style by John Dews and Richard Greer. June saw Gordon Kennett suffer a foot injury in a four-team tournament at Eastbourne, which caused him to miss a few matches, and then John Dews was injured in a spill against Newport. With Bob Kilby on the injured list, it was somewhat surprising when the Rebels defeated Coventry on 27 June, with Richard Greer scoring a fine maximum and Ulf Lovaas displaying good form for 10 points. Rick Timmo, who had been absent for a month, now returned to racing, but suffered a broken thigh in an off-track accident, which meant he was sidelined for the rest of the season. There was still no luck on opponents' tracks, although the Rebels managed a draw at Cradley United in a challenge fixture. The meeting had begun as a league fixture, but was later changed to a challenge by officialdom.

July provided a month of mixed fortunes, with home wins against Wolverhampton and Leicester, but defeats at the hands of Ipswich and Cradley United. Away from Cowley, the Rebels won a challenge fixture at Swindon, and on 27 July they secured a first away league success at Cradley United, with the 2-point victory ensuring that justice had been done. The month of August opened well, as Belle Vue were beaten 40-38 in a challenge match, but the much anticipated Test Match against the Russians was, unfortunately, lost to inclement weather. Poole were thrashed 52-26, with Gordon Kennett and Bob Kilby scoring maximums, and on Bank Holiday Monday, Dutchman Henk Steman made his British debut as a Rebel against Swindon. His presence couldn't stop a Swindon victory, however, with the Robins winning 42-36. The Rebels quickly avenged that defeat to their local rivals, when they journeyed to Swindon on 28 September and shocked everyone by winning 46-32.

The home league programme finished with a storming 50-28 win over Hull, and the next week, Oxford walloped Swindon in a challenge match by the same score. The final meeting of 1974 was to have been a speedway bonanza featuring thirty heats of racing, including the Autumn Stakes and a ten-heat challenge match between Birmingham and Eastbourne, but the weather intervened and stopped the attractive-looking event from taking place. Oxford finished the season by filling the basement position in the final British League Division One table, with Bob Kilby topping the averages, a full point ahead of Gordon Kennett.

The 1975 season began at Oxford, as in past years, with a number of team changes. Both Bob Kilby and John Davis requested transfers, while family commitments prevented Ulf Lovaas from returning to further his career in British speedway. Kilby returned to his old home base at Swindon, and a real buzz went around Oxford when it was announced that Ole Olsen had been allocated to the Rebels from Wolverhampton. The enthusiasm amongst the Oxford supporters was further heightened when it was also announced that popular Swede Hasse Holmqvist would be returning. The proposed Olsen move was quickly dashed, however, when the Control Board met on 21 March to hear an appeal by Wolverhampton over his allocation to Oxford. The result was that Olsen was allocated back to Wolverhampton, with Dag Lovaas, the young Norwegian star, joining the Rebels instead. Lovaas arrived via Reading, but part of the deal meant John Davis moved in the opposite direction and linked up with the Berkshire club. Nobody connected with Oxford minded this move though, for Dag had made it clear that he wanted to race for Oxford, whereas Ole Olsen didn't. The move that the great Dane really yearned for, of course, was to join Coventry. To complete the Rebels side, which included new skipper Gordon Kennett, Richard Greer, Hasse Holmqvist, Trevor Geer and John Dews, the promoters signed Swede Richard Hellsen, who had ridden a handful of matches for King's Lynn in 1973.

The Rebels began the campaign with two away defeats in a challenge match at Newport and a league fixture at Coventry. John Davis appeared at Coventry as a guest for himself, since the teams were still not finalized! The Rebels opened at Cowley on 28 March, with a challenge match against Coventry, and romped to a fine 48-29 victory. Holmqvist was an absentee, and was reported to be having trouble getting released from his work, so Paul Gachet, another product of the Eastbourne school, deputized and scored a creditable 4 points. New boy Dag Lovaas made a highly satisfactory home debut in a Rebels race jacket to lead the Oxford scoring with 10 points. The following week saw a truly incredible meeting when, following a snowstorm, Cradley United withdrew from the match after heat seven, despite the fact that the referee had ruled the track ride-able. The Rebels continued to ride and chalked up six successive 5-0 heat victories to win 58-14. Holmqvist was still absent for this meeting, so the rider replacement facility was used to cover his programmed heats.

Swindon raced to a draw in the Midland Cup (39-39) on 17 April, and the Rebels returned the compliment at Blunsdon on 10 May, so the fixture had to be raced all over again. In the meantime, the Rebels had lost away at Ipswich, Halifax and Cradley United, but they beat Ipswich at Cowley by the smallest of margins (40-38). Phil Crump won the Champions Trophy on 24 April, and Ray Wilson was the victor in the Midland Riders' Championship qualifying round on 8 May. Swindon returned on 15 May for the Midland Cup replay, and this time the Rebels made no mistake, winning 53-25. Belle Vue came to Cowley the following week, when Dag Lovaas was absent. The popular Norwegian was replaced by guest Terry Betts, but despite a fine 14 points from skipper Gordon Kennett, the Rebels went down to a 10-point defeat, with Betts, who usually flew around Cowley, managing just 2 points. Things were better the following day though, when the Rebels produced a spectacular 41-37 victory at Hackney.

Having beaten Swindon on aggregate, Oxford welcomed Leicester for the second round of the Midland Cup on 12 June. The Rebels took a 46-32 victory, but there was no Hasse Holmqvist, and the following week he was still absent, as was Richard Hellsen, who suffered a broken leg at Leicester. However, this did not stop Oxford from winning 60-18 against Coventry in the first round of the Knock Out Cup. Following this match, it was announced that Holmqvist was no longer available to ride for the Rebels and on 26 June, new rider Eddie Davidsson was introduced into the team. It was an inauspicious debut for the new Swede though, as he failed to trouble the scorers.

Hackney were beaten 44-34 on 3 July, but the Rebels went down at home the following week (by 8 points) to the powerful Exeter squad, for whom Ivan Mauger raced to a fine maximum. Had Dag Lovaas not been badly shaken in a heat seven pile-up, the result could well have been different. Following a challenge match victory over Reading on 17 July, the Rebels suffered a surprise home 6-point defeat to Newport. Despite putting in plenty of effort, Eddie Davidsson was having a tough time, and prior to the Knock Out Cup match against Belle Vue on 7 August, he was released. The Swede was replaced by Norwegian Hilge Langli, who had previously ridden for Newcastle in 1969. Hilge failed to score in the match, and the Rebels went down to a 6-point defeat. Leicester were beaten in the last heat the following week, with Langli showing promising form, which continued when he scored 5 points in the fine 49-29 win over Halifax on 21 August.

Wimbledon were beaten on August Bank Holiday Monday, with Dag Lovaas racing to a superb 15-point maximum. This was followed by a victory over Poole, and on 14 September there came a really sweet 46-32 success over Reading, with Lovaas racing to another 15-point maximum, this time against his former club. Wolverhampton came to Cowley on 11 September, and Langli was now an absentee, having suffered an injury. With Richard Hellsen also still absent, use of the rider replacement rule for the absent Hasse Holmqvist ensured excellent cover and the result was a fine Rebels win by 43 points to 35. With Holmqvist unavailable to ride, it was something of a strange situation that allowed Oxford to employ the rider replacement facility for him, as and when the position allowed!

Richard Hellsen returned for the match against Swindon on 18 September, when the Rebels dispensed with the rider replacement rule and ran out winners by 44 points to 34. A double-header against Coventry and King's Lynn on 2 October saw more Rebels success with 58-20 and 49-29 victories. Then came the final match of the season on the afternoon of the 5 October, namely the first leg of the Midland Cup final against Wolverhampton. Although, the Rebels achieved only a slender 2-point victory, they went on to win the Midland Cup, but their success was overshadowed by the sad death of Wolverhampton rider Gary Peterson in a track accident during the second leg at Wolverhampton on 17 October.

The final league table saw Oxford perched in a satisfactory seventh place, having jumped ten places from the previous season's wooden spoon position. There was much greater solidity about the team, with Dag Lovaas adding much needed top-end strength, scoring 354 points to finish with a tremendous 10.22 average from his 31 league matches. As the season ended, storm clouds were gathering with the news of the impending sale of Oxford Stadium, and the move of the Rebels to a new home at London's White City. It appeared to be the end of an era and that Oxford Stadium would fall to the developers. The winter break was to be full of drama, as a hardcore of Oxford fans formed the 'Save Our Speedway' committee. They were determined that Oxford Speedway would live on, and for the first time, Cowley supporters were to hear the name of Bernard Crapper, who, together with other enthusiasts, began the fight save the track.

The fact that there was speedway at Cowley in 1976 was due entirely to the efforts of the 'Save Our Speedway' committee, who had campaigned vigorously throughout the winter months. Their success in finally saving the stadium is a compliment to their hard work and the fact that they refused to give in, even though at times the odds appeared to be stacked heavily against them. However, having saved the stadium, there then came the task of re-establishing speedway racing at Cowley, and here they were in luck. Tony Allsop and Harry Bastable had promoted speedway in the new National League at Stoke, and were now looking for a new venue. They had a team, or at least a number of riders, so it seemed sensible that they should come together with Oxford, who now had a venue but no team. So, negotiations started and happily reached a satisfactory conclusion, with Stoke riders Mick Handley and Phil Bass, together with juniors Kevin Young, Harry MacLean and Steve Holden, joining their former Stoke bosses to begin a new era of racing at Oxford.

There is no doubt that Messrs Allsop and Bastable took a gamble, as the 1975 Rebels had been a British League team, but now the public would be watching National League racing and a team of new riders that they had not previously seen. So, there was always the chance that the Cowley public would not respond favourably to the racing in the lower division. The hardcore of Oxford fans were cheered by the fact that there was speedway at Oxford and they did come along to support the new Cheetahs. Reverting to their old nickname was an astute move, as Oxford had always been the Cheetahs and the change to Rebels had never felt comfortable. Another move in the right direction was the appointment of Roger Jones to look after things on the team front. His persuasive tongue soon brought new signings to Oxford in the form of Carl Askew (from Birmingham), Malcolm Corradine (from Stoke) and Brian Leonard, who had assisted Leicester during 1975.

The new-look Cheetahs took to the track on the 18 March in a challenge match against Eastbourne, with Mick Handley skippering the side. Other team members for the start of a new era at Oxford were Aussie Carl Askew (who top scored and became the darling of the Cowley crowd), Kevin Young, Steve Holden, Mal Corradine, Harry MacLean and Roy Sizmore. Oxford lost this opening fixture by just 2 points, but the fans went home happy, having enjoyed a good evening's racing – it was different from what they had been used to, but exciting, nonetheless. The following week saw an impressive Oxford win over the Swedish tourists Vetlanda, with Phil Bass and Brian Leonard now in the Cheetahs team. Peterborough won a challenge match at Cowley on 1 April, but Oxford then secured their first league points when beating Boston 42-36, a week later. In the early weeks of the season, Workington and Newcastle took points from the Cheetahs, but after a draw against Rye House on 10 June, they really found their form at Cowley and put together an impressive series of 11 home wins. Oxford also reached the quarter-finals of the Knock Out Cup, beating Weymouth and Eastbourne before going down to Berwick.

There was no doubt that the 1976 Cheetahs had settled down well and were becoming a real force at home. Away from Cowley, however, it was the old, old story with victories non-existent. The Cheetahs' best efforts were at Coatbridge on 30 April, when they lost by 2 points, and at Boston on 30 May, when they went down by 3 points.

*Oxford v. Eastbourne programme, 1976.*

Oxford's worst away performance was the match that never was on 10 September, when they refused to ride on a wet track at Peterborough. The end result was that the home riders rode eight heats, scored 40 points, claimed the league points and went home. The Oxford riders were fined for their failure to race and, surprisingly, the result was allowed to stand as Peterborough 40 Oxford 0. Harry MacLean, who had begun the season so well, was injured at Teesside on 15 April and did not ride again.

As the season progressed, riders came and went, with New Zealander Jim Wells making his debut as a Cheetah against Newcastle on 6 May. By the end of June, Mal Corradine had retired, while Colin Meredith was signed from Stoke in mid-August. Pip Lamb, a young man with a fine record on the grass-tracks, made his home debut on 16 September, scoring paid 6 points in Oxford's 41-37 victory over Scunthorpe. The Cheetahs finished fourteenth in the eighteen-team National League, with their home record of 14 wins, a single draw and 2 defeats being a very fine effort. It was their away form that let them down, as they didn't glean a single point from 17 matches. Carl Askew was the best rider, while Mick Handley was steady, and both Pip Lamb and Kevin Young looked marvellous prospects for the future.

The 1977 season was really all about one man, namely Martin Yeates, and the Oxford supporters could thank Roger Jones for the fact that the Salisbury-based racer ended up at Cowley. Jones was mindful of the fact that the Cheetahs had lacked a high-scoring number one rider during 1976, and with Carl Askew returning to Birmingham for 1977, he set his sights on Martin, and opened negotiations with his parent club, Poole. In the opening meeting of the season – a challenge match against Weymouth – Martin opened his scoring account with a fine maximum, as the Cheetahs raced to a fine 48-30 victory. Most of the team who had ridden for the Cheetahs in 1976 returned, with Kevin Young, Mick Handley, Phil Bass, Brian Leonard, Colin Meredith and Roy Sizmore all remaining on board. Gerald Smitherman arrived via Ellesmere Port, and, waiting in the wings, was Pip Lamb, so all in all, it was a useful side for the Cheetahs' second season in National League racing.

Oxford actually opened their league campaign at Teesside on 7 April, losing a thrilling match by just two points. The following day, they entertained the Teesside team at Cowley and raced to a decisive 53-25 win, with Martin Yeates scoring a paid maximum. As had happened the previous year, there were several team changes throughout the season. After losing form, the experienced Brian Leonard had gone by the end of June. Another rider to lose form, and subsequently drop out of the side by July, was Gerald Smitherman, while a similar fate befell Roy Sizmore, who was allowed to seek pastures new. Youngster Pip Lamb was subsequently given an opportunity in the side and he grasped it with both hands. With Martin Yeates continuing to dominate the Cowley scene and knocking up high scores everywhere he rode, the management were able to introduce young riders into the side with a degree of confidence. Greg Joynt, a young Australian, made his debut in the away match against Crayford on 19 July. However, it was a match where the Cheetahs could only muster 29 points, but the immaculate Yeates scored 15 of those 29 points and rode unbeaten.

Unfortunately, Joynt proved to be out of his depth in National League racing, and soon faded from the Oxford scene, but on 28 July, a young former schoolboy scrambler by the name of Ritchie Caulwell made a promising home debut against Berwick, scoring a paid 9 points from three rides. He was given an extended run in the team, but never repeated his fine debut form, his best score being a paid 6-point return against Edinburgh in late September. The home match against Boston on 11 August saw another rider make his debut for the Cheetahs. This time it was Malcolm Holloway, on loan from Swindon, and he weighed in with 6 points. The Cheetahs lost the match by two points, however, despite the normal maximum from Martin Yeates. This match was the first home league defeat for the Cheetahs, who were displaying good form at Cowley, but the following week there was another shock in store when Scunthorpe visited and inflicted a similar 38-40 defeat. Colin Meredith scored 12 points, while both Martin Yeates and Phil Bass had 11 each, unfortunately though, the Cheetahs had a long tail, with Young, Lamb, Caulwell and Holloway only mustering 4 points between them. The next home meeting against Mildenhall saw Oxford drop another point in a 39-39 draw. Winning form at Cowley returned for the match against Peterborough on 8 September though, with Kevin Young in fine form, scoring a paid maximum.

Despite their generally good home form, the Cheetahs just couldn't take league points away from Cowley. There were a few near misses at Teesside, Scunthorpe, Stoke, Weymouth and Newcastle, but all too often it was a case of Yeates against the opposition. The Cheetahs finally finished in thirteenth position, winning 15 of their home matches, including wins over the champions Eastbourne, and runners-up Rye House. Oxford eventually beat Rye House after a re-run in the Knock Out Cup, before defeating Newport, but they went down to Ellesmere Port in the quarter-final, losing both legs. Martin Yeates (who else?) was the Cheetahs' number one rider, completely dominating the season, and his win in the Weslake-sponsored Super National at Cowley on 15 September gave the Oxford fans even more to cheer about. Martin actually finished third in the overall National League averages, scoring 396 points for a massive 10.59 figure. Phil Bass and Mick Handley were good at Cowley, but only average away, while Malcolm Holloway and Pip Lamb were excellent prospects for the future. Meanwhile, Kevin Young, who had made fine progress, was dismissed after a row with the management in mid-September.

It was all change at Oxford in 1978, and very significant the changes were too. Firstly, Northern Sports purchased the stadium, and secondly, a change on the management side saw Cradley Heath promoter Dan McCormick take over the running of the speedway. Straight-talking Dan subsequently installed Chris Van Straaten as his front man, while Bernard Crapper and John Payne, who had previously played vital roles behind the scenes, now had special managerial responsibilities. A further change saw team manager Roger Jones depart, to be replaced by former rider Pete Jarman. On the team front, the immaculate Martin Yeates returned to his British League track, Poole, and Phil Bass departed for Milton Keynes. Colin Meredith, Mick Handley and Pip Lamb from the 1977 line-up remained, to be joined by Australian Carl Askew, who returned after a season away. Another newcomer to Cowley was the promising John Hack, who came on board via Cradley Heath. Trials were given to Australian Les Sawyer, while Brian Leonard returned to active speedway racing.

The Cheetahs opened the season with a challenge match against Ellesmere Port, but

*George Hunter.*

went down to a 34-44 reverse. Two National League matches followed, with the Cheetahs suffering crushing defeats at Ellesmere Port (28-50) and Eastbourne (27-51). Something drastic had to happen to revitalize the Oxford fortunes, and two days after the Eastbourne defeat, it did. In a challenge match at Milton Keynes, making his debut as a Cheetah was a pint-sized blond-haired Australian called David Shields. The fact that the Cheetahs were victorious by 43 points to 31, and that Carl Askew scored a maximum was great. What was sensational though, was the performance of David Shields, who raced to a maximum and also captured the Milton Keynes track record in a dream debut!

A couple of days later, Milton Keynes were at Oxford for another challenge match, which the Cheetahs easily won 57-20. David Shields had a quieter home debut, scoring 6 points, while Carl Askew and Pip Lamb were paid for the lot. Another new signing, the experienced George Hunter from British League Wolverhampton, made a fine home debut, scoring a paid 10 points. At last, Oxford looked to have a team able to tackle the league programme and at Newcastle on 10 April, they shook the powerful Diamonds by winning 45-32, and followed that up with a 44-34 win over Barrow. The arrival of George and David was to signal the retirement of Brian Leonard, who left to concentrate on his business affairs.

Workington were the first visitors to Cowley on league business, which resulted in a decisive 57-21 victory to the Cheetahs, and this was followed by a fine 39-39 draw at Boston. Everything was going well for the Cheetahs, but they came down to earth when Peterborough sneaked a 2-point victory at Cowley on 4 May, despite 11 points each from David Shields and John Hack. Winning form at home soon returned, however, with good victories over Weymouth and Canterbury. Away from Cowley, Scunthorpe were slaughtered 52-28 by the in-form Cheetahs, and then Glasgow were hammered unmercifully 58-19 at Cowley on 1 June. But in a Northern tour that followed at Glasgow, Berwick and Workington, the Cheetahs had no luck, losing all three matches. They did, however, enjoy success at Teesside on 15 June with a 2-point win. Three days later at Cowley, the double was completed over Teesside with a 50-27 win that featured maximums for both George Hunter and Carl Askew.

The home league match against Milton Keynes on 6 July saw the debut of New Zealander James Moore. The Cheetahs raced to a 58-20 win, with James scoring a fine paid 8 points. Oxford now had a surplus of riders, with Mick Handley departing to link up with Scunthorpe. July and August proved to be good months on the home front. Edinburgh (51-27) and Barrow (62.5-15.5) were well beaten, while Newcastle secured a 39-39 draw in a fantastic match. Berwick were thrashed 62-17, with both Boston and Rye House also falling to the Cheetahs' onslaught. Away from Cowley, however, there wasn't much luck, with the Cheetahs losing at Edinburgh, Stoke and Canterbury. September began badly, as Oxford slumped to heavy away defeats at Peterborough (22-56) and Mildenhall (33-45), but the Cheetahs still showed their superiority at Cowley by beating Stoke and Scunthorpe, before beginning the month of October with tremendous 50-28 home success over Ellesmere Port.

As the season drew to its close, Eastbourne were beaten at Cowley, and the home league programme finished with a nail-biting draw against Mildenhall. Away from Oxford, the Cheetahs secured a draw at Milton Keynes, before losing their final away meeting at Rye House on 8 October, when George Hunter scored 16 of the Oxford total of 31 points. So, a great season of speedway racing ended at Cowley with the Cheetahs rising to seventh position in the twenty-team National League. At home, they raced to 16 wins, 2 draws and had only a single defeat, whilst away, their form improved considerably with 4 wins, 2 draws and 13 losses. George Hunter scored 333 points to top Oxford's league averages with a superb 9.93 figure, while the discovery of the season, David Shields, finished on a highly impressive 8.83. John Hack and Carl Askew provided great solidity to the side, both achieving averages in excess of 7, whilst Pip Lamb came on leaps and bounds and finished with a creditable 6-point figure.

The 1979 season kicked off with a shock, when the talented Aussie, David Shields, announced his retirement from speedway. However, with Dan McCormick at the helm, the Cheetahs' supporters had little to worry about, and it was not long before good replacement riders

*John Barker.*

were signed. The first new signing was Les Rumsey via Canterbury, closely followed by John Barker, who came on loan from Eastbourne. With returnees George Hunter, Carl Askew, Pip Lamb, John Hack and Colin Meredith, plus Mick Handley back from his spell with Scunthorpe, the Cheetahs boasted a good line-up with strength in depth. Oxford opened the season with a challenge match at near neighbours Milton Keynes on 3 April, when they came away with a 42-35 victory. Pip Lamb top scored with 10.5 points, which actually included a dead-heat with team-mate George Hunter. The home season began two days later, when Nottingham were the visitors, and again the Cheetahs raced to success.

At Weymouth, on 10 April, Oxford were again successful in a challenge fixture, winning 45-33, so confidence was high in the Cheetahs camp. Prior to the start of the league campaign, Oxford enjoyed two days of international challenge matches, hammering the Swedish Under-23 touring side 49-29, before losing by three points to Red Star of Prague. Ellesmere Port were sent packing in the opening league fixture at Oxford (53-24), but at Mildenhall on 22 April, it was the Cheetahs' turn to be on the wrong end of a hammering. The Fen Tigers hit Oxford with everything they had and were decisive victors by 52 points to 26. It didn't take Oxford long to recover, however, and it was visiting Glasgow who were to suffer the power of the Cheetahs at Cowley. Oxford hammered the Tigers 52-26, and followed this up with a fine 45-33 victory at Nottingham.

Rye House came to Cowley on 24 May and shook the Cheetahs by snatching a 4-point win, although to be fair John Barker was missing, and Colin Meredith was badly off form. This match was destined to be Colin's last for the Cheetahs, for he had suffered an early season injury and had never been able to reveal his best form, so he announced his retirement from racing. After the Rye House setback, Oxford enjoyed a fine period of success, which included a great single-point victory at Weymouth and tremendous home victories over Boston, Canterbury and Crayford. The home victory over Boston on 21 June will, however, always be remembered with sadness at Oxford, for Pip Lamb, who had been enjoying a great season, crashed and received injuries which were to confine him to a wheelchair. Pip had been an ever-present in the Cheetahs' line-up and his injury was a sickening blow. Following the injury to Pip Lamb, Oxford introduced new faces into the side. Robert Doyle, a young Australian, was given opportunities, as was South African Denzil Kent, plus Colin Ackroyd, who had had some experience at Eastbourne, and John Grahame, a member of a famous speedway racing family.

Milton Keynes sprang a surprise, winning 40-38 at Oxford on 15 July, but the Cheetahs responded by defeating Newcastle by 4 points in a thrilling encounter at Cowley. A Northern tour saw losses at Glasgow and Workington, before the Cheetahs gained revenge at Milton Keynes with a thrilling single-point victory. At home, the Cheetahs became a real force in August, hammering Peterborough 50-28, with further big wins to follow – against Weymouth (58-20), Workington (57-21), Berwick (49-29) and Edinburgh (54-23). Away from home, they didn't enjoy such good fortune, however, losing 33-45 at both Rye House and Middlesbrough. September started well, with home victories over Nottingham and Stoke being followed by impressive away wins at both Scunthorpe and Crayford. Ellesmere Port and Boston halted the Cheetahs' run of away successes, but Oxford then had a great match at Stoke, where they won 40-38.

The season drew to its close with victories over Scunthorpe and Mildenhall at home, and a defeat at Peterborough. A victory at Edinburgh was followed by a massacre at Berwick, however, where the Cheetahs could only muster 18 points to the Bandits' 60. Oxford soon recovered though, and two days later, they wound up the season with a fine 41-37 victory at Newcastle. In what had been a marvellous season, the Cheetahs finished third in the final National League table, which was undoubtedly their best effort since dropping down from the British League. George Hunter was again top of the Oxford averages, with a tremendous 10.98 figure, having plundered 309 points from 28 league matches. New boy Les Rumsey enjoyed a great season, appearing in all 36 league matches and actually scoring more points than Hunter (404) for a 9.92 average. Despite being a good year for the Cheetahs, the tragic accident that cost Oxford the services of Pip Lamb meant that it was a season tinged with sad memories. The year finished on 21 October with a benefit pairs meeting for the injured rider, with Bruce Penhall and Bobby Schwartz heading a class field to win the trophy donated by Northern Sports.

## The 1980s

The 1980 season heralded a number of changes on the team front, with the Cheetahs' two leading riders from the previous year wanting away. George Hunter returned to his first love, Edinburgh, and Les Rumsey, after just one season at Cowley, joined Crayford.

Rumsey's move was a real surprise, because the publicity that followed his signing in 1979 indicated that he had come to the Cheetahs on a three-year contract. John Barker was another rider to leave after just one season at Cowley, while Carl Askew remained in his native Australia. There were changes on the promotional front too, with the likeable Bob Wasley put in charge of the Cheetahs' fortunes on behalf of Dan McCormick.

With Oxford having to virtually rebuild their side, the signing of Dave Perks from Nottingham ensured that the Cheetahs had an efficient number one rider to head the team. Two other newcomers were Chris Sully (on loan from Leicester) and

*Dave Perks.*

Billy Spiers (from Weymouth) who joined John Hack, back for his third season at Cowley, plus old faithful Mick Handley and the two promising youngsters Colin Ackroyd and John Grahame.

The season opened on 27 March, with a challenge match against Milton Keynes resulting in a 45-33 win for the Cheetahs, with 11 points apiece from Dave Perks and John Hack. Three days later, Oxford began their league campaign at Rye House and found themselves on the wrong end of a 27-50 hammering. An Italian touring team visited Cowley on 4 April, and in an interesting match, the Cheetahs raced to a 43-34 victory. Rye House were the first visitors to Cowley on league business (on 10 April) and they left with a 43-34 victory under their belts. Both Spiers and Sully failed to score for the Cheetahs, and the former disappeared from the Cowley scene after this match, soon to be followed by Sully, who was replaced by former Weymouth rider Mick Fletcher. Mildenhall gave the Cheetahs a terrible mauling at Cowley on 17 April, winning 49-28, with only the immaculate Dave Perks saving Oxford from an even bigger beating with a brilliant 15-point maximum. Oxford's first league win was a tense affair against Crayford, with the Cheetahs snatching a 40-38 win in a thrilling last-heat decider, but it was obvious that the Oxford side needed strengthening.

The following week saw Derek 'Super Ted' Harrison link with the Oxford camp, on loan from Cradley Heath. Derek had been a star with Milton Keynes the previous year, and he was just what the Cheetahs needed. Another new face was Steve Crockett, loaned to Oxford from Wolverhampton, who, following his debut for the Cheetahs at Stoke on 20 April, held his team place and became an ever-present. Oxford met the might of British League Leicester in the first round of the Inter-League Knock Out Cup on 15 May and raced to a highly creditable draw, with Dave Perks scorching to a maximum. In the replay at Leicester on 6 June, Oxford put up a great performance before going down 31-47. Again, it was that man Perks who led the Oxford scoring with a fine 11 points from 5 rides.

Having finally established a useful side, things suddenly began to go wrong for the Cheetahs. Dave Perks, who'd recorded 14 maximums in the Oxford cause, plus a string of double-figure scores, was injured and out of the side, sadly, for the rest of the season. As if that were not enough, Cradley Heath, the Cheetahs' mentors in the British League, recalled John Hack to their line-up, and by the start of August, Oxford were reduced to just one established heat-leader in Derek Harrison. It was also a busy month away from Cowley with six fixtures on away circuits, so it was small wonder that they lost the lot. The home match against Workington on 21 August did, however, give Cowley fans much enjoyment, as the Cheetahs won 50-28, but the real pleasure was to see youngsters Colin Ackroyd and Steve Crockett each score maximums. New faces to boost the Oxford team came in September via the British League. Experienced Bruce Cribb came on loan from Wolverhampton, and the former Oxford Rebel Trevor Geer arrived on loan from Eastbourne. Their arrival took some of the pressure off Derek Harrison, and ensured that the Cheetahs were at least competitive in the final weeks of the season.

With all the problems, it was no surprise that Oxford dropped to fifteenth place in the National League. They were on a high before the sensational Dave Perks was hurt,

*Derek Harrison.*

but from that moment on, any chance the Cheetahs had of league honours vanished. Derek Harrison did a great job holding the side together, while both Colin Ackroyd and Steve Crockett made excellent progress. Dave Perks' record in league matches really was something special though, with his overall average being 10.94 (the highest in the entire league), while at the Cowley circuit alone, it was an incredible 11.53.

The good news that greeted Oxford fans before the start of the 1981 season, was that skipper Dave Perks had recovered from his injuries and would again lead the Cheetahs. More good news was the fact that Derek Harrison would be back. Mick Handley also returned, as did the promising Colin Ackroyd, Mick Fletcher and John Grahame, while trials were given to Alan MacLean, brother of former Cheetah Harry. Steve Crockett was missing though, having moved to Wolverhampton, who were now members of the National League. The promoters were well aware that the side had a long tail after Perks and Harrison, and a third heat-leader was urgently needed. As things turned out though, the third heat-leader was a long time coming. To try and bring the side up to strength, Oxford turned to former Rebel Bob Kilby, who had retired following a highly successful Testimonial season at Swindon. However, the chunky Swindonian said 'No thanks' and the promotion subsequently turned their attention to Reading and local boy Ashley Pullen. But in the event, it was only in the closing weeks of the season that Ashley finally became available and joined the Cheetahs' ranks.

The early season matches emphasized the lack of a third heat-leader, with home losses in challenge fixtures against Milton Keynes, Rye House and Weymouth. It was not until 23 April, when the league campaign began, that the Cheetahs tasted success. A 42-36 victory over Boston saw the debut of Arthur Price, who moved from Nottingham, and he made a quiet start with a paid 6 points. Mildenhall beat Oxford 43-35 the following week at Cowley, but on 1 May, Oxford enjoyed a 4-point success at Workington. Narrow defeats at Stoke and Canterbury followed, with the latter match seeing Paul Evitts make a very satisfactory debut as a Cheetah with a paid 7 points. The home match against Milton Keynes on 4 May saw the Cheetahs really click as a team to record a fine 49-29 victory. Dave Perks got the lot (12 points) and Derek Harrison scored 11, while Colin Ackroyd also had a fine meeting. Four days later at Newcastle, the Cheetahs thought their third heat-leader problem had been solved with the signing of Arnold Haley from sister track Cradley Heath. Haley had vast experience and Oxford thought he'd be just the man for the job, but unfortunately, they were to be disappointed, for Haley scored just a single point from two rides, and decided that it was time to retire.

Defeat at Weymouth was followed by a good victory at Milton Keynes, where Oxford used the rider replacement facility for the injured Harrison. Dave Perks rode unbeaten for 15 points, with Colin Ackroyd recording a creditable 10. Throughout June and early July, Oxford enjoyed a period of success, with home wins against Stoke, Glasgow and Edinburgh, plus a great win at Wolverhampton. They crashed to defeat, however, at Exeter when, without skipper Perks, they lost 27-51, with Harrison and Ackroyd scoring 24 of the Cheetahs' 27 points. Newcastle then came to Oxford on 9 July and left with the league points, but when Rye House came the following week, Oxford returned to winning form. That was followed by a great 4-point win at Glasgow on 24 July, but Oxford lost the hard-riding Colin Ackroyd with a broken collarbone, which was to sideline the Sussex youngster for six weeks. Into August, and despite Oxford operating the rider replacement facility, they gained a creditable draw at Ellesmere Port, where Derek Harrison raced to a fine 18-point maximum. A 43-34 success at Scunthorpe was followed by a home victory over Wolverhampton (44-34) in a double-header on 20 August, which also saw the Cheetahs slaughter Workington 62-15 in the second match. Perks and Harrison recorded paid maximums, but more pleasing for Cheetahs supporters in this uninteresting match, was the full maximum recorded by Paul Evitts, and a paid maximum from John Grahame.

The Cheetahs came down to earth when visiting Middlesbrough on 23 August, the home side winning 54-24, and Weymouth sprang a surprise by winning at Cowley on 27 August. Success against visiting Ellesmere Port on 3 September was followed by a home defeat at the hands of Middlesbrough, this being one of the few occasions at Cowley when Dave Perks failed to record a double-figure score. Dave was back to his brilliant best for the visit to Crayford, however, scoring 15 points from 6 rides. Despite this, Oxford went down fighting, 36-42. Exeter were beaten 41-37 at Oxford on 17 September, but Canterbury came the following week and raced to a 3-point victory. The Exeter match saw the return of the hard-riding Colin Ackroyd, and the defeat by Canterbury was to be the one occasion when Dave Perks failed at Cowley, as he recorded an uncharacteristic 4 points. Dave was soon back on form though, racing to maximums against Crayford and Scunthorpe in a double-header at Cowley on 1 October. Colin Ackroyd scored a maximum against Crayford, and just for good measure, he also repeated the feat against Scunthorpe. The very next day at Peterborough, the Cheetahs were beaten, but the following Thursday, it was their turn to entertain the Panthers. It was a memorable match, not just because Oxford won 42-36, but because it marked the home debut of new signing Ashley Pullen, a man Oxford had been chasing since day one of the season. Ashley marked his Oxford debut with a well taken paid 7 points.

The league programme ended with defeats at both Mildenhall and Berwick, but the season at home finished with a 57-21 victory over Milton Keynes in the second leg of a challenge match. Oxford's final position was twelfth in the nineteen-team National League and supporters were left wondering just what might have been, had they had the services of Ashley Pullen from the start of the season. The Cheetahs won 13 home matches, and lost 5, while away from Cowley, they won 5, drew just the once and lost 12. Topping the averages again was Dave Perks (10.26), having scorched to 361 points from 34 league matches, while Derek Harrison recorded 346 points for a 9.51 average.

As usual, it was all change again at Oxford in 1982, but the Cowley faithful were used to it by now. The supporters had long since reasoned that being a sister track to the glamour club Cradley Heath in the British League, meant it was the Heathens who paid the piper, and therefore called the tune. The top two from 1981, namely Dave Perks and Derek Harrison, were missing, with Perks returning to Long Eaton, while Harrison was transferred to Mildenhall. Also Long Eaton-bound was Paul Evitts, who had been so promising for the Cheetahs in 1981, and the equally promising John Grahame moved to British League Reading. Thankfully, Ashley Pullen was back, as was the crowd-pleasing Colin Ackroyd, plus old faithfuls Mick Handley and Mick Fletcher. To bring the side up to strength, Graham Drury was signed from defunct Hull on loan, and Wayne Jackson also arrived at Cowley, following the closure of Workington.

It was hardly surprising that the season opened badly for the Cheetahs, since the side had practically been re-built and needed time to settle together. Milton Keynes won at Oxford in the season's opening fixture, having already beaten the Cheetahs at the Groveway in the first leg of a home and away challenge fixture, and in addition, Oxford lost another challenge match at Peterborough. At home against Weymouth on 1 April, the Cheetahs secured a 4-point win in the Dorsox Trophy, only to lose the second leg at Weymouth by 16 points. Things really looked up at Rye House on 4 April though, in the first league match of the season, when the Cheetahs were victorious by 53 points to 43. However, it was subsequently claimed that Graham Drury's contract had not been registered with the B.S.P.A., with the result that the match was declared void, and was actually re-run in September. On that occasion, the Rye House side made no mistakes, winning 64-32.

It soon became obvious that Oxford desperately needed strengthening, as Jackson was hurt in April and was sidelined for six weeks with a knee injury, while both Handley and Fletcher were struggling, and Drury was not getting the scores the promoters had hoped for. The signing of Simon Cross, on loan from Cradley Heath, proved a real boost to the team and it wasn't long before the talented youngster was knocking up double-figure scores. His arrival gave the Oxford public something to cheer about and the management were quick to give an opportunity to another youngster, namely Kevin Smart, who had been a Central Junior League success with Swindon. Kevin came on loan from the Robins and held his place in the side on merit, and he could be regarded as one of the few successes enjoyed by Oxford during 1982.

The experienced Brian Woodward arrived via Weymouth, but hardly had time to settle in before breaking an ankle. No sooner had he recovered, than he was sidelined with a back injury, with the result that Oxford hardly knew he'd actually been around. Ian Gledhill arrived from Cradley Heath, but proved to be most disappointing and was gone after only 17 matches. Bill Barrett, a young and likeable Australian, was given

*Colin Ackroyd.*

opportunities to establish himself, but despite his wholehearted efforts, he was never more than a reserve in the line-up. John Frankland, on loan from Long Eaton, was another arrival, and provided plenty of thrills, but was not the heat-leader that Oxford so desperately needed. By June, Oxford had collected only a single home win against Crayford, and a 48-48 draw against Peterborough, yet they shook Milton Keynes by winning there in the Knock Out Cup, following a home victory in the first leg on 6 May. Unfortunately, in the second round against Mildenhall, the Cheetahs suffered a hiding – both home and away – losing 118-73 on aggregate.

Fortunately, the month ended happily with a resounding 60-36 win at Canterbury on 26 June, but there was disappointment as the forceful Colin Ackroyd suffered injury, and Mick Handley retired after struggling to find his best form. July was a little better for the Cheetahs, and a fine win over Glasgow at Cowley was followed by an excellent 64-31 victory at Stoke. Berwick came to Oxford on the 22 July and were beaten by just 4 points, and the month ended with a home draw against Milton Keynes. The month of August was a disaster, with Boston (followed by lowly Scunthorpe) being victorious at Cowley, whilst away from home, the Cheetahs raced six league matches and lost the lot. As if that were not bad enough, the spectacular Simon Cross and the Oxford skipper Ashley Pullen were involved in a disagreement at Long Eaton on 11 August, with the result that Cross never turned a wheel for Oxford again. To help the Cheetahs' cause, Gary Chessell came on loan from near neighbours Swindon, and really played his part in the home win over Stoke on 2 September. However, it was another bad month results-wise. It was not until 30 September that the Oxford side had another success of sorts, and that was merely a home draw against Long Eaton.

A season with few memories of note, ended with a narrow victory over Canterbury at home on 14 October. Rather unsurprisingly, the Cheetahs finished as wooden spoonists in the nineteen-team league. In all, they won only 7 league matches out of the 36 raced, and secured 3 draws, while suffering no fewer than 26 losses. Ashley Pullen was Oxford's best with an average of 7.73 points a match, closely followed by Graham Drury on 7.54, and Colin Ackroyd with a creditable 7.42 figure. Oxford used a total of twenty-one riders in an effort to put together a winning combination, but it really was a terrible season, with the efforts of Simon Cross (before he left) and the tigerish Colin Ackroyd being two of the only bright spots.

The 1983 season heralded yet more changes, both on the team and the promotional front. The change of promotion was to be most significant, because the stadium owners Northern Sports (Oxford) Ltd, took over the running of speedway, with Bernard Crapper and John Payne becoming the co-promoters. Although it was not fully realized at the time, a new chapter was being written in the history of Oxford Speedway, and little did the supporters know, but it was the beginning of something very special indeed. The links with British League Cradley Heath were severed, and the new promoters had to build a team virtually from scratch. Ashley Pullen departed to join Peterborough, and sadly the exciting Colin Ackroyd was another absentee, but Graham Drury was back on loan for a further year, and he was elected as the Oxford skipper for the new campaign. Wayne Jackson, who had not enjoyed the best of luck during 1982, was signed on a full transfer from Cradley Heath, and another full transfer saw Nigel Sparshott move in from nearby Milton Keynes.

Further loans were agreed with Swindon for the highly promising duo of Kevin Smart and Gary Chessell, while Dan McCormick agreed to send the spectacular Mike Wilding from Birmingham to Cowley. Mark Summerfield came on loan from Leicester, and to complete the septet, Steve Crockett resumed his speedway career with the Cheetahs. The opening fixture against Danish touring club Kulsvierne, unfortunately fell victim to the weather, so Oxford took to the track for the opening Cowley fixture on Good Friday morning in the second leg of a Knock Out Cup fixture against Milton Keynes. Oxford had previously visited the Knights on 29 March, gaining a 2-point win, and in a very fine match in the Easter sunshine, the Cheetahs raced to a 51-45 victory, to win overall by 100 points to 92. New boys Wilding and Sparshott looked good with paid 14 points apiece, while Kevin Smart was a brilliant reserve with a paid 12-point return.

Having lost their opening league fixtures at Canterbury and Exeter, the Cheetahs' first home league match was against Boston on 7 April. The Oxford side was minus Drury, Chessell and Jackson, however, who were injured, and more bad luck hit the makeshift side when Mike Wilding crashed in heat four, breaking a collarbone. Despite this, they won 49-47, thanks to 14 points from Nigel Sparshott and a well-taken dozen from Steve Crockett. The match against Mildenhall the following week, saw new signing Ian Clark make his debut as a Cheetah, but even his 11-point tally, plus a paid 16 from acting skipper Nigel Sparshott, couldn't stop Oxford losing narrowly by 4 points. Cradley Heath's Simon Wigg won the World Championship qualifying round at Oxford on 21 April, and a week later Drury returned to action in the Cheetahs' 53-43 win over Long Eaton. Then followed league defeats at Stoke and Milton Keynes, and a 5-point defeat at Rye House in the Knock Out Cup. Scunthorpe were beaten 51-45 at Cowley in mid-May, but Weymouth took the league points, winning 53-43 at Oxford, as the month drew to a close.

Mike Wilding and Wayne Jackson were now back in action and a full-strength Oxford team took the league points from visiting Peterborough on 2 June. There was a shock though, when Rye House came to Oxford for the second leg of the Knock Out Cup and won 51-45 to secure an overall victory. Winning form returned, however, with a home league success over Middlesbrough, followed by a 56-40 victory over Milton Keynes. July was a busy month, with the Cheetahs on the road for much of it. They enjoyed a 4-point success at Boston, but visits to Edinburgh, Berwick, Scunthorpe, Middlesbrough and Glasgow proved fruitless for Oxford. At home, it was a good month with wins over Rye House, Canterbury and Glasgow.

August opened with a fine match against Newcastle, when the Cheetahs went down by 2 points in a last-heat decider. It was an incredible match, as the Diamonds were virtually a two-man side, with Rod Hunter and Joe Owen scoring 40 points between them! On 11 August, a certain John Tremblin brought his British League Swindon side, including guests Sam Nikolajsen and Andy Grahame, to Cowley for an Inter-League challenge. It was small wonder that the powerhouse Robins team won by 73 points to 22. Ian Clark had suffered a broken arm at Rye House and the promising Nigel De'Ath wore the number seven race jacket against Swindon. Martin Yeates was the winner of the Hartford Motors-sponsored Supporters' Club Trophy on 18 August, and Edinburgh went away from Cowley with a 14-point victory the following week. August had not been a good month away from Oxford, since the Cheetahs had lost at Peterborough and Newcastle in the league, but they did at least manage to secure a point in a 48-48 draw at Long Eaton.

September saw a series of home wins over Crayford, Exeter and Berwick, but this was offset by defeats at Rye House, Crayford and Mildenhall. British League sides Birmingham and Reading came to Cowley at the end of the month for a four-team tournament, with Oxford and a Martin Yeates Select side completing the field. A certain Hans Nielsen was riding for Birmingham and he had little difficulty in recording a 12-point maximum. As the season drew to its close, the whole of Oxford was buzzing with the news that 1984 would see British League racing back at Cowley. Northern Sports director David Hawkins stated that 'Only the best is good enough for Oxford' and purchased the British League licence from Hackney. 'No effort will be spared to ensure that the 1984 Cheetahs would be an attractive and competitive side,' said Mr Hawkins.

Having finished the 1983 campaign in fourteenth position, the Cheetahs' spell in National League racing was over, with a new and exciting era waiting just around the corner. With everyone looking forward to 1984, team building got underway before the 1983 season had closed. Already, fans had seen the Danish rider, Jens Rasmussen of Hackney, having a few practice spins around the Oxford circuit, and by October the Cheetahs' promoters had him signed, sealed and settled. An off-track signing followed, when Len Silver, the former Hackney promoter, joined the Oxford camp to be team manager. David Hawkins of Northern Sports had made a generous budget available to co-promoters Bernard Crapper and John Payne in order to purchase riders, and they certainly spent the money wisely. Following the signing of Jens Rasmussen, a cheque for £15,000 saw Rye House star Marvyn Cox, who was one of the top boys in the National League, join Oxford. A few days later, Messrs Crapper and Payne hit the jackpot though, when a fee, reported as a record £30,000, was paid to Birmingham for Danish international and World finalist Hans Nielsen.

The Oxford promoters' spending spree hadn't finished yet, as they further dipped in the coffers and a reported £25,000 fee brought another international rider to Cowley. This time the rider was British and one who would go on to become a legend in the sport, namely Simon Wigg, who arrived via Cradley Heath. Finally, to complete the top five of the line-up, £12,000 was paid to King's Lynn for the services of Melvyn Taylor. From the 1983 side, Ian Clark and Nigel Sparshott were retained, and initially both filled the reserve berths in the new team. With an eye to the future, Kevin Smart, who had been purchased from Swindon, and Nigel De'Ath were both loaned to National League Milton Keynes, in order to further their experience.

The 1984 Cheetahs were now ready to take on all comers, and they certainly made the speedway world sit up and take notice on 24 March. Opening with a League Cup match at King's Lynn, the Cheetahs stormed to victory by 46 points to 32. On Friday 30 March, Oxford made their first home appearance in a challenge match against Poole, and new skipper Hans Nielsen showed his undoubted class, to record the first of many full maximums as the Cheetahs won 43-35. Friday was now to be the Cheetahs' regular race night, making a change from the traditional Thursday evenings. The new race day was part of the deal when they took over the Hackney licence.

On Wednesday 4 April, Oxford journeyed to Poole and came back with another success, and they went on to record four more victories, including two more away from Cowley, at Reading and Wimbledon, to make it a marvellous start to the season. Friday 13 April was, however, to prove very unlucky for Oxford. Wimbledon with former Oxford Rebel Gordon Kennett in their side, came to Cowley and left with the League Cup points following a last-heat decider. The Dons won 40-38, and Gordon showed that he still knew the best way around his former home with a fine paid 13-point tally, which included a win over Hans Nielsen in a tremendous heat twelve. Riding as a guest for Hans Nielsen, Kennett again returned to Oxford for the visit of King's Lynn on 27 April, and proved a worthy replacement as he notched 11 points in a super home victory. Hans was back for the Knock Out Cup clash against Belle Vue the following week, but even his paid 15-point maximum couldn't stop the Aces from winning 40-38, and in the return leg, poor Oxford got a real hammering, scoring only 25 points to Belle Vue's 53.

After their great opening spell, Oxford had now come down to earth a bit. However, they were providing great racing at home, while on their travels, they were always very attractive to watch. Hans Nielsen was leading the side by example, and his team riding with Marvyn Cox was a joy to behold. 'Cocker' was riding really well in what was, after all, his first full season in British League racing, and no one at Oxford was surprised when he captured the British Junior Riders' Championship, and followed this by securing the European Under-21 Championship. Unfortunately, the injury bug began to bite, and at one time there were no fewer than eight Oxford contracted riders who were suffering injuries. To try and rid the track of this problem, the promoters invited an exorcist to Cowley, but despite a seriously conducted service, things didn't improve and this was emphasized when Mel Taylor broke an arm and dislocated a shoulder in a match against Reading.

To cover for injuries and help to strengthen the side, Oxford signed West German rider Klaus Lausch, who had a fine reputation in his homeland. Klaus certainly showed a great deal of promise, and had he decided on a British League career, he could

*Nigel De'Ath.*

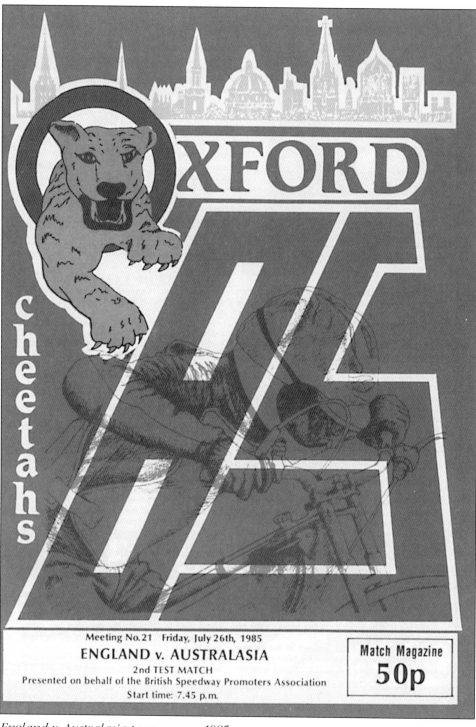

*England v. Australasia programme, 1985.*

undoubtedly have become a heat-leader. The league campaign didn't start at Cowley until 22 June, when the Cheetahs recorded a narrow victory over visitors Newcastle. They had actually begun in the best possible way, with a 6-point victory at Coventry on 9 June, and whilst generally they did very well in the quest for the league points, injuries caused them to lose some of their sparkle during the second half of the season. Despite their problems, Oxford still managed to finish eighth in the sixteen-team league and had made a fine return to top flight racing.

The Cheetahs had two riders in the Gothenburg-staged World Final, with Hans Nielsen notching 13 points to finish as runner-up to Erik Gundersen, while Simon Wigg recorded a 9-point total to finish in sixth place. The same two riders topped the Oxford scoring, with Hans notching 296 points from 26 league matches (yielding a 10.69 average, which was enough for him to finish the year on the very top of the national averages), while backing the 'Main Dane' all the way was 'Wiggy', who plundered 251 points (average 9.91). As the season finished, plans were announced for the building of a sports complex at the stadium. The super new structure would provide facilities second-to-none in speedway, meanwhile the promoters pledged to spare no effort to strengthen the team. 'We've not had a bad season, all things considered,' said co-promoter Bernard Crapper, 'Next year, we intend to show 'em a thing or two.' Little did he know how true these words would be.

1985 was a season to savour if you were an Oxford Cheetahs fan. It was the year that saw the team crowned as British League Champions, while they also won the Knock Out Cup and the Midland Cup. The Cheetahs were, without doubt, the team of the season, and it all happened in only their second season back in the British League. The foundations for success had been laid during 1984, and there were a few changes for the 1985 campaign, as money was again made available for the purpose of team-strengthening. As in 1984, the money was spent wisely and Andy Grahame was secured from Wolverhampton, where he had spent the previous season on loan from Birmingham. Nigel Sparshott and Ian Clark, who had filled the reserve berths in the Cheetahs side the previous year, were allowed to leave for Exeter and Peterborough respectively. So, to complete the side, Oxford gambled on Troy Butler, a young Australian who had caught the eye of both Hans Nielsen and Simon Wigg whilst they were touring 'down under'.

The Cheetahs team to do battle in 1985, therefore, comprised Hans Nielsen, Simon Wigg, Andy Grahame, Jens Rasmussen, Marvyn Cox, Mel Taylor and Troy Butler. In what was a nicely balanced line-up, Oxford had a fine blend of youth and experience. Len Silver had left the club and Bernard Crapper took over as the team manager of the senior side, with John Tremblin taking charge of the junior team. For one reason or another, the British League was now reduced to eleven sides, with Newcastle closing, and Poole, Eastbourne, Exeter and Wimbledon opting for National League racing. The season opened with the League Cup competition, and a narrow 2-point win over Coventry was followed by a 39-39 draw against Cradley Heath. Away success came at King's Lynn (47-30), but having won at home against Wolverhampton, Oxford went down by 2 points at Halifax, and then secured an excellent draw at Coventry. Home wins against Sheffield and Belle Vue and an away victory at Wolverhampton saw Oxford riding high, but mid-May, saw defeat at Belle Vue.

The Cheetahs suffered home and away defeats at the hands of Ipswich, before Swindon caused a surprise by winning 40-38 at Cowley on 24 May. However, the next day, Oxford gained revenge by winning 41-37 at Blunsdon. At Sheffield, Oxford went down by 6 points, but followed this with a home victory against King's Lynn and an away win at Cradley Heath. Reading beat the Cheetahs at Smallmead on 24 June, but Oxford then enjoyed home victories over Halifax and Reading to finish second in the League Cup table and qualify for a semi-final clash with Ipswich. In the Knock Out Cup, Oxford went to town with a vengeance, securing home and away victories over Coventry. A 2-point defeat at Belle Vue, followed by a 10-point home win over the Aces, saw the Cheetahs drawn against Reading in the semi-final. Things were looking very good for Oxford indeed, and an aggregate 81-74 success over the Racers meant they would meet Ipswich in the final.

The British League began at Belle Vue on 22 June, and this time the Cheetahs secured a 40-37 win. This was to be the first of many away triumphs, as Oxford strolled their way to the Championship. The Cheetahs lost only 3 matches, all very narrow defeats – 38-40 at Halifax, 37-41 at Sheffield, and 37-41 at Cradley Heath – while only Ipswich took any league points at Cowley, after snatching an excellent draw on 18 October. Happily, the team saw few changes, although Mel Taylor moved out to Mildenhall in August, which saw Klaus Lausch (the West German star) recalled, and when he broke a collarbone, there was the promising Alastair Stevens waiting in the wings. As the season moved to its close, the question on everyone's lips was 'Could Oxford secure the Grand Slam?' and having beaten Ipswich home and away in the League Cup semi-final and secured a home win against Coventry in the first leg of the final, things looked very promising. Sadly, Andy Grahame had broken his wrist on 4 September, and without him the Cheetahs crashed to defeat at Brandon in the second leg on 26 October, losing by 28 points to 50, so it was Coventry who took the League Cup honours.

The Cheetahs made no mistake in the Knock Out Cup, however, as they beat mighty Ipswich 42-35 at home, having lost the first leg 37-41 at Foxhall Heath, thereby securing a marvellous 79-76 aggregate victory. In the Midland Cup, Oxford did not taste defeat. They beat Wolverhampton both home and away, and followed it up with victory over Swindon at home, and a draw at Blunsdon. For the final against Cradley Heath, Andy Grahame returned to the side with his damaged wrist heavily bandaged, and played his part in the 45-33 home success. This was followed by a magnificent 40-38 win at Dudley Wood on 31 October. Hans Nielsen was a magnificent leader of the Cheetahs, and the whole team responded to his sheer brilliance. In British League matches alone, Hans again topped the national averages with an astounding 11.43 figure, while he was well backed by 'Wiggy', who averaged 9.70. Again, Hans was runner-up to Erik Gundersen in the World Championship Final held at Bradford, but Simon Wigg won the World Long Track title at Korskro, Denmark, and celebrated by arriving at Cowley in a heli-copter. The city of Oxford rewarded the Cheetahs' success with a civic reception to mark their outstanding speedway achievements, when the team paraded through the streets in an open-top bus. Who can forget the crowds that waited outside City Hall to receive the Oxford team that had achieved so very much? Oxford Cheetahs – 1985 British League Champions, Knock Out Cup winners and Midlands Cup winners.

At the beginning of the 1986 campaign, the Cheetahs paid the price for their achievements the previous year. In order to comply with the points limit, popular Dane Jens Rasmussen had to move, and linked up with Ipswich. Meanwhile, Troy Butler, who had won the Australian Championship, returned suffering from the after effects of a badly broken leg, which effectively sidelined him for the whole of the season. A new face at Cowley was Aussie Mark Carlson, and the introduction of the compulsory junior saw promising Jon Surman given a berth in the Oxford line-up. A further change saw Nigel De'Ath return to the team after two seasons with Milton Keynes in the National League.

Oxford did not make a particularly good start to the season, however, losing the Premiership to Coventry, with defeats at both Cowley and Brandon. Mark Carlson scored 4 points at Coventry, before finding himself the victim of an assessed average, which forced him to leave and eventually join Milton Keynes in the National League. In the League Cup, Oxford also got off to a bad start, losing by 6 points at home to Belle Vue on 4 April. Coventry also won at Cowley on 23 April, but the Cheetahs won the other 8 home meetings, and with 5 away successes, along with a 39-39 draw at Swindon, they managed to qualify for the final.

The rather shaky start convinced the promoters that the team needed strengthening. It was at Swindon on Sunday 11 May, on the occasion of the World Championship semi-final meeting, that Bernard Crapper and John Payne took the decision that was to transform the Cheetahs from a good team into a great team. Young Danish rider Per Sorensen had been forced out of the Swindon team, following the return from injury of Finn Thomsen. Per's average was such that he would fit into the Cheetahs line-up, so the Oxford management made an offer, which was subsequently accepted. The promoters reasoned that Sorensen, under the guidance of Hans Nielsen and backed by the tremendous team spirit in the Cheetahs camp, would blossom at Oxford. It was something of a gamble, but it paid off handsomely. Per was made partner to Hans Nielsen and following his signing, Oxford never really looked back. Although 2 League Cup fixtures were lost during June – at Wolverhampton by 2 points and at Ipswich by just a single point – and a 12-point defeat was suffered at Sheffield in a Challenge Cup match, from 4 July onwards, Oxford were not to taste defeat again in 1986!

It was an amazing winning sequence, and following a victory against Ipswich on 4 July, Oxford went to Cradley Heath the day after and won 45-33. Sheffield came on 11 July in the second leg of the Challenge Cup, and although the Cheetahs won 44-34, they just failed on aggregate, although that didn't matter as it was an Oxford home victory. Belle Vue were beaten at Cowley in a British League match, and this was followed by a League Cup victory at Hyde Road the day after, and July finished with a home victory over Cradley Heath. August saw King's Lynn severely mauled 60-18 at Cowley in the British League, and away wins at Belle Vue, Bradford and Reading followed. September brought more success, starting with a narrow victory over Ipswich (40-38) in the League Cup semi-final at Oxford. Swindon were beaten at Blunsdon in the Knock Out Cup, and Wolverhampton fell to the Cheetahs at Monmore Green in a league encounter.

*Oxford 1986. From top to bottom: Hans Nielsen, Simon Wigg, Marvyn Cox, Per Sorensen, Andy Grahame, Nigel De'Ath, Jon Surman, Bernard Crapper (co-promoter).*

Coventry were beaten at Cowley on 12 September and still the Cheetahs steam-rollered on. Swindon were beaten 48-30 at Oxford in the second leg of the Knock Out Cup, and Bradford were hammered 58-20. On their travels, the Cheetahs won at King's Lynn in a British League match, Ipswich in the League Cup semi-final, and finally, they took Sheffield to the cleaners by 49 points to 29. The month ended with a double-header at Cowley, which saw continued league success over local rivals Swindon and Reading. In October, Sheffield were beaten 45-33 in the Knock Out Cup semi-final, and the Cheetahs recorded the same score in the return at Owlerton to book a place in the final against Cradley Heath. Swindon were hammered 56-21 at Blunsdon in a league match, then Cradley Heath were beaten by 2 points in the League Cup final at Dudley Wood, and finally, Ipswich fell to the powerful Cheetahs in the British League.

Whilst the high-flying Cheetahs could beat anyone on the track, they couldn't defeat the weather and, sadly, the two home league matches against Wolverhampton and Sheffield were never ridden, but such was Oxford's dominance, they still emerged as Champions. Not only were the two league matches wiped out, the weather also prevented the home matches against Cradley Heath in both the League Cup and the Knock Out Cup from being ridden. The Cheetahs had actually journeyed to Cradley Heath for the first leg of the Knock Out Cup final on 1 November and had come away with a fine draw. Previously, on 18 October, Oxford had secured a 40-38 victory at Cradley Heath in the first leg of the League Cup final, but with it proving impossible to complete both competitions, the decision was made that the trophies would be shared by the two clubs!

The Oxford success story also received a tremendous boost when Hans Nielsen took the World Championship in Katowice, Poland, and it was pleasing to have Marvyn Cox as a competitor in the World Final as well. Hans Nielsen had a tremendous season, and in addition to his World title success, he took the British League Riders' Championship and never tasted defeat in all 10 British League matches away from Cowley. Hans' league average of 11.83 speaks for itself, but Oxford's overall success in 1986 was a great team effort. Also performing wonderfully well for the Cheetahs were Simon Wigg (who averaged 11.01), while Marvyn Cox achieved a brilliant 8.79 figure. Per Sorensen also covered himself in glory and recorded a maximum at Swindon, which must have given him tremendous satisfaction. Once again, Oxford City Council honoured the Cheetahs with a civic reception. As in 1985, crowds lined the route as the riders toured the city in an open-top bus.

It was asking a great deal of the 1987 Cheetahs to follow their success of the previous two years, and regrettably they couldn't do it. As in the past, they paid a price for their achievements on track, and speedway's rules ensured the break-up of the 1986 title-winning side. Although the points limit, set at 45, remained for 1987, the Cheetahs, whose total average topped 50-plus, still had to lose riders and this gave the promoters the heart-searching job of deciding who was to be retained and who had to go. Eventually it was Simon Wigg who left, joining Hackney, who decided to give British League racing another go. It was interesting to note that the B.S.P.A. were pleased to welcome another track into speedway's top competition, and pledged that help would be given to re-establish the Kestrels. Sadly, in the event, it was only Oxford who released an established heat-leader to assist them, and no one else seemed too concerned. Simon's release created other problems, because whilst the debate over his joining Hackney went on, the Cheetahs missed out on the popular Per Sorensen. The young Dane had the offer of a very good job in his native Denmark, and in the end accepted it, so he too was lost to Oxford.

Good news for the campaign came when an attractive sponsorship deal for the team was announced, with Halls Brewery backing them, initially in a two-year deal. Oxford therefore, became known as the SKOL Cheetahs, proudly displaying the Halls emblem on their race jackets. The release of Simon Wigg and the unavailability of Per Sorensen saw the return of Jens Rasmussen, and to complete the line-up, the promising Alastair Stevens came into the side after a season on loan at Rye House in the National League. Another change in the Cowley organization saw the race night changed back to Thursdays.

The season started well for the Cheetahs, as they went to Cradley Heath on 21 March in the first leg of the Premiership and won 41-37, and on 3 April at Cowley they made sure that overall success was theirs, winning the second leg 41-36. The injury bug struck in a three-team tournament, which saw Oxford, Reading and Swindon in competition over the Easter period. Alastair Stevens suffered a broken arm in a heat nine spill at Cowley which ruled him out of the saddle for a few weeks. Kevin Smart, on loan to

Milton Keynes, and Troy Butler, happily recovered from his broken leg and also on loan to the Knights, covered during Stevens' absence. The Cheetahs' bright start continued through the League Cup competition, as they gained away victories at Hackney (40-38), Reading (45-33), Cradley Heath (41-37) and Wolverhampton (40-38). At home, only Coventry took points away from Oxford, winning 41-37 on 17 July. Oxford went through to the semi-final again, and they'd done it by not only having to cover Ali Stevens' enforced lay-off, but also injuries to Nigel De'Ath, Marvyn Cox and Jens Rasmussen as well.

The only blot on the landscape came on 15 May, in a League Cup match against Belle Vue, when Bernard Crapper resigned from his job as team manager, following a row in a very stormy meeting. The Cheetahs won the match 45-33, but Bernard, whose motivation of the side had really played its part in 1985 and 1986,

*Simon Wigg.*

said 'Enough is enough', with junior manager John Tremblin taking over for the next match against Hackney. The league campaign began on 23 July with a match at Sheffield, which saw Oxford defeated 43-35. Two days later, Coventry took the points from the Cheetahs at Brandon, with a 44-34 victory. Things looked up a bit when Oxford beat King's Lynn at Cowley on 29 July, and followed it up with a good draw at Wolverhampton. Both results were achieved without the services of Jens Rasmussen, who had been hurt in the Knock Out Cup match against Belle Vue on 5 June. Little did Oxford supporters know, however, that the victory over King's Lynn would be one of only 6 home wins in the league, while the draw at Wolverhampton would turn out to be the only point achieved away from Cowley!

After beating Ipswich in the Knock Out Cup and losing to Belle Vue in the League Cup final, the rot really set in at Cowley, with the only victories being over Bradford, Sheffield, Wolverhampton, Belle Vue and Cradley Heath. The returning Simon Wigg inspired a shock Hackney victory (45-33) at Cowley on 14 October, with the HL1 Kestrels proving very worthy winners indeed, and the season ended with the Cheetahs only just avoiding the wooden spoon. Cradley Heath beat Oxford on aggregate in the Knock Out Cup semi-final, so there was nothing much to show for what had been an extremely frustrating season. However, it was not all gloom and doom, as Marvyn Cox reached the Inter-Continental Final, and generally enjoyed a good season with an average in excess of 8. There was also, of course, the magnificent Hans Nielsen, whose achievements at international level made up for Cowley fans' disappointment at club level. Hans retained the World Championship in Amsterdam in speedway's first-ever two-day World Final and, just for good measure, he also retained the British League Riders' Championship. With 30 maximums (21 full and 9 paid) and an average of 11.38 from a combined total of 49 British League, League Cup and Knock Out Cup fixtures, the 'Main Dane' was undoubtedly the man of the season. At international level, there was further success for Hans in the World Team Cup and World Pairs events when representing Denmark.

After the frustrations of the previous year, the 1988 season was better for the Cheetahs, but still not quite good enough for the ambitious Oxford management. They had promised changes in the side and, as good as their word, changes were made in an attempt to build a title-winning team. The points ceiling was raised to a maximum of 48 which helped, while the compulsory junior ruling was scrapped, so it gave Oxford room to manoeuvre. Simon Wigg returned to the team after his stint at Hackney, with the London side opting for a return to National League racing, while Peter Lloyd was another returnee, following a spell with Milton Keynes. The Cheetahs' major signing was Martin Dugard, who arrived via Eastbourne. Martin, a young rider of outstanding potential, was totally dedicated to making it to the top in speedway and had been the target of practically every team in the British League, so it was a coup when the youngster pledged his future to Oxford.

So, the Oxford team read Hans Nielsen, Simon Wigg, Marvyn Cox, Martin Dugard, Nigel De'Ath, Ali Stevens and Peter Lloyd, with John Tremblin as team manager. The combined averages of the squad was 47.37, and the re-building of the side meant that there had to be departures from the 1987 side. Thanks to the points system, the

*England v. Denmark programme, 1988.*

Cheetahs released Andy Grahame, Jens Rasmussen and Jon Surman. Andy returned to Wolverhampton on loan and Jon Surman went to National League Eastbourne, but surprisingly, no British League track came forward for Jens Rasmussen. There was no doubt that Jens could have done a useful job for any of them, and Oxford were prepared to offer him on a free loan to get him fixed up, but still no one was interested. So, being an E.E.C. rider and married to a British girl, Jens exercised his right to race in the National League and linked with Rye House, where his presence undoubtedly saved the Rockets from going under.

The season at Cowley opened with a challenge match against Swedish touring side Getingarna, which the Cheetahs won 53-37, but in the first British League match at Coventry on 30 March, Oxford crashed to defeat by 39 points to 51. The return match on Good Friday morning was a cracker, with Oxford winning 46-44 after a last-heat decider. Despite a series of home wins during the early weeks of the season, one thing became obvious: that at the lower end of the side, the Cheetahs were vulnerable. Ali Stevens was struggling to produce his best form, while Peter Lloyd was finding British League racing a tough prospect. Something had to be done, so the go-ahead Oxford promoters took a chance on Norwegian Einar Kyllingstad, who had been released by King's Lynn. His signing allowed Nigel De'Ath to drop to the reserve berth, and the promoters hoped that Kyllingstad would do what Per Sorensen had done in 1986. Ali Stevens was released to join National League Wimbledon, where he quickly found his form, but the Kyllingstad move didn't come off. The Norwegian flopped and was quickly released, but despite this failure, the promoters were not put off and they took another chance with Dane Lars Munkedal, who had been released by Wolverhampton. But he faired little better and with Nigel De'Ath still finding points hard to come by, the Cheetahs were still vulnerable in the number two position, and also in the reserve berths.

Despite their problems, the progress of Martin Dugard gave Cowley fans plenty to cheer about. It didn't take Martin long to settle into British League racing and his enthusiasm kept everyone happy. Frequently during the season, Martin came good when his team-mates (Hans Nielsen apart) were struggling, and he was undoubtedly the signing of the season in British Speedway. Overall, it was a season that promised much, but achieved little, and it ended with Oxford finishing fourth in the British League, but this was certainly an improvement on 1987. Hans Nielsen again led the scoring, with 563 points from 40 league matches, for an average of exactly 11.00. Amazingly, that was enough to see Hans top the national averages for the fifth successive year since linking with the Cheetahs. Sadly, Hans lost the World Championship title in his native Denmark to his old rival Erik Gundersen, but teamed up with him to win the World Pairs title. The triumphant Danes also won the World Team Cup, with Hans scorching to an amazing 17-point tally. Hans and Marvyn Cox teamed up to take the British Open Pairs for Oxford, which was one of the few honours in the season to find its way to Cowley. Simon Wigg, who made a welcome return to Oxford and averaged 8.66 in the British League, qualified for the World Final, where he notched 8 points. Meanwhile, Marvyn Cox seemed to lose some of his sparkle and at the end of the season, there were rumours that he fancied a move to a larger track.

During the winter break at the end of the 1988 season, the Oxford promoters began the task of strengthening the Cheetahs team ready for 1989. The points limit had been lowered to a maximum of 46, with an agreement from the B.S.P.A., that it would initially last for three years, which made the task of putting a competitive side together just a little bit harder. Hans Nielsen was quickly signed up to lead the Oxford side for the sixth successive season, with Martin Dugard and Simon Wigg quickly following to ensure the Cheetahs had as good a trio of heat-leaders as any of the nine tracks now left in the British League. An important signing for the first team was that of Paul Dugard, brother of Martin, who had come into the Oxford junior side in October 1988, just after his sixteenth birthday. This talented young rider decided it was the British League for him, and, like his elder brother, pledged himself to Oxford.

Good news for Oxford was that Marvyn Cox, after a somewhat unsettled winter where a move to another track was on the cards, agreed to stay at Cowley, to the joy of his many fans on the terraces. Andy Grahame, who'd not enjoyed a very good season at Wolverhampton and had only a 5.77 average, leapt at the chance to return home, which left Oxford with just 3.32 points to play with. It was now that the Oxford promoters' keen knowledge of the rulebook paid off, because an intense study revealed that they could include Troy Butler in the side. Troy had spent two seasons on loan at Milton Keynes and had captured the National League Riders' Championship title in 1988. There was no doubt that he was now ready for the higher level of racing, and the fact that he could legitimately return to the Oxford team on his previous British

League 3.00-assessed average was a real boost for Oxford. Naturally, Troy's inclusion in the final Oxford line-up provoked quite a bit of reaction from other promoters, but the fact that the rider's inclusion was well within the rules.

The season got off to a poor start weather-wise, when both of Oxford's opening away fixtures, a Gold Cup match at King's Lynn and a challenge match at Wolverhampton, fell foul of the weather. But the Cheetahs showed great form in their opening home fixture on Good Friday morning, recording a fine win over visiting Wolverhampton (55-35) in a challenge match. The Gold Cup began at Swindon the following day, with the Cheetahs in great form, winning 49-41. To make it a very happy Easter for Oxford, they enjoyed two

*Hans Nielsen.*

84

further wins on Easter Monday, beating Swindon 56-34 in the morning, before winning 49-41 at Reading in the evening. The Cheetahs again topped 50 points, when they completed the double over Reading on 31 March, but a surprise was in store when they went to Coventry on 8 April, and the Bees won 49-40. Revenge over Coventry came quickly on 14 April, when Oxford won 58-32 at Cowley, and the Gold Cup competition finished with a draw at King's Lynn on 15 April, plus a storming win over the Stars at home on 28 April. So, the Cheetahs qualified to meet Cradley Heath in the Gold Cup final, and the chance of their first pot of the season.

The British League campaign began well with a fine win over Cradley Heath, and a draw in the return at Dudley Wood in late April was followed by an outstanding 51-39 success at Swindon on 6 May. Oxford fans had seen Simon Wigg win the World Championship semi-final at Cowley on 5 May, and for good measure, 'Wiggy' went on to capture both the British and Commonwealth titles and book his passage to Munich for the World Final on 2 September. Talking of Munich – what a night that was! Hans Nielsen had already qualified, and an injury to Jan O. Pedersen meant that Troy Butler moved up from reserve to take his place. So, Oxford had three competitors and the joy of the Cowley supporters and management was overflowing when Hans Nielsen put in a tremendous display to score maximum points and collect his third World Championship. To complete a marvellous night for Oxford, 'Wiggy', who had already captured the World Long Track Championship, put in a great display to finish as runner-up to the 'Main Dane'.

Before the World Final, Oxford had journeyed to Cradley Heath on 26 August for the first leg of the Gold Cup final. The Cheetahs came away with a fine 6-point victory, and in the second leg on 15 September, they took the Heathens to the cleaners, winning 54-36, to clinch the trophy by 102 points to 78 on aggregate. Who can forget Martin Dugard's superb third-to-first ride in heat eleven, which set Oxford up for a storming finish? While all that was going on, the Cheetahs were still very much on course for the British League Championship, but their hopes received a setback on 20 September when old rivals Swindon came to Cowley. Marvyn Cox was absent, having broken his collarbone in an accident on 6 September in a match against Bradford, so Oxford used Belle Vue's Chris Morton as a guest. Unfortunately, Oxford crashed to defeat, with the Robins doggedly carving out a 49-41 success.

Winning form returned in the home matches against Wolverhampton and Reading, while in between, the Cheetahs gained revenge for their home defeat at the hands of Swindon, winning by 2 points at the Abbey Stadium to keep their title hopes alive. However, defeats at Coventry and Bradford, along with a home match against Coventry that fell victim to the weather, kept the Oxford camp on tenterhooks. Then came the G.M. Classic on Sunday 22 October and more frustration when the track was declared unfit, with no racing possible. Further problems with the Oxford circuit saw the important league match against Cradley Heath postponed, and it was now that stadium owner David Hawkins took a hand in events. In a meeting called to discuss track problems, the riders claimed that granite could provide a solution. Within hours, granite and the necessary equipment had arrived, with Mr Hawkins himself heading a squad of workers to ensure that the track was in perfect shape for Oxford's final meeting, a double-header British League encounter with Cradley Heath and Coventry, arranged for Wednesday 1 November.

Prior to that, Oxford visited King's Lynn on 26 October and won in tremendous style by 56 points to 34. That victory meant they had only to win one of their two remaining home matches to clinch the Championship. With the track in perfect condition on 1 November, the Cheetahs made no mistake. Marvyn Cox returned to the side, and Belle Vue's American sensation Gary Hicks replaced Troy Butler who had returned home. The first match against Cradley Heath was a tight affair, but with Martin Dugard in great form, Oxford made sure of the league title by winning 48-42. In the second match, Oxford kept up the pressure, with Andy Grahame, who had not had the best of luck against Cradley Heath, really coming into his own. In a great performance, Andy scored paid 14 points to head the scorechart and ensure a Cheetahs victory over Coventry by 49 points to 41. Oxford thus became League Champions for the third time since returning to top-flight racing in 1984. As usual, Hans Nielsen not only headed the Oxford scoring, but also topped the national averages on 10.97. Solid support was provided by 'Wiggy', who notched 233 points (average 7.82) and Martin Dugard, who averaged 7.69 in British League meetings.

## The 1990s

The 1990 season began with a real shock for all Oxford supporters. With just weeks to go, there came the news that Hans Nielsen and the Oxford management had been unable to agree a new contract, and for a time it looked as though the Cheetahs would enter the new campaign without their World Champion and number one rider. Such a thing was unthinkable, but with Hans not really wanting to leave, and the management not wanting him to go, there was a sound basis for negotiations. After further talks, everyone connected with the club was happy when the 'Main Dane' signed up to lead the Cheetahs again. It was, therefore, a very relieved bunch of supporters who journeyed to Belle Vue on 16 March and saw Hans and his new partner, Dean Barker, line up for Oxford in heat one of a challenge match. Barker had been signed from National League Eastbourne and was a rider with a very bright future, but whilst the Oxford promoters realized signing him would present problems in finalizing their side, they also knew that they could not let the opportunity of gaining such a promising rider slip away.

Putting the team together gave the promoters several headaches. However, one problem was solved when Marvyn Cox asked for a move and was loaned to Bradford for the season. Due to the 46-point limit, it still meant that another member of the title-winning side had to go and, after much soul-searching, it was decided that Andy Grahame was to be released. Somewhat surprisingly, no British League track came in for the hard-riding Grahame, with the result that he sought pastures new at National League Wimbledon. So, for 1990, Oxford lined up with Hans Nielsen, Dean Barker, Martin Dugard, Troy Butler, Paul Dugard, Simon Wigg and Alastair Stevens, who had been recalled from Poole.

The season began at Cowley, with an impressive win over Wolverhampton, and

*Paul Dugard.*

although it was just a challenge match, the Cheetahs looked impressive. New boy Dean Barker rode well for a paid 7 points and returnee Ali Stevens really shone with 11. The following day, 24 March, Oxford began the Gold Cup campaign at Swindon, and emerged convincing winners by 51 points to 38. The Premiership matches against Cradley Heath provided two excellent meetings, with a 45-45 draw at Oxford, followed by defeat at Dudley Wood, when Simon Wigg surprisingly failed to score at a track where he was usually good for double figures. On 6 April, local rivals Swindon came to Cowley for the return Gold Cup fixture, and shocked the Cheetahs by avenging their defeat at Blunsdon with a storming 51-39 victory. Hans Nielsen experienced all sorts of problems and could only muster 4 points, but Oxford returned to winning form on Easter Monday morning, easily beating Reading by 53 points to 37. Martin Dugard had been injured in an accident at King's Lynn, suffering a damaged ankle and a wrist injury, and although he returned for the evening match at Smallmead, Dean Barker was ruled unfit, with his place being taken by a junior, Sean McCullagh. Oxford were trailing 26-40 when the track lights went out, causing the match to be abandoned.

Oxford were proud to stage the first Test Match between England and Denmark on 18 April, which the home nation won 63-45. The match commemorated the Diamond Jubilee of Test Matches in this country, and many former capped riders were welcomed as guests. Most importantly, Oxford's first 'Great Dane' Arne Pander returned to Cowley as a special guest, and was given a tremendous reception.

Oxford completed their home Gold Cup fixtures with a narrow victory over King's Lynn on 27 April, and began their league matches with a fine win over Bradford at Cowley. The league campaign had actually begun for Oxford at Swindon on 21 April, where the Cheetahs had crashed to a 31-57 defeat. It was a defeat that was not totally unexpected, for the Oxford side was minus Barker, Stevens and Paul Dugard, who were ordered to compete in a re-arranged World Championship qualifying round at Stoke. Therefore, Oxford were forced to track three juniors, plus Kelly Moran as a guest for the injured Martin Dugard.

May saw a special meeting staged for the dependants of the late Paul Muchene, who had sadly died on 4 July the previous year, after a track accident at Hackney four nights earlier. There was a shock for Oxford on 18 May, when Coventry came for a re-arranged Knock Out Cup match. The Cheetahs had raced to a 45-45 draw at Coventry on 4 April, and were cruising to overall victory when the Bees staged a brilliant comeback to ride out of their skins in the last three heats and take victory by 2 points. The month ended on a happy note for Oxford, however, as both Martin Dugard and Simon Wigg made it through to the Commonwealth Final, while the league double was completed over Cradley Heath.

June began badly when Belle Vue, tracking three guest riders, beat Oxford in a league match by a single point. The Commonwealth Final at Belle Vue on 10 June saw three Oxford riders, namely Martin Dugard, Simon Wigg and Troy Butler, battle their way through to the Overseas Final. Hans Nielsen, meanwhile, was already on the World Final trail via the Nordic Final. Having secured the bonus point in the re-arranged Gold Cup match at Reading, Oxford qualified for the final where they would face Bradford, and on 22 June the Dukes came to Cowley for the first leg. Oxford raced to a narrow 4-point win, but in the return match Bradford went on the rampage, hammering Oxford 63-27 to win the Gold Cup amidst an atmosphere never before witnessed at the Odsal Stadium. The Overseas Final at Coventry saw Martin Dugard and Troy Butler progress to the Inter-Continental Final in Denmark. However, it was the end of the line for Simon Wigg, who just failed to qualify, and was riding with a collarbone injury sustained in the home hammering of King's Lynn on 15 June.

In the league campaign, July and August heralded a bad time for the Cheetahs. Reading and Coventry raced to victories at Cowley, and Oxford were shocked when Paul Dugard retired, claiming he had lost interest in the sport. The young Dugard was replaced by former Cradley Heath rider John Bostin, but he was never able to pick up as many points as Paul, and it left Oxford extremely vulnerable at reserve. Swindon and Wolverhampton tasted success at Cowley, and although Oxford raced to a win at King's Lynn on 7 July, the Zetor Stars caused a surprise by drawing at Cowley on 17 August. Reading, riding high in the league, won by 3 points at Cowley on August Bank Holiday Monday to end a lean month for the Cheetahs.

September saw Oxford back to form with a vengeance. At home, there was success against Bradford, Belle Vue, Cradley Heath and Coventry, while away from home, the Cheetahs tasted victory at Swindon, Wolverhampton and Cradley Heath. Unfortunately, there were also disappointments in September. Hans Nielsen and Martin Dugard had qualified for the World Final at Bradford but, in a tremendous meeting, Hans was unable to retain his World title, which went to Reading's Per Jonsson. Hans finished in fourth position, but Martin Dugard made a most satisfactory World Final debut, scoring 6 points. The month ended with Simon Wigg, who had retained his World Long Track Championship, suffering a serious injury to his neck whilst racing in Italy, which put him out of racing for the remainder of the season.

The season finished on a high note at Cowley, with convincing wins over Cradley Heath and Wolverhampton, and there was a fine away victory over Belle Vue to ensure that Oxford finished fourth in the final British League table. Reading emerged as Champions, and the Cheetahs were left thinking how different things could have been, had they not suffered that string of home defeats in July and August, for their away record was the best in the league. Hans Nielsen, his World Final disappointment behind him, won the British League Riders' Championship for the third time, with a superb

15-point maximum. The immaculate Hans again led the scoring for his club and in the league as a whole, reaching a 413-point tally, for a league average of 10.32. Martin Dugard continued his rapid progress to record an 8.39 figure, while Simon Wigg averaged 7.55. As the season drew to its close, the Oxford promoters opened negotiations with National League Poole for the transfer of their number one rider, Australian Craig Boyce. On 2 November, on the occasion of the Supporters' Club Dinner and Dance, it was officially announced that Craig had been signed and would line up with Oxford for the 1991 season.

There were more team changes at Oxford in 1991, as the management strove to put together a competitive side. Simon Wigg went on loan to Bradford, who in turn (and somewhat surprisingly) released Marvyn Cox, another Cheetahs asset, who was subsequently purchased by Poole. Changes to the set-up of British Speedway saw the formation of Divisions One and Two, with Poole, Ipswich, Wimbledon and Berwick opting for the higher level of racing. The Oxford team for the year was made up of Hans Nielsen, Martin Dugard, Craig Boyce, Dean Barker, Mark Carlson, plus Tony Primmer (an Australian) and Darren Grayling, signed from Eastbourne to stiffen the reserve berth. New signing Boyce had become Australian Champion at Alice Springs on 27 January recording a brilliant 15-point maximum.

The opening meeting of the season, a Gold Cup fixture against King's Lynn on 22 March, fell victim to the weather. So, Oxford opened the following day, at King's Lynn, with the return Gold Cup fixture, and to the joy of their fans, they won a thrilling encounter by 47 points to 43, with new boy Craig Boyce making a sensational debut, scoring 17 points. Oxford then opened with their now traditional Good Friday morning meeting, a Thames Valley Trophy match against Swindon, which they won by 48 points to 42. On Easter Monday, they had a home and away fixture with Reading, winning at home by 48 points to 42 (again), but suffering defeat at Reading. Oxford then lost at Swindon, the scores being 38-52 in both

*Darren Grayling.*

matches against their Thames Valley rivals. The weather prevented the Gold Cup fixture with Wimbledon from going ahead on 5 April, and it was eventually run on 17 May. It was at this meeting that it was announced that the team nickname SKOL Cheetahs had to be dropped, since Allied Breweries had decided that motor sport and alcohol did not go together, so Oxford lost the brand name, but happily retained the sponsorship.

In the meantime, Oxford had beaten Swindon and Poole at Cowley in Gold Cup matches, but unfortunately, they lost their first home league match against Belle Vue by 42 points to 47. Away from Cowley, Gold Cup results were quite encouraging, with victories at Wimbledon, Reading and Swindon, while defeats were suffered at Poole and Ipswich. Peterborough visited Oxford for a B.S.P.A. Cup match on 29 May, and whilst the Second Division side were beaten 63-27, it was Swedish rider Mikael Blixt who caught the eye with a 9-point tally. On 2 June, the Ancit Commonwealth Final was held at King's Lynn, with Oxford having two representatives in Craig Boyce and Martin Dugard. Sadly, Boyce was involved in a nasty spill, which saw him suffer back injuries and he was subsequently ruled out of the Oxford side for some weeks. Meanwhile Martin, who had qualified from the British Final on 19 May with 8 points, rode his heart out at Saddlebow Road, but could only muster 4 points.

With Boyce out of action, Oxford covered his absence in the main by using rider replacement, but when Wolverhampton came visiting for a Division One match, Boyce was replaced by former favourite Marvyn Cox. The Cheetahs used rider replacement for Hans Nielsen, who had to be at the compulsory practice for the Scandinavian Final. With a weakened team, it was not surprising that the Cheetahs lost by 20 points (35-55), despite an outstanding 18-point maximum from 'Cocker'. Hans Nielsen, however, was successful in winning the Scandinavian Final in his homeland (at Brovst, Denmark) with 13 points. Sadly, Tony Primmer had found the pace of top league racing beyond him, and Dean Barker was proving terribly inconsistent. So, with no Boyce, it was often down to just Nielsen and Dugard to score for the Cheetahs, but two men cannot cover for five, and there was also a weakness at reserve. There was a glimmer of hope on the horizon though, as medical opinion suggested that Boyce should be back in action by early August.

In the Reserve League match against King's Lynn on 14 June, young novice Glenn Cunningham (from Bristol) made a most satisfactory debut, scoring a paid 7 points. He was subsequently signed up on the spot by the Oxford management, and was definitely a rider for the future. On 2 August, Craig Boyce returned to track action, scoring a paid 6 points against Cradley Heath. Sadly, it was not enough to stop the Cheetahs losing 43-47, and this was despite a 14-point return from Hans Nielsen and 10 from Martin Dugard. Following that defeat, Oxford had a reasonable time in home league matches, with wins over Swindon, Poole and Reading, but saw the Gold Cup go to Berwick, after losing the final on aggregate.

The end of the season saw Oxford finish the league campaign in ninth position, but losing no fewer than five league matches at home certainly didn't help their cause. With 340 points, the ultra-professional 'Main Dane' sauntered to a fantastic 10.66 average, while the sensational Martin Dugard achieved a 9.12 figure. In league matches, Hans failed to top the national averages for the first time since 1983, with 'Sudden' Sam

Ermolenko finishing slightly above the 'Main Dane' on 10.74. Hans finished third in the World Final at Gothenburg, Sweden, but together with newly-crowned World Champion and fellow Dane Jan O. Pedersen, he won the World Pairs competition in Poznan, Poland. The dynamic duo were also part of a Danish success in the World Team Cup Final, held in their own back yard at Vojens.

1992 was not a good season for Oxford, yet when the side was put together, both the management and supporters had every reason to believe that a serious challenge would be made for league honours. After just one year at Cowley, Australian rider Craig Boyce was on his way back to Poole on a full transfer and this left Oxford without an established third-heat leader and, as the season progressed, this weakness became more and more obvious. There was a further change at the commencement of the season, when John Payne left and ceased to be a promoter, with Kevan Hedderly, an executive from promoting company Northern Sports, taking over the position.

In Hans Nielsen and Martin Dugard, Oxford possessed two of the best riders in the league and both did everything that was expected of them. Hans scored 315 points to achieve a 10.25 First Division average, while Martin notched 215 points for an average of 8.94. Sadly, Hans fractured a collarbone at a mid-May meeting in Denmark, and although he was quickly back in track action, he failed to make the World Final in Poland. This was the first time Hans had failed to reach the big night since 1979. Martin Dugard was another to suffer a collarbone injury, but like his skipper, Martin was quickly back in action. Martin did make it to the World Final, but only as reserve and he failed to get a ride. The back-up department of the Oxford team, on paper anyway,

looked good, with Dean Barker, Troy Butler, Mark Carlson and Glenn Cunningham, plus young Dane Morten Andersen. With Boyce gone, the Cheetahs looked to Dean Barker to fill the vacant berth of third-heat leader, but things did not work out. As the season progressed, 'Deano' developed a complex about the Oxford track, and although he had his name taken off the transfer list before the season got underway, his scoring became somewhat erratic. It was no surprise to anyone really, when 'Deano' returned to his old club Eastbourne at the end of the season.

It has to be said, however, that there was substance in Barker's feelings about the Oxford track, as it did provide some problems and this point

*Morten Andersen.*

91

was emphasized in early May when Cradley Heath were the visitors. In each of the first three heats, Cradley had a rider fall, and after a failed attempt to run heat four, the match was called off. A practice session was then held in order to prove that conditions were not that bad, and Oxford believed that they had permission for the practice, but they were called before the Control Board and fined. The Oxford promoters, however, were never happy to just sit back if they thought that team changes were necessary. Attempts to sign former star Gordon Kennett failed though, thanks to the rulebook. Gordon wanted to come, but as a backup to the heat leaders. However, if he had returned to Cowley, one of the existing heat leaders would have to be released, and that was something that just wasn't an option. Glenn Cunningham was struggling to come to terms with top-flight racing and in an attempt to strengthen the reserve berth, Spencer Timmo was signed and Glenn made way. Spencer tried very hard, but like Cunningham, he was way off the pace, and finally Daz Sumner was drafted in via Middlesbrough.

Tenth position in the First Division was something of a disappointment for everyone at Oxford. Yet despite the problems with the track, which were solved to a degree with the help of Cradley Heath promoter Colin Pratt, the racing was very exciting indeed. At home, the Cheetahs won seven matches and recorded four draws – against Belle Vue, Cradley Heath, Poole and Swindon – while losing just once, to Wolverhampton on 2 September. Away from home, it was a different story, with one single success, a 48-38 win at Coventry. The Oxford bosses tried hard to strengthen the side when they thought it necessary, but they failed, thanks to the constraints of the points limit. Had the rules permitted them to add Gordon Kennett to the side, things could have been very different. Little did the faithful supporters realize when the season ended, that they were due for a most dramatic winter, with the Cheetahs' future in jeopardy. The end of an era of success came about in October 1992, and no one realized it, but things were destined never to be the same again.

The fact that Oxford operated at all in 1993 was due entirely to Kidderminster businessman and speedway enthusiast Tony Mole, who stepped in at the eleventh hour to save the track. The club had been through a troubled winter, due to the introduction of the B.S.P.A. pay policy. Despite sterling efforts by the management, led by promoter Kevan Hedderly, Oxford were unable to come to terms with star-man Hans Nielsen. Hedderly made it clear that there was no way Oxford Speedway would risk the heavy fines (a figure of £10,000 had been mentioned) by breaching the pay code, other than through sponsorship for their multi-World Champion and the number one rider in British Speedway. It is ironic that after the decision to impose a pay policy, it was Mr Hedderly who expressed the view that he 'Just did not see how the pay policy could work', and had actually voted against it at the B.S.P.A. Conference.

With the season beckoning, Oxford had just three riders, one of whom was Martin Dugard, who were prepared to take a pay cut and had been able to agree a deal, thanks to the tremendous efforts by the Cheetahs Supporters' Club, who had secured sponsorship. The other two riders were novice Darren Andrews, and outstanding Danish youngster Morten Andersen. It was, therefore, a sad day on 23 February, when Kevan Hedderly announced that, having been unable to put together a competitive team, the

*Chris Cobby.*

Oxford Speedway club would cease to function. It was then that Tony Mole took over the promotion, having made an acceptable offer to the stadium owners Northern Sports Ltd. In the beginning, Mr Mole tried to get things moving for the continuation of First Division racing, but through no fault of the new promoter, things had moved too fast. Nielsen was on the brink of signing for Coventry, and being unable to put together a competitive Division One side, Mr Mole settled for Second Division racing. It was a new era and Oxford were, effectively, in the same position that they were in at the beginning of 1976, when they joined the National League. Bernard Crapper and John Payne were installed as the new day-to-day promoters and their first task was to put together a new side.

Mark Blackbird, one of twin brothers, was the first to sign for the new Cheetahs, with his brother Paul following a few weeks later. Further signings quickly followed in the shape of Andy Hackett from Coventry, and David Smart via Swindon. 'Smartie' in fact, could not be fitted in at his home track, Swindon, in what was actually his Testimonial year! Young Dane Rene Madsen, who was spotted by Bernard Crapper at Belle Vue in a World Under-21 meeting, came over, impressed in practice, and was duly signed. David Clarke, formerly of Coventry, was another new acquisition for the Cheetahs' camp. With the team beginning to take shape, a good number one was urgently needed and Oxford found that man in Poole rider Tony Langdon, who came on loan for the season.

Langdon was to enjoy an outstanding season and always led the team from the front.

Oxford shook the speedway world on 22 April, when their new side won the league match at Sheffield by 55 points to 53, this after beating the Yorkshire side by 10 points at Cowley a week earlier. As the season went on, the injury bug began to bite. Andy Hackett, who had struggled to find his best form, was badly injured in a match against Swindon on 9 July. Meanwhile, Mark Blackbird decided to retire and made way for a new signing, as the Oxford bosses shuffled and re-shuffled their pack. In came the experienced Alan Grahame, along with Spencer Timmo and Andy Meredith plus, as the averages determined, Chris Cobby. Unfortunately, the various team changes that the promoters were forced to make meant that the side was never settled. Throughout the traumas, Tony Langdon kept on going, scoring 451 points and 8 maximums in league matches alone, to yield an average of 9.10. Even Tony couldn't escape the injury bug though, for he suffered a knee injury, while David Smart, who was a real success, broke a collarbone towards the end of the season. David Clarke held his team place and provided excitement with his style of racing, but he ought to have done much better at Second Division level. Clarke, in fact, was actually dropped for a spell, as the Oxford bosses tried to put together a winning combination.

Having struggled all year, it was little wonder that Oxford finished at the very bottom of the Division Two table, but at the end of a difficult season, at least John Payne was able to announce that a three-year agreement had been reached with Northern Sports. With the racing during 1993 being exciting and well worth watching, John was confident that after the initial year, the promoters would seek to improve in 1994, with a return to First Division racing being the long-term objective. There was only one way Oxford could go in 1994, and that was up! The first task facing Messrs Crapper and Payne, the promoters, was team building, since many of the 1993 outfit were, for one reason or another, unavailable. A real body blow was the fact that Tony Langdon was not available. Langdon was a Poole asset, of course, and with the promoters of the Pirates also now promoting Second Division racing at Swindon, it was obvious that they would need him at Blunsdon.

It was tough for Oxford to lose their number one rider, but the closure of Rye House meant that Martin Goodwin was available, and he was quickly snapped up. Mick Poole sought a move from Peterborough and he too was quickly added to the Oxford team. An important backroom appointment was that of 1991 World Champion Jan O. Pedersen as team manager, with the Dane enjoying his first experience of life on the other side of the safety fence. The season began with a few problems, as Martin Goodwin suffered concussion and a leg injury which caused him to miss a number of matches in early May. Another matter for concern was the fact that Mick Poole was taking time to settle on the Oxford track. It turned out to be a bad month, with the Cheetahs losing all their matches, but perhaps the blackest moment was a bad injury suffered by Andy Meredith at Glasgow on 29 May. The young Coventry-based rider suffered back and neck injuries, and was out for the season, but as soon as he was able, Andy was back, cheering on his team-mates from the terraces.

It was obvious that new faces were needed, and two arrived from Sweden in the shape of Stefan Ekberg and Niklas Karlsson, although efforts to bring back former

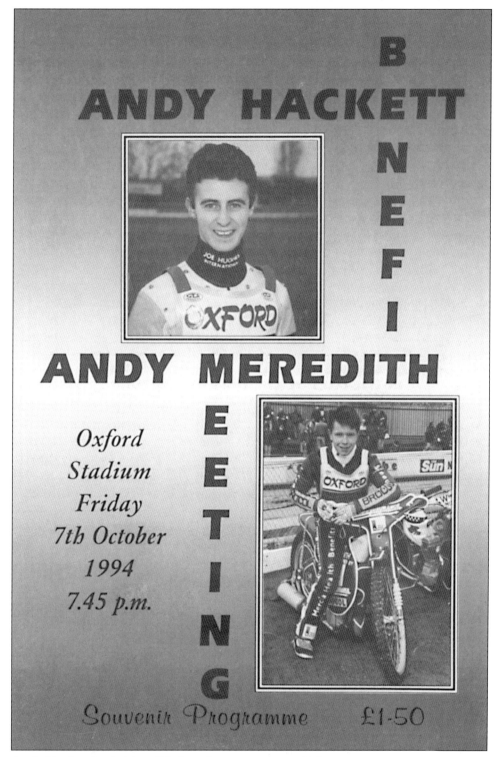

*Andy Hackett/Andy Meredith Benefit programme, 1994.*

favourite Jens Rasmussen failed. Happily for the Cheetahs, Mick Poole gradually discovered his best form, and as the season progressed, he became very much the number one around the Cowley circuit. A real highlight for the Oxford faithful was the Cheetahs' success in the Four-Team Championship at Peterborough, when Martin Goodwin headed the scoring as they beat Long Eaton, Peterborough and Edinburgh in the final. David Smart had been riding well, even though he was troubled by a series of niggling little knocks, but he was allowed to move on when Daz Sumner was snapped up via Middlesbrough. 'Smartie' wasn't altogether happy with the management and left for Exeter in late July, a rather disillusioned young man. Throughout the year, there were several changes to the team, as the management tried to juggle their riders and find the feel-good factor. At one point, they tried to replace Stefan Ekberg with Niklas Karlsson, but the B.S.P.A. vetoed the idea and ruled that 'the Cheetahs had to ride both Swedes at the same time or not at all.' One further change occurred as the season drew to its close when Alan Grahame, who had been a steady points compiler, lost form and was dropped.

Oxford finished eighth in the ten-team league, which showed a slight improvement on the previous year, but although they had good riders, the problem was getting them all to strike form together and successfully gel as a team. The Cheetahs would certainly have fared better in their quest for league honours had they been able to track a settled side, but this was not to be. Mick Poole took over the mantle of top man at Oxford, scoring 398 points from 36 league matches for an average of 8.59. Giving good support to Mick was the solid scoring 'Burt' Goodwin, whose point tally reached 285, producing a 7.72 average. Both Mick Poole and Alan Grahame rode in the Jawa/Barum-sponsored Division Two Riders' Championship, scoring 10 and 9 points respectively. Perhaps, the most bizarre of accidents happened to promoter Bernard Crapper, when he was accidentally knocked over in the Oxford pits by junior team manager Colin Clarke, who was moving his car at the time. The end result was that the Oxford boss suffered fractures in both legs.

It was all change again in 1995, with Tony Mole, who had saved the club from going under in 1993, putting the promoting rights up for sale. The former Ipswich promoter Chris Shears was subsequently named as the new boss, however, as this change came within weeks of the new season beginning, it gave the incoming promoter little time to put together a side, but somehow he succeeded. All the tracks from both the First and Second Division had joined forces to form one big Premier League, with Oxford taking their place amongst no fewer than twenty-one teams, so it was imperative that Chris Shears put together a competitive team. Martin Goodwin and Rene Madsen remained from the 1994 line-up, and were joined by Swede Jimmy Nilsen, who came via Bradford, and the exciting Italian Armando Castagna, who arrived from Reading. Linking up with these signings were former Belle Vue rider Michael Coles, and David Steen, who had turned up for a practice session and was handed a reserve berth. Once the season was underway, Shears pulled off a grand signing when young Swede Daniel Andersson (known as Dalle) came to Cowley and was an outstanding success.

Former Oxford and Coventry rider Mick Bell became the team manager and there is no doubt that he instilled a grand fighting spirit amongst his charges. Oxford opened with a well-deserved win in a Bank Holiday challenge match against Wolverhampton, but lost their opening Premier League match at Reading in the rain (42-52). However, in the first leg of the Knock Out Cup at Poole on 19 April, Oxford rode brilliantly to keep the Poole victory down to a 3-point margin (51-54), with David Steen notching a brilliant paid 15-point tally. In the return leg at Cowley, the Cheetahs really went to town, with a thumping victory by 72 points to 36, with Nilsen, Coles and Madsen each recording double-figure scores.

Oxford continued to put up great performances and the team came together well, even when Goodwin suffered a shoulder injury at Hull in May and was sidelined for some weeks. The Cheetahs became a pretty formidable outfit at their Cowley base, and on 10 May produced their biggest win of the season, when they hammered visiting Sheffield 62-34. The match was memorable for the marvellous 13-point tally from Swedish sensation Dalle Andersson. The young Swede enjoyed a tremendous year and looked a real world-beater, but he moved to Cradley Heath the following year, and subsequently tried to make it at a number of other venues, although sadly, he never repeated the outstanding promise and ability he had shown at Oxford.

After beating Poole in the opening round of the Knock Out Cup, the Cheetahs defeated Arena-Essex in round two, before losing to Cradley Heath in the quarter-final by 12 points on aggregate. In the league, Oxford won fifteen matches at home, while losing five, but their form tended to be patchy away from Cowley, where they won just a single match (at Coventry), and gained a draw (at Long Eaton). Oxford ended the campaign in seventeenth position, after a poor time in mid-season when Mick Bell had to ask for more commitment from his men. With the season ending and everything

*John Tremblin, Martin Goodwin and Jan O. Pedersen.*

looking good for 1996, it came as a shock when Jimmy Nilsen indicated that he wanted to go back home to Swindon, the track where he made his name in British Speedway. There was further drama when Tony Mole, within the rules of speedway, reclaimed the promotion, and within weeks, had sold it on to former Ipswich and Hackney boss Dave Pavitt. Just how this happened, few of the long-suffering Oxford supporters knew. Rumours were rife, but apart from Tony Mole's announcement, nothing was said, and no statement was ever forthcoming from Chris Shears. One cannot help but pay tribute to the hardcore of Oxford fans who, despite the many promotional changes, still stuck by their team and gave them, in whatever level of racing they rode, the very maximum of support and encouragement.

So, 1996 heralded a new promoter in Dave Pavitt, and he was joined in the running of the club by Keith 'Buster' Chapman, since his own track (King's Lynn) had temporarily closed down. Chapman brought with him Czech riders Tomas Topinka and Bo Brhel, while former Oxford favourite Marvyn Cox, along with Mark Lemon, both arrived on loan from Poole. Lawrence Hare joined via Ipswich, and Martin Goodwin was retained from the outgoing promotion, with young Poole loanee Martin Willis being brought in to complete the side. John Tremblin became clerk of the course and assistant team manager, whilst 'Buster' Chapman took on the role of team manager. Oxford started the season well and were impressive at home, but their away form

*Oxford 1996. From left to right, back row: Martin Goodwin, Lawrence Hare, Martin Willis, Mark Lemon. Front row: Bohumil Brhel, Marvyn Cox, Tomas Topinka.*

remained suspect. Swindon forced a 45-45 draw in the opening Premier League match of the season, before Oxford went on a winning streak at Cowley, which ended on 3 May when composite side Cradley Heath/Stoke beat them.

Shortly after the season began promising youngster Mark Frost was signed, after being recommended to Oxford by London rider Paul Hurry, who had spotted Frost during a tour of South Africa. Frost forced his way into the side and replaced Martin Willis. In the end, he only appeared in 13 league matches for the Cheetahs, scoring 35 points, and was injured before the season ended. Although Frost was initially retained in 1997, he was subsequently released without donning a Cheetahs race jacket again. He then disappeared from the speedway scene, but in 1999 he was seen in the World Team Cup semi-final at Poole, when he rode for Hungary under the name of Attila Stefani! Frenchman Philippe Berge was signed, but found himself in and out of the team, when an extended run could have worked wonders. The Cheetahs, sponsored by John Tarr of J.T. Commercials from Poole, won by 10 points at near neighbours Reading, and then raced to impressive draws at Poole and Exeter. The divisional Four Team Championship commenced on 14 June, and the Oxford boys did brilliantly to qualify for the final at Peterborough on 4 August. As they had done in 1994, the Cheetahs went on to win the tournament, with the result being: Oxford 23, Peterborough 17, Hull 16, Ipswich 16.

In the league, Oxford finished in thirteenth position, having won just twelve of their thirty-six-match programme. When the statistics were calculated at the end of the campaign, Tomas Topinka was the Cheetahs' top man with 287 points (average 8.63) from his 27 league matches. The Cheetahs could point to being somewhat unlucky with injuries, for besides the aforementioned Mark Frost, four regulars suffered injury during the course of the season, namely Bohumil Brhel, Mark Lemon, Marvyn Cox and Martin Goodwin. An example of Oxford's bad luck with injuries occurred on Friday 13 September! The Cheetahs were racing against London and looked to be in with a good chance of winning. However the match was only a quarter of an hour old when Oxford were reduced to a five-man team. Both Bo Brhel and Marvyn Cox suffered falls in their first outings and were taken off to hospital, with Oxford subsequently losing 43-53.

Talking of Marvyn Cox, it is worth remembering that he became the first Oxford rider to make it through to the Grand Prix series in 1996. Sadly, 'Cocker' found the going too tough, and could only muster 15 points from the five rounds in which he participated. At the end of the season, promoter Dave Pavitt claimed to have lost money during the course of the campaign, but said that Oxford would run in 1997, albeit in the re-vamped Premier League. In other words, Oxford would not be joining the ten teams that opted to form an Elite League (or First Division), but would compete in the lower level of racing offered by the Premier League. So, for the third time in little over twenty years, Oxford supporters would have to settle for Division Two-style racing, as had happened previously in 1976 and 1993.

Mr Pavitt acted quickly to assemble an attractive and competitive team for the 1997 season of Premier League racing, retaining Lawrence Hare, Philippe Berge and the promising Mark Frost from the 1996 team. The promoter made his top priority a number one rider, and whilst his search went on, he signed Krister Marsh on loan from Swindon. Rumour was rife around Oxford as to the name of the number one signing, so much so that Pavitt was forced to admit his target was Neville Tatum. Neville duly signed, and was closely followed by Swede Mikael Teurnberg, which certainly made the Oxford side look very good on paper. In the event, Frost was not retained, his place being taken by Jason Bunyan (on loan from Poole), who had spent the greater part of 1996 on the injured list.

The J.T Commercials Cheetahs began the season well in the Premier League Cup, with the months of April and May being particularly successful. A draw at Long Eaton on 2 April was followed by four victories, including a 2-point success at Exeter. On 5 May, Oxford lost 44-46 in a very tight encounter with near neighbours Reading, although the result was later amended to a draw by the Control Board. That was quickly followed by more success, which included a draw at Reading in the Premier League Cup on 19 May. The Cheetahs' opening league match was on 25 May, and it was a surprise when Oxford lost by 2 points (44-46) at home to Edinburgh. Winning form quickly returned though, with success at Peterborough against Skegness. On 8 June, Oxford lost a controversial match at Newport 48-50. The Cheetahs were upset by the constant track watering on a hot afternoon, which was done without their consent or any reference to them. Promoter Pavitt claimed that the conditions certainly upset Neville Tatum, who returned just paid 7 points, and that, in many respects, the Oxford season began to change from that point.

Certainly, the months of July and August were not good for Oxford. A 46-43 home win against Long Eaton was followed by a Premier League Cup defeat at Hull. Newcastle came to Cowley on 11 July, and left on the wrong end of a 50-39 defeat. Then came the crunch, a home league match against Reading, with the Cheetahs suffering another close defeat (43-47), despite a real captain's part being played by Neville Tatum with paid 15 points. Krister Marsh, who was taking a long time to settle, suffered a shoulder injury at Newport and although he returned to track action, his form let him down and he soon disappeared from the Oxford scene. Another rider to depart was Jason Bunyan, who moved to the Isle of Wight, and was replaced by local boy Darren Andrews.

Two sides operated from Cowley in 1997, for apart from the main Cheetahs team, Oxford Cubs took part in the British Amateur League. This junior side completed 12 league matches and ended up in ninth position out of thirteen teams. The afore-mentioned Krister Marsh and Darren Andrews were regulars in the Cubs side, while other riders who appeared included Phillip Ambrose, Lee Driver, Simon Wolstenholme, Lance Sealey, Jason Newitt and Jason McKenna. With 167 points, Ambrose topped the Cubs' scoring, receiving good support from Driver (120 points) and Wolstenholme (111).

Back to the Cheetahs, and Exeter were well beaten on 8 August, but sadly this was to be the only Oxford victory for some time. It wasn't until 5 September that Oxford again tasted success with a good win against Sheffield, however, the Cheetahs followed that up with three more league victories against Newport (52-38), Berwick (55-34) and Arena-Essex (56-34). It had been a season of two halves for Oxford, and if only they had finished the season as they had began, they might well have taken league honours. As it was, they finished eleventh in a fourteen-team league. The Cheetahs couldn't escape the injury bug, with Mikael Teurnberg being affected. Oxford finished third in the Four-Team Championship at Peterborough, and Neville Tatum won the World Championship (British semi-final) at Exeter, and subsequently qualified for a British Final place by scoring sufficient points at Sheffield in the second semi-final.

Oxford reached the final of the Knock Out Cup, only to lose a real thriller against Edinburgh by 86 points to 94 on aggregate. Lawrence Hare was Oxford's best, having been selected as the club's Rider of the Year by the loyal Cheetahs supporters. Promoter Pavitt, at the end of the season, claimed he would be returning for his third year at the helm, but in the event, it was yet another traumatic winter for Oxford, with the promotion changing hands again. This time, the promotional rights were bought by Southampton-based businessman Steve Purchase and his wife, Vanessa. The Cheetahs would, it was explained, be joining the Elite League, so yet again, it was a case of all change at Cowley, but the loyal Oxford public had seen it all before and were used to it.

Steve Purchase was determined that the club should be participating in Elite League racing when he took over as promoter at Oxford in 1998. He knew the importance of putting together a good, competitive team and set about it with great gusto. Lawrence Hare, a star of the 1997 side, was taken over by Purchase, who also came up with a new team skipper in Steve Schofield from Poole. Other incoming riders were Paul Hurry (via King's Lynn) and Jan Staechmann, who had been sacked by Peterborough after a few matches in '97. Steve Johnston also came on board, after a spell at Ipswich, while former Oxford favourite Martin Goodwin, was brought in as team manager.

There was a need for an established number one rider, and Jason Crump was signed when the Peterborough management opted for Premier League racing. Sponsorship arrived when Gresham Computing agreed to back the Cheetahs, so it was all systems go down Cowley way. As the season kicked off for the new Gresham Cheetahs, there was a home draw against Coventry on 3 April, in the Knock Out Cup, and their first home win in the competition was against Belle Vue on 3 May. Local rivals Swindon came the following week, and Oxford recorded their most convincing home victory to date, with a 58-32 success.

Success away from home was non-existent in the early weeks of the season, while a couple of home league defeats in June (against Coventry and Eastbourne) convinced Steve Purchase that his side definitely needed strengthening. For the away fixture against King's Lynn on 24 June, Australian Todd Wiltshire (who had been out of British speedway since 1991, following a bad injury in his native land) made his debut as a Cheetah. Todd scored a single point in four outings, but this was to be his poorest score in an Oxford race jacket. Todd scored paid 9 points in a home league win over Swindon on 3 June, and as the season progressed, he just got better and better, until in late August, he recorded a marvellous paid 18 points from 6 outings in a home victory over Eastbourne.

On 16 July, Oxford made the short journey down the road to old rivals Swindon, and there was great joy when the Cheetahs came away with a 52-38 victory, thanks to an 18-point return from guest Billy Hamill, who was standing in for Jason Crump. The following day, however, there was a real shock in store, when Wolverhampton came to Cowley and left with a 2-point victory, and although Hamill again stood in for Crump, his 14 points couldn't help the Cheetahs to victory. July was greeted with mixed feelings by all those associated with Oxford. Jason Crump was hurt in the home match against Swindon on 3 July, and had an unfortunate confrontation with team-mate Todd Wiltshire. The World Long Track Championship at nearby Abingdon saw excellent performances from Paul Hurry (who finished as runner-up), Steve Schofield and Jason Crump. Having apologized for his attack on Wiltshire, 'Crumpie' returned for the home match against Poole on 24 July, and quickly showed his best form with paid 15 points in 47-43 home success for the Cheetahs.

Coventry beat Oxford at Cowley on 31 July, but the following week saw a cracker of a match when Ipswich visited. The Cheetahs grabbed victory in the final heat, with the Crump and Johnston pairing scorching to a magnificent 5-1 over the Ipswich duo of Tony Rickardsson and Tomasz Gollob. This so inspired the Cheetahs that they went to King's Lynn on 12 August, and came away with a 10-point victory, thanks to a 15-point maximum from Jason Crump and 13 points from Paul Hurry. Crowd favourite 'Lol' Hare left for Newport in early July, but in his very first home meeting for the Wasps, he suffered a serious injury and was out of action for the rest of the season. With Elite League teams now being made up of six riders only, Lawrence did not have to be replaced, and the arrival of Wiltshire enabled him to move on.

Oxford completed the season in seventh position and Crump was, as to be expected, the Oxford number one, emphasized by 292 league points and an average of 9.10. 'Crumpie' was also a big success in the Grand Prix series, actually winning the British round at Coventry on 7 August and scoring a series total of 62 points to finish eighth overall. To round off a brilliant season, Jason finished as runner-up to the victorious Tony Rickardsson at Swindon in the Elite League Riders' Championship. At the end of the season, it was a very disappointed Steve Purchase who, having done all he could to re-establish top league speedway at Oxford, announced that he had lost a great deal of money, and in order to complete the season, had to cancel a fiftieth anniversary meeting. Nevertheless, he was prepared to give speedway a go again in 1999, when once again, he would endeavour to put together a winning side.

Oxford promoters Steve and Vanessa Purchase had every reason to be optimistic in their second season in charge of the club. True, the return of Peterborough to the Elite League saw top man from 1998, Jason Crump, return to his parent track, but the backbone of the side was still there, led by the immaculate Todd Wiltshire. With Crump gone, Steve Purchase looked for a top-class replacement, and took a chance with former Cheetah Craig Boyce, on loan from Poole. To strengthen the reserve berth, the promoter added another Poole rider (again, on loan) in the

*Simon Wigg's Farewell programme, 1999.*

shape of perky Alun Rossiter. Team manager Martin Goodwin was forced to step down due to pressure of business, and to replace him, Purchase appointed track supremo Colin Meredith, together with centre-green presenter Richard Palmer in a dual role.

Oxford began the campaign with a Craven Shield match at Ipswich, but with Craig Boyce an absentee, still suffering from the after effects of an injury, the Gresham Cheetahs crashed to a 38-52 defeat. A week later, Oxford visited Coventry (again, in the Craven Shield competition) and with reserve 'Lol' Hare giving the best performance of his speedway career to record an unbeaten 15-point tally, the Cheetahs were victorious by 54 points to 34. As the Craven Shield progressed, the Cheetahs got better and better. Their run in the competition was outstanding, and it really was no surprise when they finished first in the qualifying table and met old rivals Coventry in the semi-final. Unfortunately, the semi-final encounter wasn't held until October, and by that time, the Cheetahs had run out of steam, losing on aggregate by 80 points to 100. One thing worth mentioning regarding the Craven Shield was the match against Hull at Cowley on 9 April. This was when Alun Rossiter, who certainly had his critics on the terraces, recorded an unbeaten 12 points – the first time he'd scored a maximum in top league racing. 'Rosco' was, in fact, offered another ride, but declined, and was reported as saying 'I didn't want to push my luck!'

The season's opening meeting at Oxford had been a big farewell for former Cheetahs legend Simon Wigg. The meeting on 28 March, saw a world-class field turn up to pay tribute to 'Wiggy', including meeting winner Greg Hancock, along with Jason Crump, Armando Castagna, Billy Hamill, Jimmy Nilsen, Sam Ermolenko, Tony Rickardsson, Hans Nielsen and Leigh Adams. The Cheetahs' league campaign began at Ipswich on 27 May at Ipswich, when Oxford went down fighting by 41 points to 48, with Steve Johnston and Paul Hurry giving excellent performances. At home, Oxford began well, with victories over Belle Vue and King's Lynn, and their good form at home lasted into the month of August, with a fine 56-34 win over Hull. Away from Cowley, the Cheetahs' form wasn't as dominating as it had been in the Craven Shield, and they were hammered 29-61 at Poole on 1 September.

Just prior to that (on 27 August), Eastbourne came to Cowley for a league match and the Cheetahs lost by a single point (46-47). However, little did the supporters realize, but that was the beginning of the end as far as any title aspirations were concerned. After that evening, Oxford didn't enjoy any kind of success until 8 October, when they raced to a thrilling draw against Coventry in the home leg of the Craven Shield semi-final. The Cheetahs did finish their league fixtures with a narrow home win over visiting Ipswich (47-43), but by that time, most folk on the Oxford terraces had lost interest in the Elite League competition.

In summary, it was a season of two halves, for in the Craven Shield, the Oxford boys were magnificent, but when the Elite League came along, Oxford were found wanting. Sometimes, it was hard to think that the team of riders struggling was in fact the same side that had been so dominant in the early months of 1999. However, the racing was very exciting, and Todd Wiltshire gave Oxford fans much to cheer about. It was Todd's first full season in Britain for a number of years, and he upped his overall average to just over 8 points a match. Todd, to add to his honours in 1999, won the Inter-Continental Final at Poole, and gave a polished performance when feeling far from well in the Elite League Riders' Championship, finishing second.

Craig Boyce, an ever-present in league matches, showed patchy form and wasn't quite the force that had been expected. Steve Johnston looked like a world-beater on occasions, but the post-July period often saw him struggling. Both the reserve riders (Hare and Rossiter) averaged over 5 points a match and were capable of doing anything, the problem being that no one was sure just when they were going to do something really special. However, to be fair, they gave of their best at all times. Sadly, the final position for the Cheetahs was eighth in the ten-team Elite League, but the good news at the end of the season was that the promoters indicated they would be prepared to carry on, with the priority for the team being an established number one rider.

## 2000 Onwards

The 2000 season was promoter Steve Purchase's third year in charge, and he again worked hard to assemble a winning side, but whilst he had not met with the success his efforts deserved, Steve should be congratulated for his endeavours. On the team front, Boyce had gone, snapped up by King's Lynn, and to replace him came Jimmy Nilsen, a former Cheetah on loan from local rivals Swindon. Steve Purchase then took a chance by signing the young Czech brothers Ales and Lukas Dryml. Russian boy Roman Povazhny came to Cowley from Eastbourne, with Paul Hurry going in the opposite direction. The brilliant Todd Wiltshire returned, along with Steve Johnston, who was to skipper the side, while to keep within the points limit, young Jon Underwood, a grass-track rider and a member of the Oxford Junior team, was drafted into the side to fill the second reserve berth. Sponsorship of the team came from Poole company J.T. Commercials, who had previously backed the side in 1996 and 1997.

*Jon Underwood.*

Straight away, Oxford opened their league programme with a match at Coventry on 25 March and promptly lost by 34 points to 55. Todd Wiltshire and Jimmy Nilsen looked good, but both the Dryml boys and Jon Underwood looked way off the pace. Cowley subsequently opened for business on 31 March when a challenge fixture was staged against Wolverhampton. The Cheetahs took a narrow 46-44 victory and lost the second leg at Monmore Green by just 4 points. Before the Oxford public saw another meeting at Cowley, the Cheetahs were to race a league fixture at Ipswich, which they lost 38-52. Already a pattern was emerging, but it was telling promoter Purchase something that he already knew, or at least suspected. The Dryml brothers, whilst displaying plenty of promise, were not yet of Elite League standard. Meanwhile, young Jon Underwood was in desperate need of a stint at Premier League level, and Roman Povazhny hadn't built on his experience at Eastbourne the previous year.

Team strengthening was a top priority, and as soon as the Oxford boss could, he made changes to the line-up. Some juggling saw Mark Lemon return, on loan from Poole, while Jan Staechmann came back from exile. Moving in the opposite direction, Jon Underwood was posted to Premier League Arena-Essex, where he began to settle down, but then tragedy struck. Jon was killed in a motor accident whilst returning to this country from a grass-track meeting on the continent. Everyone was shocked at the loss of such a popular lad, and condolences poured in to his family and friends from everyone connected with both speedway and grass-track racing. To accommodate the team changes and stay within the points ceiling, Steve Purchase was forced to let Roman Povazhny go out on loan to Wolverhampton, but at least (on paper) the Oxford boss had strengthened his side. However, there was an early exit from the Knock Out Cup, when a thrilling draw at home to Poole was followed by a 4-point defeat in the second leg at the Dorset venue.

As the season progressed, Oxford proved to be very inconsistent at home and didn't have much luck on their travels. They enjoyed a 50-40 away success at Belle Vue on 25 June, but during July, Oxford lost six away matches in a row. July was a bad month at home too, because although just two matches were raced (against Wolverhampton and Poole), the Cheetahs lost them both. To break up the fixtures, a Young England *v.* Young Australia Test Match was held at Cowley on 28 July, when the English lads enjoyed a good win in a rain-affected match that, disappointingly, just didn't pull the punters. Business interests were taking up more and more of Steve Purchase's time and it became obvious that he was getting increasingly disillusioned with speedway. It came as little surprise when he subsequently resigned from the B.S.P.A., with his wife Vanessa taking over the promotion at Oxford.

August began in promising style for the Cheetahs when they won a gripping league match by 2 points against Eastbourne early on and followed it up with a tremendous 47-43 victory at Wolverhampton. Sadly, the rest of the month was a disaster, with losses against Coventry, Peterborough and Ipswich. The month also saw the arrival of Brian Andersen, on loan from Coventry, as Vanessa Purchase worked hard to put some more pep into her side. Andersen actually made his home

*Leigh Adams.*

debut against his old club, scoring paid 16 points, but it couldn't stop an Oxford defeat.

As the season drew to its close, the Cheetahs rode out of their skins to take a league point from Poole on 6 September, before defeating the Dorset side in a very wet match at Cowley. The season ended with Oxford finishing eighth in the nine-team league, with a match at Belle Vue being declared null and void by the Control Board. The Cheetahs were, however, awarded the aggregate bonus point as a result of their home victory. Looking back, it has to be said that the Oxford management tried so hard to do their best for the supporters. Amazing comeback man Todd Wiltshire topped the Oxford scoring with 322 points (average 8.29), while Jimmy Nilsen attained an 8.12 average despite a shoulder injury sustained on 16 June, which completely disrupted his season. In the Grand Prix series, Oxford boasted three representatives, with Todd Wiltshire proving to be the best. It was a great credit to Todd that he could live with the world's best and 63 points from the six rounds was sufficient to see him finish in eighth position. Jimmy Nilsen scored 42 points for eleventh place overall, while Brian Andersen had to be satisfied with just 15 points from his six rounds.

There was great sadness when former Oxford legend Simon Wigg died on 15 November 2000, following a long battle with illness. Simon was an all-round professional motorcyclist and his record was tremendous, having been crowned World Long Track Champion on no fewer than five occasions. 'Wiggy' also won the British Championship twice and was runner-up to Hans Nielsen in the 1989 World Final. His record with Oxford was marvellous, as he helped the side to the British League Championship in 1985, 1986 and 1989. In league and Knock Out Cup matches, Simon made 176 appearances for Oxford, scoring 1,732 points (including bonus).

During the winter, Oxford promoter Vanessa Purchase made clear her intentions for the 2001 season. The first priority would be a world-class number one rider to lead the scoring, and the second was to win the Elite League Championship. Happily for the Cowley faithful, the Cheetahs succeeded on both fronts, securing

Leigh Adams (the Australian international and Grand Prix rider) on loan from his parent club Swindon and, after a nail-biting finish to the domestic campaign, capturing the Elite League title by just a single point.

The signing of Leigh Adams was a masterstroke. The talented Aussie had been at King's Lynn for two seasons, during which time he had established himself as the master of the Saddlebow Road circuit. However, Leigh lived just outside Swindon and it was obvious that if Vanessa Purchase could agree terms with him, then a track just down the road as a home base would surely appeal to him. That, of course, was just what happened and Adams put pen to paper and became an Oxford rider for the 2001 campaign. There were the so-called speedway experts who believed that the Cowley circuit wasn't Adams' type of track and that he would never be able to master it the way he had King's Lynn. However, they should have known better, as Adams quickly became the new Cowley King, giving the Oxford team a stability that the club hadn't enjoyed since the days of 'Main Dane' Hans Nielsen.

Mrs Purchase also kept faith with her two Czech signings from the 2000 season – the Dryml brothers, Ales and Lukas, who had both gone through a tough first year in the Elite League. The Oxford promoter reasoned that if she had stood by them as they came to terms with the high standard of Elite League racing, then she should stand by them after they had enjoyed a season's experience. This was another shrewd move: Lukas, although suffering from a leg injury that actually required surgery (which he kept putting off), rose to the rank of heat-leader, and his brother Ales also had his moments in 2001, being a more than useful reserve-cum-second string for the Cheetahs during the season. Backing the efforts of Leigh Adams and the Dryml brothers were Grand Prix riders Todd Wiltshire and Brian Andersen (who was on loan from Coventry). The fast-gating Australian, Wiltshire, was a steady scorer for the Cheetahs, who as a club were backed by J.T. Commercials and a local radio station, Fox FM. However, as the season drew to its close, Todd suffered a painful shoulder injury, but kept going for the sake of the club with the injury strapped up, when he really ought to have been resting it.

Steve Johnston skippered the 2001 Cheetahs, and proved to be a popular captain. You never knew just what 'Johnno' would do, as he was somewhat inconsistent in his scoring, but he created a fine team spirit and gave of his best in every race. The team was completed with young Andrew Appleton, who had done much of his early training at Cowley, but came back on loan via Premier League side Newport. It was a baptism of fire for the youngster, but he stuck to his task and made such an impression that the Oxford bosses were keen to make his move a permanent one.

The Cheetahs began the season with a 37-53 defeat at Coventry, but it was just a challenge match, with the Australian duo of Adams and Johnston showing good form. Oxford then went to Belle Vue for an Elite League encounter on 26 March, and lost by just 5 points, despite a superb 18-point maximum from Leigh Adams. Their first Elite League success came on 30 March, when they defeated Wolverhampton (47-43) at Cowley. After that, the Cheetahs put a great run together and did not taste defeat again until 30 April, when they lost the return match against Wolverhampton 37-53. In between, Oxford had shown that they were a force to be reckoned with, having raced five matches in the league, winning three and drawing two – against Eastbourne (home and away), plus Belle Vue, Ipswich and King's Lynn (all at home). However, the real purple patch began on 18 May, when they beat visitors Poole 54-36, after which they did not lose again until 15 August. Ironically, that was when they travelled to Poole and found the Pirates in a mean mood, and succumbed to a heavy 38-52 defeat.

During their fantastic unbeaten run, Oxford raced 15 matches, winning 14 and drawing a superb match at Poole on 27 June. Success was tasted away from home at Coventry, Peterborough, King's Lynn (twice) and Wolverhampton. After such a period of triumph, speedway pundits were talking seriously of Oxford as Elite League Champions, but these hopes received a nasty jolt on 24 August, when visiting Eastbourne stole the points in a thrilling 2-point (46-44) victory at Cowley. Coventry then beat Oxford 47-43 the following night, but the Cheetahs came back strongly, taking revenge at Eastbourne with a 51-41 victory, which was closely followed up with a 48-42 success at Belle Vue. In the Knock-out Cup, Ipswich came to Cowley on 14 September, and rode to an exciting draw. Meanwhile Poole, who were quietly picking up points and were to prove that they too had an interest in the final destination of the Championship, scuppered any hopes Oxford may have had in the Craven Shield competition, beating the Cheetahs both home and away. It was a trying time for Oxford, who appeared to lose a little of their early season sparkle. However, they dug deep, and even though Poole won their final two Elite League matches – both, incidentally, at Peterborough – Oxford had matches in hand, although, of course, they still had to be won.

Finally, the great day came. Tuesday 9 October saw a double-header at Ipswich, and in a thrilling match that went right to the wire and a last-heat decider, Oxford secured a draw and the Elite League point that gave them the Championship by the narrowest of margins. The final heat of the match saw the Australian pairing of Leigh Adams and Todd Wiltshire keep the ever-pressing Chris Louis behind them, while Scott Nicholls sailed off into the night air to win the race. The Cheetahs had secured a total of 58 league points with a match to go, whereas Poole had finished with a total of 57. The second part of the double-header then saw the teams turn around and do the whole thing again, in the second leg of the Knock-out Cup. This time, however, it was success for the Witches, who won another nail-biting contest by 46 points to 44, thereby gaining a place in the final. Having already made sure of the league title, few of the Oxford fans in the large crowd were too bothered about going out of the Knock-out cup.

On 19 October, Oxford raced their final Elite League match of the season at Cowley, against visiting Coventry. Sadly, it was the visitors who raced to victory, and they did it brilliantly by 53 points to 37, with only Leigh Adams showing anything like normal Cowley form on his way to a 14-point tally. The result didn't dampen the celebrations after the match though, when television presenter Kirsty Gallacher handed over the Sky Sports Elite League trophy to jubilant Oxford skipper Steve Johnston. The Cheetahs were worthy winners, since they had set the pace in the

Elite League right from the opening weeks of the season. It was a just reward too for the Vanessa Purchase, who had spared no effort or expense to bring the title back to Cowley.

Looking through the riders, the brilliant Leigh Adams led the way, scoring an amazing 411 points from 32 league matches for a 10.07 average. As a measure of the Cheetahs' solidity, they then boasted no fewer than five riders who finished the season with averages between 6.05 and 7.45. The highest of these was Aussie Todd Wiltshire, while the others were Brian Andersen (7.19), Lukas Dryml (6.82), Steve Johnston (6.49) and Ales Dryml (6.05). Oxford had three representatives in the Grand Prix series, with Leigh Adams enjoying his highest ever finish in the event, scoring 69 points to finish a very creditable fifth overall. After starting well in the first three rounds, Todd Wiltshire tailed off a little, although he could still be reasonably satisfied with 56 points and eighth position. Like his fellow Cheetahs, Brian Andersen took part in all six rounds, scoring a total of 23 points for eighteenth place in the final reckoning.

# 2

# READING

## The Early Days

Long before racing was held at Tilehurst or Smallmead, the sound of speedway bikes could be heard on the outskirts of Reading, at Longmoor Speedway, Little California-in-England, Nine Mile Ride, Wokingham. The track was situated in the middle of a wood, with nearby amenities such as a boating lake, miniature railway and swimming pool. It is difficult to be exact about when the track actually opened, but upon close inspection of various magazines, several clues are given. For instance, an article in *Motor Cycle* (dated 5 November 1931) states that 'Reading is to have a speedway next year'. A further article in *Speedway News* (dated 10 June 1932) indicated that Stamford Bridge were to visit Longmoor on 10 July that year, and that the circuit was a sand track, used for motorcycle scrambles.

The clear evidence provided by programmes shows that the track most certainly staged speedway meetings from 1936 onwards. Thirteen meetings were staged that year, the first one an open event comprising of scratch races was held on 3 May. Interestingly though, the meeting did included a one-heat challenge match between Reading and London. Most of the meetings in 1936 were of the open or individual type. However, one full team match did take place on 27 September, when a challenge between Reading and Barnet was staged. These were the days when large crowds generally attended speedway meetings, but California's attendance varied between 2,000 and 3,500. However, in order to make a comparison with modern-day speedway, we are talking of a level of racing somewhere between Southern Track Riders and Conference League standard. Meetings were organized by the Reading and District Motorcycle Club, who were affiliated to the South Midlands A.C.U. Centre.

A further fifteen meetings were held at the Wokingham venue in 1937. The following year, the track record for the 310-yard circuit stood at 69.4 seconds (held by Jim Boyd) and adverts for the meetings that were held on Sunday afternoons called it sand track racing. One can just imagine the problems that would be created by a sandy track on a hot and sunny day! Indeed, this was borne out by a magazine quote from the era, which stated that the Reading announcer, Bill Hitch, was 'in bed with a sore throat' and that it 'must be the kind of dust they race on at Longmoor'.

A total of thirteen meetings took place in 1938; again, most of them were on an individual basis, although two-team meetings were also included in that total. On 17 July, Reading faced Oxford in a challenge match, winning 41-30, and two weeks later, on 31 July, Reading were challenged by a team from High Beech. The latter match resulted in a 59-24 victory for Reading, with Jim Boyd and Jack Adams both recording 12-point

*California programme, 1954.*

maximums for Reading. On 7 August, Reading made the trip to High Beech for the return fixture, and from what is known, this appears to be the club's first-ever away match. Incredibly, Reading's big first-leg victory wasn't enough to win on aggregate, for High Beech won the match 60-22, with the only resistance coming from Boyd, who scored 10 points! The last recorded meeting prior to the outbreak of war took place on 20 August 1939 and was an individual battle for the California Cup. It was like a bakehouse at California that day, and crowd favourite Bill Newell went on to record a 15-point maximum and claim the trophy.

## The 1940s

After the war, racing resumed at California on 8 August 1948, but only three further meetings are confirmed for that year. The following year, ten meetings were staged, the majority of them being team challenge matches, the first two of which were between teams calling themselves Easterners and Westerners. The last meeting that year, held on 16 October, featured California against Chalfont & Amersham. Away from Longmoor, California also took part in a grass-track challenge match at Newbury on 22 May. In 1950, six meetings were staged, all of them team challenge matches – including California *v.* Rye House; California *v.* High Beech (result 51-33) and an interesting sounding tussle between the Vampires and the Meteors! California also rode a single away fixture that year, at Rye House on 8 October.

## The 1950s

Again, just six meetings were held in 1951, split equally between individual events and team matches. The team events pitched California against the Rest and the Beachcombers and they also received a return visit from Chalfont & Amersham. It is also known that midget car racing was staged at the Wokingham venue that year. In a programme dated 13 April 1952 (the first meeting of that year), the dirt track racing, as it was then called, was organized by the California Motor-Cycle Club, but still affiliated to the South Midlands A.C.U. Looking at that programme, several riders who were in action would go on to appear in league teams of the future, including Jim Tebby, Roy Bowers and Ron Sharp. Only a further three meetings took place that season, the last one being an individual event on 20 July.

The following year (1953), just four meetings were promoted, two of them featuring California against Maidment's Team – a side led by St Austell's Cyril Maidment. The other two meetings were a best pairs event and an individual tournament for the Coronation Trophy. A new track record was set on 19 April, when Jim Tebby burned up the track in 65 seconds dead. From 1954-56, California rode with the team nickname of Poppies and took part in the Southern Area League. In 1954, the league originally started with six participating teams, however, Aldershot closed down after completing ten matches from their programme, citing a lack of support, and their record was subsequently expunged from the league table.

Despite a poor start, the Poppies finished the season as runners-up to Rye House. In

Gil Goldfinch (154 points and top scorer in the entire league), Jimmy Gleed (139 points) and Peter Mould (114 points), California boasted the best heat-leader trio in the league. Backing them up were Eric Hockaday, Bob Andrews, Tommy Sweetman, Ron Sharp and veteran George Bason. Apart from nine league matches (including one against Aldershot), a further six events were staged in 1954, mainly of the individual type, although a challenge match between the Probables and Possibles also took place. No doubt the riders taking part were all vying for a place in the Poppies league side. For the record, the first Southern Area League match at California took place on 25 April and the visitors were Ringwood. It was a losing start for the Poppies though, with Ringwood running out victors by 45 points to 38.

In 1955, California again claimed the runners-up spot behind Rye House, and still boasted the heat-leader trio of Goldfinch, Gleed and Mould. Other team regulars included several from the previous year, namely Tommy Sweetman, Eric Hockaday, Ron Sharp and Bob Andrews, plus newcomer Ross Gilbertson. Sixteen meetings were staged in 1955, including a league match against Ringwood, who closed down in June, claiming that track alterations had to take place. However, the picturesque Matchams Park venue in the New Forest failed to re-open and their record was expunged from the league table.

Due to the Poppies' success at bringing on new talent, California finished with the wooden spoon in 1956, as several of their riders moved into National League racing. Most notable among these were Gil Goldfinch and Bob Andrews, both of whom went to Wimbledon during the season. Leading the way for the Poppies was Peter Mould with 86 points, closely followed by Ross Gilbertson, who recorded 83 points. Other team

*Racing at California in 1954.*

members that year were Ron Sharp, Jimmy Gleed, Phil Sheppard, Ron Webb, Roy Gutteridge and Mike Keen. The league comprised only four teams and one of them (Southern Rovers) actually had no home track and had to complete their 'home' meetings at a variety of venues, including California, Rye House, Eastbourne and Swindon! It must be said that Southern Rovers did well to keep going and complete their fixtures, as it is difficult to see how the Southern Area League would have been able to survive with just three teams, had they folded. Another sixteen meetings were staged at California that year, including two of Southern Rovers 'home' fixtures. Sadly though, 1956 was to be the last year of regular speedway action at the scenic Wokingham venue.

Speedway at California had become unviable due to the call for Sunday observance. The situation could be overcome by charging supporters for a programme instead of an admission fee, but that idea fell flat when several people travelled in the same vehicle and only purchased one programme between them, thereby significantly reducing the incoming revenue. Therefore, in 1957, the California promotion staged speedway meetings at Tongham Stadium in Aldershot, which was not a Sunday venue. The Wokingham venue was then taken over and occupied by campers for much of that summer. One meeting, however, did take place at the circuit in 1957, when the California Championship was staged on Monday 5 August, with Eric Hockaday emerging as the winner and scoring a 15-point maximum. Three riders tied on 12 points to force a run-off for second place, with Ross Gilbertson winning, ahead of Ron Walton and Phil Sheppard. This proved to be the last proper meeting ever staged at the quaint Wokingham venue.

The promotion of 1957 obviously had an identity crisis, created by the move to Aldershot. At their first team fixture of the year against Rye House on 27 April, they were called the Poppies. At the next meeting (a four-team tournament against Eastbourne, Southern Rovers and Rye House) they went back to being known as California Poppies. By the next meeting on 11 May against Eastbourne, their name had changed again, this time to Aldershot Poppies! 22 meetings were staged at the Aldershot venue in 1957, as the team once again took part in the Southern Area League. Attendances at Tongham were disappointing though, as many people favoured a move back to California, but it was not to be, save for the single meeting back at the old venue in August. On track, the team didn't fare too well (particularly away from Tongham) and they had to settle for third place in a league of just four teams. Top man was Ross Gilbertson with 89 points, who was ably backed by Pat Flanagan and Ron Walton. Other riders used that season included Peter Mould, John Day, Phil Sheppard, Jimmy Gleed, Jim Tebby and future Racer Ted Spittles.

Sadly, the Southern Area League was no more after 1957, and with its demise went the Poppies – never to be seen again. The caravans were cleared from California in 1958 and a few junior training meetings were staged, including (on 15 June) a practice session in which Ted Spittles looked particularly impressive. There is no further evidence of any form of speedway at the venue since 1958 and the track is now overgrown with trees and bushes. Programmes from meetings staged at California have proved to be very collectable and are known to have

115

fetched anything up to £40, particularly the one from the last-ever meeting in 1957, but keen enthusiasts can expect to pay an average price of around the £30 mark.

## The 1960s

Moving on a few years, Reading Racers were formed and had their first meeting at Plymouth on 7 June 1968, when they went down 36-42 in a British League Division Two match at Pennycross Stadium. Prior to 1968, there had only been the one division of the British League, so Reading and nine other tracks were founder members of the brand new Second Division. Under the promotion of Allied Presentations Ltd and fronted by Reg Fearman, Reading Greyhound Stadium at Tilehurst staged its first-ever speedway meeting ten days later, on 17 June, when Nelson were the visitors for a league match.

Moving back in time briefly, an old local newspaper reports that speedway actually took place at Tilehurst Stadium on 16 May 1932. The relevant newspaper actually has photographs from the meeting, and the old stadium is clearly recognizable in the background. However, what is also clear is the fact that they were not riding on a cinder track, but on grass!

Going back to the opening night in 1968, admission prices were 5s for adults and 3s for children. Despite a reported crowd of some 5,000, the opening night turned into a bit of a shambles, as referee A.W. Day ordered a re-run of heat thirteen after Gary Peterson of Nelson had won it! Peterson, programmed at reserve, had already had 4 rides and the referee decided that he had been ineligible to take an additional start in the final heat. Despite the fact that the Reading team manager Dick Bailey had not protested, Mr Day ordered a re-run with the original programmed riders, which meant that Gerry Birtwell took the place of Peterson. When the race got underway again, there was a three-man pile-up involving Nelson's Terry Shearer and Birtwell, along with the Racers' Joe Weichlbauer. The race was stopped and Shearer was excluded; however, Birtwell was unable to take his place in the next re-run and was subsequently replaced by…Peterson!

Captain and coach of the Racers in that first season was the vastly experienced John Poyser, who had also helped with the laying of the track, and leading by example, he had a tremendous season, piling up 230 points in just 23 league and cup matches. Poyser was well supported by Ian Champion early on, but a succession of injuries wrecked his season, restricting him to just 14 matches and less than 100 points. Joe Weichlbauer – born in Graz, Austria, but a naturalized Australian – managed only 13 matches, thanks to a broken collarbone and rib injuries. Another Aussie, battling Dene Davies, bounced back after foot injuries to record 81 points from 18 matches, becoming a firm favourite with the Tilehurst faithful in the process. Vic White arrived at the end of the season and proved to be a shrewd signing, rattling up 54 points in the five Knock Out Cup matches that he rode in, and helping the Racers to reach the final, where they went down to Canterbury by an aggregate score of 80-112. The other mainstays of the Reading side in that first year were Ted Spittles (who proved that he had the makings of a decent rider), Stuart Wallace (who made a comeback after a stint

# READING ★ ★
## ★ ★ SPEEDWAY

### READING GREYHOUND STADIUM - TILEHURST

**OFFICIAL PROGRAMME - ONE SHILLING**

1st Meeting - 1st Season          British League Division II

# READING v. NELSON

MONDAY, 17th JUNE, 1968 at 7-30 p.m.

BETTING AND UNAUTHORISED PHOTOGRAPHY PROHIBITED

*First Tilehurst programme, 1968.*

*Reading 1969. From left to right, back row: Mike Vernam, Alan Jackson, Reg Fearman (promoter), Phil Pratt, Mick Bell, Dene Davies. Front, on bike: Dick Bailey (team manager), Ian Champion (captain).*

in the Merchant Navy) and young Phil Pratt (who found the going very tough).

All in all, it was a good initial season for Reading, as the side finished eighth in the league and made it to the Knock Out Cup final, after a marvellous semi-final success over League Champions Belle Vue. There was certainly plenty of enthusiasm on the terraces as Tilehurst boasted one of the biggest regular crowds in British speedway. There were 2 individual meetings staged in 1968 – the Reading Open Championship and the Stadium Trophy, both of which were won by Middlesbrough's Graham Plant. John Poyser was runner-up in the Open, while Dene Davies finished second in the Stadium Trophy.

For the 1969 campaign, the Racers only retained the services of Ian Champion, Phil Pratt and Dene Davies from their inaugural season. Coming into the side was Mick Bell, on loan from Oxford, and the drop down a division was to prove a shrewd move for both rider and club. He went on to top the Reading averages, recording 277 points in the process. Also joining the Racers were Mike Vernam (via Weymouth), Alan Jackson and Australian Bob Tabet. Alan Jackson suffered several crashes and was replaced by young rookie Richard May, son of the former Wembley and Southampton rider Charlie May. The signing of May turned out to be a blessing in disguise, as the novice ran out second in the side's averages, scoring 181 points from his twenty-four league and Knock Out Cup matches.

Ian Champion left the club to join Rayleigh after sixteen matches, and into the team came another youngster destined for a long career with the Racers, namely grass-tracker Bernie Leigh. Bernie made steady progress and was definitely one for the future. Phil Pratt made progress after struggling the previous year, while Dene Davies continued to entertain the crowds with his on-track battling qualities. Despite all the rider changes, Reading had a tremendous season, finishing second in the league to double-winners Belle Vue, and enjoyed 6 away victories to boot! In the Division Two Riders' Championship, Mick Bell took the runners-up spot, scoring 13 points, to finish just a single point behind winner Geoff Ambrose.

A bizarre occurrence worthy of note happened on 19 May at Tilehurst in a league match against Plymouth, when heat eight resulted in a 0-0 draw! In the original running of the race, Chris Roynon was excluded for foul riding after Bob Tabet had fallen. Roynon's team-mate, John Ellis, was also a non-starter in the re-run, having suffered an engine failure first time around, and was quite rightly excluded from the re-start for not being under power at the time of the stoppage. In the re-run, Reading's Tabet and Dene Davies looked odds-on to record a 5-0 heat win until, in separate incidents, both fell and neither was able to finish the race!

An international meeting was staged at Tilehurst on 25 August, when England took on the Czechoslovakian tourists. The visitors won 57-51 and were led by Miroslav Verner with 18 points and Vaclav Verner, who scored 14. Future Racer Jiri Stancl also rode for the Czechs, scoring 7 points. Meanwhile, leading scorers for England were Martyn Piddock plus two Racers – Richard May and Mick Bell – who all recorded 10 points apiece. Sadly, in August, popular Tilehurst announcer Peter Arnold died following a car crash. Two months later, a memorial meeting was staged in his honour and won by John Harrhy of Ipswich. One other individual meeting was staged in 1969 – the Stadium Trophy – which was won by Barry Crowson, with Racer Dene Davies taking third spot.

## The 1970s

After finishing second in the league, big things were expected in 1970, but they never materialized as the Racers slumped to ninth position in a seventeen-team league. Mick Bell went back into the top league with Oxford and was never really replaced, although the Racers did, however, retain the services of Richard May and Mike Vernam. May piled up 302 points and Vernam collected 265, but it was the lack of a third heat-leader, which cost Reading dear. Richard May, in fact, had a tremendous year, winning all three individual tournaments staged at Tilehurst. In a marvellous treble, May took the Reading Open Championship, the Stadium Trophy and the second staging of the Peter Arnold Memorial Trophy.

Bernie Leigh continued to make good progress, and Dene Davies easily outscored his point contribution from the previous year, but Phil Pratt's form headed in the wrong direction as he only managed to complete 14 matches. Aussie Bob Young joined the Racers camp and proved to be a good middle order man, scoring 141 points from his twenty-six matches. John Hammond and Cec Platt rode in the majority of Reading's fixtures, but neither produced the hoped-for points. Several youngsters were given a

*Reading v. Swindon programme, 1971.*

trial in the side, but none looked like pulling up any trees as the Racers languished in mid-table mediocrity.

Allied Presentations had also promoted at First Division Newcastle in 1970, but falling attendances spelt a quick end to this venture and the decision was made to switch the Diamonds' top league licence to Tilehurst in 1971. This move resulted in Dag Lovaas, Geoff Curtis and super Swede Anders Michanek joining the Racers from the Brough Park venue, and after the mediocrity of 1970, all of a sudden things looked much brighter for the good speedway folk on the Tilehurst terraces. And bright they turned out, as the Racers finished sixth in their first attempt at Division One racing, led brilliantly by Anders Michanek, who rattled up 294 points for his new club. It was a great year for 'Mich', as he also went on to reach the World Final in Gothenburg, where he scored 11 points, finishing in fifth position.

Norwegian Dag Lovaas showed his form to be much improved from what he had experienced at Newcastle previously, finished second in the Racers' scorechart with a very healthy total of 235 points. Backing the top two solidly was the third member of the ex-Newcastle trio, Geoff Curtis, who weighed in with 214 points from his 36 league and Knock Out Cup matches. The rest of the regular 1971 Racers were: Richard May (although he found it hard work in the top league, he never stopped battling away and did very well to record 183 points), the returning Mick Bell (who had possibly been expected to do better, although he did show flashes of brilliance), Bernie Leigh (who showed continued promise, despite only returning 114 points) and ex-Poole rider Geoff Mudge (who missed half the season with a serious knee injury, but when riding showed great courage).

Many guest riders were used during Geoff Mudge's absence and this only served to highlight how much Anders Michanek had carried the side throughout the season – indeed it is anybody's guess as to what might have happened without the brilliant Swede. Anders made it to his fourth World Final, held in his native country at the Ullevi Stadium, where he scored 11 points to finish just outside a rostrum position. Ray Wilson won the Peter Arnold Memorial Trophy, with Geoff Curtis finishing in second place. A major new individual event made its first appearance on the Reading calendar, with the staging of the Manpower Trophy, which saw Barry Briggs take top spot ahead of Anders Michanek (second) and Reidar Eide (third).

In 1972, Reading did something rarely seen in speedway, tracking the same seven men who had served them the previous season. The seven riders gelled brilliantly as Reading climbed up to the runners-up spot in the league and also, despite being drawn away three times, reached the semi-final of the Knock Out Cup. Anders Michanek, although missing a third of the Racers' fixtures due to his Swedish commitments, still scored 270 points and led by example. Dag Lovaas hammered home 287 points, which was more than any other Racer and he continued to make rapid progress as a rider. Meanwhile, Aussie Geoff Curtis ably backed up the top two with solid scoring throughout the year.

Geoff Mudge, given an injury-free run, showed what a useful rider he was and weighed in with over 200 points. Bernie Leigh battled on gamely, despite a broken shoulder and Richard May progressed further – his 187 points spoke volumes for his

*Dag Lovaas.*

tenacity. Many Racers fans still talk about the match at Swindon on 6 May when 'Dickie', as he was affectionately known, twice beat the great Barry Briggs. His first super victory over 'Briggo' came in heat one, after 'Mich' had been excluded for breaking the tapes; then, for good measure, in heat nine, 'Dickie' repeated the dose after 'Briggo' had been brought in as a tactical substitute. It certainly was a great night for Reading as they ran out 44-34 victors at the home of their local rivals.

Mick Bell scored more solidly throughout the year and it was the improvement from the middle-order men that formed the basis for Reading's success. The Racers did make one signing during the year, bringing in Graeme Smith from Sunderland as a number eight, and he never let the side down when called upon to ride. Ivan Mauger won the prestigious Manpower Trophy, ahead of Anders Michanek, who was runner-up for the second year running. The other big meeting at Tilehurst in 1972 was the Peter Arnold Memorial Trophy, which saw Reidar Eide emerge as the winner. Ray Wilson was second and there was a three-way tie for third spot between Ronnie Moore and the Racers duo of Dag Lovaas and Richard May.

One of the meetings from the Inter-Nations Championship took place at Tilehurst on 10 July, when Sweden beat a combined Norway/Denmark side 40-38, with Dag Lovaas scoring a brilliant 12 points for the losing side. In the World Final at Wembley, super Swede Anders Michanek did well to score 8 points, following a fall in his first race. 'Mich' was also the Reading representative at the Belle Vue-staged Division One Riders' Championship, where he scored 9 points and finished fifth.

1973 was a roller-coaster year of success for Reading Speedway, as the Racers took the League Championship and reached the Knock Out Cup final. And what a cup final it was, for having beaten Belle Vue 47-31 in the first leg at Tilehurst, Racers had one hand on the cup, but it was not to be, as Belle Vue won by the same score at Hyde Road to force an aggregate draw. In a tremendous run-off to decide the outcome, it was Peter Collins who won the cup for the Manchester outfit, when he defeated Anders Michanek. That run-off has been described by many folk as the greatest race of all time, as both stars passed and re-passed each other on every bend.

'Mich', though, had put in another brilliant season, even better than before in fact, plundering a mighty 439 points in league and Knock Out Cup matches, and he also notched up a mammoth 26 maximums! Dag Lovaas, in support of Michanek, was

# READING SPEEDWAY

Manpower '73—Anders Michanek the winner, with Ole Olsen 2nd and Reidar Eide 3rd. Three of the world's top Stars who have thrilled us here at Tilehurst. Photo: Alf Weedon

# GRAND FINALE
## Reading v Ole Olsen's United 7
### Monday, 8th October, 1973 at 7.30 p.m.
OFFICIAL MAGAZINE PROGRAMME 10p

*Final Tilehurst programme, 1973.*

*Reading 1973. From left to right, back row: Bob Radford (team manager), Mick Bell, Bobby McNeil, Bernie Leigh. Front row: Richard May, Dag Lovaas, team mascot, Anders Michanek, Geoff Curtis.*

*Tilehurst Stadium, just after the bulldozers had moved in.*

absolutely tremendous, putting his average up to over 10 points a match. Again backing these two was Geoff Curtis, who battled away and belied his critics with 323 points. Sadly, Geoff was killed in a track crash at the Sydney Showground in December 1973. Smallmead today still has, dedicated to his memory, The Geoff Curtis Bar.

Richard May, despite niggling injuries, managed to collect more points than in 1972 and continued to make progress in the sport. Mick Bell, appointed club captain, also upped his points plundering, despite having to ride at number two. Bernie Leigh battled away in his own inimitable style and was a firm favourite with the crowd. Peter Murray was brought in to replace the retired Geoff Mudge, but after just three official matches, he opted for the somewhat easier life in Division Two. Jack Millen arrived as the Racers' number eight and did well in the twelve matches in which he rode. Reading used a string of Division Two loanees and guests throughout the season, but no matter what, Racers cruised to the league title led by team manager Bob Radford. The on-track success, however, was marred by the news towards the end of the season that the site of the stadium had been sold for re-development. The wheels turned for the last time at the venue on 8 October, when the Racers beat Ole Olsen's United Seven in a challenge match.

The *Daily Mirror* International Tournament was held at tracks all over England in 1973, and Tilehurst staged the match between New Zealand and the Soviet Union. The Kiwis won the meeting, with Ivan Mauger scoring 12 points, Ronnie Moore 11 and Barry Briggs 9. For the Soviet Union, the top rider was Vladimir Gordeev, who recorded 10 points. In the World Final at the Slaski Stadium in Katowice, Poland, Anders Michanek had a disappointing night, as he was excluded from one ride for tape breaking and could only muster a total of 6 points. Anders fared better in the Division One Riders' Championship at Belle Vue, scoring 11 points to earn himself a place in the four-man run-off for second place, behind the majestic Ivan Mauger. Unfortunately, Ray Wilson took the flag in the run-off, but Anders was second, beating Ole Olsen and Arnold Haley to take third place overall.

After the closure of Tilehurst in 1973, very few people believed the Racers would ever get back on track. However, Reg Fearman (along with the assistance of Bill Dore, Frank Higley and Len Silver) never gave up, and with the help of the local council, a new site was eventually found. A new stadium was then built from scratch on the site of a rubbish tip on Bennet Road, situated in the Smallmead district of Reading. The Racers had hoped to move into Smallmead Stadium in 1974, but their new home was not ready on time, so they had to apply for their licence to be put on ice for a year, with the riders being loaned out. The one bright spot of the year that never was came on 6 September, when Anders Michanek became World Champion at the Ullevi Stadium in Gothenburg, scoring a brilliant 15-point maximum in front of 40,000 partisan fans.

Come 1975 and Reading Speedway was back, and 10,000 shale-starved fans crammed into the new stadium for the first match of a new era on 28 April, as the Racers faced Hull in a British League match. The meeting was due to start at 7.30 p.m., but eventually started over half an hour late in order to let the huge crowd in. The opening heat saw Jim McMillan, the Hull skipper, inflict a rare defeat on Reading's top man Anders Michanek. Jimmy Mac's race time was 64.6 seconds, which stood as the track record

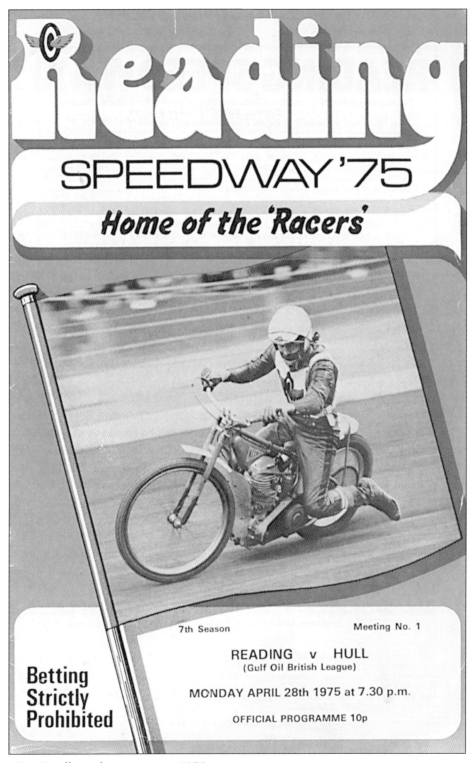

*First Smallmead programme, 1975.*

throughout the meeting. Anders was unable to race again in the match, due to an injury sustained the previous day in a grass-track meeting, however, the rest of the Racers pulled together to win 48-30.

The Racers team on that historic day was: Anders Michanek from Sweden (1974 World Champion); Mick Bell (who also rode for Oxford, Coventry and Leicester during his career); Bengt Jansson (Swedish international and 1967 World number two – behind Ove Fundin); Richard May (1960s grass-tracker and son of ex-Southampton rider, Charlie May); John Davis (English international, who also appeared for Oxford and Swindon among others); Bob Humphreys from Australia (hero of the opening Smallmead meeting with a paid 15-point maximum from the reserve berth); and Bernie Leigh (all-round motorcyclist from Hampshire, who became one of the most loyal Racers of all time). Officials at that first meeting were: Tony Silk (referee), Dick Bailey (clerk of the course), Frank Higley (team manager), John Homer (timekeeper), 'Diddy' David Hamilton (master of ceremonies) and Dave Lanning (announcer).

Opening night referee Tony Silk, who lives at Highworth (just outside Swindon), had been a regular fan at Reading Speedway, having attended the first meeting at Tilehurst in 1968. Tony remembers that he went up to Smallmead on the day before the opening meeting to have a look around. On race night, Tony vividly recalls walking around the track before the meeting with timekeeper John Homer. Tony felt very honoured to be the referee at that first meeting and he refers to it as one of the highlights of his speedway career.

Overall then, 1975 was a good start to racing at the new venue, as the Racers finished in sixth place in the British League, enjoying large attendance figures. Anders Michanek led the scoring, despite missing a third of the Racers' fixtures, again achieving an average in excess of 10.50. John Davis was runner-up to 'Mich' in the scoring stakes and showed tremendous improvement in his all-round game, having been a second-string at Oxford the year before. 'JD' had, in fact, arrived at Smallmead in an exchange deal, which saw Dag Lovaas join Oxford. Third in the team's scoring was 'Banger' Jansson, who had a poor season by his standards, exacerbated by mechanical gremlins.

Bernie Leigh, after a year on loan to Swindon, came back and continued to be a crowd-pleaser with his on-track battling. Bob Humphreys struggled to hold on to his opening night form, but achieved a steady 5-point average, recording 175 points. Richard May was another returnee, but having finished the previous season as a 6-plus man at Poole, he barely managed 5 points a match in a disappointing year for him at Smallmead. Mick Bell remained a steady team man, despite an injured hip late in the year. Mighty 'Mich' took ninth place in the British League Riders' Championship at Belle Vue with 8 points. Anders lost his World title to Ole Olsen at Wembley, but still took the runners-up spot and retained his World Pairs crown with partner Tommy Jansson. On the individual front at Smallmead, Newport's Phil Crump won the Manpower Trophy from Malcolm Simmons (second) and Ole Olsen (third). Home rider John Davis, won the Geoff Curtis Memorial Trophy with Tommy Jansson (second) and former Racer Dag Lovaas (third).

The major change in 1976 was Anders Michanek opting out of the British League, to be replaced by new number one, Dave Jessup, who arrived via Leicester. Anyone who

*Boley Proch.*

thought that 'DJ' wouldn't be able to replace mighty 'Mich' soon changed their minds. Three 12-point scores in as many matches and also taking the *Daily Express* Spring Classic at Wimbledon quickly won the Racers fans over. Pint-sized Jessup went on to top the Reading averages and also won two further big individual meetings during the year, namely The Yorkshire TV Trophy at Hull and The Geoff Curtis Memorial Trophy at Smallmead. In pairs competitions, 'DJ' also took victories in the Skol Classic at Wimbledon (with John Davis) and the Nulli Secundus Trophy at Reading (with Bob Humphreys).

With Richard May also leaving after over 200 appearances for the club, a new name appeared at Smallmead: Eugeniusz Blaszak from Poland. He did start to progress, but following a shop-lifting problem, was ordered back to his native land, never to be seen again! In his place came Polish Junior Champion Boleslaw Proch, and 'Boley' certainly proved to be one of the better Poles to race in British Speedway during the 1970s, recording 121 points from his 29 league and Knock Out Cup matches. Bengt Jansson had another nightmare with his engines and, after just ten matches, he was gone. Luckily for Reading, battling Bernie Leigh was riding better than ever and this, coupled with the use of guest riders, covered the loss of Jansson. Bob Humphreys had an excellent season and was one of the best second-strings in the country, notching over 200 points.

The highlight for Mick Bell in another steady season, was a reserves 9-point maximum against Halifax in June, as the 'Dukes' were sent packing by 56 points to 22. John Davis had another good year, finishing second to Dave Jessup in the Racers' averages, and he was triumphant in the Smallmead-staged Marlboro Southern Riders' Championship with a 15-point maximum. In the home match against Hull on 26 April, 'JD' featured in one of the best races ever witnessed at Smallmead, as he and four-times World Champion Barry Briggs diced for the lead in a four-lap, wheel-to-wheel battle. 'JD' won the epic heat eleven by half a wheel on the line, amidst an electric Smallmead atmosphere. 'Briggo' though, had his revenge in heat thirteen, but that heat eleven was worth the entrance money on its own.

The big individual meeting at Smallmead, The Manpower Trophy, was won by 1976 World Champion Peter Collins, with a scintillating 15-point maximum. Runner-up on 12 points was Reading's former 'King' Anders Michanek, who was making a rare appearance in Britain. In June, Reading played hosts to the USSR in an international team match, which the Racers won 46-32, with John Davis topping the England scoring on 11 points. Meanwhile, Reading lost out to Hackney at the first hurdle in the Knock Out Cup. Overall though, it was another good season for Reading as they again finished sixth in the British League, with inconsistency being the reason for not finishing higher. The Racers did actually head the table at one point, but sadly were unable to maintain the position.

It wasn't just speedway and greyhounds at Smallmead in 1976, as Trevor Redmond, along with promoters Allied Presentations Limited, introduced stock cars, plus some sidecar racing to the circuit. During the 1970s, Smallmead witnessed massive crowds for speedway, helped in a huge way by the local press in the shape of the *Reading Evening Post* and the *Reading Chronicle*. Both newspapers have been fantastic in providing support and publicity for the Racers over the years, and that continues right up to the present day with coverage by Dave Wright at the *Post* and Nick Dyer at the *Chronicle*.

For several years, the *Reading Evening Post* produced a special edition to mark the start of the speedway season at Smallmead, and 1977 was no exception, with a 24-page special which included a full 8-page picture feature on the Racers. The special sold for just fifteen pence and the two people who brought all the latest news to the Reading fans were Bob Radford and the very same Dave Wright. On the team front there were not a lot of changes, as back came the double spearhead of Dave Jessup and John Davis, while regulars Bernie Leigh and Bob Humphreys also returned. Bengt Jansson also came back to have another go, but Mick Bell had retired (although he later made a comeback at Coventry) and 'Boley' Proch was unable to start the season due to injuries. New faces in the Reading line-up were Australian Glyn Taylor (the son of former Aussie international Chum Taylor) and Sweden's Bo Jansson (brother of the legendary Tommy).

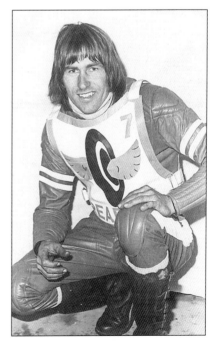

The opening meeting of the season at Smallmead brought an international flavour, as Polish side Stal Gorzow arrived for a challenge match. The Racers took a comfortable 47-31 victory against a side that included internationals Marek Cieslak, Edward Jancarz and Jerzy Rembas. Reading's new signings Bo Jansson and Glyn Taylor struggled and were soon gone. 'Boley' Proch eventually returned, and was joined in the Racers camp by Ian Gledhill. Later on in the year, Doug Underwood joined Reading from Leicester, with Proch heading in the opposite direction. However, it was West German international Hans Wassermann who really got the crowd buzzing

*Bob Humphreys.*

when he arrived. He produced some daredevil stuff and certainly livened up the proceedings, finishing the season with a home average in excess of 7 points, which was very good for a first season.

Reading hosted an England *v.* the Rest of the World Test Match, with the World Select winning 62-46, but the big shock of the meeting was Racers' number one Dave Jessup failing to score a single point from four starts. Among those riding for the World team were Ole Olsen (15 points), Phil Crump (11), Ivan Mauger (7) and Egon Muller, who also failed to score. More international action took place at Smallmead on 19 June, in the shape of the British round of the World Team Cup. This saw an England side featuring Dave Jessup and John Davis defeat Australia, Scotland and New Zealand.

Dave Jessup had another fantastic year, recording a mammoth 489 points for an average in excess of 10. John Davis wasn't far behind wee Dave, scoring 433 points, as the two of them became one of the most potent heat-leader duos in the land, but it was the lack of a third top man that was to cost the Racers dearly in the end. Bengt Jansson was both unpredictable and inconsistent, and his return of 234 points should surely have been greater. Australian Bob Humphreys had a good, steady season and was an excellent number two to Dave Jessup. Meanwhile, good old Bernie Leigh put in another fine season and was one of the best middle-order men in the business.

The British League title went to White City with 55 points, but Reading were not far behind in the Championship chase, finishing on 53 points along with Exeter. But for some unwanted politics during the season, it could have been another Championship year for the Racers. Promoter Reg Fearman was, at one point of the season, ordered to release a rider, as the Racers were accused of being too strong! This was the reason why 'Boley' Proch was allowed to leave Smallmead, thus upsetting the balance of the side and ultimately costing Reading the league title. Reading were also the nearly team in the Knock Out Cup, losing out in the final to King's Lynn by a mere 2 points on aggregate. Having won the first leg at Smallmead by just 2 points, the Racers performed heroically in the second leg, going down by 4 points to lose by the narrowest of margins overall.

On the World Championship trail, John Davis just missed out after a controversial race with Ivan Mauger in the Inter-Continental Final at White City. 'JD' finished on 7 points, the same as the other Racer in the big meeting, Dave Jessup. Davis did get to the World Final, however, but only as British reserve, and he failed to get a ride. Both Racers did become World Champions though, as part of the England team that took the World Team Cup in Poland. On the domestic individual front, Dave Jessup won the Dews Trophy at Halifax, while John Davis took the Bass Yorkshire Open Championship at Sheffield.

1978 was a disastrous year, as the Racers finished the league campaign in fourteenth place out of nineteen teams, their worst position since joining the top league. This was due to a combination of injuries and a lack of on-track strength in depth. The top two riders were again Jessup and Davis, but 'DJ' fell and broke a leg at the start of the season and missed several vital matches. Later in the season, having qualified for the Golden Jubilee World Final at Wembley, Hans Wassermann had a bad track smash, breaking his neck at Ipswich. Sadly, that spill was to end the little German's career at Smallmead. A

*Reading's ingenious 'postcode' poster.*

fit Jessup did take fourth place in the World Final, but it could have been so different for the diminutive rider, as a minor mechanical problem definitely cost him a rostrum place, if not the Championship itself.

The World Team Cup UK round was again held at Smallmead, with England defeating Australia, USA and New Zealand. Reading's Dave Jessup scored 9 points for England, while young Racer Roger Abel recorded 2 points for New Zealand. The second half of the World Team Cup round featured the competing riders racing for individual glory, with former World Champion Peter Collins showing his class in a tremendous race, as he caught and passed fellow England international Malcolm Simmons to win. Individual honours went to John Davis, who won Reading's big meeting, The Manpower Trophy. 'JD' also took the famous Wimbledon Laurels and the third round of the Master of Speedway series in Sweden. Dave Jessup was also a winner in 1978, as he took the Bass Yorkshire Open Championship at Sheffield.

The Racers had a reasonable home record, but it was a different story away from Smallmead with just two victories all season. Reading won at Cradley Heath in the Knock Out Cup, but lost the home leg to the Heathens to crash out in the first round. The only other away success came at Hackney in a league match. The biggest home win of the year was also against Hackney, as the Racers ran out comfortable winners by 53 points to 24. Despite his injury misfortune at the start of the year and his bad luck in the World Championship, Dave Jessup led the way again for Reading, with a 10-point average. John Davis was slightly down on his form of the previous year, but still backed 'DJ' all the way with the bulk of the Racers' scoring.

Bernie Leigh ended the season as Racers' third heat-leader on an average of just under 6 points a match, and also recorded his first British League paid maximum. Hans Wassermann started the season well, but had tailed off and was just getting it together again, prior to his smash at Ipswich. Of the other Racers in 1978, Bob Humphreys was having a right old nightmare until he opted for life in the National League with Milton Keynes. Doug Underwood came up with the odd good showing, but was generally inconsistent. New boy for 1978 was former World finalist Henryk Glucklich from Poland, but he struggled badly, scoring just 41 points from the 20 matches he appeared in. Young Kevin Bowen showed promise, but was out of his depth with the big boys of British League racing. Mel Taylor did well enough to warrant a return in 1979 and Roger Abel looked useful, but it was the lack of a real third heat-leader that lead to Reading's worst-ever season thus far.

It was all change at Smallmead in 1979, as top rider Dave Jessup moved to King's Lynn for £20,000. New riders signed were Jan Andersson (a 1978 World finalist from Swindon) and veteran Terry Betts (the idol of King's Lynn, who was talked out of his retirement plans). Also joining the Racers in 1979 was Norwegian Reidar Eide, via Exeter, while another Nordic signing was Sigvart Pedersen. There were also new people in charge for the 1979 campaign, with Brian Constable installed as promoter and Mick Blackburn taking up the position of new team manager. Meanwhile, John Davis, Bernie Leigh, Bob Humphreys and Mel Taylor all returned, along with youngster Ashley Pullen.

John Davis took over the vacated number one race jacket and had a brilliant year, scoring 335 points, for an average not far short of 10.50 per match. Jan Andersson

# READING SPEEDWAY

## BERNIE LEIGH TESTIMONIAL MEETING
Sunday, August 12th, 1979

Price 10p

*Bernie Leigh Testimonial programme, 1979.*

enjoyed his best season thus far in British speedway, as he plundered nearly 300 points and won the Swedish Championship. Jan went on to retain his Swedish crown in both 1980 and 1981. Thirty-six-year-old Terry Betts put in a steady season for the Racers, but it was to be his last year in the sport. Bob Humphreys was an ever-present in the National League with Milton Keynes, but he also doubled-up to help the Racers in no fewer than 27 of their 38 official league and cup matches. Mel Taylor also doubled-up, riding for Mildenhall in the National League and also appearing in thirty of Reading's matches and achieving a useful 5-plus average.

Injuries played havoc with the Racers though, as first Pedersen broke his leg at Exeter in May, never to return, and a month later, Eide broke a leg in a grass-track meeting. Reidar returned to action three months later, but he understandably found it hard going after so long out of the saddle. Czech Champion Jiri Stancl arrived in August, but he didn't pull up any trees, and failed to average 6 points a match. West German long track racer Alois Weisbock agreed to join the Racers, but after just a single meeting, he returned home and never came back again. Seventh position out of eighteen teams wasn't bad for the new-look Racers, considering all the problems that they endured along the way. In the Knock Out Cup, Reading went out to Halifax at the quarter-final stage, losing 82-134 on aggregate. Special mention is due to young Ashley Pullen, who in the first round cup-tie at home to Eastbourne recorded a brilliant paid 15-point maximum. This was definitely one of the high points of a rather mediocre season for the Racers.

Two international meetings were staged at Smallmead in 1979, the first of these being held on 16 April, when the Racers gained a 52-26 victory over Getingarna from Sweden, who included Anders Michanek (scorer of 8 points) in their side. The other international fixture was the UK round of the World Team Cup on 20 May. This produced a real shock for English speedway fans in the wet at the Berkshire circuit, as New Zealand won the round ahead of the USA, with England down in third position and Australia last. It was the start of an amazing run for the Ivan Mauger-led Kiwis, as they went on to win the Inter-Continental Round, before taking World Final glory at London's White City Stadium.

On the individual front, home rider Jan Andersson won the Geoff Curtis Memorial Trophy with a 15-point maximum, ahead of John Davis (14) and Bernie Leigh (13), making it a clean sweep for the Racers. It was good old Bernie Leigh's year though, as he averaged over 6 points a meeting for the side, won the Strongbow Nulli Secundus Best Pairs with John Davis in May, and enjoyed a very successful and fully deserved Testimonial meeting at Smallmead on 12 August. The Bernie Leigh Select team won the four-team tournament, staged to honour the then 'Mr Reading Speedway'. Bernie was a top all-round motorcyclist, for as well as speedway, he was a trials rider of note and a national grass-track star, who won the Southern Centre Grass-Track Championship on many occasions. In November 1979, John Davis and Bernie Leigh went off to the Middle East to ride in three individual meetings at Cairo, Kuwait and Abu Dhabi. Both riders celebrated their birthdays while on the tour – 'JD' celebrated his twenty-fifth, while Bernie reached the veteran stage with his thirty-fifth. Bernie did well though, scoring a total of 31 points from the three rounds, meanwhile 'JD' gathered a total of 19 points.

The overall winner of the event was Belle Vue's Chris Morton, who won all three rounds, scoring 14 points in each.

## The 1980s

1980 was a golden year for the Racers as they took the British League title ahead of Hackney and Belle Vue. It must be said though, that Hackney pushed Reading all the way, and it was not until the end of October that the Championship was finally in the bag. There were changes at Smallmead, as Dave Lanning took the role of speedway executive. Uniquely in speedway, Lanning took out a special insurance premium that resulted in a £40,000 bonus for the team, having won the League Championship. Mick Bell returned to Reading, this time as team manager. Other officials in 1980 were Dick Bailey (clerk of the course), John Homer (timekeeper) and Dougie Harris (track maintenance). Dick Bailey had, of course, been with the Racers since 1968, in one capacity or another. Bill Dore's daughter, Pat Bliss, also joined the promotion team in 1980 and, of course, she would go on to become the rock of Smallmead in later years. John Davis, Jan Andersson and Bernie Leigh were still part of the furniture, but joining the Racers camp for the Championship year were American Bobby Schwartz, Czech Jiri Stancl and Kiwi Tony Briggs, son of the legendary Barry Briggs. Also joining Reading in 1980, for a fee of £4,000, was former England international Martin Ashby, via local rivals Swindon, where he held (and, indeed, still does to this day) all the club records for appearances and points.

It was reported in the Racers programme of 5 May that super Swede Jan Andersson kept himself fit by running four miles in the morning, followed by another four-mile jaunt in the evening! It obviously worked, as Jan had his best-ever season in speedway, scoring 321 points from his 33 league and Knock Out Cup matches to reach the top of the Racers' averages with a figure of just over 10 points per match. 'Boogaloo' Bobby Schwartz, after his £8,000 transfer from Cradley Heath, backed Andersson all the way and was a tremendously enthusiastic man to have around. Bobby scored more points than Andersson, but his average was ever-so-slightly less than the Swede's, at exactly 10 points a match. It is easy to see how Reading won the league, as not only did they boast two 10-point men, but they also had a 9-plus man in John Davis. 'JD' was a touch down on his 1979 scoring, but with three big points men, Reading didn't need a lot more from the rest of the side.

Good old Bernie Leigh went about his job in much the same way as usual and must be regarded as one of the best team-men in speedway of all-time. Young 'Briggo' had a lot to live up to, but it was a huge learning curve. Even so, he impressed on several occasions and to finish his first season with a 5-point average was an big achievement for the lad. Jiri Stancl, despite numerous trips back home, did very well indeed, scoring 200 points and backing his heat-leaders admirably. Martin Ashby found the going hard and spent much of the season at reserve, not helped by a broken collarbone. Sadly, this was to be Martin's last season and it was a great shame to witness the downfall of such a great servant to British Speedway, but at least he went out with a British League Champions' medal to his name. During Martin's enforced lay-off in order to get his

*Reading v. Swindon programme, 1980.*

collarbone mended, Reading brought in a couple of National League loanees to cover the gap. Steve McDermott and Dave Trownson could not be faulted for their efforts, as both scored useful points on the Racers' relentless march to the league title. Among others, two young men who got plenty of second-half rides, plus the odd senior outing, were Mark Leslie from Dorset and Andy Campbell from Surrey. Reidar Eide had started the season with Reading, but he was off to Wolverhampton after just a couple of matches for the Racers.

In May, seven-year-old Darius Goodwin, the World's youngest and smallest motor-cycle stunt rider, launched a series of live shows at Smallmead. His jump over eight Reading riders was watched by a reported crowd of some 9,000, as well as being filmed by the cameras of ITV! In June, at the Smallmead staged *Daily Mirror* Grand Prix meeting, tennis star Sue Barker was a guest of honour. It wasn't the first time that a famous personality had visited Reading Speedway though. In 1973, at the height of his fame, Gary Glitter was persuaded by the then master of ceremonies David Hamilton to parade around Tilehurst on top of a Rolls Royce with team captain Mick Bell and Racers number one Anders Michanek.

Although the Racers went out of the Knock Out Cup by just 2 points on aggregate to Cradley Heath at the quarter-final stage, they did boast three World Final qualifiers. In the big meeting, staged at the futuristic Ullevi Stadium in Sweden, Jan Andersson did very well, scoring 11 points to finish fourth. Fellow Racer John Davis recorded 9 points and was equal fifth with future World Champion Bruce Penhall. The third Reading man in the pack was Jiri Stancl, but he finished well down the field after yielding just 5 points. Young Tony Briggs brought some glory to Berkshire, finishing as runner-up to Tommy Knudsen in the European Junior Championship, as it was then known. In 1988, this tournament was upgraded to what we know it as today: namely the World Junior Championship.

In the big individual meetings of 1980, John Davis won the *Daily Express* Spring Classic at Wimbledon and Bobby Schwartz won three of the season's 'biggies', taking the Geoff Curtis Memorial Trophy at Smallmead, the Champion of Champions Trophy at Wolverhampton and the Metro Stadium Trophy at Ipswich. As usual, an all-star line-up was assembled for the annual Manpower Trophy at Smallmead, and this was won by Belle Vue's brilliant Chris Morton, ahead of new World Champion Michael Lee and 'Boogaloo' Bobby Schwartz. As is the case nowadays, 'Monday Monday' by the Mamas and the Papas was played at the stadium, these days as the parade music, but in 1980 it was the signature tune. Meanwhile, the opening parade music was the 'Post Horn Gallop', followed by the parade anthem 'Rocking Goose' by Johnny and the Hurricanes.

During the season, the promotion organized a competition entitled 'Hudson's Historical Humdinger'. It was a speedway quiz and in the Racers match magazine for 8 September, the winner was named as Pete Butler, who scored 128 points out of a possible 132. In second place was Tim Sugar, who won £7. Yes, *the* Tim Sugar, a lifelong supporter of the Racers, who was later to become a legend as an ace team manager, helping to bring many trophies to the Smallmead coffers. Another lifelong supporter, Emily Brakespear, celebrated her seventieth birthday by having a ride on the back of

Bernie Leigh's bike!

It was a big drop down the league to eleventh place for the Racers in 1981. On the team front, replacing Martin Ashby and Jiri Stancl were youngsters Denny Pyeatt and Ashley Pullen. There were changes on the promotional side too, as Dave Lanning moved on, with co-promoters Bill Dore, Frank Higley and Pat Bliss taking more of an active role. Roger Ware took over as meeting presenter, while Mick Bell stayed on as team manager. Celebrities have played a big part in the history of Reading Speedway and 1981 was no exception, with the press day having a special guest to open the season. Miss World, Kimberley Santos, along with competition organizer Julia Morley, helped to launch the new campaign in great style. The match programme in 1981 cost just twenty-five pence, and at the souvenir shop you could purchase a Racers badge for seventy-five pence and a programme board for £1.25.

After only ten league matches, the Racers were dealt a cruel blow, when the popular Tony Briggs piled up at Coventry, breaking his neck. Sadly, that crash was to spell the end of 'Briggo' junior's career. Jan Andersson was top man for the season, both in terms of average (10.13) and points (395), and his riding of the white line at Smallmead was nothing short of brilliant. 'Jan the Man' received solid support from 'Boogaloo' Bobby Schwartz, who rattled up 313 points in spite of a back problem. The other member of the Racers' tremendous trio from the previous season, John Davis, was there again, piling up the points until a £20,000 transfer to Poole. 'JD' had only ridden

*Reading 1981. From left to right, back row: John Davis, Bobby Schwartz, Jan Andersson, Tony Briggs, Ashley Pullen. Front row: Bernie Leigh, Denny Pyeatt.*

in fifteen league and Knock Out Cup matches for Reading, and following his departure, the rot set in as the Racers were left with just two top men and a selection of middle-order riders.

Ashley Pullen joined Reading on a full-time basis from Rye House and tried very hard, achieving a 4-point average. However, before the end of the season, young Ashley was off, back into the National League, joining his hometown club, Oxford. Twenty-three-year-old Denny Pyeatt came from California, and the previous year had finished fifth in the USA National Championships, later visiting Australia and receiving coaching from former England international Nigel Boocock. Denny, a close friend of team-mate Bobby Schwartz, put in a steady year, somewhat in the Bernie Leigh mould, battling away for those all-important points. Bernie himself though, struggled a little with machine troubles and a niggling knee injury, but by and large, was as dependable as ever.

Pole Andrzej Huszcza was brought in, but he could only manage 10 points from the five matches he appeared in. Several other riders were used by the Racers, especially towards the end of the season, and these included German duo Peter Wurterle and Max Schollhorn, but a special rider who returned for just five meetings was the great Swede Anders Michanek. Super 'Mich' did enough to show that the old magic was still there, scoring 34 points and a paid maximum from his handful of appearances. Despite their torrid league season, the Racers did well in reaching the semi-final of the Knock Out Cup, only to narrowly lose to Birmingham, 91-101 on aggregate. Prior to that, the season had kicked off with a brand new League Cup competition. Reading found themselves in Group B (which was basically the southern section) and they fared well, finishing second to King's Lynn and only just missing out on a place in the final.

The World Team Cup UK round was staged at Smallmead in May, and England came out on top with 36 points, ahead of USA (32), Australia (20) and New Zealand (8). Tony Briggs scored 4 points for the Kiwis, meanwhile Bobby Schwartz recorded 8 points for the USA. This was the fifth time that Smallmead had staged the prestigious World Team Cup meeting. An England *v.* Denmark Test Match was also staged at Smallmead on 22 June. England won the match 58-50, with the late and great Kenny Carter leading the Lions' scoring on 14 points. There was some joy in the Reading camp, however, as Bobby Schwartz became a World Champion in 1981, partnering Bruce Penhall in the World Pairs title in Poland. On 28 September, following a 49-47 victory over Birmingham, some quad races took place at Smallmead, although the bikes used were three-wheeler ATCs. Bruce Penhall, who had recently become World Champion, made an appearance on the unusual machines, taking a win and a couple of second places.

Belle Vue took their fourth British League title in 1982, with Reading only managing ninth position out of the fifteen teams. Flamboyant American Bobby Schwartz led the Racers' scoring, with 294 points from his twenty-seven league and Knock Out Cup matches. Bobby was backed by super Swede Jan Andersson and fellow Americans Steve Gresham and Denny Pyeatt. Tim Hunt arrived in the Reading camp via Ipswich, and was joined by John Grahame, brother of Alan and Andy. Czech Champion Jiri Stancl made a return to the Racers, but sadly, it was a fond farewell to a few familiar faces. 'Mr Reading Speedway' of the 1970s, Bernie Leigh, had decided to retire. Also moving on was team manager Mick Bell, along with meeting presenter Roger Ware. Timekeeper

John Homer also left to become a referee, and was replaced by Roger Nettlefold. Roger went on to become one of speedway's leading timekeepers, officiating at big meetings and he is still an integral part of the Smallmead set-up today. Two other new faces in 1982 were Barrie Matthews as announcer and John Smith as team manager. Later in the year, Ross Williams came along as a roving commentator, in order to increase the fans' entertainment.

Going into the season, the track record stood at 59.7 seconds for the 307-metre circuit, and was held by the 'Main Dane' Hans Nielsen. Media coverage was good in 1982, with Radio 210 helping out with some sponsorship, plus regular live reports from meetings at Smallmead. Meanwhile, the *Reading Evening Post* organized a rider of the month competition. The Racers also had a lottery running in conjunction with Wokingham Town Football Club. Dave Wright of the *Evening Post* was writing in the match programme of the time, under the banner of 'Wright's View'. Meetings were filmed by KM Videos, and spectators could view the action in the bars afterwards.

The season had started at Smallmead with a challenge match against Poole, when Jan Andersson was in fine form, scoring 14 points. Jan's only defeat came at the hands of flying American Scott Autrey. However, it wasn't a good start for the Racers as they went down by 37 points to 41. Rubbing salt in the wound was ex-Racer John Davis, who top scored for the Pirates with 10 points. Tony Briggs was a spectator at the meeting, and was making steady progress after his horrific injuries of the previous year. On 5 April, Ipswich came to Reading and left with a 40-38 victory in the bag, but rather interestingly, riding at number six for the Witches was Jeremy Doncaster. 'Donkey' only scored one point that night, but it was enough to tip the meeting in favour of Ipswich. However, he certainly showed no sign of the major role he was later to play in the Racers' golden years! Promoters Bill Dore and Frank Higley praised track maintenance man Dougie Harris in the programme of 17 May for the excellent way in which he prepared the track. Also in May, the first auditions were held at the Caversham Dance Centre for the Racers cheerleaders.

Tragedy struck the Racers on Friday 16 July, when young American Denny Pyeatt crashed into a lamp standard at Hackney, in heat nine of a British League match. Early the following morning at Hackney Hospital, Denny sadly died without regaining consciousness after sustaining serious head injuries. Denny

*Christchurch*
*Christchurch Road*
*Reading*

**READING**

# Denny Pyeatt

(Reading Races and United States of America)

*Died 17th July 1982*

*Memorial Service*
*29th July 1982*

*Denny Pyeatt's memorial service card.*

*Reading 1982. From left to right, back row: Bobby Schwartz, Denny Pyeatt, Jiri Stancl, John Smith (team manager), Steve Gresham, Tim Hunt, John Grahame. Front row: club mascot, Jan Andersson (on bike).*

was badly missed by everyone, but nobody was more upset than his girlfriend Hazel Sillence and his close buddy Bobby Schwartz. A memorial service was held at Christchurch Church, Whitley Wood, Reading on 29 July. On 2 August, the Denny Pyeatt Memorial meeting was staged at Smallmead, when a Jan Andersson Select defeated John Davis' team by 47 points 30. A second meeting followed, when a Bobby Schwartz team was defeated 35-43 by a Bruce Penhall Select. The results however, were not important, for it was a tribute to the life of young Denny and a 'Who's Who of Speedway' turned out in force to pay their respects. Among the gathered stars were Hans Nielsen, Phil Crump, Scott Autrey, Malcolm Simmons, Tommy Knudsen, Lance King, Billy Sanders and, of course, the team captains already mentioned.

On to brighter things in the summer of 1982, as the Reading Racers cheerleaders made their first appearance. Their choreographer was Monica Cleaver and the young ladies included Zoe Gardiner, Josephine Hayward, Sarah Gardiner, Paula Anderson, Alison Cooke, Rachel Kemsley, Joanna Kay, Gail Fisher, Tracey Kay and Mandy Clarke. In August, the Racers met local rivals Swindon in the Sarjents Tools-sponsored Silver Spanner Trophy. The Racers won at Swindon, but the Robins took the victory parade at Smallmead; however, it was Reading who took the honours on aggregate. On 27 September, Smallmead played host to the second round of the Inter-Nations four-team tournament. This resulted in a victory for the USA, who scored 46 points. Second place went to England (29 pts), who were closely followed by Denmark (23), while somewhat adrift were Australia on 10 points. Reading's Bobby Schwartz scored

11 points for the Americans, with his only defeat coming in heat eighteen at the hands of England's Kenny Carter. Tim Hunt was reserve for England and he recorded 3 points from his two starts.

Reading's Jiri Stancl won the prestigious Czech Golden Helmet, and on 11 October the Racers defeated Czech touring side Ruda Hvezda 48-30 at Smallmead. Top man for the tourists was the same Jiri Stancl with 11 points, proving he hadn't forgotten the quickest way around Smallmead. The last home meeting of the season was a Southern Cup match against Eastbourne, with the Racers coming out on top by 43 points to 35. The second half included grass-track style 1000cc sidecar outfits, and among those competing were Pete Head, Dick Packham, Roger Cant and Norman Hames. In summary, it was a poor season for the Racers, with only two genuine heat-leaders in Jan Andersson and Bobby Schwartz, both of whom received very little support. It was a season of struggle for Steve Gresham, who battled on gamely, despite thigh and back injuries, but his scoring was well below the expected mark. Meanwhile, poor Denny Pyeatt was starting to make real progress when tragedy struck.

Tim Hunt found the going tough and could only muster 94 points from his 28 league and Knock Out Cup matches. Jiri Stancl was in and out of the side, depending on his trips to and from Czechoslovakia, and a 5-point average was a poor reflection on his true ability. Young John Grahame tried hard, but understandably found it difficult against the best riders in the world, week in, week out. Dave Trownson, the number one at National League Edinburgh, appeared in thirteen matches for the Racers and never let the side down, but several others came and went without pulling up any trees, including Uno Johansson, Colin Ackroyd, Derek Harrison and Brett Saunders.

Reading went out of the Knock Out Cup at the first hurdle, hammered on aggregate by Belle Vue. The Racers fared little better in the southern group of the League Cup, winning just six of their fourteen matches, to finish sixth out of the eight teams. Two Racers made it to the World Final in Los Angeles, with Jan Andersson scoring 8 points, while Jiri Stancl collected 7. But the season was overshadowed by the death of Denny Pyeatt, following that horror smash at Hackney on 16 July.

1983 brought the return to Smallmead of Bob Radford, as team manager and press officer. Meanwhile, Brian Talbot became meeting co-ordinator and deputy team manager, with the post of junior team manager going to Martin Hudson. One of the early matches at Smallmead featured a visit from Swedish side Getingarna. The Racers only just managed to win the meeting 40-38, and top man for the visitors was old friend Anders Michanek, with 8 points. Bob Radford's boys did well with fourth spot in the British League, while also reaching the semi-final of the Knock Out Cup, before losing to eventual double-winners Cradley Heath. Meanwhile, in the southern group of the League Cup, Reading finished third, and just missed out on a semi-final place.

Mitch Shirra, who was signed from Coventry, became the Racers' new number one, rattling up 329 points from his 33 league and Knock Out Cup matches, and recording 8 maximums along the way. Mitch had a brilliant year, also reaching the World Final in Norden, where he scored 7 points. The diminutive Shirra was well backed up by Racers stalwarts Jan Andersson and Bobby Schwartz, and it was easy to see the difference that having three top-end men instead of two made. Jan plundered 310 points, and Bobby

*Glyn Taylor.*

scored 279, as all three heat-leaders ended the campaign with averages in excess of 9 points per match.

Bob Radford also introduced a new super Swede in Pierre Brannefors, who finished his first full season with an average in excess of 7. Pierre had ridden for King's Lynn in 1981, but had struggled in the ten league and Knock Out Cup matches he rode, and in fact only averaged 3.60 for the Stars, so his 1983 return was a tremendous boost for the Racers. Pierre's father Bengt, a former rider, had actually been one of the reserves for the 1966 World Final. Several riders were tried during the year, but none was a particular success. New Dane Peter Glanz arrived on the Smallmead scene, but despite plenty of promise, a 3.82 average was disappointing. Czech Stanislav Urban also showed some good signs, but never made it and ended up with an average of under 3 from his 23 matches.

Finn Jensen was brought in from Leicester, but failed to score from two matches. Having qualified for the Overseas Final, Glyn Taylor was also given a spin, but again this was a move that didn't work out, either for the Racers or the rider. John Grahame battled on and found it hard to say the least, scoring just 17 points in 14 meetings. Tim Hunt also found it a struggle, and near the end of the season he opted for a change of track and linked up with local rivals Swindon on loan. So, to sum up the season, with three good heat-leaders plus Pierre Brannefors, the Racers were nearly there, but just needed a little more strength in depth.

The Reading Rivets junior team saw plenty of action throughout the season and included amongst their ranks were Chris Chaplin (son of vintage speedway historian John), Michael Warren, Chris Hunt, Graham Andrews, Andy Passey, Brian Bain, Mike Bacon, Ian Dowie and two grass-track aces in Mark Edwards and Phil Ranson. During the season, the Racers 400 Club was launched, in order to provide funds for the running of the Rivets junior team. This was organized by Alan Chandler and Tim Sugar. Yes, that man Tim Sugar appeared behind the scenes again, before, in later years, being thrust into the limelight.

The World Team Cup UK Round made a welcome return to Smallmead, and this resulted in a victory for the USA with 38 points. England were runners-up (scoring 27), followed by New Zealand (20) and Australia (11). The meeting included two Racers, with Mitch Shirra scoring 8 points for the Kiwis, while Bobby Schwartz grabbed 7 for the victorious Americans. Making a return for the meeting was John Homer as judge/timekeeper, and John Ballard's name first appeared in the programme, making a one-off appearance as machine examiner. John, of course, took over the job full-time in 1985 and still does it to this day! Fittingly, on American Independence Day (4 July), the Denny Pyeatt Memorial was staged at Smallmead. The event featured a four-team tournament and was won by the Boogaloos with 37 points, ahead of the Vikings (28), the Bulldogs (24) and the Anzacs (19). In the second-half individual final, Shawn Moran retained the Denny Pyeatt Memorial Shield, which he had won the previous year.

In the Smallmead match programme for 5 September, 'Bob Radford's Race Talk' page quotes 'Tonight we welcome Cradley Heath, hailed in many quarters as the finest side ever to compete in the British League.' The Heathens' team of superstars proved that comment to be spot on, as they beat the Racers 43-35. The six-man Cradley team scored solidly throughout, as follows: Simon Wigg (9); Erik Gundersen (8); Phil Collins (7); Peter Ravn (7); Simon Cross (7) and Alan Grahame (5). The only Racer to withstand the onslaught was Bobby Schwartz, who only suffered defeat once at the hands of Simon Wigg. Later that same month, Cradley returned for the Knock Out Cup semi-final, and won even more handsomely, by 46 points to 32! On 26 September, 'Boogaloo' Bobby Schwartz won the Battle of Britain Trophy, presented by RAFA (Royal Air Force Association). This is an award that still gets presented at Smallmead on the night of the annual RAFA collection.

On 4 October, Smallmead hosted the Marcus Williams Benefit meeting, in aid of the young rider who was badly injured in the early part of the season. This saw the Racers record 49 points to win a three-team tournament, while an All-Stars Select side was second on 37 points, with Exeter third on 21 points. The second half of the meeting featured another demonstration of 1000cc grass-track style sidecar racing. The Smallmead season ended on 10 October, with the Racers defeating Wimbledon 44-34 in what was the twenty-ninth home fixture of the year. Reading old boy Dave Jessup top scored for the Dons with 10 points. Also making an appearance for the Dons at number six was future World Long Track Champion Kelvin Tatum, who scored 4 points. It wasn't all speedway action at Smallmead in 1983, for a thirty-race moto-cross meeting took place on 30 October, with one of the competitors being Tony Mattingly, the son of former Glasgow rider Maury, who was later to try speedway at Exeter.

The 1984 season started with a 45-33 win over local rivals Swindon in a challenge match, and this was achieved without American star Bobby Schwartz, who had moved on to Eastbourne. Following his win down under during our winter, new Kiwi Champion Mitch Shirra took Reading's number one race jacket, and was backed up by Swedes Jan Andersson and Pierre Brannefors. Dane Peter Glanz was back for a second year, along with new signing from Swindon, the 'Mad Wellie' Malcolm Holloway. Tim Hunt was recalled, after his short loan spell at Swindon, and Barry Thomas agreed to be the Racers' number eight for the year.

A certain young Swede by the name of Per Jonsson was also expected to sign for Reading. However, the major headline in 1984, as far as the Racers were concerned, was that the Speedway Control Board had refused Per permission to ride, doubting that he would achieve a 6-point average. The 6-point figure was required in order for any foreign rider to obtain a permit to race in Britain, and so it was that the Department of

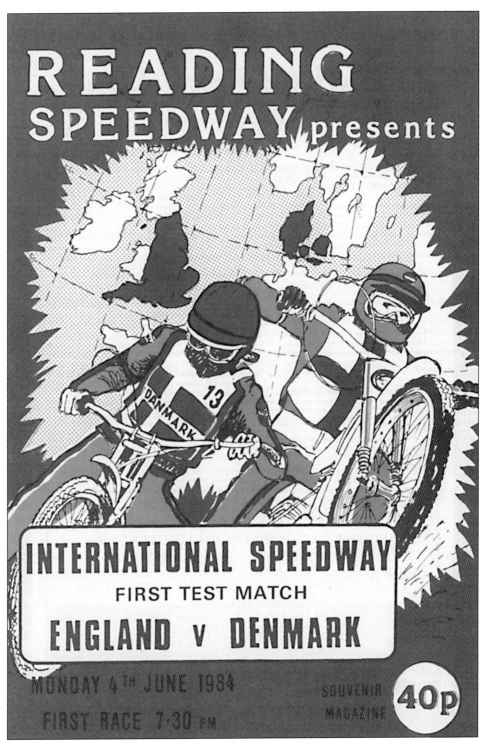

*England v. Denmark programme, 1984.*

Employment turned down Per's application for a work permit! This was in spite of the fact that the BSPA and the Speedway Riders Association had agreed to the teenager joining Reading.

In the programme for the meeting between the Racers and a Shawn Moran Select on 26 March, the then team manager Bob Radford, stated in his 'Racertalk' column, 'So if there is no work permit for Per Jonsson by next Monday, I feel I must tender my resignation as Reading team boss.' This was a bold statement indeed, but it all ended happily after a strong case was put forward in Per's defence by Bob Radford and former legends of the track, Anders Michanek and Torbjorn Harrysson. Per finally lined up for the Racers to face Poole the following week in a Southern Cup match, scoring 8 points. It was a great start for Per and included a race win in heat five, ahead of Pierre Brannefors and former World Champion Michael Lee, the Poole skipper.

Bob Radford did, however, step down as team manager later in the season, due to a combination of poor health and the need to concentrate on his day job. On 4 June, Reading hosted the first match in a four-round Test series with England taking on Denmark. The sparkling match ended in a 54-54 draw, with former Racers Dave Jessup (11 points) and John Davis (8) riding well for England. The Reading Rivets junior side also saw league action in 1984, with Laurie Starke joining the management team. The Rivets took part in two leagues (British Junior League and Wessex Junior League) and the riders included Andy Passey, Trevor Williams, Dave Johnson and Michael Warren.

In July, the Geoff Curtis Memorial meeting took place, and it was a Racers one-two, with Mitch Shirra notching a 15-point maximum, ahead of Jan Andersson, who scored 13. On 6 August, Reading defeated Oxford 41-37 and in the second half, the grass-track sidecar outfits took their place on the track. Among those competing were Ray Blackall and Martin Coxhead, who were later to appear at Smallmead in the 1990s when full-blown sidecar meetings were staged.

Later on in August, following the thrashing of King's Lynn (50-28), Reading's Jan Andersson took on Hans Nielsen for the Golden Helmet. Hans took the first heat in the very fast time of 60.4 seconds, not far outside Shawn Moran's track record, which had stood since June 1982. Jan won the second leg, but Nielsen wasn't to be denied as he took the decider. Incidentally, a young man who was riding for King's Lynn that night was future Racer Ray Morton.

On Saturday 1 September, Smallmead played host to the British Masters Stadium Cross Championship, which was duly won by world moto-cross star Dave Thorpe. Cradley rider Erik Gundersen became World Champion in the Gothenburg staged final, but in fifth spot was Racers' own Mitch Shirra with 10 points. Mitch had more success when he joined Tim Hunt to take second place for the Racers, behind World Pairs Champions Peter Collins and Chris Morton (representing Belle Vue) in the British Open Pairs Championship at Wolverhampton. Another winner in 1984, was Super Swede Jan Andersson, who won the annual Battle of Britain Trophy at Smallmead.

Backing promoters Bill Dore and Pat Bliss in 1984 was their very able body of officials in the shape of Dick Bailey (clerk of the course), Roger Nettlefold (timekeeper), Barrie Matthews (presenter), Alan Bowler (starting marshall), Tim Fox (machine examiner), Dougie Harris (track manager) and meeting co-ordinator Brian Talbot, who also designed the match-day programme cover. Photographs for the programme were supplied by the legendary Alf Weedon (established 1947), who of course has done this from the 1970s right up to the present day.

It was another good season for the Racers, as they finished the league campaign in fourth spot. In the League Cup, Reading topped the nine-team southern section to progress into the semi-final, only to lose out to Cradley Heath by an aggregate score of 68-88. It was also that same Cradley team that dumped the Racers out of the Knock Out Cup at the first hurdle! On the team front, Jan Andersson had a superb season, leading the way with 334 points for a British League and Knock Out Cup average of 10.24, scoring eight full maximums along the way. Mitch Shirra was slightly down on his scoring power of the previous season, hampered by an injury to his neck, but still averaged over 9. New Swede Per Jonsson proved he was well worth his work permit, as he rattled up 179 points for a 6.31 average. The remaining Racers all finished with averages of around the 5-point mark, so despite this, fourth place in the league was a notable achievement.

Tim Hunt had a better year and actually put a point on his average, but his aggressive style of riding was not always well received by his opponents or his team-mates, for Tim had a falling out with Jan Andersson, which resulted in a change to the Racers' team pairings. Pierre Brannefors had a poor season, seldom showing the form of 1983, and his final average of 5.10 would obviously create problems in trying to obtain a work permit for the following year. This was rather ironic, following the problems of fellow Swede Per Jonsson at the start of the season! Malcolm Holloway was a good scorer at Smallmead, but found the points hard to come by on his travels. He was, however, a good man to have around the pits with his enthusiasm and sense of humour. Inconsistent was a good word to describe Peter Glanz, as the Dane struggled to find any sort of form, but a few good meetings suggested that he might be worth persevering with.

1985 wasn't a good season for the Racers, as they finished ninth in an eleven-team league. However, it was good to see former star John Davis return to the fold, via Wimbledon. On the other hand, Kiwi ace Mitch Shirra was unable to start the season, due to a broken thigh sustained while racing down under at Western Springs, Auckland in December 1984. Cool Swede Jan Andersson, the 'Mr Reading Speedway' of the 1980s, was back for another stint and he again led by example. The other Swede, Per Jonsson, was also back, but only after another battle to obtain a work permit. This time, the Department of Employment would not issue a work permit to any foreigners with an average of under 8 points until all the British riders had found a team place for the season!

Tim Hunt was retained, along with Malcolm Holloway, while young Mark Chessell was given his chance during the League Cup campaign, later to be replaced by Peter Glanz. A rider from National League Canterbury appeared at Smallmead several times during 1985, and was embarking on a love affair that would see his name become a part of Racers folklore, along with the likes of Anders Michanek, Bernie Leigh and Jan Andersson. His name was, of course, David Mullett and he is still at Smallmead today, piling up the points and appearances.

*Jan Andersson chases Erik Gundersen.*

Another rider with National League links at Arena-Essex, who also made several appearances for the Racers, was Neil Middleditch. It was a great year for Neil, as he won the National League Riders' Championship at Coventry in August. Not unexpectedly, Mitch Shirra struggled upon his return to the saddle, and it was a season-long battle for the plucky rider to rediscover his best form. He did, however, partner Ivan Mauger to fourth place in the World Pairs Final in Poland and, by the end of the year, was almost back to his best. He also partnered John Davis in the British Open Pairs Championship at Wolverhampton, as the Racers took the runners-up spot behind Chris Morton and Peter Collins of Belle Vue. Mitch did actually win a pairs event in 1985, as he and Malcolm Simmons took the Denny Pyeatt Memorial Pairs title at Smallmead in August.

Jan Andersson was top man again, scoring 213 points for another 9-plus average. Jan was tremendously loyal to the Racers and one of the finest riders ever to grace the Smallmead circuit. John Davis also achieved a 9-point average and obviously enjoyed being back with Reading, and the highlight of his year must have been second place in the British Final at Coventry, behind the late Kenny Carter. John's season was curtailed by a shoulder injury, and as a result, he only rode in fifteen of the Racers' league and Knock Out Cup matches. Per Jonsson won the European Under-21 Championship in Abensberg, West Germany, but his form for Reading showed only a slight improvement on the previous year. As the season ended, Per actually put in a transfer request and Reading slapped a £20,000 fee on his head for any would-be takers.

Peter Glanz, once he had forced his way back into the side, showed better form, particularly at Smallmead. Glanz did have a spell out though, in late September/early October, with torn ligaments. 'Mad Wellie' Malcolm Holloway, suffered a wrist injury and struggled badly as a result, gleaning only 51 points from his twenty-two matches. Tim Hunt was also injured in September, and missed the rest of the season with multiple injuries sustained in a crash at Sheffield. Several other riders were used in an effort to plug the injury gaps, including Norwegian Einar Kyllingstad, Aussie Mark Fiora and another National League boy, David Blackburn of Milton Keynes. So, ninth in the British League and eighth in the League Cup, but at least the Racers had a decent Knock Out Cup run, reaching the semi-final, before going down on aggregate to local rivals Oxford. Speaking of Oxford, the Smallmead track record was broken for the first time in three years on 24 June, as top Cheetah Hans Nielsen stormed to a new best time of 59.2 seconds.

In the British Junior League, the Rivets finished bottom of the pile, as King's Lynn took the title. Just for the record, the junior side of 1985 featured Stuart Williams, David Main, Trevor Williams, Phil Ranson, Alan Wilson, Shaun Whiting and Dave Johnson. The aforementioned Stuart Williams (from Yate, near Bristol) also rode for Exeter, but had much more success on the West Country grass-track circuits. David Main from Swindon was the son of former grass-tracker Dave Main, while Phil Ranson went on to appear in the Conference League in the 1990s, and also enjoyed success on the grass. Others racing in the junior league of 1985 that present-day fans will undoubtedly have seen in action included Paul Fry, Wayne Broadhurst and Ray Morton.

However, back to the Racers and the problems of their season. On 6 May, Wolverhampton arrived for a League Cup match, but with Reading leading 24-14, the visiting riders walked out and their supporters decided to sit on the track in protest about the conditions. The meeting was abandoned and was eventually ordered to be re-run, a decision that was not well received by the Reading promotion. When the match was finally re-staged, on 17 September, Reading ran out winners by 46 points to 32, with Bill Dore allowing the supporters to gain free entry. There was more controversy on 28 October, when Cradley Heath were due to visit Smallmead for a league match, only for the Heathens to race in a local Dudley/Wolves Trophy match at Wolverhampton instead. The Racers management acted quickly to arrange an alternative meeting for the fans, and so a Geoff Curtis Memorial Pairs event took place, with the winners being Peter Glanz and Neil Middleditch. The original match against Cradley Heath was never actually staged, as no other suitable date could be found so late in the season.

Aside from the controversy, the season was blighted by rain and lots of it! A total of eight meetings were rained off and many more were rain-affected. In the end, the number of spectators coming through the turnstiles suffered as a result. Other events saw Dave Moss become the new starting marshall, while Jeff Sealey became track manager and John Ballard took over the job as machine examiner. As well as greyhound racing, Smallmead staged afghan racing and American football, with the local Thames Valley Chargers playing against such teams as the Heathrow Jets, Bournemouth Broncos and Portsmouth Warriors.

The 1986 season started with little change on the rider front. Tim Hunt had retired, with youngster Gary Tagg coming into the side at reserve, meanwhile off the track, Bob Radford returned to the club as meeting announcer. The junior team had a sponsor and became known as the 210 Rivets (after the local radio station) and the side had two new faces in the shape of Billy Pinder and new Racers reserve Gary Tagg. Malcolm Holloway started the season, but soon went out of the Racers line-up with a leg injury, giving an extended run to Canterbury's David Mullett.

On 19 May, Reading took on the mighty Belle Vue Aces and thrashed them 54-24, with former World Champion Peter Collins a shadow of his former self at Smallmead, scoring just 2 points. In the programme for that meeting, Tim Sugar started a new series with part one of 'Eighteen years of Reading Speedway'. Edna Chandler was a vital part of the back-room staff, keeping a watchful eye on the '400 Club', a weekly competition that was run to raise funds. Former team manager John Smith was back in 1986, looking after the advertising side of things.

In July, Mitch Shirra qualified for his third World Final, while Jan Andersson qualified as reserve for the big night in Poland. The final proved a big disappointment for Mitch though, as he collected just a single point. On 4 August, a sidecar demonstration took place after the Racers had entertained Bradford, and featured top drivers Paul Pinfold, Pete Drakeford and Rob Henderson. In September, John Davis found himself sidelined after Wimbledon had demanded that Reading pay up the outstanding balance of his 1985 transfer fee. The situation dragged on, so Reading swooped to sign another Swede, Tony Olsson, in order to plug the gap in the side. Recommended by Jan Andersson, Olsson rode for Bysarna in the Swedish league and was runner-up in the European Under-21 Championship. Tony soon proved his worth, as on 13 October he recorded a paid maximum in an international challenge match, when the Racers defeated Czechoslovakia 46-32.

In the final meeting of the season, Jan Andersson teamed up with David Mullett to win the Denny Pyeatt Memorial Pairs, while in the second half Gary Tagg won the JMS All-Stars-sponsored Geoff Curtis Memorial Junior Championship. The Racers had to settle for seventh place in the league and eighth spot in the League Cup, while in the Knock Out Cup they were beaten by Cradley Heath at the quarter-final stage. Super Swede Jan Andersson was, once again, the model of consistency, plundering another 231 points for a 9.63 average. Jan qualified for the British League Riders' Championship at Belle Vue, and in a star-studded field, he rode brilliantly to score 11 points for a place in the four-man run-off for second position. Unfortunately, Jan was beaten by both Erik Gundersen and Shawn Moran, but he did finish ahead of Chris Morton to claim the overall fourth spot in the meeting.

John Davis rode in only eleven league and Knock Out Cup matches, having missed several meetings through injury, before being sidelined over his transfer from Wimbledon. Even so, 'JD' still finished second in the Racers' averages on 8.74. The diminutive Mitch Shirra had to have an operation to remove the plate from his previously injured thigh, and this undoubtedly affected his form as he saw his average dip below the 8-point mark. Despite the transfer talk at the end of the previous season, Per Jonsson did return for his third season as a Racer and although his overall form had improved, a 6.76 league and Knock Out Cup average was not quite the hoped-for return. Per did become Swedish Champion though, and everyone knew that the potential was still there. In fact, Per was unable to finish the season at Smallmead, due to a stint of national service in the Swedish Army.

Malcolm Holloway missed a large chunk of the season through injury, but when he came back, he scored over twice as many points as he had managed the season before. Dane Peter Glanz had a steadier year, recording 131 points, and it was certainly a step in the right direction. Young Gary Tagg had what can only be described as a nightmare, and so too did Billy Pinder, who also had a run in the team, but both youngsters suffered from a lack of confidence. However, a bright spot on the horizon was the form of David Mullett, who did very well when brought into the Racers team and was sure of a long association with the Berkshire track.

Off-track changes in 1987 saw the former West Ham, Oxford and Swindon rider Brian Leonard join the promotional team of Pat Bliss and Bill Dore, with Leonard also taking over the team manager's duties from Bill Dore. Meanwhile, Swindon's Clive Fisher arrived to do the radio microphone work. John Davis was back on track for the Racers, but in order to keep the side within the 45-point limit permitted by the authorities, Mitch Shirra had moved down the road to Swindon. Per Jonsson was back for a fourth term, and the Swedish Champion was given a heat-leader's berth for the first time. Another Swede and late season signing in 1986, Tony Olsson, kept his place in the Racers septet and also returning, as usual, was the third Swede in the line-up, the ever-reliable Jan Andersson. The team was completed by another three men who had also worn the famous 'Winged Wheel' the year before, namely Malcolm Holloway, Peter Glanz and Gary Tagg.

The Racers' theme tune for 1987 became the Bangles hit 'Manic Monday', replacing the old favourite 'Monday Monday' by the Mamas and the Papas. However, when Dave Stallworthy became the announcer in later years, many supporters asked him to re-introduce the Mamas and the Papas tune as the parade music, and this he eventually did in 1996, and it is now very much part of the history of Reading speedway. The Reading Rivets were still in junior league action, with several new names appearing in the side managed by Laurie Starke. Among the riders used in 1987 were Dean Walker, Rodney Payne, Nick Bates, Troy Smith and Bruce Richards. Bruce was, in fact, the son of the spares van salesman and former grass-track racer Max Richards.

On 12 July, Smallmead hosted the British Open Pairs Championship, with the Racers pair of Jan Andersson and Per Jonsson surprisingly failing to progress to the second round of the meeting, which was eventually won by Oxford's Hans Nielsen and Andy Grahame. In the first-ever two-day World Final, staged in Amsterdam, Reading were represented by Per Jonsson, and he rode brilliantly to finish equal fourth overall (with his great buddy Jimmy Nilsen), scoring a total of 22 points. Meanwhile, Racers old boy Mitch Shirra finished ninth on 12 points, the World Crown going, of course, to the 'Main Dane' Hans Nielsen. In a season that was again affected by rain, although not as badly as the previous year, the Racers consolidated their mid-table league position, again finishing seventh. They fared slightly better in the League Cup, finishing one place better in sixth spot. Meanwhile, in the Knock Out Cup, the Racers overcame their local rivals from just down the M4, Swindon, before going out to Coventry in the semi-final.

The form of Per Jonsson was a revelation, as the Swede finally lived up to all his expectations to achieve an average of 9.45 from his 22 league and Knock Out Cup meetings. As a rider, Per was nothing short of breathtaking on a bike, being a super and stylish entertainer. His performance in the World Final was the icing on the cake and was a benchmark for the future. By the end of the season, Per had lowered the Smallmead track record to 58.1 seconds, a feat he achieved in the league match against Coventry on 12 October. A slight dip in Jan Andersson's average could be attributed to a series of bike problems, the like of which the phlegmatic Swede had never before experienced. Even so, Jan still piled in another 229 points, exactly the same number as Jonsson, but from eleven more rides for an average of 8.69. Jan again did well in the end-of-season British League Riders' Championship at Belle Vue, scoring 10 points to finish in equal sixth position with Richard Knight of King's Lynn.

The Racers' other Swede, Tony Olsson, did very well in his first full season of racing over here, proving himself to be an excellent team-man, and despite several crashes, he always came back for more. John Davis' season got off to a bad start before it had even begun, when he injured a leg while riding in West Germany. 'JD' probably returned to the saddle sooner than he should have and aggravated his injury, thereby missing several key fixtures. 'JD', in fact, only ended up riding in 14 out of the Racers' 26 league and Knock Out Cup fixtures, and would surely have achieved more than his 6.53 average had he steered clear of injury. Young Gary Tagg continued to find the going tough, but kept at it through thick and thin, proving, if nothing else, that he was a gutsy character. Rodney Payne was given a run in the team, but as with Tagg, he found the points hard to come by. Both Peter Glanz and Malcolm Holloway had a much better

time of it, with the Dane pushing his average above 6 in an ever-present campaign. In terms of points scored, 'Wellie' had his best Racers season since 1984, and also managed to finish with an average in excess of 6. A number of guests were used during the year, along with some of the National League boys, most notably David Mullett, Miles Evans, Gary O'Hare and Nigel Crabtree.

The 1988 campaign saw Mitch Shirra come back to form a powerful spearhead with the super Swedes Per Jonsson, Jan Andersson and Tony Olsson. A strong-looking Racers side was completed by Malcolm Holloway, Rodney Payne and David Mullett, who joined the team full-time after his

*Jan Andersson.*

previous appearances while attached to National League Canterbury. The Smallmead season opened with a 57-33 victory over Swedish touring side Getingarna. What was interesting about this meeting was that the tourists side included a youngster by the name of Tony Rickardsson, who failed to score a point! Who would have thought he would go on and follow in the wheel tracks of Swedish greats Ove Fundin, Bjorn Knutsson, Anders Michanek and Per Jonsson as a World Champion?

1988 saw the Diamond Jubilee celebrations of British Speedway, which involved a Test Series featuring England, Sweden, USA and Denmark. The all-conquering Danes were the overall winners, but the man of the series was undoubtedly Per Jonsson, who rattled up scores of 12, 13 and 17 respectively, in his three matches for Sweden against Denmark (at Wolverhampton), against USA (at Swindon) and against England (at Reading). The Sweden *v.* England meeting at Smallmead took place on 25 April, with England winning 58-32. Among the England scorers was future Racer Jeremy Doncaster with 4 points. For Sweden, Tony Olsson scored 6 points, but the brilliant 17 points recorded by Per Jonsson proved that he had arrived on the world circuit.

The Denny Pyeatt Memorial meeting took place at Smallmead on 9 May, and was won by Shawn Moran with a 15-point maximum. Jan Andersson enjoyed a richly deserved benefit year and although his Testimonial meeting was originally rained off on 4 July, it did go ahead on 24 July, when an Oxford & Swindon Select beat the Jan Andersson Select 44-40. Per Jonsson won the second-half Superstar Knockout, but it was good to see some of the Racers greats back on track in a Golden Oldies race, with Anders Michanek winning ahead of Martin Ashby, Bernie Leigh and Mick Bell. Talking of golden oldies, on Sunday 23 October the National Vintage Speedway Championships, organized by the Vintage MCC, were staged at Smallmead. Bill Barley, an all-round motorcycle rider, who had raced in scrambles and grass-track, won the pre-war class. The post-war class was won by former 1960s Wimbledon rider Steve Chilman. This meeting was a special one for Dave Stallworthy, as he took the microphone for the first time at Smallmead. Dave was subsequently invited to join Bob Radford at race control the following evening for a challenge match between Jan's Swedes and Malc's Mixtures, and the rest, as they say, is history!

Despite a run of wins at the start of the season, Reading could only finish fifth in a league won by a strong Coventry side, managed by former Racers team boss and rider Mick Bell. In the Knock Out Cup, the Racers went out to the same powerhouse Coventry team at the quarter-final stage, losing 86-94 on aggregate. Reading, represented by Jan Andersson and Per Jonsson, finished third in the British Open Pairs Championship, which was held at Smallmead on 17 July. Per and Jan also represented the Racers in the British League Riders' Championship, the first to be staged at the original Belle Vue track on Kirkmanshulme Lane, with both recording 5 points. The Rivets junior side did well to reach the final of the Knock Out Cup, before losing 77-102 to Cradley Heath on aggregate.

Proving he had really arrived, Per Jonsson won the Champions Cup at Krsko, Yugoslavia, with 14 points, ahead of Gerd Riss and Zoltan Adorjan. The Champions Cup brought together all the national Champions for a big individual event, so this really was a prestigious win for Per. The Super Swede also made it to the World Final in

Vojens, Denmark, where he did well to finish fifth with 9 points, following a somewhat controversial exclusion in his first race after a clash with Hans Nielsen. Per also scored 9 points in the World Team Cup, as Sweden finished in third spot – a position secured by Per after he had beaten England's Kelvin Tatum in a run-off. In the World Pairs Final at Bradford's Odsal Stadium, Per recorded 12 points as Sweden finished fifth. One place above the Swedes were New Zealand, for whom Racer Mitch Shirra plundered a mammoth 24 points.

On the domestic front, Per was a bit 'in and out' and this was substantiated by his final league and Knock Out Cup average of 8.98, a drop of around half a point on his 1987 figure. Even so, he still had a superb year and was top man for the Racers. Backing Per all the way was the consistent Jan Andersson, who piled up another 371 points in the cause of the 'Winged Wheel'. In fact, Jan's final average of 8.93 was only a fraction behind that of his Swedish team-mate. Jan enjoyed a successful Testimonial year, but his end-of-season form was hampered by a broken collarbone sustained while jet-skiing! Had that not happened, he may well have finished above Per in the Racers' averages. Prior to the start of the season, Jan had maintained his dominance of the indoor ice events, taking the Ice International Individual at Telford in February with a 15-point maximum. This was a title that Jan had previously won at Telford in November 1986, as well as winning the Yugo Classic at Murrayfield in February 1987.

Reading's third Swede Tony Olsson saw his average dip, due to a succession of niggling bike problems, but even so, he had a good year and scored 260 points, still looking like a great one for the future. Mitch Shirra, back after a tremendous year on loan at Swindon where he averaged over 9.5 points, saw his form drop back by well over a point a match. Mitch still scored 359 points for a solid 8.20 average though, and was a good man to have around. Malcolm Holloway had a steady year in the backbone of the side, and David Mullett, in his first full year, did well enough, scoring 194 points, although he was besieged with engine troubles, which ultimately curtailed his scoring. Rodney Payne started the year at reserve and found the going tough, eventually losing his place to Gary Tagg, who fared only slightly better in what was, after all, the toughest speedway league in the world.

1989 was not a good year for the Racers, as they slipped to seventh place in a nine-team league. The Rivets junior side fared no better, finishing the league campaign in eighth position. In the Knock Out Cup, Reading went out at the semi-final stage, losing by just 4 points on aggregate to Cradley Heath. Team changes saw both Jan Andersson (retired) and Per Jonsson (remaining at home in Sweden) not riding, and there was also no room at the start of the season for Malcolm Holloway or Gary Tagg. Taking over the captaincy was Kiwi Mitch Shirra, cleared to ride after gaining a reprieve against a two-year suspension for drug offences. Joining the side were ex-Ipswich boys Jeremy Doncaster, Carl Blackbird and the 'Italian Stallion' Armando Castagna, following the Witches' decision to run in the National League. Added to these were 1988 team members David Mullett and Tony Olsson, plus youngster Steve Chambers.

Chambers was also a member of the Rivets team and he was backed in the junior side by Lance Sealey, Troy Smith, Scott Pulleyn, Darren Boulton and new boy David Steen, who was later to feature in several Racers teams. Bill Dore, who had taken on the

*Jeremy Doncaster and Armando Castagna.*

Racers' team managing duties again in 1988, eventually stood down, with Tim Sugar taking over fully as the season progressed in 1989. Tim had, in fact, become joint team manager with Bill the previous year, and his shrewd knowledge of the rulebook had earned him the job outright. Sadly though, in the spring, Dick Bailey, the former team manager and latterly clerk of the course, passed away.

During the summer, the Racers made an historic trip to Italy, riding in two matches and winning 73-35 at Lonigo and 70-38 at Udine. Top Reading scorers at Lonigo were Jem Doncaster (14), tour guest Marvyn Cox (14) and Tony Olsson (11), meanwhile at Udine, top men were Cox (15), Mitch Shirra (15) and another tour guest Martin Dugard (13). The trip was marred though, when Armando Castagna, riding for the Italian Select side at Lonigo, crashed and broke a leg. It was an injury that signalled the end of the season for the Italian, who had only just returned to the saddle after breaking a collar-bone in the Austrian-staged Champions Cup. Armando only completed nine matches, and his extended absence meant a return to the side for Malcolm Holloway, who had been riding in the National League at Mildenhall. It was not a happy return for 'Wellie' though, as he struggled for points and ended the season on the injured list after a horror smash at Bradford on 5 October.

Jem Doncaster emerged as the Racers' top scorer in league and Knock Out Cup matches, with 391 points for an 8.61 average. This represented something of a drop in Jem's form, for his 1988 average at Ipswich was 9.34, but then he had been with the Witches for so long that it was probably a little difficult to settle in at a new home base. Mitch Shirra's season was blighted by the wagging of tongues over his failure of drug

*Sidecar programme, 1990.*

tests at two World Championship meetings the previous year. There were many calls for him to be banned, but despite the hassle, Mitch got on with the job, and although a final average of 7.62 was down on pre-season expectations, it was a credit to the rider for refusing to give in.

Tony Olsson, the only remaining Swede in the Racers camp, failed to progress any further: in fact, his return of 207 points was 53 less than he had recorded in 1988. David Mullett maintained his 5-point average and was obviously taking time to settle into the rigours of the British League. Carl Blackbird had a very inconsistent year, only reaching double figures once (at Oxford in August) and finished up with a 5-plus average. David Steen was given a chance in the side towards the end of the season, but found it hard going, as did the other youngsters who had a run-out during the year, namely Steve Chambers, Troy Smith and Scott Pulleyn.

On 14 August, the Denny Pyeatt Memorial was won by Troy Butler, ahead of Martin Dugard and David Mullett in a six-lap main final. In the second half, Steve Chambers won the Geoff Curtis Memorial. The following week (21 August), England defeated Australia 43-35, in only the second ever sidecar Test Match between the two countries, the first one having taken place at Coventry two days previously. The top drivers on the night were Alan Artus (England, 11 points) and Darren Treloar (Australia, 10 points), while, interestingly, one of the members of the Australian team was Bernie Koppe, brother of the ex-Swindon and Exeter speedway rider Steve.

In the Champions Cup, Mitch Shirra took second place behind Jan O. Pedersen, while in the World Final, the Racers had three qualifiers! The 'biggie' was staged in Munich and Jem Doncaster rode out of his skin to score 12 points and subsequently partook in a run-off for second place with Simon Wigg. Unfortunately for Jem, 'Wiggy' won the run-off, but even so, number three in the world was a great achievement for 'Donkey'. Of the other Racers, Mitch Shirra gathered 10 points to finish seventh, one place ahead of Tony Olsson, who scored 8. So it was a great night all round for Reading Speedway.

In a highly successful year on the individual front, Jeremy Doncaster won the Battle of Britain Trophy, top scored for England's World Team Cup-winning squad, and emerged victorious from the prestigious Czech Golden Helmet. In October, Smallmead staged the Dick Bailey Memorial Trophy for junior riders and this resulted in a Rivets one-two, with Steve Chambers winning ahead of David Steen. The second staging of the National Vintage Speedway Championship was won by Mike Coombes (pre-war) and Manuel Hughes (post-war).

## The 1990s

1990 was the Racers' Golden Year! In the history of Reading Speedway, this has to be the most outstanding season of them all. Although the Racers won the league in both 1973 and 1980, this was the first time they had done the double, taking the British League title and winning the Knock Out Cup. But that wasn't all, for at Bradford Per Jonsson became the World Champion, with another Racer, Todd Wiltshire, finishing in third position. That World Final will, of course, always be remembered for the first place run-off between Per and Shawn Moran, which was brilliantly won by the Racers' super Swede. In fact, it was a great year of success all round for several members of the team. Here are some of the major achievements: Jeremy Doncaster was winner of the British semi-final and Czech Golden Helmet, Overseas Champion and runner-up in the World Team Cup with England; Todd Wiltshire was third in the World Championship, second in the World Pairs Championship with Australia and the SWAPA Rider of the Year; Armando Castagna was the Italian Champion; and Per Jonsson was the World Champion and winner of the Denny Pyeatt Memorial Trophy. The Drews Cobra Rivets junior team of David Steen, Troy Smith, Christian Howell, Lance Sealey and Mark Seabright did well too, taking the runners-up spot in the British League Division Two. It really was some season!

Just to show how strong the XXXX Racers were, Per Jonsson could only manage third in the Reading averages, behind 'Donkey' and 'Hot Toddy', while David Mullett (6.31 average) and Tony Olsson (6.29) were sixth and seventh in the averages. Other riders to wear the famous 'Winged Wheel' during this triumphant season were Armando Castagna, Jan Andersson, David Steen, Nathan Murray, Troy Smith and Christian Howell. Worthy of a special mention too, for the brilliant work done throughout the season, was team manager and master tactician Tim Sugar. The season had started with Mitch Shirra banned for a year by the Speedway Control Board; however, Jan Andersson came out of retirement and Per Jonsson was recalled. Todd Wiltshire was signed from National League Wimbledon for a reported fee of around £20,000 and the rest is history.

Jem Doncaster was back to his best, pushing his average back up above 9 points. The form of Todd Wiltshire was a revelation, his lightning gating had to be seen to be believed, and a final average of just under 9 was a marvellous achievement in his first year at British League level. Jan Andersson was a great man to have back at Smallmead, and an inspiration to everyone in the camp as he plundered another 250-plus points in the Racers' cause. Tony Olsson proved to be a very solid team-man, but was badly injured while guesting for Cradley Heath on 25 August. Tony was out for the rest of the season and this meant a return for the 'Italian Stallion' Armando Castagna, who although only riding in eight matches did a solid job, and proved he had recovered from his broken leg of the previous season. David Mullett had a much better year, as he got to grips with the pace of the British League, proving to be a very reliable second-string as he gathered nearly 200 points. During the year, David passed the 100 appearances milestone for the Racers, on his way to a club record total of well over 400.

Per Jonsson fulfilled all his early potential with the World Championship triumph, and the luxury of three top-class heat-leaders definitely tilted things in the Racers' favour. Nathan Murray began the year in the reserves, but found the pace too hot and, eventually, David Steen was given an extended run. David also found it tough, but the potential was there. Troy Smith and Christian Howell were also pressed into action when injuries decreed, but only rode in three and two matches respectively. Two sidecar meetings were staged at Smallmead and saw England defeat the World All-Stars 45-44 in an exciting encounter on 4 June, before Gary Moon won the Empire Classic two weeks later, on 18 June. The latter meeting was the unofficial World Championship

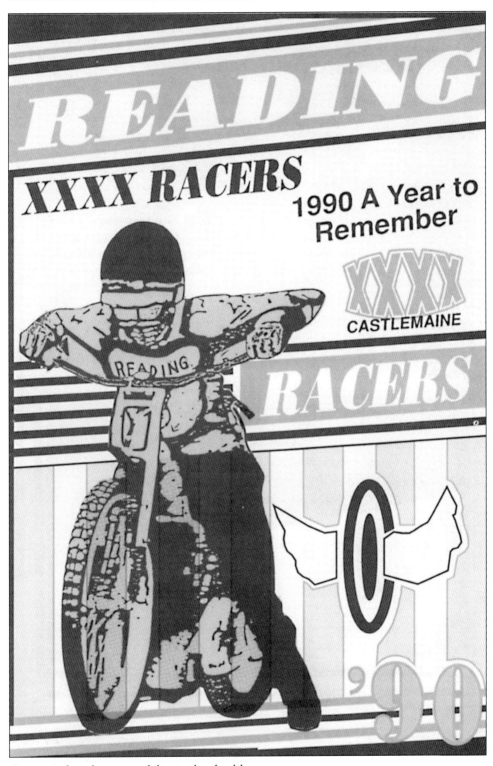

*Souvenir brochure to celebrate the double.*

*Reading 1990. From left to right, back row: Tim Sugar (team manager), David Mullett, Armando Castagna, Bill Dore (promoter), Tony Olsson, David Steen, Jan Andersson, Nathan Murray. Front row: club mascot, Todd Wiltshire, Jeremy Doncaster, Per Jonsson.*

of sidecar speedway, and was followed by a demonstration on 500cc Rotax mini desert racing cars, with the drivers including American speedway star John 'Cowboy' Cook.

The atmosphere at Smallmead was fantastic throughout the year, and the large attendances seemed to grow with the success of the team, right up to the end of the season, culminating in the brilliant Knock Out Cup final victory over Bradford. The rampant Racers took on the Dukes in the first leg on 8 October at Smallmead, winning 51-39. Todd Wiltshire led the scoring with a brilliant 15-point maximum, backed by a superb paid 14 return from Per Jonsson. That left the second leg balancing on a knife-edge, however, on 13 October, the Racers went up to the Odsal Stadium and produced a marvellous 47-43 victory, to win by 16 points on aggregate. All the riders were heroes on the night and it would be wrong to single anyone out, so here is the full list of scorers from that most memorable of nights: Todd Wiltshire (13), David Mullett (11+1), Armando Castagna (6+2), Jeremy Doncaster (6+1), Jan Andersson (5+1), Per Jonsson (4+1) and David Steen (2).

Another special memory is of the Denny Pyeatt Memorial meeting on 22 October, when Todd Wiltshire produced one of his super-fast starts to lead the final, but what a finish there was, as Per Jonsson caught and passed him to win in fantastic style. The Vintage Speedway Championship was again staged at Smallmead, with the victors being Mike Coombes (pre-war) and Vic Lonsdale (post-war). For the latter part of the 1980s and the early part of 1990, Vic Lonsdale was the video man at Smallmead, filming under the guise of LTV Productions. Sadly, Vic passed away in December 1991.

Vic was a former rider from the North, who had moved down to Buckinghamshire, and in 1990, as well as filming at Smallmead, he used to assist David Steen. Vic had won the Halifax Cycle Speedway Championship three years running (1950-52), before moving on to conventional speedway at Bradford in 1956. It was then that he earned his 'Wildman of Speedway' tag, following nasty crashes at Bradford, Motherwell and Liverpool. He may have been a bit on the wild side, but he was dedicated, even interrupting his honeymoon to ride in a meeting at Bradford! Vic rode for Middlesbrough and Newcastle in the 1960s, before moving on to Sheffield, his final track being Workington in 1970, when he was brought in to captain the new Comets side. Something of an extrovert, among Vic's hobbies was collecting jars of shale, portions of safety fence and scraps of wire from various tracks – he really was quite a character.

Towards the end of the season, Mike Leach of ML Video Sport took over the meeting videos and he has done an excellent job of filming all the action at Smallmead ever since. On 11 June, a special Malcolm Holloway Farewell four-team tournament took place. The stars came out to pay tribute to the 'Mad Wellie', who had called it a day following a bad track crash at Bradford in 1989. After Reading and Oxford had tied on 27 points, Jem Doncaster beat Martin Dugard in a run-off for first place. A British League Select side was third with 25 points and Swindon came fourth on 16 points. Among the stars on show were Marvyn Cox, Graham Jones, Leigh Adams and Jan Staechmann, plus Malcolm himself, who made an emotional return to the track.

The plan was to start the 1991 season at Smallmead on Monday 18 March with a Thames Valley Trophy match against Swindon, but that was cancelled due to the rain. The first home match turned out to be a win against Poole in the Premiership, by 51 points to 39. Four days later, in the second leg at Poole, the result was reversed, leaving the scores tied at 90-90 on aggregate. Sadly, this was a season without Per Jonsson, who stayed at home in Sweden. Per was greatly missed, but the Racers also had to dispense with the services of two other favourites, due to the points system in speedway. Because of the team's success in 1990, Armando Castagna and Tony Olsson were loaned out, as the Racers were left in a situation whereby they had to de-strengthen! Losing three loyal riders didn't help and the Racers dropped to eleventh place in the league. Another contributory factor was a nasty injury suffered by star rider Todd Wiltshire in July. In the Gold Cup, Reading finished second in their group, just missing out on a place in the final. The Racers did have a good run in the Knock Out Cup, however, reaching the semi-final before going down to Cradley Heath on aggregate.

It may not have been a good year in the league, but the racing was still close and exciting, never more so than when near neighbours Oxford came to town in a Thames Valley Trophy meeting. A tremendous race took place between Todd Wiltshire and multi-World Champion Hans Nielsen. 'Hot Toddy' flew out of the gate to lead, only for Hans to catch him and overtake, but it wasn't over, as Todd fought back to win in breathtaking style. Later in the season, on Bank Holiday Monday (6 May), Oxford were again the visitors for a Gold Cup match, and another superb race was witnessed. Heat eleven saw Jan Andersson gate ahead of Hans Nielsen and Martin Dugard, but both Cheetahs managed to get through on the inside of the first turn. Jan then broadsided right around the Oxford pair to take the lead, which he held for the rest of the race. It didn't end there though, for in heat thirteen, Ray Morton pulled off the best win of his career, defeating the 'Main Dane' and Craig Boyce in tremendous style.

*Jeremy Doncaster Testimonial programme, 1991.*

Part of Dave Stallworthy's microphone duties took him to the British Youth Grass-Track Championship and the Welsh Open Youth Championship, where he saw for the first time a fifteen-year-old Welsh boy take victory in the senior A1 categories. Little did he know at the time that he was watching a rider destined to become a major player in Smallmead history. That rider was, of course, Phil Morris, and by the end of the summer, having turned sixteen, he had made his debut in the Racers' team. On 18 June, the Racers went to Poole for the first leg of the replayed Premiership, going down narrowly by 41 points to 49. In the second leg at Smallmead on 8 July, the rampant Racers won 54-36 to secure an aggregate victory and win their only trophy of the season. Hero of the second leg was 'Ripper' Ray Morton, who notched a brilliant paid maximum.

In the Four-Team Championship at Peterborough on 21 July, David Mullett suffered a groin injury, and Todd Wiltshire took an awkward spill, which resulted in wrist and elbow injuries that were to rule him out of action for the duration. On 5 August, it was the turn of Jem Doncaster to be honoured with a Testimonial meeting. The weather stayed fine and there was excellent racing, as well as a good turnout of supporters. Australian stunt rider Matt Coulter from Melbourne also put on a great show for the Smallmead faithful. Matt, the world's number one quad motor-cyclist, was known as the 'Kangaroo Kid', and at Jeremy's meeting, he entertained the crowd until nearly eleven p.m.

Mitch Shirra qualified for the World Final in Sweden, and joining Mitch for the big night were Jem Doncaster and former Racers Per Jonsson and Armando Castagna. It wasn't a good night for any of them though, as Per scored 7 points, Armando 6, Mitch 4 and Jem 2. In August, the International Sidecar Super Prix was won by Paul Pinfold and Keith Wall, while in October, the National Vintage Speedway Championship was held for the fourth (and final) time at Smallmead, with Manuel Hughes (post-war) and Paul Fudge (pre-war) being the winners.

The main men in 1991 were Todd Wiltshire, Jeremy Doncaster, Jan Andersson and David Mullett. Backing the top four were Ray Morton, David Steen and young Danish rider Tim Korneliussen. Tiny Tim found the pace too hot though, and after a few early-season matches, he was replaced by the exciting Australian Scott Humphries. Former Wimbledon junior Terry Mussett also had some outings at number seven. Jem was top man for the season, scoring 296 league and Knock Out Cup points, ahead of the brilliantly consistent Jan Andersson, who weighed in with 251 points. New boy Ray Morton fully justified his signing from Wimbledon, finishing as Racers' third highest scorer with 183 points, while David Mullett had another good year, piling up 171 points. Mitch Shirra was brought back in to replace the injured Todd Wiltshire and did extremely well, and was almost back to his very best.

The Drews Cobra Rivets team included Jason Green, Mike Tomlin, Nick Upton, David Steen and Terry Mussett, with Paul King taking an active part in junior management. Like the Racers, the Rivets also managed to finish eleventh in the Division One Reserves League. On 2 September, Terry Mussett scored a 9-point maximum to win the Dick Bailey Memorial Shield, ahead of Garry Sweet and Darren Spicer. This took place after the Reading *v.* Cradley Heath match, but before any action took place, World Champion Jan O. Pedersen was paraded around the Smallmead circuit with his trophy. Although a

Cradley rider, Jan O. was a popular champion, and the Smallmead fans showed him their appreciation.

1992 was another golden year in the history of Reading Speedway. Per Jonsson was back and the Racers became League Champions for the fourth time, won the B.S.P.A. Cup and were runners-up in both the Knock Out Cup and Gold Cup! On the individual front, Per nearly won his second World title, finishing second to Gary Havelock at Wroclaw, Poland, while in the British League Riders' Championship, Per was again second, this time behind Joe Screen. Kiwi Mitch Shirra had moved on to Swindon again, but produced a tremendous effort to finish as runner-up in the World Long Track Championship, behind Marcel Gerhard of Switzerland.

The Racers' Championship team consisted of Tim Sugar (team manager), Jan Andersson, Per Jonsson, David Mullett, Jeremy Doncaster, Armando Castagna, Ray Morton and Phil Morris. Many supporters remember the night at Smallmead though, when thousands packed into the stadium to witness a double cup final on 26 October. The first part of the double-header saw the Racers beat Poole 52-38, to win the B.S.P.A. Cup by an aggregate score of 92-88, having lost the first leg in Dorset by 10 points. The second match was against Bradford in the Knock Out Cup final, with the Racers having a 20-point deficit from the first leg. Amid a great atmosphere, Per and the boys gave it all they had, but unfortunately they could only manage a 53-37 win on the night, thereby losing 88-92 on aggregate. But what a night of high drama!

The Reading junior side finished seventh in the Reserve League and included Phil Morris, Mike Tomlin, Jason Green, Garry Sweet, Mark Sayer and Lance Sealey, son of track manager Jeff. Other officials backing up promoters Bill Dore and Pat Bliss were Andy Griffin (clerk of the course), Roger Nettlefold (timekeeper), Bob Radford (announcer), Clive Fisher (radio microphone), Dave Moss (starting marshall), John Ballard (machine examiner) and Tony Porter (staff manager). Not forgetting the major contribution from the St John's Ambulance Brigade, plus Dr Budd (in the 1980s) and Dr Gargav (throughout the 1990s), without whom speedway simply could not run.

A special meeting took place at Smallmead on 15 June, when England defeated Australia 55-23 in a Test Match. Top man for England was David Mullett with 14 points, while Ray Morton scored an exceptional 11 points and Jem Doncaster chipped in with 6. This was the Second Test of the series, which England won overall by 2 matches to 1. Another terrific meeting in 1992 was David Mullett's Testimonial on 21 September, when Dave's Testimonial Racers defeated Cocker's Magnificent Seven by 52 points to 38. The stars came out to pay tribute to David, and it was just reward for a rider who has always given 100 per cent effort for the Reading cause.

Highlights of the league campaign must surely have been the away wins at Cradley (47-42, headed by a brilliant paid 14 points from Per); at Belle Vue (47-43, with a marvellous paid 13 points from Ray Morton); at Swindon (50-40, led by a faultless 15-pointer from Per and 15 from Jan); at Eastbourne (49-41, including paid 14 points from David Mullett); at Ipswich (48-41, featuring a paid 15-point maximum from ex-Witch Jem); and at Arena-Essex (46-44, which included 14 points from Per). The Speedway Control Board also awarded the Racers a 75-0 victory at King's Lynn, after the meeting had not gone ahead on its scheduled date. That made 7 away wins for the season and was the

*David Mullett Testimonial programme, 1992.*

foundation for a successful assault on the League Championship.

So, it was another fabulous season for the Racers, led brilliantly by Super Swede Per Jonsson with 372 points and a 10.04 average. Evergreen Jan was as consistent as ever, weighing in with another 261 points – what an amazing servant to the Racers this fellow was. 'Donkey' had another superb year, achieving an 8.36 average and leading the side superbly. The backbone of the Racers' powerhouse side was filled by David Mullett, Armando Castagna and Ray Morton, each of whom did all that was expected and more. The top six didn't have a weak link and they were backed up by young Phil Morris, who obviously found the pace of the British League very fast, but never stopped plugging away. Mark Sayer, Lance Sealey, Garry Sweet and Mike Tomlin had odd outings in the Reading side when needed, and all struggled of course, but it must have been nice to have played a small part in another magnificent Racers team.

Sidecar racing was again staged at Smallmead in 1992, with a Thames Valley Team Championship on 8 June which saw Reading score 27 points to defeat Oxford (23) and Swindon (21). The Reading team was managed by Tim Sugar, and their top scorers were Gary Moon (who recorded a 12-point maximum) and Richard Moore (who yielded 9 points). The side also included former French speedway rider Thierry Hilaire. In the second half, a vintage speedway contest was won by Jim Gregory, while John Stallworthy finished as runner-up. One other sidecar event was held on 3 August, when the Tigers defeated the Kangaroos 47-43, with Roger Measor topping the winning team's scoring (12 points), while Gary Moon recorded an outstanding 18-point maximum for the losing side. Finally for 1992, praise must go to the *Reading Evening Post*, for on 26 October, they produced a special *Speedway Post* cover, highlighting the double-header cup meeting and featuring a colour picture of Per Jonsson. The back page included a full A3-sized colour picture of Tim Sugar and the league winning Racers, entitled 'Simply The Best'.

After their great success, the Racers team had to be broken up in order to comply with the points limit for the 1993 campaign. Thirty-seven-year-old Jan Andersson half-solved the problem by deciding to retire in order to build his own house in Sweden. Everyone involved with the club would miss Jan, who was quite rightly referred to as 'Mr Reading Speedway', having ridden 392 league and Knock Out Cup matches for the Racers. He also held the all-time club record of 3,712.5 points, garnered on behalf of the 'Winged Wheel'. The rest of the team jigsaw fell into place with Ray Morton being loaned out to Poole, leaving the way open for Tony Olsson and Peter Glanz to return to the Racers. Tony had been away from Reading since the golden year of 1990, plying his trade on loan at several tracks, including Hackney and Belle Vue. Dane Peter Glanz made the return to top league racing, following a stint at Second Division Milton Keynes.

The race formula was different in 1993, with eighteen-heat matches and eight-man teams. This meant a team spot for Mike Tomlin, who had previously ridden for the Rivets junior side. On paper, the team still looked strong, with the remainder of the side retained from the previous year. This meant that Per Jonsson, Armando Castagna, Jeremy Doncaster, David Mullett and Phil Morris were all back for another term, as was team manager Tim Sugar. However, there was sadness during the winter with the news

*Peter Glanz.*

that Joy Warne had died. Joy had been a dedicated member of the backroom staff at Smallmead and would be greatly missed.

The season started well at Smallmead when the Racers beat Bradford 58-50 in the first leg of the Premiership on 22 March. Five days later, Reading went to Bradford for the second leg and performed magnificently to draw 54-54. Armando Castagna was the star at Odsal, recording a brilliant paid 18-point maximum, as the Racers completed an aggregate victory by 112 points to 104. There was good media coverage throughout the season, not only from the *Reading Chronicle* and the *Reading Evening Post*, but also from Meridian TV and Radio Berkshire. Clive Fisher was the usual Smallmead roving microphone man, but Peter York had his first stint at Smallmead when Clive was on holiday. This was, of course, a prelude to 'Yorkie' becoming the full-time centre-green announcer in 1994.

The Reading Racers Social Club had a stand in the Butts Centre Shopping Precinct and Phil Morris spent all day there promoting the Racers. The club had been in full swing throughout the winter, organizing many events such as a Christmas dinner, video night and a talk. In April, they presented a much-needed cheque to Phil Morris for just over £325. Throughout the season, the club sold raffle tickets and ran a penny sponsorship scheme, as well as organizing coaches to away meetings. They also staged a six-a-side soccer tournament and fun day at Hartley Wintney Football Club later in the season on 31 July.

Off-track, it was not a good start to the season for David Mullett, who suffered a violent burglary which left his parents and his dog injured. David was also suffering from an attack of shingles but, despite his problems, his performances were as reliable as ever. It was reported in the Reading programme that during the winter, 'Italian Stallion' Armando Castagna had sampled two other forms of sport. Firstly, he had tried bobsleigh racing on an Italian Olympic course, and this was followed by boxing, with an Italian Championship contender! Armando was certainly fit for the season ahead, and that performance at Bradford in the Premiership showed it was paying off. Also from abroad, good news was received from former Racer Todd Wiltshire and his wife Linda in Australia, who had a baby son called Anders – a good choice of name from a Reading point of view!

The end of 1992 spelled the end of the Reserve League, although an English Junior League was formed for 1993. This new league comprised just six teams – Reading, Belle Vue, Long Eaton, Oxford, Cradley Heath and Wolverhampton. The three-man Reading side was now entitled Young Racers, and featured Lance Sealey, Garry Sweet and Mark Seabright. After only a handful of meetings in the Racers team, Mike Tomlin quit, having been unable to cope with the pressure. Tomlin was quickly replaced by Lance Sealey, whose father had been responsible for setting up the training track adjacent to Smallmead Stadium. The sidecar boys were back at Smallmead on 7 June, when the Mark Goodyer Memorial Trophy was held. The event was staged in memory of the rider who unfortunately died on 15 March 1992, the day after a track accident at Waikaraka Park in his native country. Richard Moore and Roger Measor tied on 12 points apiece, with the former taking the trophy after a run-off.

On 11 July, David Mullett joined the England team for the first Test Match *v.* Sweden at Exeter. The Swedes won the match 56-52, courtesy of a last-heat 5-1 from Tony Rickardsson and Racer Tony Olsson. Per Jonsson collected 14 points for Sweden, and Tony Olsson chipped in with a paid 5-point return. But it was a fairytale for David Mullett, despite the result, as he romped to a paid 11-point haul. Six days later, David rode in the second Test Match at Eastbourne, where England stormed to a 60-48 victory. On this occasion, David scored 3 points, meanwhile for Sweden, Per scored just a single point, but he was not helped by an early crash which put him out of the meeting. Fellow Racer Tony Olsson collected 4 points for the Swedes. The deciding Test Match at Newcastle resulted in a 57-48 victory for England, but there was only one Racer on show, namely Tony Olsson, who recorded another 4 points.

On 18 July, the Stars of Tomorrow was staged at Smallmead, and was won by Eastbourne's Mark Bruton. The meeting was rain-affected and had to be reduced from twenty heats to twelve as a result. The following night, a sidecar challenge match was staged at Smallmead, between Reading and King's Lynn. The visitors, managed by Dingle Brown, romped to a 54-33 victory, with the tremendous duo of Roger Measor and Shane Lapham recording a superb 21-point maximum.

In the H.E.A.T.-sponsored Four-Team Championship, Reading stormed through the qualifying rounds to the final at Peterborough, and what a great day it turned out to be for the Racers at the East of England Showground on 25 July. Per Jonsson and David Mullett led the way with 8 points apiece, as Reading won the tournament (27 points) ahead of Wolverhampton (25 points), Belle Vue (11) and Arena-Essex (9). Per and David were well backed up by Armando, who scored 7 points and Tony Olsson with 4 points. It was a great team effort, overseen as usual by Tim Sugar. Incidentally, let's not forget that Phil Morris was team reserve on that glorious day, although he didn't get a ride. Prior to the Fours triumph, Peter Glanz had decided to quit the Racers, and a replacement was sought. On the recommendation of Racers legend Jan Andersson, newcomer Kenneth Nystrom arrived, but failed to score on his debut against King's Lynn on 16 August.

On the global stage, Per Jonsson and Armando Castagna reached the World Final in Pocking, Germany, with Per scoring 7 points and Armando 5. In the World Team Cup,

Per recorded 6 points as Sweden finished third overall. The World Pairs brought further success for Per, as Sweden took the gold medal, with Per scoring 5 points, to back up Tony Rickardsson (15 points) and Henrik Gustafsson (6 points). On 31 October, there was further success for Per when he won the British League Riders' Championship at Swindon with a 14-point tally, ahead of Henrik Gustafsson.

So, despite a drop to sixth in the league, it wasn't a bad campaign for the Racers, as they won the Premiership and the Four-Team Championship, and then, of course, there was Per's success in the British League Riders' Championship. Per had a tremendous season for the Racers, piling up 466 points for an average of 10.34. The super Swede was now certainly the master of the Smallmead circuit, and some of his passing was quite astounding. There was one other success for Per in 1993, as prior to the start of the season, he had won the British Open Championship at Telford Ice Rink in February, scoring 14 points. Incidentally, Phil Morris took third place at Telford, becoming the youngest ever competitor in the event. Phil's success was due in no small way to Jan Andersson, who had prepared a special machine for the battling Welshman.

Armando Castagna had a very solid season, rattling up 367 points, and he was always popular with the fans. The ever-reliable David Mullett had his best-ever season in terms of scoring, running up a massive 348 points. A fourth member of the Reading squad also topped the 300-points mark, as Jem Doncaster passed the magical total. That was some team effort when you think about it, and when bonus points were included, Tony Olsson also topped 300 points! Phil Morris continued to progress, moving his average above 5.5 points. Putting it bluntly, Kenneth Nystrom struggled, but he did put in two double-figure scores, with 11 at Cradley Heath, and 10 at home to Ipswich. Lance Sealey found it tough going, but plodded away and did have a personal best of 9 points against Poole in May.

The 1994 season can only be described as a disaster for the Racers. The start of the season was difficult, with Jeremy Doncaster wanting to go back 'home' to Ipswich and Per Jonsson unsigned. Tony Olsson had decided the previous November that a move into the Second Division would be beneficial to him, and he moved to Swindon in a loan deal. Ray Morton came back after his year at Poole, while joining the camp was Shane Bowes, on loan from Glasgow. Following an impressive performance at Smallmead in 1993, young Swindon rider Matthew Cross was also signed on loan. There was one off-track change too, as Clive Fisher moved on, to be replaced by Peter York as meeting presenter.

The season opened at Smallmead with a challenge match against King's Lynn on 21 March. It should have been a league fixture, but King's Lynn agreed to the change in view of the Racers' team problems. Tony Olsson and Leigh Adams guested for Reading in that opening fixture, but they were unable to save the Racers from going down to a 47-49 defeat. On 18 April, the British semi-final of the World Championship was held at Smallmead, with David Mullett storming to victory with a marvellous 15-point maximum. This was a tremendous performance from David, as the field included the likes of Chris Louis, Jeremy Doncaster, Kelvin Tatum, Martin Dugard and Ben Howe. This was definitely one of the highlights of a troublesome season for the Racers.

Tony Rickardsson had decided to have a break from racing in the British League in

*Shane Bowes.*

order to concentrate on his Swedish, Polish and Danish League commitments. However, Tony did agree to help out Ipswich for a month, while the deal was sorted out to take Jem Doncaster back to Foxhall Heath. In April, Jem got his wish and was on his way back to Ipswich, with the Racers acting quickly to agree terms with Per Jonsson, enabling him to come back to Smallmead. Ironically, Per made his first appearance of the year at Smallmead on 25 April against Ipswich, for whom Jeremy Doncaster rode. Per top scored for the Racers with 12 points, meanwhile Jem also topped the Witches' scorechart with 11 points!

On 1 May, David Mullett took his place in the British Final at Coventry, but in a meeting won by Andy Smith, he could only muster 3 points. Right through May, Per Jonsson was in unstoppable form around Smallmead, as he reeled off five consecutive 15-point maximums, and his theme tune of 'Perfect' by Fairground Attraction was certainly getting plenty of airplay! Per's superb run came to an end at Smallmead on 5 June against Wolverhampton, when a dead-heat with Peter Karlsson was all that stopped another 15-pointer. What turned out to be Per's final meeting at Smallmead was on 20 June, in a qualifying round for the Four-Team Championship, when he notched 10 points. The following week, Per rode in further Fours qualifying rounds at Poole (22 June) and Ipswich (23 June), but tragedy struck on Sunday 26 June in Poland. Per was riding for Apator Torun in a Polish League fixture at Bydgoszcz, when after winning his first three rides, he was involved in a horrific crash with two other riders. Per was rushed to hospital and it was diagnosed that he had suffered crushed fourth and fifth vertebrae and pressure to his spinal cord. This meant that Per was paralysed from the chest downwards and would never walk again.

The Racers' season went downhill from this point on, and they almost gave up the ghost. Matthew Cross and Phil Morris suffered with injuries, David Mullett was injured in that Fours round at Ipswich, Armando Castagna broke a vertebra in Italy and Phil Morris broke a leg in a French grass-track meeting in July. The crash-weary Racers struggled on though, winning the odd match but losing in the main, as Jan Pedersen was brought in to help out in August. Prior to Per's injury, Smallmead had again heard the roar of the sidecars when the Mark Goodyer Memorial Trophy was run on 13 June. The format was changed for the event, and featured a qualifying round along with the semi-final and a grand final. John Bowkett emerged as the winner, while Ray Blackall had to be satisfied with the runners-up position.

Plans were made to stage a special benefit meeting in order to raise funds for Per Jonsson. A non-profit making body was set up to organize things, headed by Jimmy Nilsen, Pat Bliss and Bob Radford. Of course, Jimmy Nilsen and Per had been friends for years and who can forget some of the epic races the two of them had, particularly around Smallmead? Armando Castagna had taken over the number one race jacket and was doing a great job for the beleaguered Racers, as well as becoming the Italian Champion again, but the cruel hand of fate struck again when he broke a leg in September. Reading had already used numerous guests and loanees and this meant even more would be employed before the end of the season.

On 26 September, the Per Jonsson Benefit meeting was staged at Smallmead, and over 4,000 fans turned out to pay tribute to a rider cut down in his prime. Many top stars rode in a four-team tournament, which was won by Team Mullett with 40 points. They comprised Tony Rickardsson, Jason Crump, Mark Loram, Jan Andersson and David Mullett. Second with 37 points were Team Nielsen, led by Hans, while third with 19 points were Team Ermolenko, led by Sam, and fourth with 12 points were Team Castagna, led by Armando. Other stars on show included Greg Hancock, Billy Hamill, Craig Boyce, Leigh Adams and the Karlsson brothers. Past masters Peter Collins, Anders Michanek and Barry Briggs also rode in two special heats, while the legendary Ivan Mauger did a demonstration four laps on one of Per's bikes.

Against doctors' advice, Per courageously flew over from his Gothenburg hospital to attend the benefit meeting. It was a night that Per and his wife Maria found equally emotional and enjoyable. If only it had been a Testimonial and not a benefit meeting

*Per Jonsson leading the way.*

*Youngsters at a Reading training school, including Lee Richardson and Blair Scott.*

held under such tragic circumstances. A few weeks later, Jimmy Nilsen, Pat Bliss and Bob Radford journeyed to Stockholm and presented Per with a cheque for just over £50,000. It was hoped that the money would go towards making Per's life as comfortable as it could possibly be under the circumstances.

The Racers finished the year in tenth position out of eleven teams and it was scant reward that Per Jonsson finished on top of the overall British League averages. That fact just went to emphasize his loss even more, for he was riding at his peak when that dreadful crash occurred in Poland. The hugely popular Armando Castagna had a brilliant year in between injuries, piling up 349 points for an impressive 8.44 average in league and Knock Out Cup matches. David Mullett battled away in his usual style, having taken over the club captaincy and scored another 337 points for the Racers' cause. After a spell with Arena-Essex, Jan Pedersen came to Berkshire, but didn't really pull up any trees and generally he was better away from home than at Smallmead. The returning Ray Morton struggled with minor injuries throughout the season and never really got going as a result, in what was a difficult year for all concerned.

Shane Bowes had always proved himself to be a tremendous racer while at Second Division Glasgow, and he was certainly a thrill merchant around Smallmead. In what was an unhappy year for the Racers, Shane plugged away to notch 273 points for an average of 5.83, and was the only ever-present rider at the club. Taking everything into account, it must be said that 'Bowsie' did very well in his first year of top league racing. Matthew Cross started the season brightly, but found it progressively hard as the season wore on. This was borne out by the fact that he only managed to score 69 points from the 37 matches that he appeared in. Phil Morris' form took a slight backward step in

1994, but then again, he only rode for half the season due to the broken leg he sustained in France. Of course, Phil was always interesting to watch, with his enthusiastic hustle-bustle style of riding. Finally, in a season to forget, Reading used some forty guests and loanees in an effort to plug the gaps created by the seemingly non-stop injuries.

1995 saw the dawn of the British Premier League, whereby all the teams from the previous British League Divisions One and Two joined forces to form one big league. There were several changes in the Racers camp, with Armando Castagna electing to stay in Argentina, although he did join Oxford later on. Not surprisingly, Shane Bowes was recalled by parent track Glasgow, and that left just three members of the side from the year before, in the form of 'Welsh Wizard' Phil Morris, 'Ripper' Ray Morton and long-serving David Mullett. David Norris did not want to leave Eastbourne, but was forced out by the points limit and duly arrived at Smallmead. Tony Olsson returned for his Testimonial year, following a good season at Swindon in Second Division racing. 'Flying Finn' Petri Kokko was signed on a full transfer from Newcastle, who had closed down, and the final team place was taken by Jason Gage, but this was only on a temporary basis, while Reading waited for Lee Richardson to reach his sixteenth birthday.

The Racers programme was now being produced by Cheney Graphics, a company run by Terry Cheney, who was a former speedway promoter at Milton Keynes. Nick Dyer started to write in the programme, but Tony Porter had to relinquish his position

*Reading 1995. From left to right, back row: Jason Gage, Ray Morton, Petri Kokko, Tim Sugar (team manager), Phil Morris, David Morris. Front row: Lee Richardson, Tony Olsson (on bike), David Mullett.*

*Tony Olsson Testimonial programme, 1995.*

of staff manager at Smallmead due to becoming the publican at The White Swan in Aldershot. Ex-rider Barry Allaway was appointed as the training officer, with Steve Blay becoming pits marshall and understudy to clerk of the course Andy Griffin. All the other off-track posts were much the same as they had been before, with Bob Radford as announcer, Roger Nettlefold as timekeeper, Peter York as presenter, Dave Moss as starting marshall, John Ballard as machine examiner and Jeff Sealey as track manager. Of course, Alf Weedon (established 1947) was resident track photographer, and was always an interesting man to talk to. Incidentally, Alf actually attended his first speedway meeting at Lea Bridge, way back in 1932!

The Smallmead season opened on 3 April with a 48-48 draw against Poole, but the biggest cheer of the night was reserved for a very special visitor indeed, none other than Per Jonsson. On 10 April, Hull came to Smallmead for a league encounter and included in their ranks ex-Racer Glyn Taylor. Glyn did well scoring a paid 7-point total, which included a win first time out. This wasn't bad for a man who first rode for Reading in 1977, some eighteen years previously! The British semi-final of the World Championship was staged at Eastbourne on 16 April, and David Norris produced a dazzling display to finish as runner-up to Martin Dugard. David Mullett was also in the meeting, and he too did well, recording 10 points. Talking of David Norris, he had proved himself to be a real crowd-pleaser at Smallmead, being quite brilliant from the back and he really was something else to watch.

Come the end of April, Jason Gage's stint in the side was over and he made way for Lee Richardson. It was a baptism of fire for young Lee though, as he struggled through the rest of the season. Some supporters seemed to get on his back, but if only they could have known how he would turn out, for Lee went from being somewhat off the pace in 1995 to World Under-21 Champion in 1999! Back to 1995 and Phil Morris took part in the British Under-21 Final at Ipswich on 27 April, winning a couple of heats in a 9-point haul. It wasn't a bad performance, for the field included the likes of Ben Howe (who won the meeting), Paul Hurry, Savalas Clouting, Scott Nicholls and James Grieves.

The British Final was staged at Coventry on 30 April and by notching 8 points, David Norris did well enough to qualify for the Overseas Final. Unfortunately, David Mullett was unable to take his place in the meeting after suffering a double fracture of the ankle in a crash at Poole just four days previously. It was a real blow, as the Racers had pulled out all the stops to win 49-47 at Wimborne Road and were led brilliantly with 13 points from David Norris and 10 from 'Ripper' Ray Morton. Sadly, the season was over for David Norris following an innocuous-looking fall at the Coventry-staged Overseas Final on 11 June. Having run two lasts, David came out for his third ride in heat twelve, but a simple spill resulted in a fractured right leg.

David Mullett had quickly returned to the side following his ankle injury, but in the home meeting against Arena-Essex on 26 June he crashed again, this time damaging knee ligaments. As in 1994, guest riders were the order of the day and there were plenty of them as the season wore on. At the end of July, Marvyn Cox was brought in to plug the gap left by the injury to David Norris, and David Mullett also returned after a month on the sidelines. Tony Olsson enjoyed a successful Testimonial meeting on 23 July, when a star-studded line-up turned out to honour a very popular Racer. Tony's Select won a four-team tournament with 37 points. Managed by Exeter press officer Tony Lethbridge, the winning team comprised Chris Louis, Lars Gunnestad, Ronnie Correy, Alun Rossiter and Mark Simmonds. Reading were second on 33 points, while Oxford scored 29 points and Swindon brought up the rear with just 9 points. Other riders on show included Armando Castagna, Jimmy Nilsen and Craig Boyce, while old favourites Malcolm Holloway and Peter Glanz made a welcome track return to Smallmead. At the end of the season, it was announced that Tony would receive a cheque for £14,000. It was a welcome bonus for a rider who had been struggling with an overactive thyroid gland for much of the season.

At the end of August, Marvyn Cox left the Racers due to the cost of travel from his German base and the lack of sponsorship. Marvyn had actually become German Champion and rode in the revamped World Championship Grand Prix series, scoring 54 points from his six rounds. It wasn't enough to guarantee him an automatic place in the 1996 Grand Prix though, so 'Cocker' had to try and get through the Grand Prix Challenge at Lonigo in October. In a tense meeting, Marvyn rode superbly, scoring 13 points and finishing as runner-up to Leigh Adams.

So it was another difficult season for the Racers, who were again plagued by injuries and saw crowd levels drop off, probably more as a direct result of losing Per Jonsson the previous year than anything else. Thirteenth place out of twenty-one probably wasn't too bad, all things considered, and the riders battled away gamely. David Norris was 'Mr Entertainment' prior to his injury, as was Marvyn Cox during his short spell as a Racer.

David Mullett put in another tremendous year, quickly recovering from two injuries to notch up 268 points for an 8.31 league and Knock Out Cup average. Petri Kokko did well in his first full year of British Speedway, finishing with an average a shade under 6, and the potential was obviously there for the future. Phil Morris continued to plug away as ever, always giving maximum commitment. Captain Tony Olsson had a good Testimonial year, despite his health problems, and Ray Morton too had a very consistent season, banging in over 300 points for a 7-point average. Finally, Lee Richardson (as mentioned before) found it an uphill struggle, but the future certainly looked bright.

Quite simply, 1996 was the Racers' worst-ever season in top-flight racing, as they finished bottom of the league for the first time in their history. On the

*Jan Pedersen.*

team front, David Norris went back to Eastbourne, but the task of finding a new number one rider seemed almost impossible. Eventually Erik Stenlund was brought in, but he could only manage to ride for eight days due to other commitments. The remainder of the side was pretty much as it had been in 1995, with the only other change seeing David Steen replace Lee Richardson in order to comply with the BSPA average ceiling. A special mention is due to Tony Olsson, who didn't receive the necessary surgery on his thyroid gland until February, but still took his place at the start of the season. This was absolutely typical of Tony's loyalty to the Racers; meanwhile, Ray Morton became the third different club captain in as many years.

The opening Smallmead meeting, a challenge match against Swindon on 25 March, was abandoned after just four heats due to rain. The following week, Peterborough arrived for a Premier League fixture, and left with the league points following a 50-46 victory. Erik Stenlund did well enough, scoring paid 9 points. However, Erik could only fit in one more match, the following Monday against Long Eaton, when he scored paid 10 points. In mid-April Jan Pedersen, who had helped out in 1994, re-joined the Racers on loan. It was a short and unsuccessful stay for the Dane though, who rode in twelve league and Knock Out Cup matches, scoring just 47 points. By the end of May, Jan made way for the return of the 'Italian Stallion' Armando Castagna. After a troublesome start against Ipswich on 3 June, when he just couldn't get his machinery going properly, Armando set about adding some much needed bite to the Racers.

The World Championship trail had started early, with the British semi-final stage being held in April. Ray Morton did well, scoring 10 points at Poole and 11 points at Oxford, to qualify for the British Final at Coventry on 28 April. Joining Ray at Brandon Stadium was David Mullett, who was seeded direct. David scored 6 points at Coventry, but Ray continued his merry march forward with 8 points and a place in the 'B' final. Unfortunately, an engine failure cost him a higher placing, but eighth overall was enough for a spot in the Overseas Final, which was again staged at Coventry on 9 June. Ray tried everything he knew in the Overseas Final, scoring 7 points, but the meeting was marred by controversy, however, as many of the competing riders refused to use the newly-introduced solid block tyres, with the meeting being held up for an hour or so while arguments raged.

By the middle of June, Ray Morton had given up the team captaincy, with Petri Kokko taking over. Shortly afterwards, Ray was snapped up by Hull, who moved quickly to sign him on loan, with the Racers bringing in leggy German Jorg Pingel as a loaned replacement from Exeter. 5 August was a special day for Dave Stallworthy, as he took over permanently from Bob Radford as meeting announcer. Bob had decided to stand down and was the leaving the microphone in very capable hands. That special night for Dave featured a Premier League match against Hull, which the Racers won 54-42, with Petri Kokko leading the scoring on 13 points. Peter York was also away that night, working on the Isle of Wight as commentator for a jousting competition.

Reading Ravens surfaced in 1996, joining the British Conference League. Among the riders used by the new side were Youth Grass-track Champion Roger Lobb, and another grass-tracker in the shape of the extrovert Darren Andrews. Other team members included Carl Checketts, Mick Hester, Bill Haynes, Rob Cooling and Steve Targett. Lee

Richardson also appeared in five matches for the Ravens, as did Lance Sealey. The side eventually finished eleventh out of thirteen teams, with the top man being Roger Lobb, closely followed by Darren Andrews. Lee Richardson is worthy of mention, for he achieved an average in excess of 11.5 from the handful of matches he rode in. With Reading having a team in the Conference League, it meant a first-ever visit to Smallmead of the Wight Wizards, who hailed from Ryde on the Isle of Wight. Included in the Wizards side for that first visit on 19 August was future Racer Justin Elkins, who roared to a 15-point maximum, as the visitors took a 40-38 victory. The second half of the meeting featured pre-war and post-war speedway machines, including Douglas, Rudge and early Jawas.

The Racers were covered by cable television throughout the season by a company called Tele Cential and the man providing race commentary was none other than a great friend to Reading Speedway over the years, Nick Dyer. Every so often a race sticks out in your mind and one such occurred at Smallmead on 2 September when Coventry visited. Going into heat fifteen, the Racers held a slim 2-point advantage as the riders came to the line. Armando Castagna and Tony Olsson represented Reading, while the Andersen brothers Brian and Jan, lined up for the Bees. Armando and Brian Andersen proceeded to trade places throughout the race in a wheel-to-wheel, shoulder-to-shoulder battle, with Armando coming home just in front to give the Racers a hard-fought 50-46 victory. It was an absolutely incredible race and the 'Italian Stallion' received a standing ovation from the Smallmead faithful.

On 14 October, the Per Jonsson Appeal meeting was held at Smallmead and the idea behind this and a previously-staged charity ice hockey match was to try and raise funds to buy Per a remarkable bed, which turned into a mobile chair at the flick of a switch. Sadly, the meeting between a Reading Select and a Swindon Select was abandoned due to heavy rain after just seven heats, with Reading leading 27-15. Several top stars had turned up to help this worthwhile cause, including recently crowned World Champion Billy Hamill, along with Jason Crump, Brian Karger and former Racers Jeremy Doncaster and Ray Morton. Fortunately, the bad weather came too late to stop the appeal from reaching the necessary amount to purchase the much needed equipment to make Per's life a little more comfortable.

The Premier League Riders' Championship took place at Bradford on 19 October, and Armando put on a terrific show, scoring 8 points from his four qualifying rides. His tally included a win in heat thirteen over Leigh Adams, Steve Johnston and Brian Andersen (again). Reading's favourite Italian then lined up in the first semi-final against Adams and Andersen once more, plus Jason Crump. Sadly for Armando, he could only manage third place behind the flying Australians Crump and Adams, but it was a gallant effort as he just missed out on a place in the grand final.

Summing up the year, Tony Olsson finished as top man and how many times in the Racers' history has a Swede done that? Tony rattled up 371 points for the 'Winged Wheel' and was obviously fitter than he had been the previous year. Armando Castagna was a little less consistent than in his last year at Smallmead (1994), but he still piled up over 200 points and was as popular as ever with the fans. The ever-loyal David Mullett completed his ninth full year as a Racer, but he was dogged by a series of seemingly endless bangs which knocked 1.5 points off his final average. Thankfully, David seemed to have ridden through the worst of it by the end of the year though. Petri Kokko found things hard and failed to progress from his excellent first year, but the potential was obviously still there. David Steen put in a steady season to score 180 points for a very creditable 5-point average. Likeable Jorg Pingel also did well in his 18-match stint for the Racers, averaging over 4.5 points. Phil Morris had a year to forget though, only reaching double figures once – at Cradley & Stoke on 17 July. Phil's average actually dropped for the third season in a row, although it had consistently hovered around the 5-point mark since 1993.

It was all change in 1997 as the one big league was split into two, with the formation of a ten-team Elite League (i.e. First Division) and a fourteen-team Premier League (i.e. Second Division). Due to the falling attendances at Smallmead, Reading opted to go into the Premier League. Initially, many Racers supporters were dismayed at this decision, but once they had witnessed the superb standard of racing, they warmed to the idea. After three difficult years in the top league, it proved to be the right decision, as the Racers stormed to the league title and the glory days were back at Smallmead!

There were several changes to the on-track personnel, which saw Phil Morris spend the season on loan to Stoke, while Tony Olsson moved on to Swindon for a year of Elite League racing. Petri Kokko was the other non-returning rider, and he ended up sitting out the entire British season. David Mullett remained at Smallmead to lead the side and also staying on was David Steen from the 1996 line-up. Lee Richardson came back after a year on loan at Poole, and was joined by new boys Paul Pickering via Bradford, and Glenn Cunningham from Swindon. The format of teams was somewhat different in 1997, as six-man sides were tracked including one reserve rider, plus a track reserve in case of injuries. The reserve rider was allowed to take as many as seven rides in a match. Making up the Racers six was Tara O'Callaghan, who had previously had a handful of meetings with Eastbourne

There were off-track changes too, as ex-Racer Malcolm Holloway came in as speedway administrator. Further changes saw Bill Taylor join Alf Weedon as the second track photographer, while Doug Plester became the new starting marshall. The Smallmead season opened on 31 March with a challenge match against Oxford and a 48-42

*Steve Targett.*

*Reading 1997. From left to right, back row: Pat Bliss (co-promoter), Lee Richardson, Krister Marsh, Tim Sugar (team manager), David Steen, Bill Dore (co-promoter). Front row: Glenn Cunningham, David Mullett, Paul Pickering.*

victory, which included double-figure returns from David Mullett, Glenn Cunningham and Paul Pickering. This really did bode well for the season ahead, however, the next home match against Arena-Essex in the Knock Out Cup on 7 April, saw Tara O'Callaghan crash out in the first heat. It was a bad crash and Tara was taken away in the ambulance nursing a broken leg, and his season was over almost as soon as it had started. The Racers rallied though, and Lee Richardson took extra rides to cover for the injured rider and ended up with paid 12 points, his best-ever performance up to that point. Glenn Cunningham also rattled up his first-ever 15-point maximum, as the Racers ran out winners by 53 points to 37.

The Racers opted to operate the rider replacement rule to cover for the injured Tara O'Callaghan, which meant a couple of meetings for Roger Lobb, before Bobby Eldridge came in as track reserve. Led magnificently by David Mullett, the Racers continued on their merry way, topping the southern group of the Premier League Cup, winning 7 of their ten matches to progress into the semi-final. Double-figure scores were coming thick and fast from David, and he was well backed by Glenn Cunningham, who became known as the 'Bristol Bomber' as he stormed around Smallmead and piled up the points. Lee Richardson was improving all the time and was helped in no small way by ex-Racer John Davis.

On 26 May, Edinburgh visited Smallmead and David Mullett top scored with 14 points as the Racers won 50-40. David's performance earned him the right to challenge Peter Carr for the first Silver Helmet match race to ever take place at Smallmead, and he didn't disappoint the home fans as he roared to victory. The following week though, after the Racers had seen off Sheffield 59-31, David unfortunately lost the helmet to the flying Robbie Kessler. The Racers then notched up away league wins at Hull (49-41), Sheffield (46-44) and Newcastle (48-41) in a brilliant five-day spell which saw them move to the top of the league table. The victory at Newcastle on 8 June was marred by a heat seven crash though, which saw Paul Pickering taken to hospital with a broken collarbone. Incidentally, in the match at Sheffield on 5 June, Glenn Cunningham challenged Robbie Kessler for the Silver Helmet, but had to concede second-best to the German ace.

On 4 July, the Racers travelled up to Edinburgh for the first leg of the Knock Out Cup semi-final, and despite a brilliant 14 points from David Mullett, they went down by 12 points (39-51). David did have the satisfaction though of smashing the Armadale track record in the first heat. 'Pickers' was back by the time Edinburgh came down to Smallmead for the second leg on 21 July, but the Racers could only manage a 48-42 victory on the night, with the Monarchs going through by an aggregate victory of 93 points to 87. The end of July saw Krister Marsh come into the side to replace Bobby Eldridge, who had been having a tough time of it.

No matter what, the Racers continued on their march to the League Championship, suffering rare defeats at Glasgow and Long Eaton, before going right through August and into September with nine straight wins. A defeat at Edinburgh on 12 September was followed by a league-clinching victory over Newport at Smallmead on 15 September. It was a real party night as the Racers beat the Wasps by 52 points to 38. Glenn Cunningham led the way with 14 points and was well backed by David Mullett's 12 points, as Reading claimed their fifth league title. The final league match of the year was at the Isle of Wight five days later, and saw the Racers suffer what was only their fourth league defeat of a glorious campaign.

David Mullett was the dominant rider, finishing on top of the overall Premier League averages with a staggering 10.68 figure. Glenn Cunningham had his best-ever year in speedway, finishing fourth in the PL averages on 10.06, proving he had well and truly arrived in his chosen sport. Great team-man David Steen had a tremendous year, notching 300 points in league and Knock Out Cup matches, and Lee Richardson also plundered

*Female mascot Charly Kirtland.*

300 points in a season of real progress for the youngster. Paul Pickering was probably expected to do a little better, but certainly wasn't helped by the collarbone injury at Newcastle – even so he still rattled up 276 points. Finally, Krister Marsh only rode half the season and found it tough going, but never stopped plugging away.

In the Premier League Riders' Championship at Coventry on 13 September, the Racers had two representatives. David Mullett top scored in the qualifying heats with 12 points to gain a place in the semi-final, and Glenn Cunningham also made it to the semi-final, scoring 10 points. The 'Bristol Bomber' then scampered into the final by finishing second behind Peter Carr in the first semi-final. However, David wasn't quite so fortunate as he came in third, behind Brett Woodifield and Robert Eriksson in the second semi-final. The final saw a first-bend clash which left Brett Woodifield in a heap. The race was stopped with the exclusion of Woodifield, but Peter 'The Motor' Carr made no mistake in the re-run, as he came home ahead of Glenn and Robert Eriksson. But all the same, second place for Glenn was a tremendous achievement.

The Premier League Pairs Championship was staged at Oxford on 26 September, with the Racers being represented by David Mullett and Lee Richardson. Despite a brilliant effort from Lee (who scored 19 points) and David (12 points), the Racers had to settle for the runners-up position, just 2 points behind the Long Eaton duo of Carl Stonehewer and Martin Dixon. The end-of-season Young Shield play-offs resulted in a quarter-final aggregate victory over the Isle of Wight by 113 points to 67, but the Racers lost out to Exeter in the semi-final, going down 84-96 on aggregate.

Smallmead also staged Amateur League racing in 1997, but due to there being thirteen teams in the league, it would have been impossible to stage a full home league programme of twelve fixtures. This problem was solved by Reading and Swindon teaming up under the banner of the M4 Raven Sprockets to stage six home meetings each. The Amateur League side did reasonably well to finish in seventh position, winning three of their home meetings at Smallmead and four at Swindon. The Raven Sprockets also enjoyed success on their travels at Lathallan, Buxton and against Belle Vue (although the match was staged at Buxton). Gary Phelps, John Jefferies, Keith Lansley, Steve Targett, Wayne Holloway, Simon Moon, Shane Colvin, Martin Williams, Ian Clarke and Karl Bainbridge all received an extended run in the side, with Jefferies topping the averages.

As the 1998 season started, everybody wondered how the Racers would follow the golden year of 1997. As it turned out, they did pretty well, finishing second in the league, behind the powerful Peterborough side, but they had some revenge, beating the Panthers over two legs to lift the Knock Out Cup. Conventional seven-man teams were the order of the day, as the format returned to the traditional way. Team changes saw Phil Morris return after a year at Stoke, while also returning was the popular Finn Petri Kokko. As usual, David Mullett was back, and joining him from the previous year were Lee Richardson and Krister Marsh, while completing the team were Justin Elkins and Lee Driver. From the previous season, Glenn Cunningham moved on to Peterborough, while David Steen linked up with Glasgow, and Paul Pickering spent the year at Stoke.

The season started at Edinburgh in the first leg of the Premiership on 27 March, but David Mullett was missing with a virus. Jesper Olsen stepped in as a brilliant guest, scoring 16 points, but it wasn't enough to stop the Racers from going down to a 37-52 defeat. The

*Reading Knock Out Cup final programme, 1998.*

tapes went up at Smallmead on 30 March with the second leg of the Premiership. Despite 14 points apiece from Petri Kokko and the fit-again David Mullett, Reading lost the opener by 42 points to 48, and the mighty Monarchs took the trophy by a handsome 100-79 scoreline on aggregate. The Racers got a much-needed win under their belt the following week though, when the Isle of Wight were sent packing 54-35 at Smallmead in a Knock Out Cup match. A solid team performance saw paid double-figure returns from Lee Richardson, Petri Kokko, Phil Morris and Justin Elkins. On 12 April, Reading notched up a brilliant 49-41 victory at Newport, which included a magnificent 15-point maximum from the 'Flying Finn' Petri Kokko.

The British Under-21 Championship Final took place at Arena-Essex on 24 April, with Scott Nicholls emerging victorious on 14 points. However, in second spot was the Racers' sensational Lee Richardson on 13 points. This was a superb performance from Lee, as the line-up of riders included Paul Lee, David Howe, Andre Compton, Simon Stead and Blair Scott. It was made all the more remarkable by the fact that Lee broke his hand in a heat seven crash, but got back up to ride in the re-run and complete the rest of his rides! Unfortunately, Lee's injury put him out of action for a month, with the Racers having to call on several guests to plug the gap.

May saw the Racers complete their Knock Out Cup fixtures, but not before they had suffered home and away defeats to Peterborough in the competition. How ironic it was that they should eventually turn the tables on the Panthers in the final at the end of the season. The match at Peterborough was a disaster, for not only did the Racers get hammered 27-60, but young Lee Driver was involved in a dreadful heat two crash, which left him with a broken thigh and crushed vertebra. To summarize briefly the Racers' Knock Out Cup record in the southern group section, 5 wins and a draw were enough to claim second spot and a place in the semi-final. Sadly, Lee Driver was out for the rest of the season and was subsequently replaced by Ian Clarke. Thankfully, by the end of May Lee Richardson was back in the saddle and he never looked back, rattling up double-figure scores everywhere the Racers went.

A Honda challenge match was staged at Smallmead on 22 June, as the Racers took on Newport. The visitors adapted better to the Honda machinery, winning by 51 points to 39. The racing was somewhat slower than normal and there was not much of interest for the supporters to enthuse over. At the start of July, Phil Morris joined the injured list when he broke an elbow in a French grass-track meeting. Phil was out of action for two months, during which time the Racers operated the rider-replacement facility. A further team change saw Paul Clews joining (via Peterborough) to replace Ian Clarke, who had struggled with the pace of Premier League racing. On 16 July, the Racers journeyed up to Sheffield for the first leg of the Knock Out Cup semi-final and a brilliant performance saw them return with a 45-45 draw. Heroes of the night were Justin Elkins (with a quite superb paid 13 points) and skipper Petri Kokko (who weighed in with 13 points). The second leg was held at Smallmead on 20 July, and the Racers ran riot with a 56-34 victory. Lee Richardson plundered 17 points and was ably backed by David Mullett (paid 14) and Petri Kokko (11), as the Racers marched into the final with an aggregate victory of 101-79.

The Premier League Pairs Championship was held at Newport on 26 July, with Reading being represented by David Mullett and Petri Kokko. David scored 9 points and Petri

8, as the Racers qualified for the semi-final. Petri went on to win the second semi-final, but unfortunately David fell off and although he remounted, he was unable to catch the Peterborough pair of Brett Woodifield and former Racer Glenn Cunningham. Under the scoring system, that meant a place in the final for Peterborough, who went on to win the event ahead of Exeter. David Steen celebrated his Testimonial at Smallmead on 3 August in a meeting entitled 'Bike Mania'. This featured speedway, moto-cross, quads and sidecars, with a crowd of over 3,000 in attendance. The speedway section of the event was won by David Mullett, after he had beaten Chris Louis in a run-off. Other riders taking part included Joe Screen, Todd Wiltshire, Armando Castagna, Carl Stonehewer, Jeremy Doncaster and Ray Morton.

The Racers had done well in the Four-Team Championship qualifying rounds, earning themselves a place in the semi-final at Peterborough on 30 August. Led by Lee Richardson with a maximum 6 points, they easily won their group for a place in the final, where they were joined by Edinburgh, Hull and Peterborough. Sadly, Reading couldn't reproduce their semi-final form, as Peterborough stormed to victory with 24 points, ahead of Edinburgh (19), Hull (19) and the Racers on 10 points. Thirty years of Reading Speedway was celebrated at Smallmead on the evening of 31 August, when many ex-riders, team managers and officials turned up for the league match with Exeter. The reunion was organized by the Racers' team manager Tim Sugar and was a roaring success. Bob Radford made a return to the microphone, interviewing many of the assembled guests, who witnessed the Racers run out winners by 59 points to 31. Reading were led quite magnificently by Lee Richardson with an outstanding 18-point maximum. This followed up an identical performance by Lee at Exeter in the morning, but it hadn't been enough to stop the Racers from losing 41-49. There surely can't be many riders who have scored 36 points on a single day in the whole history of speedway!

After beating Sheffield in the Knock Out Cup at Smallmead on 20 June, the Racers put together a marvellous run of eight wins in nine Premier League fixtures, to consolidate themselves in second position behind powerful Peterborough. The only reverse was the match at Exeter (previously mentioned), when Lee Richardson went through the card. Sheffield staged the Premier League Riders' Championship on 13 September, with Lee Richardson taking his place in the line-up. It wasn't Lee's day though, as he scored 6 points and was excluded from one ride in a meeting that was sensationally won by former Racer Glenn Cunningham.

The first leg of the Knock Out Cup final was staged at Peterborough on 18 September, and what a showdown it promised to be between the best two teams in the Premier League. Phil Morris had just made his track return, so the Racers were at full strength, and they produced a brilliant performance at the home of the League Champions. Lee Richardson roared to 14 points and Petri Kokko scored 12, as the Racers won in brilliant style by 46 points to 44. The second leg was held at Smallmead on 21 September and the Racers ran riot, winning 57-33 amidst a great party atmosphere. Lee Richardson again led the way with an immaculate 18-point maximum, while backing him up with 10 points apiece were David Mullett and Petri Kokko, as the Racers stormed to an aggregate 103-77 victory. The cup was subsequently presented to skipper Petri Kokko by former Racers legend Jan Andersson. David Mullett also claimed a place in the Reading history books for being the only Racer to win two Knock Out Cup finals with the club, in 1990 and 1998.

After the cup joy, the end of season Young Shield play-offs were something of an anticlimax, as the Racers went down to Glasgow by 88 points to 91 on aggregate. At the end of the season, Reading boasted no fewer than three men in the top ten of the overall Premier League averages. Lee Richardson was in third place with a staggering 9.96 figure, and had been absolutely brilliant throughout the season – he was by far the most improved rider in the league. Not quite so dominant in 1998, but fifth in the overall PL averages was David Mullett on 9.69, who completed his eleventh full-time season for the Racers. Seventh in the PL averages was Petri Kokko on 9.41, and he led the side by example in what was his best-ever year in the sport.

Backing up the top three was Krister Marsh, who notched up 190 points from his 37 league and Knock Out Cup matches, and showed great improvement throughout the season. Justin Elkins accumulated 164 points, but it could have been so much more, if only he could have solved his mechanical problems. Battling Phil Morris had a year to forget however, as he spent the bulk of it on the injured list following the aforementioned grass-track spill in France, but the potential was still there, if only he could stay injury-free. Paul Clews came into the side late on and proved popular with the crowd, who appreciated his non-stop battling efforts. The final Smallmead fixture of the season was a challenge match against Newport on 12 October. The Racers ran out winners by 56 points to 34, and the match featured a 15-point maximum from Petri Kokko, and a paid 15-pointer from the sensational Lee Richardson.

A Southern Track Riders meeting was held at Smallmead on 15 November, with Shane Colvin winning the open event, while all-rounder Les Rowlands won the Over-40s event. The year ended on a very sad note in early December, when Bill Dore died in Radcliffe Hospital, Oxford, at the age of seventy-six, almost a month after being admitted following a stroke. Tributes poured in from riders past and present for the man who had been the backbone of Reading Speedway, and there is no doubt that Bill was sorely missed by everyone connected with the club.

Pat Bliss started the 1999 season as sole promoter after the sad death of her father, but after two fantastic seasons of on-track success, the Racers came down with a bump. Team changes saw Krister Marsh link with Swindon, and Lee Richardson moved on to Poole in the Elite League. This was a quite understandable move for Lee after his superb year in 1998. Youngsters Peter Collyer and Shane Colvin were brought into the side, the rest of which was made up from 1998 regulars Phil Morris, Justin Elkins, Paul Clews and the evergreen David Mullett. Meanwhile, one off-track change in 1999 saw Reg Willis take over as the new starting marshall at Smallmead.

The tapes went up on the 25th consecutive season at Smallmead on 15 March when Newport arrived for the first leg of the Severn Bridge Trophy. It was a bad start for the Racers though, with the Wasps winning 51-38. Top man for Reading was David Mullett with 9 points, meanwhile Craig Watson collected a 15-point maximum for the visitors. The second leg, six days later, resulted in another Newport victory, by 54 points to 36, meaning an aggregate success of 105-74 for the Wasps. The Racers then got going with an aggregate success over old rivals Swindon in the Thames Valley Trophy. A 43-50 reverse at Blunsdon was followed by a 52-41 victory at Smallmead on 22 March, with Petri Kokko grabbing 14 points. A new competition, the Premier National Trophy, then started the season officially and Marc Norris, having just turned sixteen, took over from Peter Collyer in the team. The Racers won all four of their home group matches in the new competition, but unfortunately, lost all the away meetings to give them a final group position of fourth out of five teams.

The league campaign kicked off at Workington on 8 May with the Racers forcing a splendid 45-45 draw. The following day, they won 48-42 at Glasgow. Things looked even better the day after that, as the Racers won 49-44 at Newcastle with Petri Kokko recording a 15-point maximum at his former home track. Further success followed with home and away wins against Glasgow in the Knock Out Cup and Smallmead victories against Exeter and Glasgow (again) in the Premier League. The away Knock Out Cup match at Glasgow on 23 May was marred, however, by a heat fourteen crash which left Marc Norris nursing a broken arm. This meant an enforced lay-off for the youngster, who had been riding extremely well up to that point. Finn Jarno Kosonen was subsequently drafted into the side as his replacement. The following day, a Stars of Tomorrow meeting was held at Smallmead, and this resulted in a win for Jon Underwood with a 15-point maximum. Graig Gough finished second on 13 points, ahead of Simon Moon, who notched 11 points and beat Gary Phelps in a run-off for third place.

Three Premier League defeats at Edinburgh, Berwick and Newcastle followed, with the match at Berwick ending in controversy as Petri Kokko fell and suffered back injuries in heat thirteen. Rain had fallen throughout the day and the Racers refused to complete the match, due to the condition of the track. Disaster struck at Smallmead on 21 June, and the league match against Sheffield would be remembered for one thing only, a frightening horror smash in heat ten involving David Mullett and Andre Compton. Poor David Mullett ended up going through the fence and hitting the uprights as he went, suffering a broken left thigh and right ankle. The injury was to put David out of action for well over a year. The result of the meeting was academic, with the Racers going down by 40 points to 49.

The Racers then had three riders out injured and were in trouble as league defeats followed at the Isle of Wight and Sheffield. The Racers then made a quick exit from the Four-Team Championship, finishing bottom of their group. The Fours qualifying rounds were marred by an injury to Shane Colvin in the reserves race at Smallmead on 5 July though. This meant a return to the side for young Peter Collyer. Brief respite came in the second round of the Knock Out Cup against Sheffield at Smallmead on 12 July, as Petri Kokko and Marc Norris returned to help the Racers take a narrow 46-44 victory against the best team in the league. Three days later, however, they were well beaten (35-55) in the return at Owlerton. There was great news on 7 August, as former Racer Lee Richardson won the World Under-21 Championship in Vojens, Denmark, ahead of Ales Dryml and Nigel Sadler. This was a tremendous achievement for young Lee, as he took victory with a 13-point tally. There was a marvellous array of talent in the field, which apart from the top three included Hans Andersen, Charlie Gjedde, Bjarne Pedersen, Scott Nicholls, David Howe, Simon Stead and Chris Slabon.

Three weeks after the terrible accident to David Mullett, a new Swede was brought in to replace the veteran in the Racers' beleaguered side. His name was Per Wester, who arrived on the recommendation of former Racer Jan Andersson, and he was to prove a great acquisition. A further change saw Justin Elkins, who had been having continuous problems with his machinery, announce his decision to quit, although he later linked up with Edinburgh. On 12 September the Premier League Riders' Championship was staged at Sheffield, with Phil Morris representing the Racers. Against the cream of the Premier League, Phil battled away, but 5 points were all he could muster on the night.

It wasn't until the last home league match of the year on 20 September that the Racers won again. Edinburgh were the visitors and a superb paid 15-pointer from Petri Kokko – ably backed by paid 14 from Per Wester and 13 from Phil Morris – led the Racers to a 51-39 victory. This, in fact, was the first home league victory since 7 June, when Glasgow were defeated. The Racers won only five league matches all season and slumped to the bottom of the league, but despite this, the standard of racing seen at Smallmead was quite brilliant throughout the year. The regular fans seemed to appreciate the racing, none more so than the girls in the middle of the grandstand, who created a superb atmosphere all year long. As the season ended, long-serving Racers team manager Tim Sugar announced his decision to quit the post, stating that he needed to take a break having done the job since 1988. Tim had been a wonderful team manager, leading the Racers to the British League and Knock Out Cup double in 1990; the Premiership in 1991; the Division One League Championship and BSPA Cup double in 1992; the Premiership in 1993; the Premier League Championship in 1997; and the Premier League Knock Out Cup in 1998 – a truly brilliant record.

Quickly running through the 1999 boys, Phil Morris had his best year in the sport and realized all his early potential with greatly improved confidence. It was magic to watch Phil slice his way through the opposition at Smallmead as he rattled up 239 points and stayed free from injury. Petri Kokko was solid and led the team's scoring with 258 league and Knock Out Cup points, despite one or two injury problems. Good old David Mullett had settled back into the scoring groove, until he suffered that terrible injury against Sheffield. It was an awful thing to happen to a man who had given so much for the mighty 'Winged Wheel'.

Per Wester came in and was a revelation, scoring 140 points from the 13 matches he appeared in. Per had actually been known as Per Karlsson previously, but took his girl-friend's name upon the birth of their baby! Smashing lad Paul Clews battled away gamely and improved as the season wore on, scoring 157 points from 28 matches. Marc Norris burst on to the scene, but took that nasty bang at Glasgow, which took the steam out of his sails. When Justin Elkins was on form, he looked like a tiger hunched over the handle-bars and was wonderful to watch, but sadly his equipment let him down all too often. Finally, popular Finn Jarno Kosonen showed glimpses of form in some races, but was sadly off the pace in many others.

There was sad news in November, with the death of long-serving track marshall John Hook. It was also announced that Edna Chandler had died. Edna had for many years done so much work behind the scenes for the club and been a loyal supporter of the team. That same month, Channel 4 screened a fly-on-the-wall look at Reading Speedway and very good it was too, looking particularly at the careers of Phil Morris and Peter Collyer.

## 2000 Onwards

In the year 2000, Phil Morris started off his Testimonial year in great style by winning the New Year Classic at Newport on 2 January. Phil continued his great form from the previous year, scoring 8 points in the qualifying round to grab a place in the grand final. There he made no mistake, beating Brent Werner, Steve Masters and Robbie Kessler in the final and celebrated by jumping in the pond on the centre green! Later in January, it was announced that Pat Bliss would be helped in the season ahead by Chris Shears and Bernard Crapper, former promoters at Ipswich and Oxford respectively. It was stressed that they would not be coming on board in a promoting capacity, but would help out in an official capacity on meeting nights.

On 6 February, the Southern Track Riders staged a meeting at Smallmead. It was a pairs event and although Seemond Stephens was unbeaten, the scoring system meant a victory for Adam Pryer and Gary Fawdrey. Phil Morris continued his great start to the year by winning the Speedway Star Pairs event, along with Alun Rossiter, at Telford Ice Rink on 13 February. It wasn't an easy run to the Pairs Championship though, as the final had to be re-run twice, after Phil had taken a couple of tumbles. Wayne Broadhurst, who later went on to win the British Open Championship, eventually won the second re-run, but with 'Rosco' second and Phil third, it was enough to take the Pairs Championship. Sadly though, after those falls, Phil didn't contest the British Open Championship, but perhaps he was just giving all the others a chance!

Things looked bright for the Racers to bounce back in the season ahead and a great team had been assembled, with David Mullett taking over as team manager while recovering from his horrific injuries. The 'Italian Stallion' Armando Castagna made a very welcome return to the Smallmead camp and he was backed by Per Wester and Testimonial man Phil Morris in the heat-leader department. Returning after a steady year at Swindon was Krister Marsh, and also back for another term was the ever-improving Paul Clews. The final team spots went to youngsters Marc Norris and Shane Colvin, so everything was in place and looking good.

The pre-season optimism came crashing down right from the start, however, when the Isle of Wight arrived for Smallmead's opening fixture on 27 March, and stole away with a 47-43 victory in the Premier Trophy. On a night of problems, Armando Castagna only scored a single point and was unable to get his

*Krister Marsh.*

machinery going properly, while Per Wester could only muster an unconvincing 7-point tally from five starts. Reading bounced back with a 48-42 success at Stoke on 1 April, when the Potters' Neville Tatum suffered four exclusions for exceeding the 2-minute time allowance and didn't make it on to the track all night. The Racers' fortunes soon dipped again though, with a 42-48 reverse at Arena-Essex, and then a 43-47 home defeat at the hands of local rivals Swindon on 17 April. A further defeat followed at Newport (42-47), before Exeter thrashed the Racers by 66 points to 24 at their sweeping County Ground home.

Reading then beat the Falcons at Smallmead, before journeying to the Isle of Wight the following day and earning a surprise 46-44 success. Things seemed to be back on track, but the Racers then travelled to Swindon and lost 39-52. This was when things really started to go badly wrong, for Per Wester took a nasty looking spill on the back straight in heat four and was ruled out of the remainder of the meeting. Although Per was back for the following week at Smallmead, when Reading beat Newport 46-43, he only yielded 5 points and looked far from happy. Per rode on, complaining of headaches as the Racers lost at home to Stoke and then defeated Arena-Essex, but he was clearly not the rider he had been in 1999. The match against Stoke on 8 May was memorable for what happened afterwards, when David Mullett received the biggest cheer of the night as he donned his leathers for an after-match practice session. Despite his terrible injuries and such a long lay-off, David looked as if he had never been away, as he stormed around the Smallmead circuit in his old familiar style.

The home match against Arena-Essex had signalled the end of Reading's Premier Trophy fixtures, but with only five wins from their twelve matches, the Racers could only

*Armando Castagna leads from Swindon's Martin Dixon.*

finish sixth in the southern group table. The league campaign began with a 50-40 victory over Berwick at Smallmead on 22 May, with Per Wester looking much better as he notched a 10-point tally. However, a week later, Sheffield forced a 45-45 draw at the Racers' home, with Per struggling to score a 4-point tally. Defeats at Edinburgh and Berwick followed, before another embarrassing home defeat to local rivals Swindon in the Knock Out Cup on 5 June. Per Wester only scored 6 points against the Robins, and his evening included another frightening crash at the start of heat thirteen. Although the Swede took his place in the re-run, he was clearly far from fit and he stood down from the Reading team following the match.

Using David Walsh as a guest, the Racers battled hard in the second leg of the Knock Out Cup at Swindon, but a 2-point defeat meant an aggregate reverse of 87-93, as the Robins continued on their merry way. Guest riders became the order of the day, as Reading collected a 2-point home success over Newport, before suffering defeats at Hull and Sheffield. The racing at Smallmead was just as good as it had been the previous season, if not better, especially when the Racers gained a 47-43 victory over Stoke on 19 June. More defeats followed at Workington and Glasgow, as Reading struggled to find any consistency whatsoever.

Then on 3 July, Reading unveiled a new signing in the shape of eighteen-year-old Matt Read, who arrived on loan from Arena-Essex. The youngster notched just 3 points on his debut, as the Racers defeated Edinburgh 49-44, but the talent was obviously there and boded well for the future. There was then a two-week gap in the fixtures, before the Racers suffered a 43-47 home defeat at the hands of Newcastle, for whom Bjarne Pedersen was absolutely brilliant. Matt Read, unfortunately, fell in his opening ride, before running a last and then falling again in heat eight. Sadly, that was the end of Matt's spell with the Racers, as he suffered a shoulder injury, and preferred to concentrate on grass-track racing, rather than getting back into speedway when his injuries cleared. Reading were forced to use the rider-replacement facility for the youngster, and defeat followed at Arena-Essex, prior to a depressing loss at home to Glasgow.

Thankfully, there was some respite from the stress of team matches when Phil Morris staged his Testimonial meeting on 31 July. Despite several withdrawals, it was an enjoyable and successful night, boosted by the appearance of a number of Reading's finest from the recent past. As well as speedway, the large crowd was treated to sidecar and youth grass-track racing, as well as a football penalty shoot-out! Among the riders filling in for absentees was David Mullett, who made a terrific return and scored 8 points, including 2 race wins. Craig Watson went on to win the meeting, ahead of Todd Wiltshire, with Phil Morris finishing third in his own big event. Among those competing were ex-Racers Petri Kokko, Jeremy Doncaster and Ray Morton, but the night was all about the 'Welsh Wizard' and his ten loyal years of service to the 'Winged Wheel'.

League action resumed at Smallmead on 7 August, and in order to fit David Mullett back into the side, a complete revamp was necessary. This saw Reading continue with the rider-replacement facility for Matt Read, while both Krister Marsh and Shane Colvin were unfortunately sidelined. With the sport governed by averages, this was the only permutation that allowed the Racers to accommodate David on his green sheet figure of 8.77. Taking the remaining slot at reserve was Lee Herne, signed on loan from Newport, while replacing David as team manager was Tim Sugar, back in his old role. Sadly, all the moves failed to work, with Reading falling to a 39-53 loss to a rampant Hull side. David Mullett, riding with a pin in his left thigh, got through his return match safely, though notching a win in his 6-point tally.

A win came the following week against Arena-Essex, as Reading found themselves only one place off the basement position in the Premier League table. The match was a personal highlight for Phil Morris, however, as he went through the card to record the first full 15-point maximum of his long career with the Racers. Things then got worse for Reading as Swindon ran riot, winning 58-32 at Smallmead, before coasting to a 62-28 victory at Blunsdon. The rot had set in, and the only victory from the next 5 matches was a 2-point success over Exeter at Smallmead on 28 August. Following an 11-point haul in that match against Exeter, David Mullett's season came to a premature end as he had to return to hospital in order to have the pin removed from his thigh. Unfortunately, this meant that the Racers would have to complete their fixtures by employing guest riders.

The Premier League Riders' Championship took place at Sheffield on 10 September, but in a meeting won by Workington's Carl Stonehewer, the Racers' representative Phil Morris could only muster 3 points. The following evening, both Phil Morris and Armando Castagna were on hand to present Racers superfan Emily Brakespear with flowers and a gift to mark her ninetieth birthday. The evening marked a rare Reading victory, with a 48-41 success over the Isle of Wight, but it was too late to halt the Racers' slide, as they then occupied bottom position in the league. Reading completed their league schedule with defeats at the Isle of Wight and Newcastle to claim the unwanted statistic of finishing bottom of the pile for the second successive season, having won only seven matches out of twenty-six.

Amid pouring rain, Smallmead staged the seventh Test Match in the series between Young England and Young Australia on 18 September. It was a credit to all concerned that the meeting was completed and saw the English lads secure a 49-39 victory. As an indication of the atrocious conditions, the second heat was won by Swindon's Mark Steel in a time of 77.62 seconds, which was almost 20 seconds slower than Per Jonsson's track record, which was set in 1987! It is worth noting that the England side included the Racers' own Paul Clews, as well as some of the sport's up-and-coming stars such as Simon Stead, Danny Bird and Chris Neath.

It wasn't all gloom for Reading in 2000, for they finished off the season with a 91-89 aggregate victory over Newport to lift the Severn Bridge Trophy, with the second leg of the encounter bringing the curtain down at Smallmead on 2 October. After initially struggling to find his feet, 'Italian Stallion' Armando Castagna emerged as Reading's top man, plundering a total of 307 points from twenty-six league and Knock Out Cup matches for an impressive average of 9.12. Welsh number one Phil Morris carried on where he had left off in 1999, with 287 points and his first full maximum. Paul Clews developed into something of a thrill merchant, earning himself the nickname of the 'Smallmead Master', as time and again he came from the back. 'Clewsey' ended the season as Reading's third highest scorer with a total of 182 points. The brave David Mullett managed only seven matches before had had to have more surgery, and an average of 4.39 would prove to be very handy when the 2001 team was assembled. David's seven matches took his total appearances for the club to 405, just twelve short of Bernie Leigh's all-time record.

Prior to the start of the 2001 campaign, spirits were further lifted in the Racers camp when it was revealed that promoter Pat Bliss had agreed a deal that would see dashing Dane Charlie Gjedde join Reading on loan from his parent club Swindon. The twenty-one-year-old had originally linked up with the Robins in 1998, before spells with both Coventry and Wolverhampton in 1999. A broken kneecap had forced the youngster to sit out the following season, but apparently back to full fitness and raring to go, 'Champagne Charlie' would undoubtedly add strength to the Racers' top end. The remainder of the side was completed with familiar faces David Mullett, Armando Castagna, Phil Morris, Paul Clews, Marc Norris and Shane Colvin. The team looked pretty solid, so after two seasons of occupying the basement position in the Premier League, optimism was high that Reading would again aspire to their past glories and make a serious challenge for any silverware that was on offer.

The first track action of the year took place on 26 March, with the staging of an individual event, entitled the Smallmead Classic. This gave the riders a chance to shake off any rustiness and ease themselves back into the groove. To the delight of everyone present, David Mullett showed no ill effects from his leg surgery and rode well throughout, before roaring to victory in the final ahead of team-mates Charlie Gjedde, Phil Morris and Armando Castagna. The Premier Trophy campaign began the following week, with the Racers defeating local rivals Swindon 48-42 in a hard-fought Smallmead encounter. Reading's all-round strength throughout was enough to see them home, and the result emphasized that the Racers were a renewed force to be reckoned with. Another narrow home win (46-44) followed against Newport, before a stunning 51-39 success at the Clay Country Moto Parc, home of new boys Trelawny. On a night of superlative racing at the 230-metre circuit, 'Italian Stallion' Armando Castagna shattered the track record, while Charlie Gjedde sped to a brilliant paid maximum.

Although losses followed at Arena-Essex and Exeter, the scores were close and Reading were confident of collecting the bonus point in the return fixtures. They certainly achieved that goal when crushing Exeter 64-26 at Smallmead, before going down 40-49 at Swindon, losing out on the bonus by just 3 points on aggregate. Quickly returning to winning ways, Trelawny were the next to get a hiding at Smallmead, as Reading chalked up a huge 68-22 victory. That particular match saw Charlie Gjedde collect a 12-point maximum, with the 'Smallmead Master' Paul Clews racing brilliantly to a paid 15-point maximum. With Marc Norris appearing at Wolverhampton in the Under-21 Championship, youngster Chris Schramm stepped into the Reading line-up, and as things would turn out, 'Schrammy' was soon to become a regular in the side. A 4-point defeat at the Isle of Wight followed, but the Racers then charged to a 59-31 success over Arena-Essex, making sure of another bonus point along the way. The match against the Hammers marked one of the turning points of the season for Reading, however, with Marc Norris stepping down from the side after deciding to take break from speedway. In the event, Marc was to miss the remainder of the season, which was a great shame as he had such potential, and many thought he was on the verge of a major breakthrough. At the time of his departure, Marc had completed just eight Premier Trophy matches, scoring 19 points for a 3.59 average.

In a break from the Premier Trophy, the Racers enjoyed a 99-81 aggregate success over Newport to retain the Severn Bridge Trophy. With 23 points over the two legs, Danish superstar Charlie Gjedde proved to be Reading's top man, and it could safely be assumed that the starlet had indeed fully recovered from his horrendous knee injury. Back in Premier Trophy action, the Racers were shocked when the Isle of Wight came to Smallmead and stole away with a 46-44 win. The Islanders were to go on and enjoy a successful season, with most pundits labelling them as the dark horses and rightly so. Despite completing their Premier Trophy fixtures with a 47-43 win at Newport, that defeat at home to the Isle of Wight was to cost Reading dearly, and a third-place finish in the southern section table was not sufficient to see them progress to the semi-final stage.

In the Knock Out Cup, the Racers began well with a 45-45 draw at Arena-Essex, before completing a fine aggregate success with a 48-42 win at Smallmead. The league campaign then got underway, and with Shane Colvin missing after receiving a knock at Newport in the final Premier Trophy match, M4 neighbours Swindon forced a 45-45 draw, in a typical blood-and-thunder local derby that ended amid controversial circumstances. Charlie Gjedde was adjudged to have knocked off Robins star Alan Mogridge in the final heat, although many people, including Charlie himself, claimed there had been no contact. In the re-run, Swindon's top man, Paul Fry, was joined by the aforementioned Mogridge for maximum points to give the Robins a dramatic share of the points.

With Shane Colvin back on board the following week, Reading's Premier League hopes took another jolt, as pre-season favourites Hull became the second team in succession to force a draw at Smallmead. A 4-point defeat at Hull followed, before Reading received another bolt out of the blue, when Shane Colvin decided that his future lay elsewhere. Like Marc Norris before him, Colvin ended up sitting out the remainder of the campaign. Reading acted quickly and signed Tommy Palmer, who had been released by Newport. Shane would prove hard to replace, for he had been gating well and riding with more determination than ever before. When he stepped down, the nineteen-year-old had ridden in a combined total of fifteen official meetings, recording 70 points for an impressive 5.38 average. Sadly, although Chris Schramm showed plenty of promise, and the all-action Tommy Palmer harried away constantly, Reading battled on without the fire-power at reserve they had possessed at the season's beginning. Home wins followed against Trelawny and Edinburgh, while a 4-point defeat at Workington was quickly forgotten when the Racers secured a superb 2-point success at Glasgow.

Defeat at the home of eventual Champions Newcastle was followed by a Smallmead victory over the Isle of Wight and another win at Trelawny, as the Racers maintained their challenge in the top five of the Premier League table. The quarter-final of the Knock Out Cup provided a rest from the rigours of the league, but Reading were shocked when a fast-gating Exeter side restricted them to just a 10-point victory in the first leg at Smallmead. Although Reading dug deep in the second leg, they were unable to stop the Falcons from swooping to a 12-point victory and aggregate success. Reading were then represented by Charlie Gjedde and Phil Morris in the Premier League Pairs Championship at Workington. The duo performed heroically, battling through to the semi-final, only for Charlie to be excluded for a tapes infringement. Unfortunately, that meant a place in the consolation final, but at least they had the satisfaction of finishing third overall, after seeing off the challenge of Exeter pairing Lawrence Hare and Mark Simmonds.

On 15 July, Smallmead played host to a Testimonial for Armando Castagna. The popular Italian had first joined Reading in 1989, and was an integral part of the Championship winning sides of both 1990 and 1992, so his benefit meeting was richly deserved. A well-organized meeting attracted a good attendance, who witnessed Australian Jason Crump take victory in the final, ahead of Phil Morris and Steve Johnston, while Armando himself pulled up with mechanical problems. Back to league action, and Reading's hopes of challenging for the title went right off the rails on 19 July, when Paul Clews crashed in the final heat at Sheffield, suffering a painful broken thumb. Reading lost the match 40-52, and were subsequently forced to operate the rider-replacement facility for 'Clewsey'. Although the Racers managed to win the majority of their home matches, crucial late season Smallmead defeats were suffered at the hands of Workington, Exeter and Newcastle, as the rider-replacement system failed to cover Paul's rides adequately. The Racers managed one further away success at lowly Newport, plus a draw at Arena-Essex (the latter, ironically, with 'Clewsey' back in the saddle) on 21 September. They had missed Paul's brilliant racing and scoring ability for fifteen league matches, which, on top of their other problems, had been one mountain too many for Reading to climb in 2001.

Paul had, in fact, returned to the track five days before the match at Arena, when he appeared in David Mullett's Testimonial at Smallmead. David, who had adopted the nickname of the 'Smallmead Bullet' during 2001, was a most deserved recipient of what was actually a second Testimonial, having worn the 'Winged Wheel' with pride since first appearing for the club in 1985. His honours with Reading are recorded as follows: League Championship – 1990, 1992 and 1997; Knock Out Cup – 1990 and 1998; B.S.P.A. Cup – 1992; Four-Team Championship – 1993. In terms of Reading's all-time records, by the close of 2001, David had taken his total club appearances (in league and Knock Out Cup) to 437, putting him into first place, ahead of previous record-holder Bernie Leigh, who had made a total of 417 appearances. With regard to to David's special meeting, a good crowd turned out to pay homage and they witnessed an entertaining event, with victory going to former Racer Lee Richardson, who defeated Jeremy Doncaster, Phil Morris and Armando Castagna in the final.

The Racers ended the season in ninth position, and although it was a great improvement on the previous two seasons, it was almost as disappointing after so much more had been hoped for. Armando Castagna, who had announced his retirement from the

*Brendon Mackay.*

sport, bowed out superbly, scoring 291 points to top the league averages on 9.10. Charlie Gjedde was next in line with an average of 8.51, and this would surely have been much higher, but for his inability to consistently get out of the gate on level terms with the opposition. Skipper Phil Morris had another solid year, plundering 199 points for an 8.46 average, while David Mullett well and truly proved he had overcome those terrible injuries (scoring 220 points and attaining an 8.26 average), as well as being Reading's only ever-present rider. Mr Entertainer, Paul Clews, only appeared in thirteen league matches due to his injury, but he still managed to attain a solid 7.33 average, whilst Tommy Palmer finished with a figure of 3.56, and Chris Schramm averaged 2.87.

Finally, the home match against Workington on 13 August saw Reading introduce Australian Brendon Mackay to the side. The youngster came in on an assessed green-sheet average of 7.00, and in the event, he found this impossible to live up to. The potential was obviously there, but it was a struggle for points having started so late in the season, and Brendon ended up with a 0.94 average from 11 matches. However, with the young Aussie's services again required in 2002, he could well turn out to be a real trump card, starting the campaign at reserve with a more realistic assessed average of just 3.00.

# 3

# SWINDON

## The Early Days

Speedway was still enjoying the post-war boom when Bert Hearse (a Swindon businessman) along with his partner, L.R. Clark, plus Reg Witcomb (who had successfully promoted speedway at Bristol), conceived the idea of a track at Blunsdon. The late 1920s had seen dirt track racing held at the Swindon Autodrome, situated behind the Duke of Edinburgh public house in Gorse Hill. The track opened on 4 August 1928, when C. Harman, mounted on a 350cc O.K. Supreme machine, won both the Swindon Scratch Race and the Gorse Hill Scratch Race. A total of 12 meetings were staged that year; however, after an initial burst of support, interest faded quickly and the track disappeared after a few meetings in 1930.

## The 1940s

Early in 1949, work began on the construction of the Abbey Stadium in Blunsdon, and a track measuring 410 yards was eventually constructed with a cinder surface. It was on the warm summer evening of Saturday 23 July that the Swindon Robins (who were to operate as a non-league club) first took to the track in a challenge match against Oxford, who at the time were riding in the Third Division of the National League. Reg Lambourne (formerly with Fleetwood) was captain on that historic day, with the rest of the side being Bill Downton, Ginger Nicholls, Harry Hughes, Bob Jones, Ivor Atkinson and the two reserves, Paul Best and Tom Wilson.

The attendance was recorded as some 8,000 people, although former stadium general manager and speedway promoter Ted Nelson always believed that the crowd was nearer 10,000. Those present witnessed nineteen-year-old Patricia Dainton, the star of the Ivor Novello film *The Dancing Years,* cut the tape and declare the stadium open. Some two hours later, after fourteen heats of exciting speedway racing, the Robins had lost by 39 points to 45. Ginger Nicholls was very much the main man of the show – having got married earlier that day in Poole, he dashed back to ride for the Robins and top-scored with 11 points, winning the first-ever race and setting the track record of 82.8 seconds.

On 27 August, the track surface was changed from cinders to red shale and it certainly suited Bob Jones and his style of riding, for he immediately set a new track record of 77.6 seconds in the opening heat of a challenge match against Plymouth. 'Joner', as he was affectionately known, was to go on and become a legend at Swindon and is widely regarded as 'Mr Swindon Speedway'. Bob was born in Swindon in 1919,

# 2d.

# PROGRAMME

AT

# SWINDON SPEEDWAY

## Saturday, 14th June, 1930.

### Meeting Conducted by

## SWINDON SPEEDWAYS STADIUMS, Ltd.

**OFFICIALS :**

A.C.U. Steward—Mr. Allan

Judge—Mr. H. G. Newman.

Timekeeper—Mr. Yeoll.

Starter—Mr. H. Field.

Medical Officer—Dr. Gordon Young.

Clerk of the Course—Mr. T. Moseley.

Track Manager—Mr. W. J. Roper.

**NOTES.**

This meeting is held under the General Competition Rules of the A.C.U.

The total distance round this track is 356 yards.

Track Licence by A.C.U.

NO BETTING is allowed at any meeting.

The Management reserve the right to alter this programme if it deems necessary.

## NEXT SATURDAY AT THIS TRACK

# SPECIAL INTERNATIONAL MATCH RACE.

## Coming soon—CYCLONE BILLY LAMONT.

SWINDON
PRESS LTD.

*Rare Gorse Hill programme, 1930.*

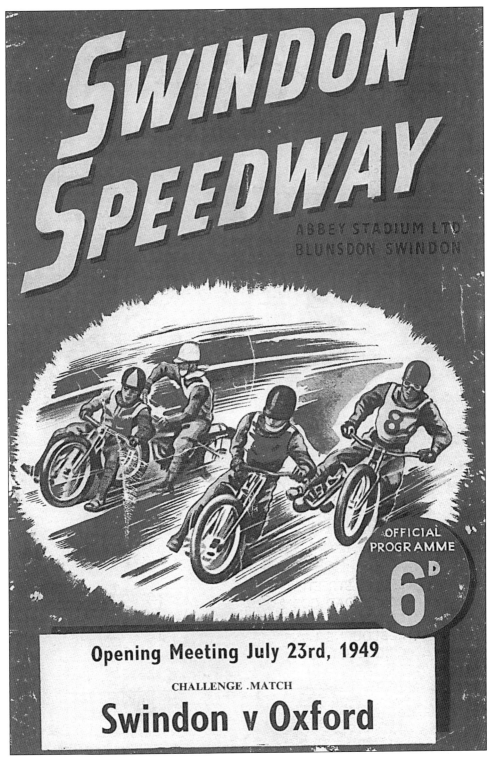

*First Blunsdon programme, 1949.*

and was, in fact, the first rider to sign for the Robins. Indeed, it was said that he actually sat out the 1948 season, having ridden for Bristol in 1947, in order that he would be free to join his hometown track! Over the years, Bob served the club as a rider, mechanic, team manager and machine examiner. Right up to his death in December, 1996, Bob proudly claimed that he had never missed a meeting at Blunsdon in 48 seasons of racing!

After just two months of open licence racing, Swindon received an unexpected boost when Third Division Hull were forced to close down and the Robins were invited to take over the remaining fixtures of the East Yorkshire side. Managing director Reg Witcomb was only too pleased to accept the offer on behalf of Swindon. In order to strengthen the Robins team, four of the defunct Hull side joined the Blunsdon set-up, those riders being Mick Mitchell, George Craig, Alf Webster and Derek Glover. Five of the existing pool of riders were retained, namely Reg Lambourne, Bob Jones, Bill Downton, Harry Hughes and Tom Wilson, while the rest were given free transfers. The biggest surprise was the failure of Ginger Nicholls to continue his good form of the opening meeting. Ginger, whose real name was actually Stan, struggled badly and it was a major disappointment after his early success: indeed, by late August, he was down to just second-half rides.

The Robins began their league campaign with an away fixture at Poole on 5 September. They lost that first official match 31-53. The line-up from that historic meeting is recorded thus: (1) Mick Mitchell; (2) Bill Downton; (3) Derek Glover; (4) Allan Briggs; (5) Alf Webster; (6) Reg Lambourne; (7) George Craig; (8) Bob Jones. Mitchell topped the Swindon scoring with 10 points, but received very little back-up against a powerful-looking Poole outfit for whom three riders scored double figures – Ticker James (12), Cyril Quick (11) and Fred Pawson (10). A further four away defeats followed at Hastings, Hanley, Plymouth and Leicester, before Swindon staged their first home league match. Hastings were the visitors to Blunsdon for the occasion on 17 September, but the Robins lost a thrilling meeting by just 2 points (41-43). The following week, however, they did register a first league victory when defeating local rivals Oxford (42-41) in a thrilling encounter.

Swindon only completed 13 league matches that year, as Hull had already ridden 35 of their scheduled fixtures at the time of their withdrawal. The combined record of the two tracks was enough for Swindon to finish in eleventh position in the thirteen-team league, with Mick Mitchell topping the Robins' averages on 7.13. George Craig was next in line (6.69), with Bob Jones (6.08) being the only other rider to achieve an average in excess of 6 points. One thing, however, was very clear: the fans of the Robins had shown their love of the sport in a very short time, with membership of the Supporters' Club topping the 5,000 mark.

## The 1950s

During the winter break, floodlights were installed and for the opening match of the 1950 season, before an estimated 10,000 crowd, speedway racing took place under a blaze of light. The meeting was a challenge match against Second Division Cradley

Heath, but the Robins unfortunately went down to a 38-45 defeat. New signing Alex Gray, a Londoner who moved down from Liverpool (exchanged for Alf Webster and Derek Glover), rode well, as did Danny Malone, a Bristol lad who had originally been noticed practising in a field by Reg Witcomb. The *Robins Monthly* magazine, which was published for members of the ever-expanding Supporters' Club, urged fans to refrain from showering the riders with gifts, as sweets, apples and pears regularly had to be cleared from the circuit!

A first-ever individual meeting was held at Blunsdon on 3 June, when Tamworth's Brian Wilson was triumphant with 14 points in the Swindon Silver Trophy. Oxford's Frank Boyle was second, while Harwood Pike of Leicester was third in the thrill-packed event. Two weeks later, a qualifying round of the World Championship was held at Blunsdon, with Liverpool's Reg Duval emerging victorious on 14 points. Bill Clifton of Cradley Heath was second, with Sheffield's Jack Chignell in third place. For some time, Swindon topped the Third Division table, but injuries to Danny Malone and Ron Clark, who had been signed from defunct Hastings, put paid to their chances of success, although a final position of fourth in their first full season was a highly commendable achievement. The Robins' league record included away wins at Exeter, Leicester, Rayleigh and St Austell, although that was somewhat offset by 3 home defeats during the season.

Team changes during the campaign saw Frank Evans and Hugh Geddes join the club, while Bill Downton and Mick Mitchell moved on to pastures new. Mitchell had, in fact,

*Swindon 1950. From left to right, back row: Reg Witcomb (promoter/team manager), Bill Downton, Ron Clark, Reg Lambourne, Alex Gray, Bob Jones. Front row: Mick Mitchell, Danny Malone, George Craig.*

started the season as team skipper, but upon his departure, the vacant position was taken over by Alex Gray. Second Division Walthamstow visited Blunsdon on 23 September, and although it was only a challenge match, the gulf between the two divisions was quite apparent, with the Robins suffering a 33-51 defeat. Jimmy Grant (11 points), George Newton (10) and Jim Boyd (9) led the way for the free-scoring Division Two side.

By the end of the season, the Blunsdon track record had been lowered to 75.2 seconds by Oxford's Pat Clarke, who established the time on 7 October. Reg Lambourne and Bob Jones remained ever-present throughout the year, while three members of the team finished with 8-point averages – Hugh Geddes (8.44), Mick Mitchell (8.21) and Alex Gray (8.18). Both Gray and Geddes made it through to the Division Three Riders' Championship at Walthamstow, but could only muster 6 points and 3 points respectively.

With Buster Brown, on loan from Wembley, added to the team strength in 1951, the Robins had strong league title aspirations, but their hopes were to be dashed by a series of injuries. Firstly, Ron Clark fractured a leg at Long Eaton on 29 March, which sadly spelled the end of his speedway career. Then Dennis Newton, a young novice who had shown brilliant form with a 16-point tally against Cardiff in a Festival of Britain match on 14 April, unfortunately broke a thigh in the very next home match against Exeter. Sadly, that brought his season to a premature end. That wasn't the end of Swindon's problems though, as Alex Gray suffered with poor health and Reg Lambourne missed several meetings with a damaged shoulder.

There was an unwanted first at Blunsdon on 11 August, when the league match against Wolverhampton was rained off. Prior to that, the Abbey Stadium had hosted 65 consecutive meetings since opening in 1949. Under the captaincy of Bob Jones, the remaining Robins plugged away gamely to finish the season in fifth position, without any real top-end strength. Fifth place was a reasonable position though, considering the Robins boasted five riders with 7-point averages, the highest of which was Buster Brown on 7.87. The others were Alex Gray (7.69), Hugh Geddes (7.54), Danny Malone (7.35) and Frank Evans (7.13). The side also battled past both Long Eaton and Poole to reach the Third Division final of the

*Buster Brown.*

*Bob Jones.*

National Trophy, before going down by an aggregate score of 92-124 to Exeter.

Despite the injuries, support remained healthy and this was borne out by the fact that 1,500 Robins fans followed their favourites down to Poole for a league match! The Abbey Stadium played host to two big individual meetings in 1951, with Hugh Geddes romping to success in a World Championship qualifying round with a 15-point maximum, while Bristol's Billy Hole won the Silver Trophy, also with maximum points. Two 'C' Test Matches were staged at Blunsdon late on in the season, against New Zealand and America. On 1 September the Kiwis defeated England 57-51, and although Ken Middleditch plundered an 18-point maximum for the English, the rest of the homesters had no answer to New Zealand's three-pronged attack of Trevor Redmond (15 points), Bruce Abernethy (12) and Mick Holland (10).

England bounced back to beat the Americans 57-48 on 14 September, however, with Gerald Jackson scoring 14 points and Ken Middleditch 12. It was a much more solid England performance, although having said that, the visitors did boast three men in double figures, namely Ernie Roccio (13), Nick Nicolaides (12) and Don Hawley (12). Swindon riders Bob Jones, Buster Brown and Frank Evans proudly received caps during the Test Match series but, sadly, Ray Ellis, an early-season signing from Harringay, missed out after he had suffered a fractured skull in a match at Exeter on 20 August.

By the end of the season, Trevor Redmond had the distinction of being the track record holder, having scorched around Blunsdon in 74.2 seconds while riding for Aldershot on 14 July. Buster Brown was one of three Swindon representatives at the Cardiff-staged Division Three Riders' Championship, but he only managed to score 6 points, while Danny Malone and meeting reserve Hugh Geddes recorded just a single point each.

The 1952 season was due to open at Blunsdon with a challenge match against Swedish side Kaparna, but unfortunately the weather intervened and the meeting was never staged. The following week (on 5 April), however, the tapes went up on the season with a match against Smederna, another Swedish team. Smederna were a powerful outfit and had finished the previous year as runners-up in their own First Division, so it was no surprise that they walloped the Robins by 55 points to 29. Rune Sormander and Bosse Andersson both stormed to paid maximums for the tourists, while Olle Segerstrom chalked up paid 10 points. For the sorry homesters, the most points came from Buster Brown, and even he could only muster 7.

The Third Division was renamed the Southern League, but after starting with eleven teams competing, the number was reduced to ten when Long Eaton withdrew after 21 matches. Changes in the Robins' nest saw Hugh Geddes leave for Cardiff to be replaced by Bob Wells, a veteran rider purchased from Wembley. However, perhaps the most significant signing was Welshman Ian Williams, younger brother of the Wembley riders Freddie (who was to become a double World Champion in 1950 and 1953) and Eric. Ian made his debut against Long Eaton at Blunsdon on 12 April and scored 3 points. He was to develop into one of the finest riders ever to wear the Swindon colours and remained with the club all the way through until the end of 1963.

Individual success during the year at Swindon went to Cradley Heath's Harry Bastable in a World Championship qualifying round, and Dick Bradley of Bristol, who scooped the Silver Trophy. A representative match was staged at Blunsdon on 6 September, when Young England lost 46-62 to Young Overseas. Robin Hugh Geddes appeared for the Overseas side, but failed to score from either of his rides. Following a fall in his first outing, Maurice Dunn reeled off 5 straight wins to top-score for the victors, while England's best were Alan Smith (12 points) and George Wall (11).

The Robins finished in sixth position in the Southern League and, at the end of the season, Reg Witcomb, who had done so much to make speedway a success in the town, left the club to be replaced by Bill Dutton. Frank Evans remained ever-present throughout Swindon's 36 league matches and topped the Swindon averages on 8.09, with Danny Malone finishing on 7.37, and Bob Jones on 7.32. 'Joner', who also remained ever-present, plundered an impressive 5 full maximums during the campaign. After the end of the speedway season, a first-ever midget car meeting was held at Blunsdon on 11 October. Greyhound racing was also introduced shortly afterwards, on 1 November 1952.

Early in 1953, Swedish side Filbyterna visited the Abbey and Swindon supporters had their first glimpse of Ove Fundin, who raced to a 12-point maximum. Fundin was well supported by Joel Jansson's 11-point haul, but Swindon battled hard and eventually lost by just 4 points (40-44). During Bill Dutton's time at Swindon, a number of youngsters from New Zealand and Australia joined the club, namely John Lee, John Lawrie, Les Saville and Bluey McCoy. However, none of them stayed very long, with McCoy being the most successful of the bunch. Blunsdon again held a Young England versus Young Overseas match, with the English going down to a 36-47 defeat. Three Swindon riders appeared for England, with both Ian Williams and Danny Malone collecting 4 points apiece, while Bob Jones failed to score. The previously mentioned Bluey McCoy rode for the Overseas outfit, but could only muster a single point. Johnny Chamberlain was the pick of the riders on show, scorching to a 12-point maximum for the victors.

Swindon and Oxford raced for the Supporters' Cup, and over the two legs the local rivalry was evident, as the Robins clinched a narrow aggregate victory by 101 points to 90. Swindon finished fourth in the eight-team Southern League and enjoyed some very good crowds. Ian Williams was at the helm of the scoring with 220 league points and a highly satisfactory 8.39 average. Danny Malone had a solid year, scoring 208 points for an 8.15 average. Ron Swaine, signed from Harringay, developed into a most useful rider and Mick Holland, who was signed following the early closure of Cardiff, was an

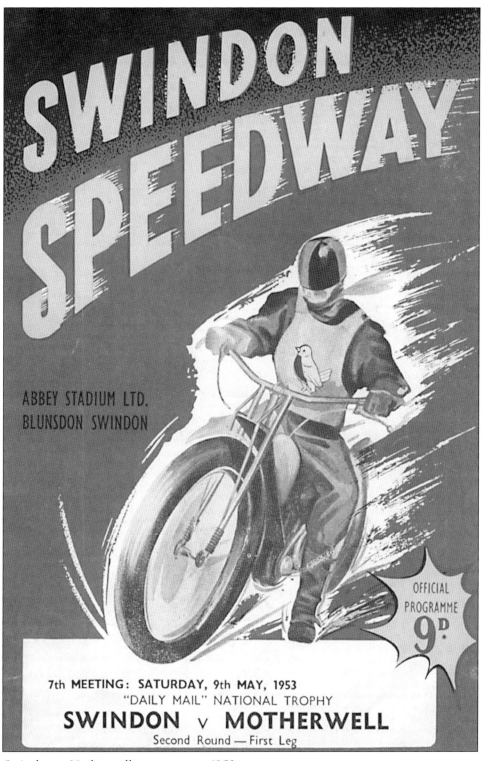

*Swindon v. Motherwell programme, 1953.*

*Ian Williams.*

excellent scorer, although his appearances were restricted by injuries.

The mid-1950s were difficult times for speedway, with the introduction of television gripping the nation. Swindon continued to enjoy good support though, and 1954 saw the Second Division and the Southern League join forces to form a National League Division Two, consisting of fifteen teams. Sadly, Glasgow and Wolverhampton closed prior to riding any league matches, with Edinburgh and Plymouth closing after only a handful of meetings, thus reducing the league to just eleven sides.

At Swindon, an important signing was made when Norman Parker, the former Wimbledon rider and an international of note, joined the club as manager in place of Bill Dutton. Parker immediately began a team-building programme that saw Frank Evans, Bob Wells and Reg Lambourne move on and Bob Roger (from Birmingham), Ray Harris (from Stoke) and George White (from New Cross) come in as replacements. Parker had been impressed by 'Chalky' White when he saw the diminutive rider winning an open meeting at Norwich the previous year, and his signing would prove to be a shrewd one. Bob Roger, too, was a marvellous rider to have on board, and he showed his paces when victorious in the Blunsdon-staged World Championship qualifying round on 10 July. Three weeks later, Poole's Ken Middleditch showed his liking for the Blunsdon bowl when scorching to victory in the Jack Parker 100 Guineas Trophy.

Earlier on, the season at Blunsdon had opened with a first-ever visit of the legendary Belle Vue team. Somewhat surprisingly, the Robins sent their illustrious visitors packing, winning 46-37. Ian Williams and Ron Swaine yielded 10 points apiece for the super Swindon side, with the Aces' top men being Ken Sharples and Harry Edwards, who each scored 9 points. 'Wizard of Balance' Peter Craven only managed to score 6 points in what was a somewhat disappointing Belle Vue display. Swindon finished the season in third position and used just nine riders during the campaign. Bob Roger was the leading rider, scoring 161 points for a brilliant 9.71 average. Ian Williams (8.26) and Mick Holland (8.00) provided solid backing, while George White had a year of steady progress, scoring 109 points from his 20 league matches. The Robins boasted two riders on the rostrum at the Belle Vue-staged Division Two Riders' Championship, with Ian Williams finishing second on 13 points, and Bob Roger joint third with 11 points. The Supporters' Cup probably meant as much as anything else to the fans of Swindon and Oxford, and to the delight of the Blunsdon faithful, it was the Robins who held on to the trophy with a brilliant 118-73 aggregate victory.

Swindon's track record was further lowered in 1954, with Bristol rider Dick Bradley being credited with a remarkable time of 71.0 seconds. Bradley's time was set on 8 May, a night when all the other heat times fluctuated between 75.0 and 78.8 seconds. To this day, many people still question the time given for his heat five ride. Some four years later, when nobody had got close to Bradley's time, it was decided that due to the introduction of a different type of tyre, a new track record should be established. Finally for 1954, another sport was introduced to Blunsdon on 25 September, with the first-ever stock car meeting at the stadium.

In 1955, much was expected in an eleven-team Second Division, but things sadly went wrong. On the main speedway front, both Bristol and Weymouth closed, and Swindon were shocked when Mick Holland retired after just three matches before returning home to his native New Zealand. As if this wasn't enough, Norman Parker resigned early in the season, due to pressure of business. Vic Scales, who had joined Swindon to take care of the mechanical side of things, took over as team boss. To add insult to injury, soon after Parker's resignation, George White suffered a broken wrist. Jimmy Gooch subsequently joined the Robins on loan from Wembley and did very well, but George was replaced in the main by guest riders, which was fine, except that the popular 'Chalky' was simply irreplaceable. Nobody was quite able to get the crowd on their toes like wee George.

Three big open meetings were staged at Blunsdon during the season, the first of which was a World Championship qualifying round on 9 July, which was won by Ian Williams with a brilliant 15-point maximum. Dick Bradley was triumphant in the Jack Parker 100 Guineas Trophy the following month, while Exeter's Neil Street lifted the Sir Noel Arkell Trophy in September after plundering a full 15

*George White.*

points. Swindon's final home meeting of the season saw the first-ever visit of the brilliant Wembley side to Blunsdon. To say that Swindon were pulverized would be an understatement, for they crashed to a 29-67 defeat. Bob Roger and Danny Malone did their best to stem the tide with 11 points apiece, but they received very little backing. For the free-scoring visitors, Brian Crutcher bagged a 15-point maximum, while Eric French recorded a paid 15-pointer and Freddie Williams plundered paid 13.

In an average sort of season, Swindon just avoided the wooden spoon, which went to Exeter. Bob Roger (with 327 league points) and Ian Williams (with 239) did their best to keep the Swindon flag flying, but with an endless string of guest riders and some mediocre performances, the Robins didn't really deserve to finish any higher. The only good news in a difficult season was an aggregate 125-91 victory over local rivals Oxford in the Supporters' Club Cup.

In 1956, there were but seven teams in the Second Division of the National League, and the Robins boasted as fine a heat-leader trio as any club in Bob Roger, George White and Ian Williams. Vic Scales had moved on, and Swindon replaced him from within their own ranks by offering the team manager's post to Bob Jones, who had been an essential part of the club since the very first meeting. The opening meeting didn't bode well for the season ahead, with the Robins losing 42-53 to Swedish touring side, Monarkerna. The visitors were superbly led by a full-house from the legendary Ove Fundin, while Bernt Nilsson was paid for 15 and Olle Nygren picked up 12 points after suffering an engine failure first time out. The Robins scored solidly throughout, but none of them reached double figures in a very disappointing start.

However, once the league programme got underway, Swindon definitely looked the part, beating all-comers to the Abbey, as well as picking up away wins at Oxford, Ipswich (twice), Coventry and Leicester. The Robins won 16 of their 24 league matches to pip Southampton by a point and win the Championship. A home defeat at the hands of Rayleigh in June almost upset the apple-cart, but the riders just about held their nerves in a nail-biting finish to the season. Fearless Bob Roger led the Swindon averages with a massive 9.53 figure, which included 7 full maximums along the way. There wasn't much to choose at the top end of the Robins' attack, for Ian Williams finished with a 9.52 average, only fractionally behind Bob Roger's figure. 'Chalky' White also boasted a 9-point average, having yielded 262 points from his 24 matches.

Winning the league was a team effort though, and the 'big three' were ably backed throughout the year by Ernie Lessiter, Ray Harris and Ron Swaine. Others who made appearances as and when required were Al Sparrey, Roy Taylor and Glyn Chandler, but the saddest event of the year was the retirement of stalwart Danny Malone, who was forced to quit after just 6 league matches, due to injury. Not satisfied with topping the averages, Bob Roger stormed to maximums as he took victory in both big meetings at Blunsdon during the year – the World Championship qualifying round in July and the Jack Parker 100 Guineas Trophy in September.

In a welcome alternative to the cut and thrust of National League racing, the homeless Southern Rovers side used the Blunsdon circuit for one of their Southern Area League fixtures on 25 August when they defeated California 42-41. Once again, Swindon retained the Supporters' Club Cup with an aggregate 113-102 success over

*Bob Roger.*

Oxford. Wembley returned to Swindon in an end-of-season challenge match, and as a measure of the Robins' improvement since the famous Lions' previous visit, it was the homesters who ran out winners by 49 points to 47. Bob Roger blitzed the opposition with a full 15 points, while George White gleaned 12, and Ian Williams took 10. Brian Crutcher (13) and Eric French (12) were top scorers for a Wembley team that also included future Swindon star Mike Broadbanks. Long after the dust had settled on the season's racing, Wimbledon staged a meeting on Boxing Day, namely The Christmas Vase, which was won in fine style by Robins throttle merchant, Bob Roger.

1957 was an unhappy year for speedway in general, although an excellent one for Swindon. The First Division lost Wembley, Poole and Bradford (although Bradford would later replace Birmingham in mid-season). The withdrawal of those teams had much to do with the remaining First and Second Division teams amalgamating to form the National League. In an equalization of team strengths, Swindon signed Ken Middleditch (who had long been one of the most popular visitors) from Poole, and for £50 secured the services of Mike Broadbanks from Wembley. This must rank as the bargain of the decade, as 'Broady' went on to become a brilliant rider, a fine team skipper and World Finalist during his time with the Robins. Later on, Neil Street, who had stayed in his native Australia following the closure of Exeter in 1955, returned to begin a career of distinction at the Abbey Stadium.

*Ken Middleditch.*

Swindon, once the league campaign began, did not have a weak link. For the first time they completed their home league programme with a 100 per cent record, which included several thrashings, most notably against Birmingham (77-19), Coventry (70-26), Leicester (64-32), Belle Vue (63-33) and Rayleigh (63-33). Away from Blunsdon, the Robins chalked up victories at Ipswich, Oxford, Rayleigh, Southampton and Wimbledon. In a quite stunning campaign, which went down to the wire, it was the Swindon men who took the Championship, finishing just a single point ahead of second-placed Belle Vue.

Bob Roger had a great season, scoring 250 league points, and his team riding with Ken Middleditch during the season was a joy to behold. Ray Harris and Ron Swaine had moved out and Swindon used just nine riders during the season, plus a guest appearance by Dick Bradley at Coventry (where he scored 15 points). Ever-present Bob Roger's final average was a monumental 10.27, and his fantastic riding also yielded 8 full and 2 paid maximums. George White scored 195 points for an 8.61 average, while Ian Williams finished on 8.17. Super team-man Middleditch posted a 7.54 figure over the course of the season, while Neil Street (6.70), Ernie Lessiter (6.44) and Mike Broadbanks (5.21) all played major roles. Al Sparrey made 2 appearances, with Glyn Chandler partaking in just a single match. What a wonderful season, with Bob Jones doing the team managing and taking care of any mechanical problems.

With a 121-71 aggregate victory over Oxford, Swindon yet again retained the Supporters' Club Cup – that being the Robins' fifth consecutive victory over the old enemy in the competition. Meanwhile, in the Britannia Shield, Swindon failed to go beyond the group stage after only winning 4 of their 10 matches. A single individual meeting was held at Blunsdon during the year, with Ian Williams recording a maximum when winning a World Championship qualifying round. Swindon boasted three World Finalists in Bob Roger, George White, and Ian Williams: indeed, they were unlucky not to have four, as Ken Middleditch just missed qualifying by the skin of his teeth. The final at Wembley on 21 September saw Roger score 8 points, while White collected 4 and Williams claimed 3. The meeting, incidentally, was won by a man who would later become a real Robins legend, namely Barry Briggs, who beat Ove Fundin in a run-off after both had finished on 14 points. Bob Roger also challenged Peter Craven for the Golden Helmet and having won in brilliant style at Swindon, lost out to Peter at Belle Vue and in the subsequent decider at Norwich.

Everything seemed to go wrong for Swindon in 1958. Firstly, Ken Middleditch wanted to retire to concentrate on his business interests and Swindon sportingly let him return to his former base at Poole. Having run with an open licence the previous season, Poole had reopened under promoter Vic Gooden, who had moved his Rayleigh set-up lock, stock and barrel to the Dorset track. The second disaster of the year occurred on Easter Monday (7 April) and again involved Poole. While guesting for Poole against Southampton at Wimborne Road, Swindon's main man, Bob Roger, was involved in a very nasty heat eight crash with Split Waterman and Brian Crutcher, which left him with a fractured skull. Sadly, although Bob later attempted a track return, the accident prematurely finished his speedway career.

Swindon welcomed Swedish tourists Monarkerna to Blunsdon again, but the visitors failed to provide any spark, with the Robins racing to a 63-30 victory. Olle Nygren and Birger Forsberg collected 8 points apiece for the Swedes, but received little support against the rampant Robins, for whom George White scorched to a paid maximum. Heat fourteen of the match was farcical though, as all the riders stopped at the end of the first lap after seeing the red lights switched on. However, this was apparently because Roy Moreton had been excluded for a tapes offence and eventually Mike Broadbanks continued on his way. Olle Nygren and Bengt Brannefors were not as quick to react and before they had got going again, 'Broady' had lapped them. Mike went on to win in a time of 139.2 seconds – the slowest ever recorded at Blunsdon!

There was controversy in the away league match at Belle Vue on 21 June, when the fixture was run in far from ideal conditions. The Swindon boys were unhappy to continue riding after heat six and asked the referee to inspect the track. The meeting official refused to do this and put the riders for the next race on 2 minutes. With neither Swindon rider (Mike Broadbanks and guest Ken McKinlay) making it to the start, Belle Vue rode to an untroubled 5-0 race victory. Swindon then decided to contest the rest of the match, but asked that heat seven be re-run with its original line-up! The referee agreed and the race subsequently ended as a 3-3, much to the disgust of Belle Vue, who then rode under protest. Swindon went on to win the match 51-45, but following an appeal, the original result of heat seven was reinstated, but although this affected the final result, Swindon still won by 48 points to 47.

The Abbey Stadium played host to two big individual meetings during the year, and these saw George White win the Midland Riders' Championship qualifying round, while Ron How took the honours in a World Championship qualifying round. On 11 June, Blunsdon staged the prestigious first Test Match between England and Australasia. The spectators were treated to a feast of speedway, which saw the Australasians claim a hard-fought 57-51 victory. The great Barry Briggs led the victors' scoring with a superb 18-point maximum, while Neil Street and Peter Moore weighed in with a dozen points apiece. England were led by 16 points from Peter Craven, but he received scant support. Three Swindon riders appeared for the English, namely George White (8 points), Mike Broadbanks (7 points) and Ian Williams (4 points).

Swindon also entered a side in the Junior League, and although they ran 2 home matches, none of the competing teams fulfilled their quota of fixtures and the competition ended in disarray. In August, it was decided that as a different type of tyre had been introduced to the sport, a new track record should be established at Blunsdon. Nobody had ever got near to Dick Bradley's record that was set in 1954, and frankly, this seemed like a good excuse to wipe the slate clean. Peter Craven was quick to establish a new record time of 74.8 seconds on 23 August, although this was 3.8 seconds slower than Bradley's previous record!

Swindon had to rely on guest riders throughout the year, and with George White and Ian Williams slightly down on scoring power, the Robins slumped to sixth position in a ten-team league. However, it was not all alarm at the Abbey, as Mike Broadbanks continued to make excellent progress, actually topping the league averages with an impressive 8.42 figure. Neil Street was a model of consistency

# ABBEY STADIUM
## BLUNSDON · SWINDON

■

### *Junior League Speedway Match*

# Swindon Juniors

## *v.*

# Yarmouth Juniors

## Saturday, July 12th, 1958

■

## PROGRAMME . . . SIXPENCE

*Swindon Juniors v. Yarmouth Juniors programme, 1958.*

scoring 166 points. Ernie Lessiter, such a brilliant reserve during the 1957 season, retired after completing 10 league matches for a disappointing 3.89 average. Ron Swaine came out of retirement to help the Robins during an injury crisis and the experienced Roy Moreton also made a comeback at Blunsdon.

The Robins made it through to the semi-final of the National Trophy, but they were unable to contain Norwich and went down to a 111-129 aggregate defeat. Swindon did much better than they had done the previous season in the Britannia Shield, finishing second in the southern group. However, only the top position was good enough for a passage through to the final and that honour went to Wimbledon. The whole club was given a great boost when Mike Broadbanks qualified for the World Final at Wembley, where he scored 5 points. It was the first of five full World Finals for the popular 'Broady', a real speedway stylist and one of the most loyal riders to ever don a Swindon race jacket.

The start of the 1959 season saw Swindon fans rocked when the 'Red Devil', Mike Broadbanks, asked for a transfer, a request he thankfully withdrew in July. Swindon signed Gerry King from Wimbledon and gave opportunities to the promising Leo McAuliffe. Trevor Redmond was also signed, and although he had vast experience, sadly he failed at Swindon, while King suffered a very bad injury and was out of action almost as soon as he arrived. Another signing was fence-scraping Australian Johnny Board, who made the 12,000-mile journey to this country after being recommended by Neil Street. One lucky break came with the signing of Tadeusz

*Swindon 1959. From left to right, back row: Glyn Chandler, Tommy Sweetman, Tadeusz Teodorowicz, Mike Broadbanks, Neil Street, Johnny Board, George White. Front, on bike: Ian Williams (captain).*

Teodorowicz, a Polish international who was seeking political asylum and living in Holland. The popular 'Teo' quickly overcame an international ban and went on to score 111 league points for Swindon.

A National Reserve League was formed to brighten the second half of meetings and Swindon finished in the cellar position, but having started late, the league was never completed. On the individual front, three top meetings were held at the Abbey Stadium during the season. Firstly, Leicester's Jack Geran was victorious in the Midland Riders' Championship qualifying round on 23 May, when he saw off strong challenges from both George White and Mike Broadbanks. 'Broady' made sure of success in the next 'big-one' at Blunsdon though, defeating Poole's Les McGillivray in a run-off to win a World Championship qualifying round on 11 July. The Jack Parker Trophy on 7 August saw a marvellous field of riders assembled, with the great Ove Fundin taking the plaudits after notching a magnificent 15-point maximum. Just to show how strong the line-up was, Peter Craven finished second, while Ronnie 'Mirac' Moore was third.

There was a general decline in some of the riders' performances, culminating in the Robins slipping to eighth place in the nine-team league. Mike Broadbanks proved to be the top man, scoring 187 league points for an impressive 9.40 average. Second in the team figures was 'Chalky' White on a 7.78 average, with Ian Williams third on 7.22. George White rode in the World Final at Wembley and scored 7 points, which was one of the few bright spots of a hugely disappointing season. Local rivals Oxford finished one place above Swindon in the final league table and just to rub salt into the wound, it was the Cheetahs who plundered the Supporters' Club Cup for the first-ever time, following a 116-100 victory over the Robins. Swindon again failed to progress beyond the group stage in the Britannia Shield, having to be satisfied with fourth position out of five teams.

The final meeting of the year at Swindon was the third Test Match between England and Australasia. In a superb encounter, it was England who scraped home to record a narrow 55-53 victory, with Peter Craven heading the scorechart on 13 points. Mike Broadbanks and Ron How yielded 8 points apiece, with Ian Williams collecting 8. For the Australasians, the mighty Barry Briggs amassed 16 points and, just for good measure, reduced the track record to 72.0 seconds in the opening heat. Track alterations began in the winter of 1959, reducing the 410-yard Blunsdon circuit to 395 yards in time for the opening of the 1960 season.

## The 1960s

Ronnie Moore wasted no time in setting a track record for the new 395-yard circuit, scorching around in 72.0 seconds in the opening meeting of the 1960 season. His record time was subsequently equalled by both Ken McKinlay and Peter Craven later on in the year. Speedway in general was on the up-and-up with the formation of the Provincial League, which boasted ten teams, the same as the National League. However, it was not to be a very happy year for the Robins – they were wooden spoonists for the first time, with a team that desperately needed some new faces. Swindon lost 4 home matches during the league campaign, as well as losing all 9 of their away fixtures. That left them languishing 4 points adrift at the foot of the table, behind Coventry.

The Robins had a very long tail, although this was significantly improved by the signing of Brian Brett from Southampton and Brian Meredith from Coventry. Young Australian Johnny Board, who had joined the Robins camp the previous year, returned for another go, while Ron Taylor, a very promising lad from the grass-tracks, was also signed. Taylor started well, but should have enjoyed more rides than he did in order to further his progress. Mike Broadbanks was the top scorer for Swindon with 161 league points in a pretty average side. 'Chalky' White finished the campaign with an 8.00 average, and while Ian Williams (6.92), Neil Street (6.85) and 'Teo' (6.74) all offered solid enough support, it was an out-and-out number one rider that the Robins desperately required.

Swindon again reached the semi-final of the National Trophy, but there was more heartache as they went down to a crushing 84-131 defeat at the hands of Wimbledon, for whom Ronnie Moore scored 16 points in each leg. For the second successive year, Swindon also lost the Supporters' Club Cup to old rivals Oxford. In the Britannia Shield, the Robins won 4 of their group matches, but it was only enough to see them finish as runners-up to Wimbledon, with the Dons progressing to the final. The Abbey Stadium played host to another three prestigious individual events during the year, the first of which saw 'Teo' brilliantly win the Midland Riders' Championship qualifying round on 28 May.

Chum Taylor produced a marvellous 15-point maximum to take victory in the World Championship qualifying round on 2 July, while Bjorn Knutsson plundered a full-house to lift the Jack Parker Trophy on 29 July. On 5 August, Blunsdon staged a qualifying round in the recently introduced World Team Cup. This saw Australia, New Zealand, England and a Challengers side battle it out to decide the qualifying place. England won the meeting with 33 points, from the Challengers (with 28 points), New Zealand (23) and Australia (12). Ian Williams rode for England as reserve, scoring a single point, while Neil Street rode for Australia, but failed to score. Meanwhile, Mike Broadbanks appeared for the Challengers, scoring 9 points.

The winter was a very worrying time for the Swindon fans, as Mike Broadbanks spent much of it in hospital with a respiratory complaint. The 1961 season soon came around and Swindon stepped up their search for a top rider. The Robins' management turned their eyes to Sweden and signed twenty-two-year-old Arne Carlsson, who had finished in seventh place in the 1959 World Final. As it turned out, Carlsson was something of a disappointment and only completed 7 league matches for a 6.00 average. Bob Roger, after two years of trying to convince the authorities that he was fully recovered from his injuries of 1958, tried a comeback, which ultimately was not successful and it saddened the Swindon faithful to see him struggle for points. Brian Meredith and Brian Brett were good reserves in a Robins side that had much more solidity about it than in the previous season.

Swindon moved up to fifth position in the ten-team National League, with Neil Street leading the scoring with 127 points for a 7.83 average. Mike Broadbanks,

*Swindon 1961. From left to right, back row: Brian Brett, Neil Street, Mike Broadbanks, Bob Jones, (team manager), Tadeusz Teodorowicz, Brian Meredith, George White. Front, on bike: Ian Williams (captain).*

discharged from hospital in April, battled on gamely for Swindon and achieved a 6.96 average from the dozen league matches he managed to complete. The biggest improvement in the camp came from 'Teo', who upped his average from 6.74 in 1960 to a solid 7.52. This was a much better year for the Robins, although with a bit more consistency at home, it could have been even greater. A couple of home defeats at the hands of Southampton and Wimbledon cost the side dearly, but this was slightly offset by a solitary away victory at Oxford.

Swindon reached the National Trophy final, having battled past both Leicester and Norwich, but there was disappointment for the fans when the Robins lost to Southampton, 70-98 on aggregate. There was some success though, as Swindon again beat Oxford by a single point over two legs to claim the Hutchins Cup. Then, in the Supporters' Club Cup, Swindon defeated Oxford by a comfortable 98-58 aggregate scoreline. The Swindon public were treated to no less than 5 individual events during the course of the season, the first of which saw Arne Pander win the Midland Riders' Championship qualifying round on 10 May with a superb 15-point maximum. Next up was the prestigious Speedway Internationale meeting on 17 June, and this saw Wimbledon's Ronnie Moore triumph with maximum points, ahead of Barry Briggs and Bob Andrews, who tied for second spot

Blunsdon was lucky enough to be chosen to host the final of the Midland Riders' Championship on 21 June, when an all-star field produced a firecracker of a meeting. After twenty pulsating heats, Jack Geran and Arne Pander were locked together on 12 points apiece and a run-off was required to decide the destiny of the title. It was Leicester's Jack Geran who subsequently held his nerve to take the nail-biting run-off and with it, the glory. On 8 July, Swindon staged a World Championship qualifying round, and this saw Wimbledon's Cyril Maidment scorch to an immaculate maximum and finish a point ahead of the popular 'Teo'.

The fifth and final big meeting on the Blunsdon calendar was the Jack Parker Trophy on 12 August, when a top-class line-up thrilled the packed terraces. Leicester's Ken McKinlay cleaned up with a 15-point haul, while there was a three-way tie for the runners-up spot between Barry Briggs, Ronnie Moore and the Robins' own Mike Broadbanks. 'Broady' gamely qualified for the World Final in Malmo, Sweden, but finished way down the field with just 2 points. Interestingly, the name of local youngster Martin Ashby began to feature in the second half of home meetings. Little did anyone know then, but Martin (or 'Crash', as he was dubbed) would go on to become the all-time number one at Swindon, making more appearances for the club than anyone else and, of course, scoring the most points as well.

1962 saw the Robins slip down the league table, handicap racing was introduced and George White retired. Former Bristol rider Roger Wise, a local man from Highworth, became team manager, with Bob Jones concentrating on the mechanical side. There were but seven teams in the National League and Swindon could only manage to finish in sixth position. As mentioned, George White had retired, in order to concentrate on his business interests and to provide for his family, but 'Chalky' was never really replaced and the Robins found life difficult as a result. Once again, Swindon were vulnerable at home, losing both league matches against Southampton, as well as being held to draws by Belle Vue and Wimbledon. On their travels, they lost 11 of their 12 matches, the only success being a 40-37 victory at Oxford.

Swedish international rider Olle Nygren had a couple of matches when Arne Carlsson was injured, and when Ipswich closed down after 15 league matches, their Australian rider, Peter Moore was allocated to Swindon. Buster Brown returned for the odd match, and Howard Cole (riding under the pseudonym Kid Bodie), Brian Leonard, Stuart Wallace and Martin Ashby were also used, as Swindon desperately tried to put together a winning combination. Mike Broadbanks was the number one rider, scoring 190 league points for an 8.21 average, but the support he received was scant, as reflected in the finishing averages of the main body of the side: Neil Street (6.81); Arne Carlsson (6.06); Ian Williams (6.00); Brian Brett (5.42); Tadeusz Teodorowicz (4.61); Martin Ashby (4.28).

For the second year running, Swindon reached the National Trophy final, after aggregate victories over Ipswich and Oxford. Unfortunately, they again lost, this time to Wimbledon by an aggregate score of 74-94, but the highlight in the second leg at Blunsdon was the quite brilliant 15-point maximum from young Martin Ashby, riding off scratch. Meanwhile, the Robins maintained the upper hand over Oxford, retaining the Hutchins Cup by an aggregate score of 86-69. Ronnie Moore was triumphant in the Blunsdon-staged World Championship-qualifying round on 30 June, romping to a full maximum to finish ahead of Les Owen and Bob Andrews,

*Tadeusz Teodorowicz.*

who finished joint second. 'Broady' didn't compete in the Swindon round, but again made it through to the World Final at Wembley on 8 September, where he again scored 2 points. One other big individual meeting was held at the Abbey Stadium in 1962, namely the Jack Parker Trophy, which saw the great Ove Fundin sweep to a majestic maximum and claim the first prize. Southampton star Barry Briggs was runner-up, while Peter Craven and Ronnie Moore finished level in third place.

1963 saw a virtually unchanged Swindon side in action, and although Arne Carlsson was not retained, the young Swede went on to surprise everyone, riding his way to Wembley for the World Final! Great servant Bob Jones was back in his dual role of team manager and mechanic after the resignation of Roger Wise. In only the second home meeting of the season, Wimbledon's Ronnie 'Mirac' Moore established a new track record of 71.8 seconds, bettering the previous best that was set in 1960. Although the season went on through to the end of September, Ronnie's time proved to be unbeatable and stood as the best all year long.

There were still just seven sides in the National League and the Robins finished in fifth spot. Peter 'Piccolo' Moore, the fast-starting Aussie, became the number one rider scoring 207 points to average 8.89. In what was to be his final season with Swindon, Ian Williams handed over the team captaincy to Mike Broadbanks. 'Broady' finished second in the Robins averages on 8.89, but there was quite a hefty drop to third-placed man 'Teo', whose end of term average was 6.57. There were two bright spots in the team, however, with Brian Brett moving his average up to 6.44, while Martin Ashby showed steady improvement to finish on 5.80.

Once again, it was Swindon's home form that cost them dearly, with 3 defeats and a draw, although they did win 2 matches on the road, at Oxford and Southampton. There was an interesting occurrence in the home match against Wimbledon on 8 June, when Ivan Mauger recorded 11 points for the Dons. Swindon won the match 40-38, but it was subsequently decided to deduct Mauger's points as he had started from the wrong handicap. The man who would later go on to win the World Championship more times than anyone else rode the meeting from scratch, but should have actually ridden off a 10-yard handicap! The outcome had no bearing on the destiny of the 2 league points, but the result of the meeting was amended to a 40-27 victory for the Robins.

Swindon again held the upper hand on local rivals Oxford, retaining the re-named Hutchins Challenge Trophy with a 96-72 aggregate victory. The Robins also disposed of Oxford in the quarter-final of the National Trophy, only to then go down to a 2-point aggregate defeat against Norwich in the semi-final. On the individual front, Mike Broadbanks won a World Championship qualifying round at Blunsdon on 5 July. His winning total was 14.5 points, having dead-heated for first place with Ron How in a neck-and-neck heat seventeen. 'Broady' also won his other qualifying round at Wimbledon, but unfortunately didn't make the big night at Wembley. 'Teo' qualified as reserve for Wembley, and Peter Moore also wore the Swindon colours, scoring 6 points. The final meeting of the season at Blunsdon saw a top-class field compete for the Bristol Tipped Trophy, with Oxford's Arne Pander coming out on top, while Sverre Harrfeldt was second, and Mike Broadbanks third. Southampton closed down at the end of the season, leaving the National League with just six teams. Also at the end of 1963, both Australians Neil Street (after seven seasons) and Peter Moore (after a season-and-a-half) announced that they would not be returning to race in Britain in 1964.

The National League as a whole combined to re-open West Ham in 1964, and moved to promote Provincial League Champions Wolverhampton, in order to strengthen the league. In the end though, Wolverhampton stayed in the successful Provincial League, which boasted twelve teams, while the National League struggled on with just seven sides. Mike Parker had undoubtedly been the driving force behind the formation of the Provincial League back in 1960 and was a tough nut for the Control Board to crack, as the two leagues grew further and further apart. As a result, the Provincial League rode outside the jurisdiction of the Control Board and grew even stronger as time passed by.

Swindon remained in the National League and with Southampton closed, promoter Bert Hearse brought the Saints superstar and former World Champion, Barry Briggs, to Swindon. The arrival of Barry renewed interest in speedway in the town and he made his debut for the Robins at Oxford on 27 March in an Easter Cup match. He was to dominate the season, and on 10 July, in an International Best Pairs event, which saw the first visit of Russian riders to Swindon, Barry captured the track record, reducing it to 71.0 seconds. Brian Brett had previously lowered the circuit's best time on 13 June in a league match against Norwich, but 'Briggo' made mincemeat of Brian's time of 71.6 seconds, shattering it by six-tenths of a second. Another newcomer to the Robins' nest was Colin Pratt from Provincial League Stoke, but Colin didn't stay long, never actually riding a league match for Swindon, and quickly moved on to Provincial League Hackney.

In mid-summer, Swindon had a shock when 'Briggo' threatened to retire unless the handicap system was abolished. His views were supported by international referee Cecil Telling, and on 22 August his protest was upheld and his retirement threat forgotten. The Robins looked to have a side with a good blend of youth and

*Stockcar programme, 1964.*

experience. Young local boy Bob Kilby had his first rides, and showed from the beginning that he had what it takes. Martin Ashby was also progressing along the right lines, and with Brian Brett, as well as the ever-reliable Mike Broadbanks, the future looked bright. Swindon also sprang a surprise by signing John Debbage from Norwich, where he had lost his team-place. The Robins gave odd rides to Kiwi Alan Stapleton, although he was only to ride in a single league match. Former Harringay stalwart Danny Dunton even had rides for Swindon, as did Roy Bowers and Leo Ramm.

The aforementioned International Best Pairs meeting on 10 July saw Mike Broadbanks and Martin Ashby ride to success, but all eyes were on the Russian pairing of Boris Samorodov and Anatoly Gruzintsev, who gleaned 12 points between them in spectacular fashion. Individually speaking, Brian Brett won a World Championship qualifying round at Swindon on 18 July, when plundering a brilliant 15 points. In a tense meeting, four riders finished on 12 points to tie for second place, these being Jimmy Gooch, Barry Briggs, Bob Andrews and Trevor Hedge. At Gothenburg, Sweden, 'Briggo' gave Swindon their first-ever World Champion, scorching to the title with a 15-point maximum. Mike Broadbanks also qualified for the big night on 11 September, and scored 6 points.

The wonderful successes of Barry Briggs, however, were overshadowed towards the end of the season by a terrible injury to Tadeusz Teodorowicz, sustained at West Ham on 1 September. The popular 'Teo' had made excellent progress since joining the Robins in 1959. He had been so proud to be the British reserve in the 1963 World Championship Final and, during 1964, he had qualified for the British Final at Wembley. His chances of further success ended when he took a nasty tumble in heat four of the aforementioned match at West Ham, after he had appeared at first to simply over-slide. However, he was taken to hospital, having become unconscious in the ambulance. For 142 days, 'Teo' fought for his life, but sadly, he was to lose the battle without ever regaining consciousness.

Fifth position in the seven-team National League was a disappointment, with the amazing Barry Briggs topping Swindon's scoring with 133 league points and a monumental average of 10.51. With the league only having seven teams, each side completed only 12 fixtures and 'Briggo' recorded 6 full maximums out of his dozen appearances! The other mainstays of the Swindon side finished as follows in terms of averages: Mike Broadbanks (9.80), Brian Brett (7.14), Tadeusz Teodorowicz (6.57), Martin Ashby (6.00), Bob Kilby (4.90) and Roy Bowers (2.88). As had become the norm, Swindon's home form was a let down, with 4 defeats out of the 6 league matches in front of their own fans. The Robins, however, again reached the semi-final of the National Trophy after defeating Wimbledon, but West Ham proved too strong over two legs, with the Robins going down to a 76-92 defeat. Having not been staged since 1960, the Britannia Shield made a one-off return in 1964, with the Robins managing to win half of their fixtures for a mid-table finishing position of fourth.

An enquiry conducted by Lord Shawcross happily paved the way for speedway to move forward and get out of its self-made muddle. The National League and the

*Swindon 1965. From left to right, back row: Alan Jackson, Bob Kilby, Roy Bowers, Norman Parker (team manager), Barry Briggs, Peter Sampson, Martin Ashby, Mike Keen. Front, on bike: Mike Broadbanks (captain).*

Provincial League would amalgamate in 1965, to form an eighteen-team British League, of which Swindon would be founder members. Past feuds and disagreements would be forgotten and the British Speedway Promoters' Association was formed. There would be a Rider Control Committee to watch over team strengths, and speedway was on the threshold of a new beginning.

In 1965, the British League saw a Swindon team with Norman Parker back at the helm. The Rider Control Committee originally allocated Mike Broadbanks to Oxford, leaving the Robins with a top three of Barry Briggs, Brian Brett and Martin Ashby. Brett, however, insisted he was retiring, so 'Broady' stayed at Blunsdon, captained the side and enjoyed a terrific year, scoring freely wherever he rode. Backing the efforts of the three heat-leaders were two local lads, Bob Kilby and Mike Keen, plus newcomers Peter Sampson and Alan Jackson. Roy Bowers came into the side in the beginning, but he didn't last long. Meanwhile, young Kiwi Frank Shuter arrived and his fence-scraping antics provided much entertainment for the fans.

Swindon still struggled, despite having three of the best heat-leaders in the league, as they often received scant support from the back-up department of the side. This was very much a deciding factor in twelve of the away matches, which were lost by just 4 points or less, and the Robins finished fifteenth in the eighteen-team league. Barry Briggs was magnificent throughout the season, scoring a mammoth 378 league points and 21 maximums (20 full and 1 paid). Barry's final average was an amazing 10.91, but 'Broady' wasn't far behind on 10.54. Martin Ashby continued his improvement, raising his average to 8.75, but the rest of the regular Robins all finished around the 4-point mark or below, as follows: Roy Bowers (4.29), Bob Kilby (4.11), Mike Keen (3.89), Peter Sampson (3.17), Alan Jackson (2.00) and Frank Shuter (1.53).

The home league match against Wimbledon on 3 July was shrouded in controversy, with Swindon originally winning 41-37. However, the Dons protested about Swindon's use of Clive Hitch and the result was later amended to a 36-37 defeat! The problem arose because Hitch was, at the time, without a track to ride for and was therefore in the rider pool awaiting allocation to another track by the Rider Control Committee. The Robins' use of Hitch was deemed illegal and the 6 points that he scored were expunged from the match result, with the other Swindon rider positions being upgraded accordingly. This, however, only affected Peter Sampson, whose points tally was increased from 2 to 3, to leave a final result of 36-37. Hitch, incidentally, later found himself allocated to Long Eaton by the Rider Control Committee.

On 20 August, Swindon journeyed to Wolverhampton for a league match, but suffered a humiliating 24-54 thrashing. Mike Broadbanks was magnificent in defeat, however, notching a full 15-point maximum. Mike's amazing 15-point haul amounted to no less than 62.5 per cent of the Robins meagre total of 24. After a bye in the first round of the Knock Out Cup, Swindon beat Newcastle in round two, but went down to a narrow 46-49 defeat to Glasgow in the next round. There was some success though, when the Robins recorded an aggregate 87-69 victory over old rivals Oxford in the Supporters' Club Cup.

A memorial meeting was staged for Tadeusz Teodorowicz, when a star-studded field turned out to pay their respects to the popular Pole. Barry Briggs came out on top with 15 points, with West Ham's Sverre Harrfeldt taking second place on 14. 'Briggo' also scored a maximum when winning a World Championship qualifying round at Blunsdon on 12 June, and he followed that up with a further 15-pointer to take the Wills Woodbine Trophy on 21 August. In the World Final at Wembley, 'Briggo' finished fourth with 10 points, while Mike Broadbanks was a nonriding reserve. The brilliant 'Briggo' also retained the Golden Helmet all season long, beating off the challenges of Charlie Monk, Ken McKinlay, George Hunter, Nigel Boocock, Sverre Harrfeldt and Olle Nygren. The icing on the cake for Barry though, was when he won the first-ever British League Riders' Championship at Belle Vue on 16 October.

In 1966, things really improved at Blunsdon, with the Robins finishing third in the British League and, at one stage, mounting a real challenge for the Championship. Clive Hitch arrived at Swindon, as did Pete Munday, allocated from Poole, while Bob Kilby and Mike Keen came on in leaps and bounds. Six of the team scored at least one full or paid maximum, as the Robins went unbeaten at home all season for only the second time in the club's history. Swindon also won 5 matches on their travels, these successes being at Glasgow, King's Lynn, Long Eaton, Poole and Wimbledon. Clive Hitch became a real thrill-maker – his 'Hitchy' dives on the

*Mike Broadbanks.*

third and fourth bends had the Swindon faithful cheering and Bob Kilby showed that he was not far away from British League heat-leader status.

Barry Briggs' dominance at Blunsdon continued unabated, as he roared to victory in both of the big meetings staged during the year, namely the Midland Riders' Championship qualifying round and a World Championship qualifying round. 'Briggo' went on to win the World Championship in Gothenburg, Sweden and his teammate Mike Broadbanks also rode, scoring 4 points. 'Briggo' also raced to his second British League Riders' Championship success at Belle Vue with a 15-point maximum, and again topped the Swindon averages with a 11.08 figure. The immaculate Barry rattled up a quite staggering 18 full maximums during the course of his 31 league matches! Barry also retained the Golden Helmet all season long, again defeating Nigel Boocock, Gote Nordin, Arne Pander, Mike Broadbanks, Ivan Mauger and Sverre Harrfeldt along the way. Sadly, 'Briggo' never got the chance to extend his winning streak in the Golden Helmet, as the competition was suspended at the end of the 1966 season, and did not resume until 1970.

Martin Ashby had a great year and, like Ginger Nicholls in 1949, was married in the morning before making the dash to Swindon, where he topped the scorechart for the Robins against Newport on 10 September. 'Crash', as he was affectionately known, recorded 271 league points to finish with a 9.01 average. In a much more solid Robins outfit, Mike Broadbanks averaged 9.70, with Clive Hitch on 5.91 and Bob Kilby on 5.76. Mike Keen progressed well, moving his average up to 5.39, while Frank Shuter also moved his final figure in the right direction, finishing on 4.46.

We can't finish 1966 without mentioning a really special meeting that was staged at the Abbey Stadium on 9 July. This was when a West of England team took on the tourists from the USSR in an international match. The meeting resulted in a 59-49 victory for the English team, which included 18 points from the mighty 'Briggo', as well as 16 points from 'Broady'. A third Robin also appeared in the English side, with Martin Ashby collecting a useful 6 (paid 9) points. The spectacular Russians proved to be extraordinary entertainers, with four of their septet finishing on

# KING'S LYNN

## SPEEDWAY CLUB

SADDLEBOW ROAD
KING'S LYNN   Tel. 3753

**KING'S LYNN v. SWINDON**
*British League Match*

**Saturday, 14th October - 7.45 p.m.**

MEETING No. 32    THIRD SEASON

Official Programme **1'-**
BETTING STRICTLY PROHIBITED

*King's Lynn v. Swindon programme, 1967.*

double figures – Boris Samorodov (13), Igor Plechanov (12), Viktor Trofimov (12) and Yuri Chekranov (10).

1967 was the year when Swindon became the Champions of the British League. Unfortunately, the spectacular Clive Hitch was posted to Coventry by Rider Control, which disappointed the Swindon fans, but nevertheless the team still boasted four heat-leaders in Mike Broadbanks, Barry Briggs, Martin Ashby and Bob Kilby. The race for the league title was a cliffhanger, since the Championship was not won until the very last match against King's Lynn, at the Norfolk club's circuit. Earlier in the year, Swindon had lost their league match at King's Lynn, but a protest over the homesters' use of Howard Cole earned them a reprieve. The first attempt to re-run the fixture (on 14 October) was foiled by the weather, but the following week on 20 October, the Robins raced to a 44-34 win and the League Championship was on its way to Swindon. Little did anyone know then, but it would be another thirty-three years before Swindon lifted any further major silverware!

The rampant Robins again won all their home matches, while gaining away wins at Coventry, Glasgow, the aforementioned King's Lynn, Newcastle, Newport and Wimbledon. Barry Briggs had a final league average of 11.05 points per match, and Martin Ashby (8.79), Mike Broadbanks (8.48) and Bob Kilby (8.46) provided the necessary firepower to support the legendary Kiwi all the way. Backing up the four-pronged attack were Frank Shuter (4.52), Mike Keen (4.40) and Pete Munday (4.37). The only other rider that Swindon used during this glory season was Peter Jackson, who had been allocated from Wimbledon at the start of the season, but his opportunities were restricted to just 4 league matches, from which he averaged 3.43. In the Knock Out Cup, Swindon had a bye in the opening round before defeating Exeter at Blunsdon. However, they were dumped out of the competition in the next round, when they lost 45-51 at West Ham. An 88-68 aggregate win over Coventry in the Midland Cup final, however, brought another trophy to Blunsdon in what was undoubtedly one of the best-ever years in the Robins' history.

Three prestigious meetings were held at Blunsdon during the year, the first being a World Championship qualifying round on 13 May, which saw Glasgow's main-man Charlie Monk take victory, having romped to a 15-point maximum. Jim Airey recorded a maximum when winning a Midland Riders' Championship qualifying round on 10 June, while Ray Wilson's 14 points were enough for him to emerge victorious from the Tadeusz Teodorowicz Memorial meeting on 13 September. In the World Final at Wembley, Barry Briggs had to settle for fifth place after scoring 11 points, while 'Broady' qualified as a reserve, but didn't get a ride. 'Briggo', however, did have the satisfaction of winning the British League Riders' Championship at Belle Vue, for the third year in succession.

During the winter months, Mike Broadbanks held a very successful training school at Blunsdon with Mick Bell (who was to join Swindon as team manager in 1997) and Barry Duke, another local boy, as trainees of great potential. Both 'Broady' and Bob Kilby toured Soviet Russia with the Belle Vue team, and the experience was particularly beneficial to the young 'Kilb'. The 'reward' for winning the League Championship was that Swindon lost Martin Ashby in 1968, allocated to

Exeter by the Rider Control Committee. 'Crash' did not want to leave the Robins' camp, but there is little doubt that he matured as a rider as a result of the move. He made a World Final appearance at Gothenburg, Sweden, where Barry Briggs finished as runner-up to Ivan Mauger.

On the management front, Norman Parker retired as team manager, with his place being taken by Dick Bradley, a local man and former rider with both Bristol and Southampton. Happily, Clive Hitch was back after his year at Coventry and whilst he didn't miss a match for Swindon, it was unreasonable to expect him to be a ready-made replacement for the departed Martin Ashby. Meanwhile, Bob Kilby missed several meetings while on the injured list, after he had lost the top of his index finger in a frightful-looking crash at Oxford.

The loss of Ashby and the burden of being without Barry Briggs for much of the season, due to injuries and international calls, finally took its toll. The Robins lost a home record that went back nearly three seasons, when Newcastle visited the Abbey for a league match on 29 June and won by the narrowest of margins (39-38), with the Robins using rider replacement for the absent 'Briggo'. The last time Swindon had lost at home was actually on 1 October 1965, when Halifax were the visitors. The defeat against Newcastle brought to an end an impressive run of 54-consecutive victories, which comprised 47 league matches, 2 in the Knock Out Cup, 4 in the Midland Cup and a single challenge match. Sadly, the rot set in at Blunsdon after the loss to Newcastle, and further defeats followed against Cradley

*Swindon 1968. From left to right, back row: Frank Shuter, Clive Hitch, Barry Briggs, Pete Munday. Front row: Mike Keen, Mike Broadbanks (captain – on bike), Bob Kilby.*

Heath, Hackney and West Ham.

Away from home, it was a sorry tale of 14 defeats, although the Robins managed to win at Oxford, Poole and West Ham, as well as forcing a draw at Cradley Heath. The end result was that Swindon slumped to eleventh position in the nineteen-team British League Division One. Of the 36 league fixtures, 'Briggo' only rode in 20, but he still achieved a brilliant 10.88 average and recorded 10 full (plus one paid) maximums. 'Broady' remained ever-present throughout a difficult season, and topped the Swindon scoring with 304 points for an 8.49 average. 'Kilb' averaged 8.28, while Clive Hitch (6.27), Mike Keen (6.23) and Frank Shuter (5.43) proved to be solid middle-order men. Pete Munday wrote his name in the Swindon history books on 4 May; riding at reserve in a league match against his old club, Poole, he raced to a 4-ride 12-point maximum in wet and miserable conditions. Pete had a steady season overall, with his exciting, if unspectacular riding style yielding a 4.89 average.

Swindon had hoped for some luck in the Knock Out Cup competition, having seen off the challenges of Oxford and Poole (after a replay) in the second round and quarter-final respectively. However, in the semi-final, the unfortunate Robins crashed to an almighty 28-80 defeat at Wimbledon. There was some success for the Robins though, when they gained a slender 78-77 aggregate victory over Leicester in the final of the Midland Cup. Having surprisingly failed to win a single big meeting at Blunsdon the previous season, 'Briggo' was back to form in recording a scintillating 15-point maximum to win a World Championship qualifying round at the circuit on 1 June. There was one other individual meeting at Blunsdon in 1968, and this saw Wolverhampton's Jim Airey plunder a full-house to win the Midland Riders' Championship qualifying round on 10 August. As previously mentioned, 'Briggo' was second in the Gothenburg-staged World Final but, yet again, he won the British League Riders' Championship at Belle Vue, edging out Eric Boocock in a run-off for the title, after both had tied on 14 points.

On 20 July, Blunsdon played host to an international match between Great Britain and Sweden, which featured many of the world's big stars. The British side came out on top with a 62-46 victory, and leading the way with paid 17 points was former Robin Martin Ashby. Mike Broadbanks gleaned 14 points for the British, while Nigel Boocock scored 11. For the Swedes, Bengt Jansson led the way with 15 points, with Anders Michanek scoring 14 and Soren Sjosten grabbing 10. Once again during the winter months, both Mike Broadbanks and Bob Kilby went on tour, this time to Australia with the British Lions. The highlights of the tour for 'Kilb' were 8-point returns at Brisbane and Melbourne, while Mike's best performance was 10 points at Brisbane.

On the team front in 1969, Frank Shuter was moved to Poole by Rider Control, while Peter Jackson linked with Wolverhampton. Both Mac Woolford and Barry Duke were given opportunities in the Robins team and at the latter end of the season, Norwegian Long Track Champion Jon Odegaard rode in a couple of league matches. Des Lukehurst rode in a match for Swindon and young Australian Bob Tabet also had a couple of outings. Early on in the season, on 19 April, Barry Briggs

*Bob Kilby.*

knocked a fifth of a second off his own track record, which had stood since 1964. The new best time of 70.8 seconds was set in the opening heat of a First Division match against Poole.

One of two special events staged during the season was the Twenty-First Anniversary meeting on 19 July, when Wimbledon (including Ronnie Moore) were the visitors. The night was a memorable one, for not only did Swindon win 44-34, but many former Robins riders returned to Blunsdon and a highlight was their parade around the track, throwing sticks of rock to the children. The second special event of the year was the England *v.* New Zealand Test Match, with Martin Ashby returning to Blunsdon to ride for England (and scoring 12 points). Bob Kilby was also capped as reserve, but failed to score. Meanwhile, Barry Briggs captained and top scored for the Kiwis with a paid 18-point maximum. The final result was a crushing 65-43 victory for the New Zealanders. The Abbey Stadium also played host to two important individual meetings, with Norman Hunter taking victory in a Midland Riders' Championship qualifying round on 14 May, while the legendary Barry Briggs emerged triumphant from a World Championship qualifying round on 11 June. 'Briggo' went on to finish second to Ivan Mauger in the World Final at Wembley on 13 September, after defeating Soren Sjosten in a run-off.

It wasn't the best of seasons for the Robins, who finished tenth in a nineteen-team British League Division One. Home form was again Swindon's Achilles heel, as they lost league matches against Coatbridge, Glasgow and Poole. In the Knock Out Cup, Swindon lost out to Cradley Heath in the quarter-final, while defeat in the Midland Cup came at the semi-final stage to a determined Leicester side who won both legs. 'Briggo' once again topped the averages with an 11.09 figure, scoring 425 points and recording 17 full maximums. Amazingly, for the fifth season in a row, 'Briggo' again won the prestigious British League Riders' Championship at Belle Vue. Barry lacked real support at Swindon in 1969, with Bob Kilby next in the averages on 7.80, followed by Mike Keen on 6.80. The outstanding career of Mike Broadbanks was halted in the home league match on 26 July against Hackney, when the Swindon skipper crashed heavily and was taken to hospital with a broken thigh. Unfortunately, the injury was to keep Mike out of action for over a year.

## The 1970s

In 1970, Swindon found themselves at the lower end of the league table (sixteenth, to be precise), but the standard of racing was terrific and the home matches against Sheffield and Halifax left the fans breathless. In both matches, the Robins had come from 10 points behind to force a draw against Sheffield and a win against Halifax. As had become normal though, Swindon dropped several league points at home, losing to Belle Vue, Cradley Heath, Poole and Wimbledon, while drawing against Sheffield in the aforementioned match. John Bishop joined the club from Oxford, but it was a season of struggle as he could only score 66 points from his 31 league matches, and a 3.40 average told its own story. Barry Duke was ever-present in league matches and impressed with a points tally of 155. Bob Kilby outscored Barry Briggs during the season, but to be fair, 'Briggo' rode in five fewer matches. Bob had really established himself as an international rider and his final league average was 9.64, with 10 full maximums and a paid one to boot. As ever, 'Briggo' topped the averages, finishing with a massive 10.51 points per match to his name.

The Robins battled past Wolverhampton and Leicester on their way to the Knock Out Cup semi-final, where they went down to a 34-44 defeat at the hands of Wimbledon. For the second year running, Swindon were knocked out of the Midland Cup by Leicester at the semi-final stage, with the victorious Lions again winning both legs. The Blunsdon track record was broken in successive weeks during 1970, firstly when Bob Kilby brought the time down to 70.6 seconds on 1 August. Seven days later, however, the great 'Briggo' scorched around in 70.2 seconds against Hackney in a Division One fixture and, needless to say, nobody else got near the new best time during the remainder of the season.

'Briggo' was again triumphant on the individual front, winning both a World Championship qualifying round and a Midland Riders' Championship qualifying round at Blunsdon during the year. Barry wasn't so fortunate in the World Final at the Olympic Stadium, Wroclaw (in Poland), however, where he could only muster 7 points. He bounced back in typical fashion though, yet again winning the British

*Barry Briggs.*

League Riders' Championship at Belle Vue for the sixth successive season. Barry Duke unfortunately suffered a broken collarbone, which put an end to his chances in the Junior Championship of the British Isles, which was staged at the Abbey on 2 September. The meeting was won by Barry Thomas, but the line-up also featured several other riders who would go on and grace British Speedway for many years, including runner-up Dave Jessup, third-placed Mick Bell, plus Bobby Beaton and Gordon Kennett. While on the subject of youth, Swindon sent a team billed as Young Robins on the road for three challenge matches during the summer. The fledglings were beaten at both Plymouth and Sheffield, but emerged from Shelbourne Park in Dublin with a 39-38 victory.

There was great joy on 5 September in the match against Cradley Heath, when Mike Broadbanks returned to active racing, scoring 7 points. Sadly, 'Broady' rode just one more match before ending his comeback for 1970. Martin Ashby was welcomed back to Blunsdon for the 1971 season after three years at Exeter, but the Rider Control Committee posted Bob Kilby to the Falcons as his replacement. With a spearhead of Barry Briggs and Martin Ashby, Swindon looked powerful, but often on away trips, the scoring was left solely to the dynamic duo. Mike Keen at times looked very good, but a series of niggling injuries countered his try-all-the-time efforts. Mike Broadbanks, Clive Hitch and Pete Munday all struggled to find their best form, while a young Scot, Jimmy Gallacher, appeared on the scene, and James Bond arrived via Wolverhampton.

The Abbey Stadium regulars were treated to several mouth-watering meetings during the year, the first of which saw Barry Briggs again win a World Championship qualifying round on 17 April. Great Britain annihilated Poland by 80 points to 28 in a Test Match on 22 May, with Ronnie Moore (14), Jim Airey (13), Trevor Hedge (12) and Ray Wilson (12) leading the scoring. For the beleaguered Poles, Andrzej Wygleda (8) and future World Champion Jerzy Szczakiel (7) were the best of a disappointing bunch. On 14 July, Blunsdon again played host to the Junior Championship of the British Isles, which was won by Ian 'Tiddler' Turner with a super 15-point maximum. The runner-up from the previous year, Dave Jessup, had to be satisfied with the same position again, while other competitors included Tony Davey, Gordon Kennett, Peter Collins and future Robin Geoff Bouchard. The fourth and final 'biggie' of the year at Swindon was the Midland Riders' Championship qualifying round on 16 July, which was won by Barry Briggs with a full 15-point score.

Home form again cost Swindon dearly, with defeats against Belle Vue, Exeter, King's Lynn and Leicester being difficult for the Blunsdon faithful to swallow. However, thanks to an excellent end-of-season list of triumphs at Wolverhampton, Oxford and Cradley Heath, Swindon managed to finish fifth in the league. An earlier 37-41 defeat at Exeter also turned into a victory, following an appeal after the Falcons had tracked all three of their heat-leaders and used rider replacement as well! The Robins' appeal was upheld and the points recorded from rider-replacement rides were expunged, with Swindon gaining a 42-36 victory.

'Briggo' was again top of the averages on 10.64, but for the first time he failed to

*Martin Ashby.*

retain the British League Riders' Championship at Belle Vue, finishing second to Ivan Mauger. Sadly, Barry created another unwanted record, when he missed out on a World Final place for the very first time in eighteen years. The returning Martin Ashby plundered 361 points during the campaign, for an average of 9.70, which proved what a tremendous rider he had developed into during his time at Exeter. The popular 'Crash' also set a new track record at Blunsdon, storming around in 70.0 seconds in heat five of the match against Belle Vue on 1 May. Mike Keen averaged 6.70, but after that, the other Robins' figures dropped steeply. Mike Broadbanks returned, and although he only missed a single league match, he was a pale shadow of his former self, scoring just 121 points for a 4.94 average. Clive Hitch struggled too, averaging just 4.79, while the new boys fared even more poorly, with Jimmy Gallacher finishing on 3.93, and James Bond on 3.43.

There were many changes and disappointments during the 1972 campaign. Barry Briggs and Martin Ashby again formed the spearhead, while Brian Leonard joined the Robins' nest from Wembley as a replacement for Pete Munday, who had retired. In the middle of the season, Norman Hunter got his wish and joined Swindon, following a disagreement with Wolverhampton. Barry Briggs and Martin Ashby both finished with averages in excess of 10 points. 'Briggo', however, following a run of machine problems and a disappointing display in the Wills Internationale at Wimbledon, took a two-week break from speedway. 'Storming' Norman Hunter bolstered up the middle order, averaging 6.08, while Clive Hitch and Mike Broadbanks enjoyed only average seasons. David Ashby, the younger brother of Martin, looked very promising and rode in 9 league matches. Later, he was loaned

*Edgar Stangeland.*

to Second Division Peterborough, in order to gain experience. Mike Keen's scoring took a dive and he finished the season with only 83 points and an average of just 3.96.

It was not surprising then, that the Robins could only manage fifteenth position in the final league table. As usual, Swindon dropped many points at home, losing to Belle Vue, Hackney, Reading and Sheffield, while drawing with Leicester. The theory has long since been that the track is too fair to ride and all teams have a chance of success when visiting the wide-open spaces of the brilliant Blunsdon circuit. The campaign was marred by the death of Svein Kaasa though, when Swindon visited Glasgow on 29 September. The twenty-five-year-old Norwegian had started the season at Oxford, prior to linking up with Glasgow, having lost his place in the Cheetahs side to Preben Rosenkilde. Unfortunately, in heat eleven of the match against the Robins, Svein clipped Martin Ashby's rear wheel while trying to overtake on the outside, and was thrown head-first into the safety fence. Sadly, after falling unconscious, the popular youngster died on the Hampden Park track.

A first round Knock Out Cup defeat by Exeter did nothing to lift morale, while bogey side Leicester again dumped the Robins out of the Midland Cup at the semi-final stage. This was after a controversial quarter-final replay at the home of old rivals Oxford, which had originally ended in a 36-41 defeat. However, after successfully appealing, the result was amended to a 40-38 victory. The problem occurred in heat eleven, which had ended as a 4-2 to the Robins' pairing of Barry Briggs and Clive Hitch. Inexplicably, the referee deemed that there had been a starting gate infringement immediately prior to the race and ordered a re-start! Oxford subsequently won 5-0, before going on to win on the night, but the Speedway Control Board acted quickly to uphold Swindon's appeal and reinstated the original result of the heat.

Blunsdon staged an Inter-Nations Championship match between Sweden and New Zealand on 15 July, and in a somewhat one-sided match, it was the Swedes who ran out convincing winners by 50 points to 28. The victors' scoring was led by Christer Lofqvist (11 points), Anders Michanek (11) and Hasse Holmqvist (9), while the Kiwis' top men were Ronnie Moore (9) and Bob Andrews (8). The Abbey Stadium also played host to no less than three individual meetings in 1972, with Ray Wilson taking the honours in both the Midland Riders' Championship qualifying round and the first-ever staging of the prestigious Silver Plume.

The remaining big event of the season was the World Championship qualifying round, which was won in great style by Barry Briggs. The season would be remembered for the World Final at Wembley, when, after beating Ivan Mauger in his first ride, Barry Briggs was involved in a crash with Bernt Persson and Valeri Gordeev and was forced to withdraw from the meeting with serious hand injuries. Later in hospital, the index finger on his left hand was amputated. With Barry out of action, Martin Ashby took his place in the British League Riders' Championship at Belle Vue and put in a brilliant performance to finish as runner-up (with 14 points) to Ole Olsen.

For 1973, it was the end of an era when Barry Briggs announced his retirement,

*Sumner McKnight.*

although he was later to ride again for both Wimbledon and Hull. Replacing 'Briggo' was a rider who had long expressed a desire to ride for Swindon, namely Norwegian Edgar Stangeland, who was brought to the Robins' nest via Exeter. Another newcomer who arrived with a fine reputation was American Sumner McKnight, recommended to Swindon by none other than Barry Briggs himself. Another new rider who appeared on the scene was Geoff Bouchard, who rode for Second Division Long Eaton, but made 7 league appearances for Swindon when they were short-handed. Geoff very much impressed the supporters with his never-say-die style, and would eventually go on to become a full-time Robin in 1975. Norman Hunter had a good year, finishing second in the averages (on 7.02) to the immaculate Martin Ashby, who took over from 'Briggo' and rode brilliantly, scoring 390 league points. Martin Hitch, son of Clive, joined the camp but only rode in a single Knock Out Cup match. Mick Handley was another newcomer who had bags of ability, but struggled with poor equipment. Sad to say, Sumner McKnight found the pace of British League racing far too hot and left after riding 7 league matches for just 4 points.

There was an interesting occurrence when Swindon rode their home match against Halifax on 20 April, as Mike Keen rode brilliantly to score a 15-point maximum, whilst Eric Boocock of Halifax scored a paid maximum from six outings. The Robins were again at the wrong end of the league table, finishing in thirteenth place. Away wins were gained at Coatbridge, Poole and Wolverhampton, but this was more than offset by the usual poor home form which saw 4 losses (against Hackney, King's Lynn, Leicester and Reading) and 3 draws (against Cradley, Exeter and Poole). Wolverhampton proved to be a thorn in Swindon's side, as they knocked the Robins out of the Knock Out Cup at the quarter-final stage. Then, having reached the semi-final of the Midland Cup, where Wolverhampton were the opponents, Swindon were forced to withdraw due to a congested fixture list!

Blunsdon played host to a further three high profile individual meetings during the season, and these resulted in victories for Ray Wilson (in the Midland Riders' Championship qualifying round), Jim McMillan (in the World Championship qualifying round) and Bengt Jansson (in the Silver Plume). On 30 June, New Zealand faced Sweden at the Abbey Stadium in a match from the *Daily Mirror* International Tournament. In a highly-charged meeting, the Swedes emerged with a 42-35 victory, with Christer Lofqvist (11 points) and Anders Michanek (9) leading their scoring. For New Zealand, Ivan Mauger recorded 10 points, while ex-Robin Barry Briggs scored 8. In the opening heat, Christer Lofqvist zoomed around the Blunsdon circuit in a new track record time of 69.8 seconds, becoming the first-ever rider to circumnavigate the track in under 70 seconds. In the second-half Rider of the Night competition, Anders Michanek equalled the time set by Lofqvist earlier in the evening. Martin Ashby took the Golden Helmet from Chris Pusey at Belle Vue, but

lost it a week later to Barry Thomas at Hackney. Martin again rode in the British League Riders' Championship at Belle Vue, where he scored 10 points to finish in sixth position. Swindon aimed to finish their season with a Four-Team Tournament that would have featured a one-meeting comeback by former Robins stalwart George White. Sadly, the meeting fell victim to the weather, so nothing happened and George stayed in retirement.

The 1974 season saw Swindon complete twenty-five consecutive years of speedway at Blunsdon, with the club now firmly established as being one of the premier circuits in Britain. The club marked the occasion with the publication of a lovely little anniversary handbook, priced at just twenty-five pence! With Reading closing for the season whilst their new

*Mike Keen.*

stadium was being built at Smallmead, Swindon added Bernie Leigh to their riding squad, and he proved to be an excellent addition, being an ever-present and averaging 5.26. Mike Keen celebrated his tenth year as a Robin, although the likeable lad from nearby Minety saw his average dip to 4.18. The spectacular Clive Hitch retired to concentrate on his plastering business, although he did ride at Rye House, which was just a stone's throw from his home.

Martin Ashby proved to be an inspiring leader – he was ever-present, had an average of 10.10 and recorded 9 full maximums plus one paid during the season. Edgar Stangeland was next in the Robins' averages, on 7.87, emphasizing the fact that Swindon needed more strength at the top end. Norman Hunter had a steady, if unspectacular year, averaging 6.49, while David Ashby achieved a highly creditable 4.51 figure from his 15 matches. A man who was to feature strongly at Swindon many years later made a few of tremendous guest appearances, scoring 21 points from just 8 starts – and his name was Mick Bell.

The Robins finished the league season in twelfth position out of the seventeen teams. As had happened so many times in the past, they would have undoubtedly finished higher but for some poor results at Blunsdon, where 2 matches were drawn and 3 were lost. The Knock Out Cup saw a first-round exit for them at the hands of Newport, although this was slightly off-set by an aggregate victory of the Welsh side in the Severn Bridge Trophy. The Robins reached the semi-final of the Midland Cup, only to crash out with home and away defeats to Leicester. The Twenty-Fifth Anniversary was celebrated on 13 July with a challenge match against Oxford, who were led by ex-Robin Bob Kilby. It was a grand occasion, as the two sides that first faced each other in the Blunsdon opener in 1949 once again did battle on the track. However, despite 11 points from Edgar Stangeland, and 10 from Martin Ashby, Swindon lost the match 36-42.

The Russians came for a Test Match on 27 July, with Martin Ashby skippering England to a 66-41 victory and top-scoring with 17 points. Tony Davey and Dave Jessup gave Martin great support, both mustering 16 points, while the Russians' best were Vladimir Gordeev (13), Grigori Khlinovsky (11) and Anatoli Kuzmin (10). John Louis won the Blunsdon-staged World Championship qualifying round, with victory in the other 2 'biggies' going to George Hunter (in the Midland Riders' Championship qualifying round) and Martin Ashby (in the Silver Plume). Capping what was a tremendous year for 'Crash' was a new track record time of 69.6 seconds, which he set in the opening heat of the Division One fixture against Wolverhampton on 17 August. Martin was again Swindon's representative at Belle Vue for the British League Riders' Championship, where he had to be satisfied with 8 points.

Bob Kilby was welcomed back for the 1975 season, but with Reading reopening, it was goodbye to Bernie Leigh. However, with 'Killer's' team-mates including Martin Ashby, Edgar Stangeland, Norman Hunter and Geoff Bouchard, the Robins looked to have a very solid squad. Things looked even better when promoter Ted Nelson dipped into the coffers to purchase Bobby McNeil from Second Division Eastbourne, but by the time Leicester came for a league match on 12 April,

Stangeland was already wanting away, naming lucrative weekend long track bookings as his reason. Stangeland left the Robins nest, of course, but was later to appear in the colours of Wimbledon (alongside Barry Briggs). Ted Nelson again looked to the transfer market but, having no luck, cast his eyes abroad and came up with outstanding young Swede Jan Andersson. Jan made his debut on 26 April in a match against Sheffield and won his first-ever race at Blunsdon, although Swindon lost the match 33-45. Later on, Alan Grahame was also signed on loan from Birmingham.

Despite having a useful squad on paper, a series of injuries (particularly to Mike Keen) and indifferent form, saw Swindon slide to the bottom of the league table and collect the wooden spoon. They lost every one of their 17 away matches, as well as suffering a quite staggering 9 home losses, to Coventry, Cradley, Exeter, Halifax, Ipswich, King's Lynn, Newport, Oxford and Sheffield. Martin Ashby and Bob Kilby did their best to stem the tidal wave, but there was very little in the way of support. Martin scored 385 points (average 10.13), while 'Kilb' plundered 286 points (average 8.31) and briefly, while Edgar Stangeland was around, he averaged 6.36 from 5 matches. Then the figures dropped sharply as follows: Norman Hunter (5.24), Alan Grahame (4.95), Bobby McNeil (4.23), Jan Andersson (4.20), Geoff Bouchard (4.12), Mike Keen (3.38) and David Ashby (2.89).

Swindon fared poorly in the cup competitions as well, with a second round defeat to Leicester in the Knock Out Cup and a first round exit to Oxford in the Midland Cup. The Robins overcame a potential banana skin in the Inter-League Knock Out Cup, winning 39-38 at Second Division Workington. They were then drawn at home to Boston in the next round. However, due to fixture congestion, Swindon applied to have the meeting raced at Boston, but the idea was vetoed by the powers-that-be and Boston were given a walkover into the next round. The Blunsdon track record was again broken in 1975, with Martin Ashby lowering his own record to 69.2 seconds against Wolverhampton on 5 April. That wasn't the season's best though, for Bob 'Killer' Kilby screamed around in 68.8 seconds in the opening heat of the league encounter with Cradley Heath on 20 September, Bob's new best time being eight-tenths of a second faster than the record which stood at the beginning of the season.

A total of 4 prestigious individual meetings were held at the Abbey Stadium during the season, the first of which saw Bob Kilby take victory in the Midland Riders' Championship qualifying round. The legendary Ivan Mauger recorded a brilliant 15-point maximum to win a World Championship qualifying round, while future Swindon superstar Phil Crump produced a dazzling display to win the Artdeans Mobylette Trophy. The final open event of 1975 saw racer supreme Peter Collins storm to a full maximum and win the much sought-after Silver Plume. Martin Ashby qualified as a reserve for the World Final at Wembley on 6 September, but unfortunately didn't get a ride. There was some consolation for Martin though, when he scored 11 points to finish third in the British League Riders' Championship at Belle Vue.

In 1976, Swedish rider Soren Karlsson was allocated to the Robins by Rider

Control, but fellow Swede Jan Andersson was missing at first, due to the call of Swedish National Service and a nasty collarbone injury. Having won the Golden Helmet from John Louis at the back end of 1975, Martin Ashby defeated Malcolm Simmons in his first defence of 1976, before losing to Wimbledon's brilliant Swede Tommy Jansson. Sadly, Tommy was killed shortly afterwards, when riding in a World Championship qualifying round in his home country on 20 May. The wonderfully loyal Mike Keen was granted a Benefit meeting on 19 July and, typical of 'Keener's' luck in what was a generally fine and particularly hot summer, it rained on Mike's big day. Despite the elements, a Swindon Select beat a Mike Keen Seven by 47 points to 31. Bob Kilby topped the Swindon scoring with 9 points, while the Mike Keen Seven were superbly spearheaded by a quite marvellous 15-point maximum from Dag Lovaas.

The previous week had seen the Russian riders back at Blunsdon, this time riding against the Robins in a challenge match. In an excellent contest, Swindon won 47-31, with Bob Kilby scoring maximum points. For the Soviet visitors, Grigori Khlinovsky was the pick of the bunch, netting 8 points. Bob Kilby and Martin Ashby kept up their private battle to see who was the quickest around Blunsdon, with 'Killer' lowering the track record to 68.6 seconds in the Midland Riders'

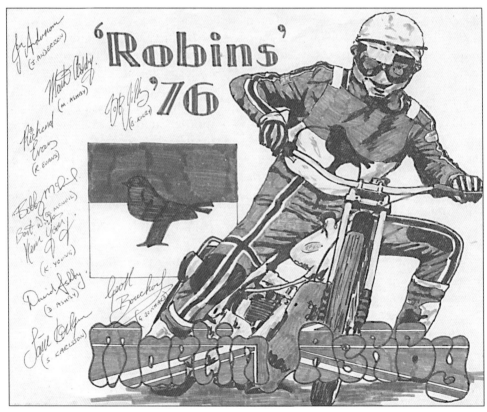

*Martin Ashby, as depicted by Pete Hackett.*

Championship qualifying round on 23 June. However, Bob's record didn't last long, as Martin blitzed around in 68 seconds dead on 10 July to set another best time. On the league front, Swindon rose to fifth place in the final table so, all in all, it was an excellent year of progress at Blunsdon, although Norman Hunter retired before the season finished in order to concentrate on his motorcycle business. The key to the Robins' rise was a far better home record, which saw 3 draws (with Coventry, Exeter and Ipswich), but perhaps more significantly, no defeats! On the road, Swindon also fared much better, chalking up 4 successes at Hull, Leicester, White City and Wimbledon.

At the top of the Robins' scoring were Messrs Ashby and Kilby, both with averages in excess of 9 – Martin on 9.89, with Bob on 9.15. Bobby McNeil had a very good year, raising his average from 4.23 to 7.55, while Jan Andersson made rapid progress, achieving a solid 6.84 figure. Soren Karlsson bolstered up the middle order, scoring 117 points to yield a 6.38 average, with the remaining regulars finishing thus: Geoff Bouchard (5.96), Norman Hunter (5.51) and David Ashby (4.12). After beating Poole in the first round of the Knock Out Cup, Swindon lost narrowly to Ipswich (77-79) in the second round. In the Midland Cup, it was the familiar story of defeat at the semi-final stage, this time to Wolverhampton. Once again, Blunsdon played host to no less than 4 first-class individual meetings during the course of the season. These saw victories for Dave Perks (in a World Championship qualifying round), Bob Kilby (Midland Riders' Championship qualifying round), Malcolm Simmons (*Daily Mirror* Grand Prix qualifying round) and Peter Collins (Silver Plume). Finally in 1976, Martin Ashby again did well at Belle Vue in the British League Riders' Championship, finishing in fourth position with a well-taken 12-point tally.

1977 was very much 'as you were' on the team front at Blunsdon, although a number of very promising junior riders appeared on the scene. Among the hopefuls were Kevin Pope, Kevin Young, Malcolm Holloway and Richard Evans. To gain experience, Malcolm Holloway was loaned to Oxford, where Kevin Young was already establishing himself, while Richard Evans joined Weymouth. Swindon were pretty formidable on their own circuit, with only Reading winning at Blunsdon, although Exeter forced a last-heat draw on 17 September when, with Martin Ashby injured, the Robins operated rider replacement and Bob Kilby rode out of his skin to score 16 points.

Both Jan Andersson and Martin Ashby suffered collarbone fractures during the season. As a result of crashing at Sheffield, Martin did not ride again in 1977, having, up to that point, enjoyed another high-scoring year yielding a 9.80 average. 'Crash' was sorely missed, no more than in a Midland Cup semi-final match against Coventry on 22 September. With the scores at 28-25 in favour of the Bees at heat nine, Ole Olsen and his boys hit the unfortunate Robins with 5-1 successes in the last 4 heats of the match, to win 48-29. Bob Kilby plundered 338 points in the British League, with his average dropping slightly to 8.68, but this was hardly surprising given all the extra rides he had to take along the way. Jan Andersson continued to progress, pushing his average up to 7.77, while Bobby McNeil's

*Jan Andersson.*

average dropped by a point, to 6.56. Soren Karlsson also had a dip in form and could only achieve a 5.74 average, while Geoff Bouchard was an ever-present and finished with a useful 5.56 figure. His battling qualities certainly endeared him to the Blunsdon faithful.

The Robins ended up in eleventh place in the league, a backward step from the previous season, probably due mainly to the injuries sustained by Jan Andersson and Martin Ashby. Their home record was impressive though, with a single loss against Reading, plus the previously mentioned draw against Exeter. It was Exeter who put paid to any hopes Swindon had in the Knock Out Cup, with the Falcons taking victory by 85 points to 71 on aggregate in their first round clash. Coventry ended the Robins' aspirations in the Midland Cup following that thumping win at Blunsdon in the second leg of their semi-final tie.

Prior to his injury, Martin Ashby further lowered the track record at Blunsdon, soaring around the circuit in 67.6 seconds on 20 August on his way to victory in the Wadworth Jubilee Trophy. Two other individual meetings at the Abbey Stadium in 1977 resulted in triumph for Jim McMillan in the Midland Riders' Championship qualifying round, while Malcolm Simmons won the Volkswagen Grand Prix qualifying round. In the absence of Martin Ashby, Swindon were represented by Bob Kilby at the British League Riders' Championship, and he didn't disgrace himself in a class field, scoring 7 points.

In 1978, Swindon signed two Polish riders, Leonard Raba and Jerzy Trzeszkowski, but unfortunately, neither was a success and within weeks both had been released. The Poles were replaced by a Norwegian and a Dane, Rolf Gramstad and Steen Mastrup respectively. Of the two, Gramstad was the most impressive, but both did enough to warrant invitations to return in 1979. In August, out of the blue, Leonard Raba returned for a further two scoreless league meetings, but he was gone again, almost as quickly as he had arrived! Martin Ashby spent the season struggling with injury and illness and it was left to Bob Kilby to head the Robins scorecharts. 'Killer' received excellent backing from Jan Andersson, who showed his undoubted class by qualifying for the World Final at Wembley, where he scored 3 points.

Soren Karlsson missed the start of the season, but returned in mid-summer; however, he was unable to find form and quickly departed. Geoff Bouchard, with his all-action riding, became the darling of the Blunsdon terraces, and scored his first-ever maximum in top-level racing with a 15-pointer against Leicester at Blunsdon on 8 April. Adding bite to the back-up department of the team, Robert Henry came on loan from National League Mildenhall, and did well in 14 league matches for the Robins. Swindon slipped further down the league table to sixteenth place, losing all but 2 of their away fixtures, with the exceptions being a win at Wolverhampton and a draw at local rivals Reading. At home, the Robins suffered 5 defeats (against Belle Vue, Coventry, Exeter, Hull and White City), with 2 matches being drawn (against Halifax and Sheffield).

Jan Andersson topped the averages on 8.18, slightly ahead of Bob Kilby on 8.15, with other regulars finishing as follows: Martin Ashby (7.69), Geoff Bouchard (6.52), David Ashby (4.57), Rolf Gramstad (4.22), Robert Henry (3.52), Malcolm Holloway (2.29) and Steen Mastrup (1.88). For the first-ever time though, Swindon had no representative at the British League Riders' Championship. In the Knock Out Cup, Swindon had a bye in the first round, but in the next round against Poole, both sides lost their home leg by the exact same score to draw on aggregate. Unfortunately, in the replay, the Robins again lost their home leg and were soundly thrashed at Wimborne Road. Swindon raced against Reading in the County Challenge Cup, but after winning 39-38 in the home leg, the Robins refused to ride in the second leg at Smallmead due to poor track conditions. The referee, however, awarded Reading the match by default, with the Racers' management then staging an impromptu Best Pairs meeting in order to keep faith with the attending supporters.

Tough Australian Phil Crump showed his liking for the Blunsdon circuit when, riding for Bristol on 29 July, he equalled Martin Ashby's track record of 67.6 seconds. On the individual front at the Abbey Stadium, Peter Collins took the spoils of victory in the World Championship/Grand Prix qualifying round, with Jim McMillan later coming out on top in the Silver Plume event. The remaining big meeting of the season at Blunsdon saw Dave Morton triumph in the Artdeans Trophy on 26 August. Little did the fans know when they left the Abbey after the last match of the 1978 season that it was to be the end of an era. In the winter conference of the British Speedway Promoters' Association, Ted Nelson, the Swindon promoter, handed over the reigns to Wally Mawdsley, a multi-track promoter and a member of the League Management Committee, who had negotiated a five-year lease. Sadly, this meant that Swindon had to say goodbye to Dick Bradley as team manager, as he was no longer required by the new promotion.

The arrival of Wally Mawdsley as Swindon promoter in 1979 brought some much-needed strength to the team. With Bristol closing down, the Robins acquired the services of Australian international Phil Crump, and American Steve Gresham. Departures from Blunsdon saw the promising and highly competent Jan Andersson move to Reading, while David Ashby went on loan to Milton Keynes in the National

League. Swindon had an excellent squad, but achieved nothing of note in the season. Martin Ashby, in a year when he was granted a Testimonial, struggled to find his best form and found himself at reserve for many matches. Every so often there were flashes of the Martin of old, but it was a disappointing year for him generally. To offset this, new Robin Phil Crump was quite brilliant, piling up a total of 340 points in league meetings for an average of 10.36. Bob Kilby, despite a period when little went right with his machinery, picked himself up and finished the year with a 7.57 average.

Rolf Gramstad's season began very well, but he seemed to lose his way as the year progressed. He did, however, have one meeting of note, away at Eastbourne on 29 June, when he scorched to 13 points. The Robins suffered a cruel blow on 28 August when the popular Geoff Bouchard crashed and was badly hurt, suffering a broken leg and a punctured lung. Unfortunately, Geoff never rode again, but he will always have a special place in the hearts of the Blunsdon faithful for his on-track battling qualities, while off-track, he was an extremely pleasant chap. Czech rider Milan Spinka was drafted in as a replacement, and did well in the 5 matches in which he rode.

This was an incredible season for fixtures at Blunsdon, with a total of 37 home meetings going ahead! This was more than had ever been staged in a single year,

*Swindon 1979. From left to right, back row: Steve Gresham, Steen Mastrup, Henry Hitch (team manager), Rolf Gramstad, Geoff Bouchard, Malcolm Holloway. Front row: Martin Ashby, Bob Kilby, Phil Crump.*

with the previous highest total being 31 in 1951. The fewest staged was 14 in the initial, short 1949 season, although only 19 meetings were held during the course of a full 1963 campaign. The quite staggering total of meetings for 1979 included no fewer than seven individual events. Also included was a Test Match between England and Australasia, which the English won by 67 points to 41. Leading the England scorers were Michael Lee (16 points), Dave Jessup (15) and Chris Morton (11), while the Australasian scorechart was topped by Ivan Mauger (12), Phil Crump (10) and Billy Sanders (10).

Martin Ashby's Testimonial went ahead on 23 September, when a star-studded individual meeting took place. The line-up read like a 'Speedway Who's Who', with Michael Lee coming out on top with a 15-point maximum. Other participants in Martin's special meeting included England internationals Doug Wyer, Peter Collins, Malcolm Simmons, John Davis, Terry Betts and Dave Jessup, which was a measure of the high regard in which 'Crash' was held. Phil Crump became the 'King of Blunsdon', shattering the track record in the aforementioned Test Match on 27 July, slicing six-tenths of a second off the previous best time in establishing 67 seconds dead as the new all-time record. Then, amazingly, on 22 September, 'Crumpie' blitzed around the circuit in 66.5 seconds in heat one of his Golden Helmet challenge with Peter Collins, which took place immediately prior to the league match with Belle Vue. Five days later though, Collins himself zoomed around the Blunsdon bowl in 66.5 seconds on his way to victory in the Silver Plume event.

Aside from Collins' victory in the Plume, other individual triumphs in 1979 went as follows: Ole Olsen (Mirrorsport Trophy), Phil Crump (World Championship/Grand Prix qualifying round), John Davis (Artdeans Knock Out Trophy), Barry Allaway (Master of Junior Speedway), Dave Jessup (Duplex Litho Press Trophy) and Michael Lee, as previously mentioned in the Martin Ashby Testimonial. Briefly going back to the Golden Helmet, Peter Collins had held the title all through the season, until Phil Crump relieved him of the coveted trophy. Sadly though, 'Crumpie' didn't hold on to it for long, losing to Bruce Penhall in his first defence.

Swindon ended the season in eighth position, with the usual indifferent home form prevailing, which saw 4 defeats and a draw. On the road, Swindon notched wins at Birmingham, Eastbourne and Hackney, while forcing draws at Belle Vue and Poole. In the Knock Out Cup, Exeter put paid to Swindon's hopes in the third round, while Leicester dumped the Robins out of the Midland Cup at the semi-final stage. Phil Crump represented the team at Belle Vue in the British League Riders' Championship, scoring 9 points. Due to the congested fixture list, Blunsdon had its latest-ever finish to a speedway season, with the Robins facing Exeter in a British League match on a freezing cold 1 November.

## The 1980s

In 1980, it was Bob Kilby's turn to celebrate a Testimonial year, and the Swindon rider, elected as captain, was in excellent form until a crash at Poole caused him to

*Bob Kilby's Testimonial brochure.*

miss half the season through injury. There were, as to be expected, a number of comings and goings, as promoter Wally Mawdsley tried to find a winning combination. Sadly, the Robins' all-time record points man, Martin Ashby, was released, and he went off up the M4 to join Reading. Martin's contribution had been immense and in league matches alone he made 452 appearances in the famous Robins race jacket, scoring 3980.5 points, plus 236 bonus. Popular Norwegian Rolf Gramstad was another to depart from Blunsdon, and he subsequently linked up with Leicester.

Two riders were signed from Exeter – Scott Autrey, the American international, and Australian Steve Koppe. Autrey finished the season as top man, scoring 329 points for an average of 9.97, but Koppe failed to find form and was gone by the end of April. Unfortunately, the high-scoring Phil Crump, didn't appear until June, having been given leave of absence by Mawdsley to remain at home in Australia, in order to set up and establish a motorcycle business. Milan Spinka was missing more times than he was actually around and John Barker, another new arrival, found the pace of British League racing far too hot. To assist the side, veterans Reidar Eide and Nigel Boocock made fleeting appearances, but the most promising name on the horizon was Mike Ferreira, who was really setting the National League on fire at Canterbury. Another bright spot was the improved form of Steve Gresham, who ceased to be a villain and became the hero of the Robins fans.

Swindon were a real Jekyll and Hyde team, managing to win no less than 5 league matches away from home, but to offset that, they lost 3 and drew 2 meetings at Blunsdon! Once 'Crumpie' had returned, he backed Scott Autrey all way, averaging 9.41, but the Robins lacked a third heat-leader as the final averages of other regular team members proved: Steve Gresham (7.40), Bob Kilby (7.23), Milan Spinka (6.46), Steen Mastrup (5.49) and Malcolm Holloway (4.93). Swindon could only manage eighth position in the league again, as Wally Mawdsley expressed concern at the fall in crowd figures. Although fewer fixtures were staged than the previous season, Blunsdon still hosted a remarkable 34 meetings throughout the year. Just 2 full-blown individual events were held in 1980 – as opposed to 7 individual meetings in 1979 – with Larry Ross tasting glory in the Artdeans Knock Out Trophy, while Michael Lee won the *Daily Mirror*-sponsored Silver Plume. The Master of Junior Speedway was also held, but only as the second half of an Anglia League representative match against the Scottish Junior League, with David Blackburn emerging as the victor.

In the Knock Out Cup, Swindon battled past Eastbourne and Ipswich to reach the semi-final, but despite a terrific effort, the Robins went down to a narrow aggregate defeat (105-111) to Belle Vue. In the Midland Cup, it was the same story, with defeat at the semi-final hurdle, to Coventry by 77 points to 79 on aggregate. The Robins did fare better in the Inter-League Knock Out Cup, however, over-coming Peterborough in the first round, Eastbourne in the quarter-final, and Leicester in the semi-final. On a bitterly cold September night at Blunsdon, Swindon flattered to deceive, going down to a 37-41 defeat in the first leg of the final against King's Lynn. Although they battled hard in the second leg at Saddlebow Road late in October, the Robins lost 36-42, with the aggregate result, unfortunately, being a 73-83 defeat.

Blunsdon proudly staged a Test Match between England and the USA on 24 May, with the Americans taking a well-earned 59-49 success to take overall victory in the five-match series. Scott Autrey and Dennis Sigalos led the Americans with 15 points apiece, while Bruce Penhall yielded 14. For England, the top dogs were Dave Jessup and Michael Lee with 12 points each. A four-team tournament was staged as Bob Kilby's Testimonial meeting on 31 August, with a Vikings team scoring 34 points to win, with the Yankees in second (scoring 30), the Union Jacks third (19) and the Global Stars fourth (13). Among the riders paying their respects to 'Kilb' in his special meeting were Hans Nielsen, Bo Petersen, Erik Gundersen, Bruce Penhall, Bobby Schwartz, Dave Jessup and Malcolm Simmons. In the big domestic meeting of 1980 – the British League Riders' Championship at Belle Vue – Scott Autrey represented Swindon and scored 8 points.

In 1981, Steve Bastable arrived via Birmingham and was made skipper of the side, in place of Bob Kilby. Bob was still getting over a back injury and, in the end, didn't ride at all. Young Swede Bjorn Andersson, brother of Jan, arrived at Blunsdon and did very well; together with the immaculate Phil Crump, plus Steve Gresham,

Malcolm Holloway and Steen Mastrup, that gave Swindon a very useful top six which virtually picked itself. Mike Ferreira, still at Canterbury, was a tremendous number eight rider, but it was the second reserve spot in the team which was up for grabs, with many riders being tried. Young Finn Veijo Tuoriniemi, who had been with Eastbourne during 1980, was given an opportunity, but failed miserably. A number of raw, but promising novices were also tried and these included Terry Broadbank (son of Mike), Steve Bishop, Kevin Smart and Martin Satchell, but like young Australian Darryl Simpson, they were out of their depth in the British League. Dane Jens Henry Nielsen (brother of Hans) and Swede Lennart Bengtsson were also given opportunities. Nielsen, who rode during his holiday period, looked as though he could be

*Phil Crump.*

the final piece of the Swindon jigsaw, but unfortunately Henry wasn't interested in a full-time speedway career in Britain.

Despite the problem reserve slot, Swindon rose to third position in a sixteen-team British League, thanks in the main to the marvellous Phil Crump. 'Crumpie' was back to his best and bagged another mountain of points (313 to be precise) to finish with a 10.39 average. He was well backed up by Steve Bastable, who also won the British Final at Coventry. 'Stevie B' attained an 8.75 average, while there was a great deal of solidity about the rest of the team, as borne out by these final averages: Steve Gresham (7.18), Steen Mastrup (6.85), Malcolm Holloway (6.83), Mike Ferreira (6.73) and Bjorn Andersson (5.01). The Robins' rise up the league table saw a marked improvement in home form, with 2 losses (against Hackney and Wimbledon) and a single draw (against Ipswich) to report. Away from the Abbey, Swindon tasted victory in an amazing 7 matches – at Belle Vue, Coventry, Eastbourne, Hackney, King's Lynn, Leicester and Reading – whilst draws were attained at Hull and Ipswich.

In the Knock Out Cup, Swindon drew Edinburgh from the National League, and a train carrying the team, management and supporters, was organized by the 'Mad Wellie' Malcolm Holloway. The journey to the Scottish capital for the second leg of the tie took place on 12 June, and in what was a thrilling match, the Robins won by just 2 points, thanks to a wonderful 18-point maximum from that man Crump. Swindon went on to beat Leicester in the next round, before losing both legs of the semi-final at the hands of Ipswich. A new competition, the League Cup, was launched, but Swindon didn't fare too well, finishing fifth in the eight-team Section B table. A couple of home defeats (against Ipswich and King's Lynn) out of 7 matches gave them little chance of progressing in the competition, and so it proved.

Test Match speedway was again held at Swindon, with England facing the USA on 2 May. England avenged the previous year's defeat, running out victors by 64 points to 43. Michael Lee topped the England scoring with 16 points, while Steve Bastable and Dave Jessup each bagged 13. For the Americans, Bruce Penhall scored 11, with Steve Gresham notching 10. Local Swindon newspaper, the *Evening Advertiser,* began the sponsorship of a big individual meeting in 1981, with Bo Petersen becoming the first *Evening Advertiser* Superstar. The only other big individual meeting at Blunsdon was the Godden-Newton 16-Lap Super, when Phil Crump showed his stamina to emerge victorious. 'Crumpie' later represented Swindon in the Belle Vue-staged British League Riders' Championship, recording 10 points.

1982 brought changes to the speedway scene at Blunsdon. The often controversial American, Steve Gresham, was posted to Reading, while Mike Ferreira moved full-time to the Robins' nest. Sadly, the rider from Zimbabwe failed to settle at the Blunsdon circuit and was, in fact, far better for the Robins on their travels. Czech rider, Jan Verner was also introduced to the team, but he struggled badly and was released after 5 league matches. Most of the old guard were back, including the brilliant Phil Crump, along with Steve Bastable and Malcolm Holloway, who was the new team skipper. The highly promising Martin Hewlett became a full-time Robin, following his loan spell at National League Exeter. Bjorn Andersson was a late arrival on the scene, thanks to a stint in the Swedish Army and a battle with the Department of Employment in order to secure a work permit. Promoter Wally Mawdsley's efforts with the D.O.E. proved to be successful and, after arriving in June, Bjorn fully justified Mawdsley's faith by upping his average by nearly 2 points a match.

The season began with the League Cup, but after a home and away winning start against Poole, everything went pear-shaped for the Robins, as they finished bottom of the Southern Section after winning only one further match! Swindon fared no better in the Knock Out Cup, with a quick-fire first round exit against Eastbourne when they lost both legs. The Robins did reach the semi-final of the Midland Cup however, only to be crushed by a powerful Cradley Heath side. After losing the first leg 29-49 at Dudley Wood, the Robins went down to an embarrassing 24-54 reverse at Blunsdon in the return leg. When the league began, Swindon just could not put it together consistently, but considering that, a final position of eighth wasn't too bad. A total of 4 defeats at home didn't help, but this was offset by 4 away victories (at Halifax, King's Lynn, Leicester and Poole). Phil Crump led the scoring as usual, and when Bjorn Andersson arrived, he played his part, but Steve Bastable's contribution was down and with Mike Ferreira failing to master the Blunsdon track, it was hardly surprising that the Robins lacked any consistency. Malcolm Holloway tried hard and had a reasonable year, reaching the British Final.

'Crumpie' piled up 272 points in the league, averaging 9.44, but he was very much a one-man band, with 'Stevie B' next in the averages with a 7.65 figure. Bjorn Andersson obtained a useful 6.47 average and 'Mad Wellie' Malcolm Holloway could not be faulted for finishing with a 6.13 figure. However, the expected performances from Mike Ferreira and Steen Mastrup never materialized, as their final averages revealed: Ferreira (5.27) and Mastrup (4.62). Phil Crump made it to Los Angeles for the World Final, but only managed 4 points, which was certainly not a true reflection on the durable Australian's ability. Steve Bastable was Swindon's entry in the British League Riders' Championship (at Belle Vue), scoring 7 points. 'Stevie B' was actually in the meeting instead of Phil Crump, who had gone back to Australia with his wrist in plaster, thanks to a track spill.

Tragedy struck on Saturday 11 September when, after scoring 8 points in a home British League match against Birmingham, twenty-year-old Martin Hewlett collapsed and sadly died a few days later. It was a terrible shock for all concerned and a Trust Fund was quickly set up to help the dependants in the young rider's family. Martin had come through the junior ranks at the club and was on his way up the speedway ladder. The youngster had impressed with his on-track battling and had done well to average 4.62 in a team that had struggled. A benefit meeting was staged for Martin at the end of the season, and this saw Swindon defeat Reading 43-35, prior to the Swindon junior team (the Sprockets) beating Exeter by the same score in the second part of the special double-header. Former Swindon favourites Martin Ashby, Barry Briggs, Bob Kilby, Edgar Stangeland, David Ashby, Geoff Bouchard and Norman Hunter also took to the track in order to help raise funds to help young Martin's dependants.

In spite of the Robins' indifferent performances, Wally Mawdsley could not be faulted for giving the public plenty of speedway action, as he staged a total of 36 meetings throughout the season. That total included the *Evening Advertiser* Superstar event (won by Phil Crump) and the Newton Oils/*Daily Mirror* Marathon (won by Alan Grahame). Among other prestigious meetings held at Blunsdon was a Test Match between England and the USA, which the Americans won by 60 points to 47. Shawn Moran and Bruce Penhall bagged a dozen points apiece for the victorious Americans, while England's best were Dave Jessup (12) and Kenny Carter (11).

The National League held their Pairs Championship at the Abbey, when supporters from all over the country converged on Blunsdon for a real feast of speedway. Eventual winners of the event were Weymouth, who were represented by Martin Yeates and Simon Wigg, while the runners-up were the Long Eaton duo of Alan Molyneux and Dave Perks. Famous Czech team Red Star of Prague visited the Abbey Stadium for a challenge match, which saw Swindon run out winners by 45 points to 33. The visitors' side included former Robins Jan Verner and Milan Spinka amongst its ranks, with the rest of the team made up of Jiri Stancl, Jiri Hnidak, Petr Ondrasik, Ladislav Hradecky and Stanislaw Kubicek. During the winter, speedway would dominate the local press, as what appeared to be a power struggle developed between promoter Wally Mawdsley and his accountant Richard Vowles. Vowles was also Mawdsley's partner and there were, it was reported, cash flow problems.

In 1983, the team (taken over by Richard Vowles, who won the battle for control) was woefully weak, and the Swindon public had much sympathy for their new promoter. The only bright spot was that Phil Crump remained a Robin, for 'Crumpie', who was due a Testimonial, had apparently refused to ride for the now departed Wally Mawdsley. Bjorn Andersson also stayed put and Malcolm Holloway, who had also been at loggerheads with Mawdsley, also remained at Blunsdon. Steve Gresham would return from Reading, but Steve Bastable was on his way to Coventry, with Danish rider Alf Busk heading in the opposite direction. Often, in the early weeks of the season, it was a case of the superb Phil Crump against the opposition. Bjorn Andersson started well in the League Cup, but then suffered injury and, sadly, no sooner was he fit, than he was injured again. To add to Richard Vowles' problems, Steve Gresham was not showing anything like his normal form, and he quickly vanished from the scene. Martin Yeates was something of an enigma, since before he left to continue his career with National League Weymouth, he had shown that he did have what it took at Swindon by beating some of the leading British League heat-leaders, while also mysteriously losing points to lesser riders.

Australian Phil Herne was signed from Leicester and showed reasonable form, and young Dane Per Sorensen came along, but he was not the heat-leader that Vowles sought. Alf Busk took time to find any sort of form, and Bob Kilby tried a brief, but unsuccessful comeback. Czech rider Milan Spinka also reappeared for a spell, but he had completely lost form, and was gone after just 11 league matches.

*Phil Crump Testimonial programme, 1983.*

Small wonder then that Swindon finished in the cellar position in the British League, but promoter Vowles learned a great deal. The Robins won just 6 home league matches and enjoyed a solitary away success at Leicester. Phil Crump carried the side all season long and finished head and shoulders above the rest, finishing at the top of the Robins' averages with an amazing 9.85 figure. The mighty Aussie also represented Swindon at the British League Riders' Championship, scoring 8 points.

Many guest riders were used throughout the campaign, but to no avail, and the support for 'Crumpie' was minimal. Behind Phil in the final analysis, the next in line were Bjorn Andersson (6.27), Martin Yeates (5.74), Malcolm Holloway (5.39), Phil Herne (5.38), Alf Busk (5.03) and Per Sorensen (3.09). In what was, quite simply, a disastrous season, Swindon also finished bottom of their League Cup group for the second year running, and suffered a first round exit in the Knock Out Cup at the hands of Wimbledon. The Abbey Stadium again played host to a Test Match, as once again England faced the USA. It was England's turn to win by 57 points to 51, Chris Morton top-scoring with 16 points. Meanwhile, Bobby Schwartz and Dennis Sigalos headed the American scorechart with 11 points apiece.

Michael Lee enjoyed himself in the wide-open spaces of Blunsdon in 1983, for on 1 July he lapped the circuit in 66.5 seconds to equal Peter Collins' four-year-old track record. The meeting in which Michael equalled the record was the *Evening Advertiser* Superstar event, and it was fitting that he should go on and take the prestigious title. 'Crumpie' enjoyed a very successful and much-deserved Testimonial year and his meeting (a three-team tournament) was staged on 2 October, with many of the world's leading riders taking part. The result was a win by a single point for the Michael Lee Select (who scored 43 points), while Ole Olsen's Vikings scored 42 and the Pacific Stars recorded 22. Showing the high regard in which he was held, many top stars turned out for Phil, and these included Erik Gundersen, Hans Nielsen, Billy Sanders, Simon Wigg and Jan Andersson.

Richard Vowles determined that things would be better in 1984, and showed that he was not afraid to spend money, paying out a hefty fee to Hackney for Danish international Bo Petersen. Other moves on the rider front saw Malcolm Holloway move up the road to Reading, while Finn Ari Koponen, along with flamboyant American Shawn McConnell joined the Blunsdon set-up. Alun Rossiter, who had been the club mascot as a youngster and had developed through the junior ranks, also moved up into a first-team slot as a useful number eight, whilst also assisting Weymouth in the National League. Sadly, injuries forced the early retirement of the very talented Bjorn Andersson, who completed a solitary league match. At the end of the season, Kevin Smith arrived on loan from Poole, riding in only 3 league matches and scoring paid 10 points.

The Robins moved up the league table to ninth place and also fared better in their League Cup section, finishing one off the bottom, handing over the wooden spoon to Exeter! Swindon's home form was much more consistent, with just 2 defeats (to Cradley Heath and Ipswich) and 2 draws (to Belle Vue and Eastbourne) to report. Away from home, however, there was just a single success at

*Swindon 1984. From left to right, back row: Per Sorensen, Alun Rossiter, Bjorn Andersson, John Tremblin (team manager), Bo Petersen, Ari Koponen, Alf Busk, Martin Yeates. Front, on bike: Phil Crump.*

Coventry, where in spite of three attempts to race the league fixture at Belle Vue, bad weather intervened and the match was never held. Ipswich won both legs to dump Swindon out of the Knock Out Cup in unceremonious fashion, but in the Midland Cup, the Robins got involved in an epic semi-final battle with Coventry. At the first time of asking, both sides won their home leg by the exact same score (45-33), thereby drawing 78-78 on aggregate. Unbelievably, both teams again won their home leg by the same score (46-32) in the replay, to again tie on aggregate. With the match going to a second replay, Swindon dug deep to only lose the first leg 38-40 at Brandon, before finishing the job off at Blunsdon with a 43-34 success. Unfortunately, there was no fairytale ending though, with Cradley Heath defeating the Robins in both legs of the final.

Phil Crump again headed the Swindon averages with a 9.94 figure, but Bo Petersen gave valuable support, scoring 239 league points for an 8.06 average. In a more solid outfit, the Robins' top two received good middle-order backing from Ari Koponen (6.23) and Shawn McConnell (5.59), while Per Sorensen improved his average from 3.09 to 4.96. Alf Busk, however, went slightly backwards, dropping his average to 4.79 in a disappointing year for the Dane. For the fifth successive year, England faced the USA in a Test Match at the Blunsdon bowl, with the Americans taking a 58-50 victory. Dennis Sigalos led them to success with a magnificent

17 points, while England's best were Chris Morton (13), Dave Jessup (12) and Kenny Carter (10). On the individual front, Bo Petersen qualified for the World Final in Gothenburg, Sweden, where he did well, scoring 9 points. 'Crumpie' represented Swindon in the British League Riders' Championship at Belle Vue, but could only muster 5 points. However, the mighty Phil did win the only open event at Blunsdon in 1984, becoming the *Evening Advertiser* Superstar on 6 July, when romping to a full 15-point maximum against class opposition, which included Hans Nielsen, Mitch Shirra, John Davis and Bobby Schwartz.

In 1985, the team became known as the Adver Robins, having received some valuable sponsorship from the local *Evening Advertiser* newspaper. With Wimbledon opting for National League racing, England international Malcolm Simmons came to Blunsdon, giving the Robins a third heat-leader alongside Bo Petersen and Phil Crump. When Swede Jimmy Nilsen finally arrived, promoter Richard Vowles had the basis of a good side. The signing of Jimmy Nilsen was a feather in the Swindon promoter's cap, since the Department of Employment had refused at first to grant the young rider a work permit. Vowles, with the help of local MP Simon Coombs, fought the decision tooth and nail and was finally successful. Jimmy proved his worth with 91 points from 16 league matches, for an impressive first season average of 6.54.

Swindon made a fast exit from the Knock Out Cup, losing both legs of their first round clash with Ipswich. In the League Cup, the Robins had to be satisfied with mid-table mediocrity in a competition they had never done well in. There was to be no chance of glory in the Midland Cup either, with Swindon losing to old rivals Oxford at the semi-final stage. The Blunsdon track record took a battering in 1985: firstly, Shawn Moran reduced the best-ever time to 66.4 seconds on 27 April, when Sheffield were the visitors in a League Cup encounter. Four months later, on 26 August, Erik Gundersen ran riot, slicing an incredible seven-tenths of a second off the record when clocking 65.7 seconds in heat two of the Robins' British League match against Cradley Heath. Remarkably, two heats later in the same match, Gundersen blitzed around the Abbey in 65.2 seconds – a full 1.2 seconds faster than Shawn Moran's record, which had stood at

*Malcolm Simmons.*

*Alan Grahame.*

the start of the meeting! Swindon once again hosted an England *v.* USA Test Match, with the Americans thundering to a 66-42 victory. Lance King topped the victors' scoring with 17 points, receiving great support from Shawn Moran (13) and Bobby Schwartz (10). Meanwhile for England, Kelvin Tatum (12 points) was the only rider to reach double figures.

19 September, however, will be remembered for all the wrong reasons, as the Robins tried to stage a home league match against King's Lynn. The referee called a halt to the meeting after a three man pile-up in the very first heat. Arguments raged and, following the abandonment, Richard Vowles sensationally quit as promoter, a decision which left doubts about the future of speedway in Swindon. Happily, peace was soon restored, with Vowles taking on former Robins rider Neil Street as team manager, in order to relieve some of the pressure. However, Vowles was a disillusioned man and, although he stayed on, he never really forgot the events of that September night.

At the end of the season, Bo Petersen said he was retiring, while Malcolm Simmons hankered after National League racing at Hackney. The Robins would miss Petersen, who actually outscored Crump and finished on top of the averages with a 9.33 figure, but 'Crumpie' did miss all the October fixtures due to a niggling wrist injury. 'Simmo', after going like a steam-train in the earlier part of the season, suffered an alarming dip in form to finish with a 6.72 league average; meanwhile Per Sorensen showed some real flashes of brilliance and upped his average to 6.59. Ari Koponen found points hard to come by, but still averaged 6.46, while Alun Rossiter slightly increased his average to 4.13. The Robins finished eighth in the sinking British League, which now boasted just eleven tracks. Home form was again Swindon's Achilles heel, with losses to Coventry, Oxford and Sheffield, while Reading stole away with a draw. Home favourite Bo Petersen won the prestigious Blunsdon-staged *Evening Advertiser* Superstar event in 1985, and also represented the Robins at Belle Vue in the British League Riders' Championship, scoring 5 points.

In 1986, Richard Vowles tried yet again to make Swindon a success. He signed Finnish star Kai Niemi from Ipswich, and Alan Grahame came on loan via Cradley Heath. Danish international Finn Thomsen, whose previous tracks included

Hackney and Poole, was also signed, but broke an ankle in pre-season practice, so Swede Richard Hellsen was quickly signed from King's Lynn to plug the gap in the side. With each team having to track a junior, Rob Fortune was also brought in. The ever-reliable Phil Crump was back, as was Jimmy Nilsen, so things looked pretty good on the team front. When Finn Thomsen was fit again, Per Sorensen, who'd struggled somewhat to find form, was released and subsequently joined Oxford. This move proved to be the making of Sorensen, as he linked up with Hans Nielsen at Cowley and learned so much from the well-titled 'Main Dane'.

Richard Vowles expressed concern at crowd levels and tried to form a company to inject more finance into the club. Due to the terms of his agreement with B.C.A. (British Car Auctions) – the owners of the Abbey Stadium – he failed, and by the end of July, he realized that he could not possibly carry on. A challenge match on 2 August against a British League Select proved to be his final meeting in charge. The team went back to the stadium owners, Kai Niemi went back to Ipswich and, for a brief but worrying week, Swindon Speedway actually closed down while the ownership of the licence was sorted out. With B.C.A. now at the helm, Ted Nelson and Bill Chandler were left in charge of speedway matters.

With the take-over, Neil Street left and Brian Talbot became team manager in his own right, having previously shared the job with Street. To replace Niemi, a very promising Danish boy called Brian Karger, was signed. On 20 September, Blunsdon staged its 1,000th speedway meeting, when Cradley Heath were the visitors for a league match. A presentation was made to Bob Jones, who was still working at the track as machine examiner, for his loyal service. Bob had served Swindon well and had never missed a meeting since the track first opened.

Veteran Richard Hellsen proved to be a shrewd signing, finishing the season with a 5.95 average. Swindon's scoring was again led by the majestic Phil Crump, with an average of 9.17. Jimmy Nilsen finished the season with a creditable 7.90 figure and Alan Grahame was a real hero. Having suffered from Hodgkin's disease throughout the season and therefore often riding in pain and discomfort, he kept going as long as he could and averaged 5.50. Of the Danish connection, Finn Thomsen was something of a disappointment, scoring just 84 league points (average 5.37), but Brian Karger looked to be a real prospect and got better with every one of his 14 matches to average 4.89. Rob Fortune tried hard, but was out of his depth in the cut-and-thrust of the British League, and a final average of 3.40 gave a fair indication of a season of struggle for the youngster.

A bitter pill for the faithful Blunsdon fans to swallow occurred in a league match against Oxford on 11 October, when the Robins' oldest rivals hammered Swindon 56-21, with former rider Per Sorensen recording a paid maximum for his new club. The Robins finished their league campaign in eighth place and, as had happened in 1984, the away match at Belle Vue was never staged due to inclement weather. The Robins kept their travelling fans happy with victories at Coventry, Ipswich and King's Lynn, but 4 defeats at the Abbey were certainly not welcomed by the beleaguered Blunsdon supporters. The opinion had long since been echoed that the Blunsdon circuit was too fair and all visiting riders were capable of turning up and doing well, irrespective of whether they had previously ridden the track. This theory could certainly be borne out by a closer look at Swindon's home results over the years!

After beating Ipswich in the opening round of the Knock Out Cup, the Robins came unstuck against the old enemy Oxford, losing both legs of their round two encounter. Swindon had their best-ever League Cup campaign however, finishing fifth in the final table and only missing out on a semi-final place by one position. The gritty Alan Grahame represented the side in the British League Riders' Championship, scoring 6 points. 'Big Al', as he was affectionately known, also won the only individual meeting held at Blunsdon in 1986, namely the World Championship qualifying round, which was run early in the season on 11 May. Jimmy Nilsen qualified for his first World Final in Katowice, Poland and rode brilliantly to finish fourth with 11 points.

The 1987 season looked like being potentially difficult as Swindon kingpin Phil Crump retired and remained in his native Australia, having been troubled for some years with a wrist injury. Coming into the Robins' nest was a new signing from Reading: one Mitch Shirra, the Kiwi with a fiery reputation. Alun Rossiter, after a very good season with Coventry, came back to race full-time for the Robins, while the services of the exciting Andrew Silver (of National League Arena-Essex) were utilized as and when required. In the backroom department, Ron Byford became

team manager, having gained valuable experience with Exeter. To the delight of the Swindon supporters, both Jimmy Nilsen and Brian Karger improved, and tireless Swede Richard Hellsen was as steady as ever and didn't miss a match. In mid-season, the services of another Swede, Conny Ivarsson, were obtained and he certainly impressed, scoring 117 points. The junior berth was filled in the main by Matthew Cross and a young rider from New Zealand, trying hard to make a good impression – Stephen Rose.

Mitch Shirra was a delight to have on board and never let the side down: in fact, he and Jimmy Nilsen fought a friendly season-long battle within the club to be the number one Robin. It was a very close-run thing, with Jimmy just nudging ahead with a

*Mitch Shirra.*

*Andrew Silver.*

9.73 average, while Mitch attained a 9.66 figure. Thanks to the two-pronged attack, Swindon rose to a very healthy third position in the final league table. The Robins became one of the most attractive sides in the country, winning 5 of their away matches (at Ipswich, King's Lynn, Oxford, Reading and Wolverhampton). At Blunsdon, however, it was the same old story, with 2 defeats and 2 draws; otherwise Swindon might have scaled even greater heights.

In the League Cup, the Robins slipped back to seventh in the table, but one wonders what might have happened had they turned around some of their slim away defeats. No fewer than 5 matches were lost 38-40, while a further 2 resulted in 37-41 defeats. Swindon saw off the challenge of Reading in the Midland Cup, but were knocked out at the semi-final stage by Coventry. Blunsdon again played host to a World Championship qualifying round, and this saw Jeremy Doncaster triumph with a superb maximum. At the British League Riders' Championship, Swindon were represented by two riders for the first time, with Mitch Shirra scoring 8 points and Jimmy Nilsen recording 4. In the two-day World Final, held in Amsterdam, Holland, Jimmy Nilsen totalled 22 points (9 and 13) to again finish in fourth place overall, while Mitch Shirra yielded 12 points (7 and 5).

It was all change at Blunsdon in 1988, as Mitch Shirra went back to Reading, and the spectacular Andrew Silver was signed, albeit on loan, from Arena-Essex. Swindon would have loved to track both riders in their side, but the points limit ruling just wouldn't allow it. With the arrival of Silver, young reserve David Smart went the other way, joining Arena on loan. Conny Ivarsson was another who did not return from the previous season, but in his place, Swindon signed another Swede, World Ice Speedway Champion Erik Stenlund. A new sponsor took over (local motor company Walker Jackson) and replaced the *Evening Advertiser*, who had done such a great job for the previous three years.

The Robins had trouble in the first home meeting of the season against Getingarna, the touring Swedish side. In heat ten, Jimmy Nilsen was involved in a nasty track spill with Jan Andersson and Per Jonsson, injuring his shoulder and wrist. Jimmy's injuries were to keep him out of the saddle for some weeks and, as if this wasn't enough, Erik Stenlund was injured in a meeting in his native Sweden. Co-promoter Ron Byford (now working full-time on speedway at the Abbey) worked hard to fill the gaps in the side, as guests were used in abundance until the return of Nilsen. There was a glimmer of light towards the end of the season however, when yet another Swede was enlisted, namely Peter Nahlin, who rode in just 6 league fixtures.

Richard Hellsen and Gary Chessell were ever-present in league encounters, as the team finished in a disappointing seventh spot. With eleven teams competing, the British League was played out with all the sides facing each other four times (twice at home and twice away). This worked out to be a mammoth forty-match programme, with Swindon suffering from their usual indifferent home form, which saw them lose to Belle Vue (twice), Coventry (twice), Cradley Heath, Ipswich, King's Lynn and Oxford. Thanks to Jimmy Nilsen's early injury, there was no real star in the camp, and Peter Nahlin actually topped the averages on just 7.68, slightly ahead of Brian Karger on 7.59 and Nilsen on 7.31.

After a bye in the opening round of the Knock Out Cup, Swindon went down to old rivals Oxford in the next round. In a two-legged battle of epic proportions, with both teams giving it their all, the Cheetahs came out on top by the narrowest of margins, 91-89 on aggregate. In celebration of sixty years of British Speedway, a

*From left to right: Bart Bast, Jimmy Nilsen, Brian Karger.*

Diamond Jubilee tournament was organized, featuring a series of matches involving England, Denmark, USA and Sweden. Swindon Speedway was proud to host the meeting between Sweden and USA, which was won by the Americans 47-43. In a thrilling meeting, the victors were led by 10 points from Lance King, while Mike Faria scored 9. The Swedes had three men in double figures – Per Jonsson (13), Erik Stenlund (12) and Tony Olsson (10) – but lacked the strength in depth of the victorious American squad.

Something very special happened at Blunsdon on 8 October, when Barry Briggs brought back all the members of the 1967 league title-winning side to race an exhibition match against the Swindon Soft Water All-Stars, a team made up of riders from the same era. It was the All-Stars who won 34-32, and the fans flocked to the Abbey Stadium in their hordes, filling the place with its biggest attendance for many years. How they loved to see their former heroes in action, with Bob Kilby showing that he'd lost none of his speed from the gate. On the individual scene, Mitch Shirra returned to Blunsdon to win the B.C.A. Classic with a gutsy display, while Brian Karger represented the Robins in the British League Riders' Championship at Belle Vue, scoring 5 points. On a wider level, the impressive Peter Nahlin underlined his undoubted potential, when he became World Junior Champion at Slany, Czechoslovakia. Also on the podium with Peter were second-placed Henrik Gustafsson and fellow Robin Brian Karger.

The British League lost two teams before the 1989 season got underway, with Sheffield closing and Ipswich opting for National League racing, thus leaving just nine tracks. American Bart Bast was welcomed to the Robins' nest, joining Peter Nahlin and the now-purchased-outright Andrew Silver. Jimmy Nilsen (elected club captain) and Brian Karger were back, with Gary Chessell and David Smart filling the reserve berths in the side. Meanwhile, Richard Hellsen and Alun Rossiter left for National League racing at Long Eaton and Poole respectively. Cruel luck hit the Robins on 6 May, in a league match against Oxford, when Peter Nahlin crashed and suffered a fractured vertebra. Danish youngster Tom Knudsen was quickly signed as a replacement, but in the event he didn't stay long, due to a contractual dispute with his parent club back in Denmark. With Bart Bast finding the pace hotter than he expected, his contract was cancelled and into the side came experienced England international John Davis.

In the league, Swindon were vulnerable at home (as usual), where they lost 6 matches – against Coventry (twice), Cradley Heath, Oxford (twice) and Wolverhampton. In a rather mediocre season, the Robins ended the season in sixth place. Jimmy Nilsen was top Robin, averaging 8.33, closely followed by Brian Karger on 8.05. Meanwhile, the figures for the remaining regular members rather fell away, as follows: Andrew Silver (7.31), John Davis (6.67), Peter Nahlin (6.42), Bart Bast (5.15), Gary Chessell (5.05) and David Smart (3.70). Wolverhampton saw to it that Swindon didn't progress beyond their opening tie in the Knock Out Cup, while in the new Gold Cup competition, the Robins finished stone last in the southern group table. The Abbey Stadium again played host to a Test Match between England and the USA and, somewhat surprisingly, the English Lions ran riot to win 75-32. In a powerful performance, England's main men were Kelvin Tatum (15 points), Neil Evitts (15), Jeremy Doncaster (14), Martin Dugard (11) and Andrew Silver (10). The only member of the USA side to offer any real resistance was Lance King, who scored 12 points.

For the first time, a full-blown 1,000cc sidecar meeting was held at Blunsdon on 23 September, when Australia defeated England by 50 points to 38 in a Test Match. Some of the world's top sidecar exponents took part in the meeting, including Paul Pinfold, Brian Ash, Alan Artus, Darrin Treloar, Gary Moon and Shane Soutar. The only individual speedway meeting held at Swindon in 1989 was run the day after the sidecar event, and saw John Davis triumph in the Bike for Life event. The meeting, organized by team sponsor Walker Jackson, was a charity event with the intention of raising sufficient money to pay for Babylog ventilators, to be installed and used at the Paediatric and Special Care Unit at Princess Margaret Hospital in Swindon. Brian Karger rode brilliantly to finish third (behind Shawn Moran and Hans Nielsen) in the British League Riders' Championship, scoring 12 points. Jimmy Nilsen also represented Swindon in the major event at Belle Vue, where he recorded 8 points to finish in sixth position.

## The 1990s

It was very much a case of repetition in 1990, with still only nine teams in the British League, and the Robins again finished in sixth position. After two years, Walker Jackson were replaced as team sponsor by Coastal, a company famous for their high quality doors and windows. An important signing for Swindon was the young Australian sensation Leigh Adams, who had previously ridden for National League Poole. Both Adams and new club captain John Davis received personal sponsorship from Coastal. The team, therefore, became known as the Team Coastal Robins. The spectacular Andrew Silver was back, as were the Swedes, Jimmy Nilsen and Peter Nahlin, plus local boy David Smart and Dane Brian Karger.

Early in the season, Brian Karger was injured and, thanks to sponsorship from a number of enthusiasts, Phil Crump flew in from Australia to fill the gap. 'Crumpie', however, was not the rider of old and his final average of 5.64 reflected this. Andrew Silver was an ever-present in league matches, and finished with a useful average of 7.53, while Leigh Adams showed he was 'on the pace' with a 6.81 figure. Top Robin was Jimmy Nilsen, who scored 285 points for an average of 8.61. From the 11 matches in which he rode, Brian Karger recorded a 7.91 average, while Peter Nahlin scored 213 points for a 7.36 average. It must be said that local lad David Smart did well though, for he only missed a single league match and averaged 5.13. Swindon had a good run in the Knock Out Cup, reaching the semi-final, before losing by a whisker to Bradford, 89-91 on aggregate. In the Gold Cup, however, the Robins finished third in the four-team southern section, with local rivals Oxford and Reading occupying first and second places respectively.

The Swindon Soft Water Classic was the only individual meeting staged at Swindon in 1990, when Jan O. Pedersen showed his class to win from a top-class field that also included Kelvin Tatum, Jeremy Doncaster, Neil Evitts and all the regular Robins. It was a great night for Pedersen, for not only did he win the meeting, but in heat two, he scorched around the Blunsdon bowl in 65.2 seconds, thereby equalling the five-year-old track record held by fellow Dane Erik Gundersen. Unfortunately for Pedersen, 'Main Dane' Hans Nielsen, annihilated his best time on 8 September, when he rounded the track in a time of 64.8 seconds, clipping an amazing four-tenths of a second off Jan O's tremendous effort. Following the success of the sidecar meeting the previous year, two events were staged in 1990, and these saw the World Stars defeat England 47-43, while Paul Pinfold won the Homefire Sidecar Masters.

Barry Briggs attempted to bring the Golden Greats to Blunsdon on 19 August, but rain caused the meeting to be postponed. However, on the rescheduled date of 16 September, the crowds flocked through the turnstiles to see their former favourites in action. Amongst others, speedway legends Ove Fundin, Gote Nordin, Anders Michanek and Bert Harkins took to the Blunsdon circuit again. Former Swindon favourites Mike Broadbanks, Barry Duke, John Bishop and 'Briggo' himself also took to the track, in what was probably the most successful meeting of an average season. Roy Trigg came out on top of the Fabulous Fifties section, while Terry Betts was triumphant in the Swinging Sixties event. Andrew Silver was one of

*Leigh Adams.*

two Swindon representatives at Belle Vue for the British League Riders' Championship, where he impressed with 8 points to finish in seventh position. Meanwhile, the other Robin, Jimmy Nilsen, could only manage 3 points, on a disappointing night by his standards. Jimmy did, however, reach the World Final at the Odsal Stadium in Bradford, where he did very well, finishing fifth after yielding 10 points.

In 1991, the league set-up was changed to Divisions One and Two, with four teams from the former National League joining the new higher section: Berwick, Ipswich, Poole and Wimbledon. There were changes at Swindon, as Jimmy Nilsen joined Berwick on loan, and John Davis linked up with Wimbledon, one of his former clubs. Aussie Rod Colquhoun moved to Blunsdon from Poole, while Paul Dugard arrived via Eastbourne. Brian Karger was made captain and, along with Leigh Adams, Andrew Silver and Peter Nahlin, the Team Coastal Robins had a good-looking side. Completing the team, the Swindon management gave another opportunity to young Matthew Cross. Unfortunately, Cross took an early knock and was replaced by another junior, Derrol Keats.

Behind the scenes, Malcolm Holloway took over the duties of team coach and the set-up at Blunsdon looked ideal. It seemed as if it was only a matter of time before Swindon were sitting on top of the league. Before long though, things began to go horribly wrong. Brian Karger, who was suffering from a loss of form, was released and joined Second Division Arena-Essex in a shock move. Dean Standing, formerly of Eastbourne and Ipswich, was brought in, and Andy Smith also arrived at Blunsdon, on loan from Bradford. The fans were far happy about Karger's release, although Dean Standing was a success, until he was hurt and lost form as a result. Then Andy Smith was injured, and so more team changes ensued. Wimbledon closed down, moving their operation to Eastbourne, and as a result, John Davis came back to Blunsdon and Danish youngster Morten Andersen also arrived, via Oxford on loan. Still the results didn't come and Swindon finished last in the league. Worse still, it looked as if the club would be relegated to the Second Division. Really, only the fact that Berwick (who had suffered severe financial problems) opted out of the First Division allowed Swindon to stay in the top league. The constitution of the B.S.P.A. stated that the Second Division should always have at least an equal number of tracks to Division One. Berwick's failure and Mildenhall's application for Second Division racing in 1992 undoubtedly saved the Robins, but it was a worrying winter for the supporters.

Top Robin in 1991 was Leigh Adams, who scored 249 league points and also represented the club in the British League Division One Riders' Championship at Belle Vue, scoring 3 points. Leigh received little backing until John Davis returned to average 8.47 from the 8 matches he rode in. Andy Smith only completed 7 matches for a 7.75 return, while Dean Standing achieved a 6.30 figure. The remaining riders were a huge disappointment, as reflected in their final averages: Andrew Silver (5.88), Paul Smith (4.49), Rod Colquhoun (4.23), Paul Dugard (4.13) and Morten Andersen (4.00). Belle Vue removed Swindon from the Knock Out Cup at the first hurdle, while the Robins could only manage fourth position (from seven) in the southern section of the Gold Cup. Swindon fared no better in the B.S.P.A. Cup, which was a revamped version of the old Inter-League Knock Out Cup, with a first round exit at Poole. Blunsdon played host to another England *v.* USA Test Match on 25 August, with the home nation enjoying a 57-51 triumph. Top scorers on the night were: Gary Havelock (16), Kelvin Tatum (9) and Chris Louis (9 for England; and Ronnie Correy (12), Greg Hancock (12) and Billy Hamill (10) for USA.

Having been granted a reprieve, Swindon hoped for better things in 1992. On the team front, Leigh Adams was retained, along with John Davis and Dean Standing. With Berwick dropping to Division Two, Jimmy Nilsen was welcomed back to the Robins' camp, while Mitch Shirra also returned. It was Shirra who recommended that Swindon gave an opportunity to German Peter Schroeck, and this they did, giving him one of the reserve berths, together with promising junior Steve Camden. Although weak at reserve, Swindon did boast a strong top five, so things should have worked out for the Robins, now backed by their stadium owners, A.D.T. Auctions. One important change at the Abbey in 1992 saw the regular race-day change from the traditional Saturday to Thursday, but this was a move that

*Swindon 1992. From left to right, back row: Steve Camden, Peter Schroeck, Ron Byford (team manager), John Davis. Front row: Leigh Adams, Mitch Shirra, Jimmy Nilsen, Dean Standing.*

certainly did not go down well with the fans.

The season kicked off with the Gold Cup competition, but Swindon could only manage to win 3 of their 6 home matches, while losing all but one away from Blunsdon. This was a disappointing start to the campaign, as Swindon finished a poor sixth in the southern section table. The Robins also suffered an early exit from the Knock Out Cup, with Wolverhampton winning both legs of the first round tie. In an effort to strengthen the reserve position, Justin Elkins, a talented junior, came from Poole, but despite the fact that he had plenty of promise, it was still hard for him. On 24 April, at Arena-Essex, John Davis broke a leg and this was the start of many problems for Swindon. Two days later, at home to Arena, the Robins lost, with former rider Brian Karger scoring a paid 11 points for the visitors. Peter Nahlin arrived at Swindon, expecting to sign for the club and ride against Wolverhampton in a Knock Out Cup fixture. However, as Nahlin waited, the management opted to sign Kelly Moran on loan from Belle Vue, and it was he who rode against Wolverhampton, scoring just 3 points, which couldn't help a 43-47 defeat. The following week, Peter Schroeck was released and in came Steve Masters from Eastbourne, who had signed former Robin Andrew Silver during the winter break.

Despite brilliant form from Leigh Adams, Swindon lost their first four away league matches, and, if that wasn't enough, shortly afterwards, they suffered a run of six home defeats on the trot, with team manager Ron Byford suffering much unjust criticism from the terraces. In early June, with Second Division Mildenhall closing, local boy David Smart returned to Swindon. Although his all-out efforts were appreciated by the fans, they often did not get the points they deserved. The rot had set in, and Swindon were in deep trouble as they plunged nearer the foot of the table. The Four-Team Championship offered a break from the stress of the league, and Swindon did well enough to qualify for the final at Peterborough. Unfortunately, things didn't go the Robins' way in the final and they finished a disappointing fourth behind winners Belle Vue, runners-up Ipswich and third-placed Oxford.

In the B.S.P.A. Cup, which ended in a draw with Poole, Leigh Adams won a run-off with Steve Schofield, but the Pirates' management protested about this way of deciding the result, and their protest was upheld by officialdom. In the replay at Poole, the Robins were thumped 32-58. It was also Poole who finished Swindon off in the league when, on 15 October in the last home match, they beat the troubled Robins 47-43. Swindon were bottom of the First Division again, and this time relegation couldn't be avoided. The final league table revealed that Swindon had won just 5 of their 24 matches, with a staggering 7 defeats suffered in front of their own supporters. As the fans trudged home after this meeting, they wondered just what the future held in store for them and their beloved Robins.

The one bright spot in a disappointing season was the form of Leigh Adams, who often carried the side and scored 298 points for a 9.55 average, as he remained ever-present throughout the league campaign. Adams also represented the Robins at Bradford in the British League Division One Riders' Championship, scoring 11 points. The young Aussie enjoyed further success when he won the World

Under-21 Championship in Pfafenhofen, Germany. Looking through the rest of the 1992 team, the riders' final averages tell their own story in a season that everyone wanted to forget as quickly as possible. Mitch Shirra was next in line to the immaculate Adams, scoring 184 points for a 7.32 average, while Jimmy Nilsen's efforts could only attain a 7.28 figure. Incidentally, despite an indifferent year on the domestic front, Jimmy did make it through to the World Final at Wroclaw in Poland, where he finished seventh.

Going back to the Robins of 1992, Kelly Moran averaged 6.25, which was a poor reflection of his undoubted class and ability. The remaining Robins all finished below the six-point mark as follows: Dean Standing (5.28), David Smart (3.67), Steve Masters (2.78) and Justin Elkins (2.65). Swindon staged two individual meetings during the season, with Glenn Cunningham scoring a 15-point maximum to take the honours in the Bee-Line Lubricants Junior Classic, while track specialist Zdenek Tesar took victory in the Super Pink Pizza Classic. The Blunsdon regulars also had a taste of Test Match action again, as England were defeated by the USA. In a meeting that was close throughout, the Americans won by 58 points to 50, with the spectacular Bobby Ott scorching to 16 of his team's total. He was well

*Jason Crump.*

supported by Greg Hancock (14 points), Ronnie Correy (12) and Sam Ermolenko (11). Meanwhile, for England, Mark Loram led the way with a dozen points, while Gary Havelock scored 10.

A new era began at Swindon Speedway in 1993. Having been relegated from the First Division, a new promotion – Betterment Properties (Leisure Activities) Ltd, headed by Mervyn Stewkesbury and Peter Ansell, who also ran Poole Speedway – took over at the Abbey Stadium and introduced Second Division racing to the public of Swindon. Saturday night racing returned and a brand new team was put together, with only Steve Masters from the 1992 line-up retaining a team place. Alun Rossiter returned to skipper the side, and Gary Chessell came 'home' from Stoke. There was also the son of a famous father in Jason Crump, who had been at Peterborough the previous season. Gary Allan also joined the ranks, along with Glenn Cunningham and Peter Jeffery, while former rider Martin Yeates was installed as the new team manager. It was just a pity that David Smart, who moved up the road to Oxford, could not be accommodated in the team plans, as he had been granted a Testimonial meeting, but he was to celebrate his special year at both Swindon and Oxford.

Early on in the season, Alun Rossiter broke a wrist and the management wasted no time in drafting in the young Dane Tom Knudsen as a replacement. As the season progressed, it became obvious that the Swindon supporters were enjoying the Second Division experience, for there was much enthusiasm on the terraces. The explosive Jason Crump was proving to be every bit as good as his father, Phil, had been in his heyday. Peter Jeffery though, found form hard to come by, and left the club to be replaced by Nigel Leaver. On 31 July, Gary Allan burned up the Abbey Stadium circuit to equal the track record (64.8 seconds) set by Hans Nielsen in 1990. Modern technology had seen race times being measured to one hundredth of a second since the start of the 1993 season, and although Allan was timed at 64.87 seconds, it was still considered to have equalled the time of the 'Main Dane'. Just to make sure there was no doubt, however, the following week (7 August), in a Knock Out Cup match against Edinburgh, Allan set a new record of 64.70 seconds!

Swindon continued to serve up excellent racing and enjoyed a marvellous run in the Knock Out Cup, beating Exeter and Edinburgh to reach the final. Unfortunately, their opponents were the powerful Glasgow side, who forced a tremendous 54-54 draw in the first leg at Blunsdon, before defeating the Robins 64-44 in the return leg at Shawfield the following night. The Robins also battled through to the final of the Four-Team Championship at Peterborough, where a determined effort saw them finish as runners-up, just two points adrift of a triumphant Edinburgh side. Swindon finished a strong fourth in the league, winning every one of their 20 home matches. This was only the fourth time that Swindon had enjoyed a 100 per cent home record since opening in 1949, with the other three occasions being in 1957, 1966 and 1967. Thrill merchant Jason Crump led the way, storming to an amazing 470 points for a 10.67 average. 'Crumpie' junior also rattled up 12 full and 3 paid maximums throughout the season. Gary Allan proved to be a revelation and gave superb support, scoring 454.5 points for an 8.98 average. Meanwhile, the solid-scoring back-up men returned averages as follows: Alun Rossiter (7.44), Gary Chessell (6.83), Nigel Leaver (6.17), Glenn Cunningham (5.91), Steve Camden (4.93) and Steve Masters (3.71).

David Smart celebrated his Testimonial meeting at Blunsdon on 5 September with a four-team tournament, won by Smartie's Cheetahs (with 31 points) from Gary's Robins (23), Dave's Falcons (22) and Leigh's Hammers (20). Among the riders who turned out to honour David were Armando Castagna and David Mullett, as well as former Robins Richard Hellsen and Leigh Adams. The British League Division One Riders' Championship was raced at Swindon at the third attempt, having twice fallen victim to the weather, with the brilliant Per Jonsson emerging as the winner. Both Gary Allan and Jason Crump took part in the meeting, scoring 6 points and 5 points respectively. One other individual event was staged at Blunsdon in 1993, and this saw Martin Goodwin triumph in a World Championship qualifying round. Super-quick Gary Allan represented Swindon in the Division Two Riders' Championship at King's Lynn and, to the delight of the travelling hordes, he won the meeting by beating Mick Poole in a run-off, after both had recorded 13 points. Jason Crump also appeared in the meeting, scoring 9 points. The 1993 season would also be remembered for rain, with the Swindon management suffering an unprecedented 8 rained-off meetings during the course of the season.

*David Smart leads from Tony Olsson.*

The previous record was 6 lost meetings, something that occured in both 1981 and 1987. Interestingly, as a guide to the changing nature of Britain's weather, a total of 47 meetings were washed out at Blunsdon between 1949 and 1979, whereas an amazing total of 55 meetings were lost to the wet stuff between 1980 and 1993 inclusive!

In 1994, it came as no surprise when Jason Crump, a revelation the previous year, moved up to Division One to race for Poole. Surprisingly, Gary Allan decided to retire and moved back to New Zealand, while Nigel Leaver was another to move on, so there were team places to be filled at Swindon. In came Tony Olsson, via near neighbours Reading, plus Tony Langdon, who had enjoyed a terrific season at Oxford. Man of many tracks, David Blackburn, added experience to the team, while a brand new Swede, Patrik Olsson (no relation to Tony), was signed following a successful series of pre-season trials. Joining Glenn Cunningham at reserve was local grass-tracker John Jefferies. The side was made up by Gary Chessell, who missed the opening matches of the season with a broken collarbone, sustained in a fall while practising at Reading's training track. A work permit application was made for the Poole asset, Australian Mark Lemon, but it was turned down, with the reason seeming more a question of politics than the rider's ability. When it appeared that the unfortunate Chessell would be out of action for some weeks, the management moved quickly to sign Finnish rider, Mika Pellinen.

Patrik Olsson started the season like a rocket by scorching to a 15-point maximum in his first-ever league match, at home to Sheffield on 9 April. Gary Chessell returned to action at the end of April, so Mika Pellinen went off to join Exeter. Later in the year, Dutchman Henk Bangma joined the club, but was very badly injured in his debut meeting at Peterborough on 1 July. The following day, in a home match against Edinburgh, Patrik Olsson crashed and suffered a broken arm. It took time to heal, but Patrik was never the same rider again. Both Tony Olsson and Tony Langdon also suffered with injuries, which cost Swindon valuable league points when they weren't available. However, both Tonys more than flew the flag for Swindon: Olsson (with 12 points) was second, while Langdon (11 points) was third, in the Division Two Division Riders' Championship at Coventry. The dynamic duo also rode brilliantly to take the Division Two Best Pairs title at Arena-Essex, beating the Glasgow pairing of Nigel Crabtree and David Walsh in the final.

In another grand season for racing, the Robins again finished fourth in the league, with Tony Olsson the top man, scoring 435 points for a 10.02 average. When you consider that Swindon lost 4 home matches and drew another, it was a disappointing fourth place finish, which could have been so much better. A total of 5 away victories – at Exeter (twice), Middlesbrough, Oxford and Sheffield – just demonstrates what a Jekyll and Hyde side the '94 Robins were. Tony Langdon was next in the final analysis, averaging 8.30, while David Blackburn plugged away well to finish with a 6.86 figure. The remaining four regulars finished thus: Gary Chessell (6.77), Patrik Olsson (6.46), Glenn Cunningham (5.44) and John Jefferies (1.96). After losing to Glasgow in the Knock Out Cup final the previous season, Swindon were unfortunate enough to draw the Tigers at the first hurdle, with the power-

*Craig Boyce.*

house Scottish side taking a comfortable victory by 106 points to 86 on aggregate. The Robins did triumph in the Midland Shield though, defeating Oxford in the semi-final, before beating Long Eaton by 9 points on aggregate in the final.

In the Four-Team Championship, Oxford easily qualified for the final, but Swindon and Peterborough tied for the second qualifying position. It was decided to stage a run-off to settle the outcome, and it was no surprise when track specialist Zdenek Tesar defeated Tony Olsson 2-0 in a match race series at Blunsdon to take Peterborough through. The Division One Riders' Championship was again allocated to Swindon, and proved to be a well-organised event, won by Sam Ermolenko of Wolverhampton. Aside from that, two further big individual meetings were held at Blunsdon, and these saw David Blackburn win a qualifying round of the World Championship, while Zdenek Tesar again revelled on the Blunsdon circuit to emerge from a classy field and take victory in the Swindon Classic.

The year 1995 saw all the teams in the First and Second Divisions come together to form a twenty-one-team Premier League, and there were the usual comings and goings on the team front at Swindon. Tony Langdon decided to stay in Australia, and Tony Olsson went back to parent club Reading. World number three rider Craig Boyce, who was unable to agree terms with Poole, came to Blunsdon and was made captain. Messrs Ansell and Stewkesbury then dipped into the coffers to purchase New Zealander Mark Thorpe from Newcastle. Thorpe had long expressed the view that Swindon was his favourite track, so it was a dream move for him. Finally, a work permit was granted for Polish star Dariusz Sledz, but in the event, he never turned a wheel for Swindon. Two more newcomers came into the reckoning for a place in the team – Swede Frank Richt and Finn Jarno Kosonen – so with Gary Chessell, Glenn Cunningham and Patrik Olsson, the Robins looked to have the right blend of youth and experience. The club also unveiled a new sponsor in Poole-based businessman John Tarr, and rode under the banner of the J.T. Commercials Robins.

Frank Richt missed the opening match due to a dispute over transport, and, in fact, only rode in a single league match, against Eastbourne – a meeting that was significant for being the first to have Martin Yeates and his partner Peter Toogood in charge. In the first instance, Peter Ansell stayed on to give welcome help and advice, but it was the new twosome of Yeates and Toogood who were now in charge. Having lost two of their first three away fixtures, the new promoters quickly realized that extra strengthening was required, and crowd favourite Peter Nahlin was subsequently brought back. This then gave the Robins three very good heat-leaders, since Mark Thorpe's form was proving to be a revelation. By early May, Martin Yeates was finding the combination of his promotional duties and managing the team too much, so back came Malcolm Holloway as team manager. On track, things were going well for the Robins, despite being hit by the injury bug. Peter Nahlin was hurt riding in his native Sweden, so in came former favourite Brian Karger on a short-term contract. Reserve Jarno Kosonen was injured and several riders were tried, including Justin Walker and Spencer Timmo, but somehow, in spite of all the chopping and changing, Swindon kept on winning.

On 10 August, after a match at Middlesbrough, Gary Chessell stunned everyone by deciding to quit racing there and then. It was a great pity, as Peter Nahlin had just returned, and the signing of Poole junior Martin Willis looked to be filling the troublesome reserve berth in the side. Then Nahlin was injured again and the Robins slumped to nine defeats out of their last eleven league matches. Swindon ended the season in eleventh spot, and were left to ponder on what might have been, especially when considering the fact that they won no less than 7 of their away matches (at Coventry, Cradley Heath, Exeter, Ipswich, Long Eaton, Poole and Sheffield). The Robins also gained 2 draws on their travels, with solid performances at both King's Lynn and Middlesbrough. However, if the away form was good, then the home results were the exact opposite, with 6 defeats and a draw being suffered at the Blunsdon Bowl.

Top Robin was Aussie Craig Boyce, who enjoyed a tremendous year to end the season with 388 points in league racing, producing a tremendous 10.05 average. Kiwi Mark Thorpe actually scored more points than Boyce, plundering 417 in all, to average a splendid 8.35. Peter Nahlin achieved a 7.79 average from his 19 matches, while Gary Chessell was averaging 6.01 at the time of his shock retirement. In a season when Swindon used a staggering total of thirty-seven riders, only two others made more than eight appearances: Glenn Cunningham, who averaged 5.60, and the highly-disappointing Patrik Olsson, who could only muster a 4.69 average. In the Knock Out Cup, Swindon had a bye in the first round, before defeating Exeter in round two. The Robins then faced Belle Vue in the quarter-final, but a heavy defeat at the Manchester venue in the first leg proved too much to overcome, and Swindon went out on the wrong end of a 95-118 aggregate defeat. Sam Ermolenko again showed his liking for the Blunsdon circuit, by recording a 15-point maximum to win the Swindon Classic on 5 August. Continuing with the individual theme, the Premier League Riders' Championship was allocated to Swindon, and saw a huge field of twenty-four riders compete for the title on 14 October. The eventual winner was Gary Havelock, who put on a terrific display of riding to beat Billy Hamill, Jason Crump and Leigh Adams in the grand final.

The 1996 season saw former Robins Jimmy Nilsen and Brian Karger return 'home', having been purchased outright from Bradford and Arena-Essex respectively. Craig Boyce rejoined Poole, and to replace his scoring power, Swindon signed Dane John Jorgensen from Coventry. Also in the team was Mark Thorpe, who had been such a success the previous year, as well as Glenn Cunningham and Jarno Kosonen, while Steve Masters returned after a loan stint with Poole. There was new team sponsorship in the shape of the local Westmead Nissan motor vehicle company, and things looked very promising as the tapes went up on the Robins' forty-eighth consecutive season of racing. Swindon began well, although Mark Thorpe seemed hampered by machine trouble, but Nilsen and Karger were showing their best form, and John Jorgensen, backing their efforts, was excellent. With the promotion keen to encourage young talent, Swindon also entered a team in the Conference League, with six such league matches and a challenge fixture taking place at Blunsdon during the season.

The Westmead Nissan Robins were doing very well, and away wins at Long Eaton

*Swindon Sprockets 1996. From left to right, back row: Keith Lansley, Simon Paget, Scott Pegler, Scott Donovan, Gary Phelps. Kneeling: Martin Williams. On bike: Krister Marsh.*

and Coventry showed that they were a team to be reckoned with. Thorpe sorted out his machine problems and began to show his old form, thus giving Swindon four riders capable of filling heat-leader slots. Sadly though, the bad luck that was to dog Mark began at Belle Vue on 31 May, when Swindon recorded a marvellous two-point victory. The Kiwi was involved in a track spill through no fault of his own, and was left nursing a broken wrist. Thorpe returned to action in mid-July, only to be injured again at Hull. Mark was soon back again, but his return didn't last long. On 17 August, in a home match against Exeter, he was injured in a bizarre accident when he turned around from the starting gate to de-mist his goggles and hit the tractor. This time it was more serious, and he was out for the rest of the season. Jarno Kosonen was injured in a match at Poole, when he and Poole rider Lars Gunnestad crashed, demolishing part of the safety fence. The fence took too long to repair, and with Swindon leading 44-34, the match was abandoned with the league points coming to Blunsdon. Swindon's leading Conference League rider, Scott Pegler, then came into the side to replace the injured Kosonen.

The Robins had a good season overall, finishing fourth in the league, and might have fared even better but for the problems encountered by Mark Thorpe. Home form was the key to a better year, with the Robins winning all but one of the Blunsdon encounters, with the odd one out being a draw against Hull. Away from home, Swindon enjoyed league successes at Belle Vue Coventry, Long Eaton, Middlesbrough, plus the aforementioned victory at Poole. Averaging 9.35, Jimmy Nilsen led the way with 377 points, ahead of Brian Karger (350) and John Jorgensen (334). The unfortunate Thorpe only completed 18 league matches, averaging 6.88, while Steve Masters battled away in his own inimitable style for a 5.37 average. Glenn Cunningham's form failed to show the expected improvement, and this was reflected in his final average of 4.60. Jarno Kosonen, although very quick from the gate, could only achieve a 4.56 average from his 20 matches, while Scott Pegler found the pace a little hot compared with Conference Leage racing and only yielded a 1.50 average from his 8 Premier League matches.

Swindon fared reasonably well in the Knock Out Cup, disposing of Oxford in the opening round, before accounting for Eastbourne in round two. Somewhat surprisingly though, Exeter came to Blunsdon in the first leg of the quarter-final tie and stole away with a 48-48 draw. The Falcons then dumped Swindon out of the competition by virtue of an 8-point victory at their super-fast County Ground venue in the second leg. Swindon hosted the British Under-21 Championship on 27 April, when Savalas Clouting beat Scott Nicholls in a run-off for the coveted title, after both riders had tied on 13 points. The line-up also included many of the sport's other up-and-coming youngsters, including Paul Clews, Phil Morris, Leigh Lanham and Stuart Robson. The Premier League Riders Championship was staged at Bradford, with Jimmy Nilsen carrying the Robins' flag and scoring 8 points in the qualifying heats, before being eliminated at the semi-final stage.

The Swindon Sprockets Conference League side finished fifth out of thirteen teams, winning all 6 of their homes matches, plus one on their travels at Sittingbourne. Scott Pegler topped the Sprockets' averages on 10.32, receiving solid support from Krister Marsh, who finished on a 9.26 figure. Other regulars in the Sprockets side included Keith Lansley, Gary Phelps, Scott Donovan, Martin Williams and Simon Paget, while former Robin Malcolm Holloway also donned his leathers again on 4 occasions. Swindon did well with the weather in 1996, holding 33 consecutive meetings without the intervention of rain, right up until the very last scheduled Ace of Aces meeting on 27 October, when, with the track under water, the event was cancelled and never re-staged!

A shock for the Swindon patrons was the decision of Martin Yeates to quit, due to the pressures of business, but it was known that he had become frustrated with many aspects of the sport. Peter Toogood pledged that he would carry on by himself, and that the Robins would operate in the highest possible league, a pledge that meant if the proposed Elite League were formed, he would want Swindon to be part of it. There was great sadness at the end of 1996, when the death of Bob Jones was announced in December. Aged seventy-seven, Bob was affectionately known as 'Mr Swindon Speedway', and proudly claimed that he had never missed a home meeting at Blunsdon!

1997 was an important year for speedway, as it saw the formation of the Elite

League, which boasted just ten tracks. A number of rider allocations took place to ensure a higher standard of racing, with nearly all of the best riders from home and abroad competing in the new league. The new set-up also saw teams comprised of just six riders, in an attempt to ensure it was literally the highest quality league in the world. With Peter Toogood now in sole charge of the Westmead Nissan Robins, he set about putting a team together that would give a good account of itself. His first signing was Mick Bell as team manager, and this was an inspired piece of business by the Swindon promoter. Jimmy Nilsen, Brian Karger and Steve Masters were retained from the 1996 line-up, and to these three were added former Robin Leigh Adams, who was available due to the closure of London. Two other riders arrived on loan, namely Tony Olsson from Reading and Alun Rossiter from Poole. Going the other way, Glenn Cunningham joined Reading on loan in the restructured Premier League, while John Jorgensen returned to his parent track, Coventry. Meanwhile, the unfortunate Mark Thorpe stayed in New Zealand, with Jarno Kosonen moving to Premier League Edinburgh.

The season began with 3 defeats in the Knock Out Cup and some of the fans began to question Mr Toogood's judgement on his team selection. However, on 23 March, Swindon won a Knock Out Cup thriller against Bradford, and from that moment they were not to taste defeat at home until Coventry won at Blunsdon on 27 September. Away from Blunsdon, Swindon had much success, and as they led

*Swindon 1997. From left to right, back row: Mick Bell (team manager), Alun Rossiter, Jimmy Nilsen, Steve Masters, Peter Toogood. Front row: Leigh Adams, Brian Karger, Tony Olsson.*

the Elite League for a number of weeks, promoter Toogood had silenced the critics. Only in the last weeks of the season did Swindon let it slip, their problems beginning at Bradford on 23 August, when Alun Rossiter was injured. Tony Olsson was then injured in Sweden, and these two occurencies proved decisive. Rossiter was very difficult to replace, as suitable guests were not always available, and the rider replacement rules put far too much strain on Steve Masters.

Swindon, therefore, finished in third place in the new league, which was a very fine effort indeed. There was just that single league defeat at home against Coventry, while the Robins collected three well-earned away successes at Coventry, King's Lynn and Peterborough, plus a hard-fought draw at Poole. In fact, Swindon could have finished second, but lost no less than three bonus-point run-offs during the course of the season! Leigh Adams had a tremendous year, scorching to 444 points and topping the averages with a tremendous 9.96 figure. Jimmy Nilsen backed the consistent Aussie with a solid 8.88 return, while Brian Karger did well to average 8.09. Tony Olsson proved to be very reliable and finished with a creditable 6.84 average, while Alun Rossiter yielded 4.49 from his season's work. Steve Masters battled away throughout the campaign, but it wasn't easy against the world's best riders and this was reflected in his final average of 2.57.

The revamped Knock Out Cup was run in two groups of five teams, with Swindon finding themselves in the northern section. Their 8 group matches produced only 3 wins, and the Robins ended up at the foot of the table. In the new end-of-season Craven Shield, the Robins reached the semi-finals, but were well-beaten by Coventry, who took both legs to win by 18 points on aggregate. Swindon did partake in one final in 1997, however, when they rode in the Four-Team Championship, but it wasn't their day as they finished joint third with Belle Vue, behind winners on their own track, Peterborough, and runners-up Bradford. Leigh Adams appeared in the Elite League Riders' Championship at Bradford, but on a disappointing night for Swindon's main-man, he could only muster a single point.

Having run a second team in the Conference League the previous season, Swindon joined forces with Reading and competed in the renamed Amateur League in 1997. The team were known as the M4 Raven Sprockets, with the fixtures equally split between the two circuits. The combination completed a total of 24 league fixtures, winning 10 and drawing 3, to finish in seventh position in the thirteen-team league. John Jefferies led the scoring with 207 points for an impressive 9.62 average. Other regulars included Gary Phelps (8.21), Ian Clarke (7.24), Karl Bainbridge (6.98), Keith Lansley (6.71), Shane Colvin (5.14) and Martin Williams (5.08).

With Swindon running Amateur League fixtures on top of the Elite League racing, it was another bumper year for the Blunsdon regulars, with a remarkable 34 home meetings being staged. One of those meetings was the Bob Jones Memorial, held in honour of the Swindon great who had died the previous December. The special meeting was won by Steve Johnston, who defeated Brian Karger, Tomas Topinka and Zdenek Tesar in a grand final. At the end of the season, Peter Toogood shocked supporters by announcing that he had sold out to the new stadium owners, the

*Charlie Gjedde.*

B.S. Group. However, Toogood would be staying on to head a promotion team which included former Robins rider Richard Evans, who was now an employee of the B.S. Group.

Swindon Speedway reached the landmark of fifty years in 1998; however, Saturday night would no longer be speedway night in Swindon, as this would now be for greyhound racing, while the super shale sport had to move back to Thursday evenings. On the team front, Jimmy Nilsen, Leigh Adams and Brian Karger all returned, having enjoyed a good deal of success the previous year. Alun Rossiter and Steve Masters were also back, while the final piece of the jigsaw was completed by young Danish prospect Charlie Gjedde, but sadly, there was no place for the extremely popular Tony Olsson. The Robins again started badly in the Knock Out Cup, winning only 2 matches and finishing bottom of their group. Charlie Gjedde looked impressive, but Alun Rossiter in his Testimonial year looked off the pace. A combination of loss of form and the fact that his leg, injured at Bradford the previous year, was still troubling him, saw 'Rosco' retire and become presenter of meetings at Blunsdon.

It had become obvious to both the Swindon management and supporters that the team badly needed strengthening. On 4 June, John Jorgensen returned to score 8 points in a 47-43 victory over Belle Vue. Steve Masters, who was having a tough time, made up his mind that he would do better in the Premier League, and with the blessing of the management, he went on loan to the Isle of Wight. Travelling in the opposite direction, Philippe Berge arrived on loan from the Islanders but, unfortunately, found the pace too hot. At King's Lynn on 15 July, the Robins lost Jimmy Nilsen with a shoulder injury and the skipper was out of action for a month, with his absence being covered by guest riders. However, luck smiled on the Robins when they learned that Andy Smith had finished with Belle Vue, and promoter Richard Evans moved quickly to sign him on loan. This proved to be the signing of the year, as Andy served up some spectacular stuff, much to the delight of the Blunsdon faithful who actually voted him Rider of the Year, despite him only riding in a dozen league matches!

Jimmy Nilsen returned to action against Eastbourne on 9 August, storming to a paid 14 points. Jimmy was having a marvellous season, both home and abroad, and his performances in the Grand Prix were sensational. Swindon, with John Jorgensen and Andy Smith, now looked very competent, but they were to lose Brian Karger under a suspension by the B.S.P.A. The Dane had missed the home match against Wolverhampton, claiming injury, but with no supporting medical certificate, the Robins were forced to use John Jefferies in his place. The following week, Karger didn't show up at Eastbourne and was duly suspended. Despite all the rider comings and goings, with Swindon actually using a staggering total of thirty-four riders in their 32 league matches, the Robins did well to finish the season in a very creditable fourth position. They would undoubtedly have finished higher, but for the usual susceptibility at home, which saw 5 defeats.

Once again, Leigh Adams topped the scorecharts with a haul of 418 points, well ahead of the next man, Jimmy Nilsen, on 241. Running through the finishing averages of the seven riders whose appearances reached double figures shows a lack of firepower at the top end, coupled with some inconsistencies: Leigh Adams (8.95), Jimmy Nilsen (8.09), Andy Smith (7.70), John Jorgensen (7.15), Brian Karger (6.32), Charlie Gjedde (4.49) and Steve Masters (3.12). After thrashing Eastbourne, Swindon reached the semi-final of the Craven Shield for the second year running, only to lose to all-conquering Ipswich, who won both legs with relative ease. The Elite League Riders' Championship was held at Swindon, with Leigh Adams battling his way through to the grand final, only to retire and have to settle for fourth position behind Tony Rickardsson, Jason Crump and Joe Screen. Jimmy Nilsen also rode in the prestigious event, but was eliminated at the semi-final stage.

One other individual event in 1998 was the Stars of Tomorrow Junior Trophy, which was won in impressive fashion by Marc Norris. The line-up featured several up-and-coming talented youngsters, including Matt Read, Glen Phillips, Chris Neath, Shane Colvin and Seemond Stephens. Dreadful weather wrecked Alun Rossiter's Testimonial plans by twice causing his special meeting to be postponed. This was cruel luck on the chirpy 'Rosco', who had to be patient for a long time before finally managing to stage his benefit meeting many months later at Poole (in March 2000). On the international front, Jimmy Nilsen, who had ridden brilliantly throughout the Grand Prix series, became world number two, finishing behind fellow Swede Tony Rickardsson. A winter of worry ensued, as the B.S. Group counted the cost of staging Elite League racing and a new pay structure for riders was to be introduced. Jimmy Nilsen and Leigh Adams could not accept the new terms, and for several weeks the future looked bleak, as rumours circulated. It was finally announced that Swindon would be applying to race in the Premier League in 1999. The application to run in the lower league was eventually accepted by speedway's hierarchy and, shortly afterwards, Peter Toogood stepped back in as sole promoter, having reached an agreement with the B.S. Group.

The Swindon side for the 1999 campaign had to be rebuilt from scratch, with Glenn Cunningham returning to his parent track as the new number one, having enjoyed two terrific seasons on loan at Reading (in 1997) and Peterborough (in 1998). Somewhat surprisingly, former England international Neil Collins became available, and Peter Toogood wasted no time in signing him up on loan from Stoke. Steve Masters also returned to the fold, following his loan stint with the Isle of Wight, and it was hoped that he would fill the third heat-leader berth in the new-look Robins septet. The Robins side was completed by Krister Marsh, along with promising youngsters Oliver Allen, David Mason and local lad Gary Phelps.

The season opened at Blunsdon with the Thames Valley Trophy against local rivals Reading, during which Gary Phelps was injured. So for the second home match against Sheffield in the Premier National Trophy on 1 April, Peter Toogood drafted in former Swindon junior Steve Bishop. 'Bish' (who was now an experienced rider and was racing for St Austell in the Conference League) was signed initially on a short-term contract, and brought the house down with an outstanding paid 18-point return in the match against Sheffield. Following that wonder display, strenuous efforts were made to ensure that 'Bish' would remain with the Robins for

*Geoff Bouchard, back at Blunsdon for the Golden Jubilee.*

the remainder of the season. By May, Swindon had dispensed with the services of David Mason, who just hadn't been able to put things together, despite having good equipment and a nice easy riding style. Cornishman Seemond Stephens, who had been a star in the second-half Youth Development League at Blunsdon in 1998, was introduced into the Robins line-up to replace Mason, and opened with a brilliant paid 13 points at Exeter on 3 May.

Swindon fared quite well at home, winning most meetings comfortably, although Sheffield forced a sensational draw. Away from Blunsdon, however, it was a different story, with a 28-62 mauling at Edinburgh on 14 May, followed by a poor display at Berwick the following evening. As it that wasn't enough, the day after that, the Robins went down by two points in a last-heat decider at Glasgow. Newport proved to be a thorn in the Robins side in 1999, as they became the only visiting side to win a league match at Blunsdon, and with Swindon winning the central section of the Premier National Trophy, it was Newport who won both legs to knock the Robins out at the semi-final stage of the competition. In the Knock Out Cup, a poor team performance saw Swindon lose 35-55 at Arena-Essex in the first leg of their quarter-final encounter. Although the Robins rallied to win the second leg, it was the Purfleet side that progressed to the semi-final with a 4-point aggregate victory.

Although Swindon impressed at home, no less than seven away matches slipped away on last-heat deciders, as the team finished the league campaign in a somewhat disappointing fourth place. Having finished his previous two campaigns with averages of 10.06 and 9.68 at Reading and Peterborough respectively, Glenn Cunningham's 1999 figure of 8.54 was not quite the expected or hoped-for return. Steve Masters always tried hard and was probably steadier than ever before, ending up with an 8.41 average. Meanwhile, Neil Collins was a revelation and finished the year with an 8.32 average and the Rider of the Year award, which wasn't bad for a rider at the age of thirty-seven. 'Olly' Allen got better and better as the season wore on, undoubtedly learning fast from being paired with Neil Collins, and a final season average of 5.87 was a tremendous achievement for the youngster. Seemond Stephens proved to be an excellent signing and a very likeable lad, whose season ended with a highly creditable 5.27 figure from his 23 league matches, while Krister Marsh (5.68) and Steve Bishop (4.77) were somewhat disappointing as the season wore on.

In the Young Shield, Swindon won both legs of their quarter-final tie with Newcastle, but were sent packing by the powerful Sheffield side at the semi-final stage. The Westmead Nissan Robins also reached the semi-final of the Four-Team Championship, but at the Peterborough-staged event, they failed to progress any further after finishing behind the Isle of Wight and Newport. Glenn Cunningham represented Swindon in the Premier League Riders' Championship at Sheffield, but could only muster 9 points in what was an disappointing performance from the rider who had won the event the previous year. Perhaps the greatest night of the season was on 9 September, when Swindon staged their Golden Jubilee meeting, which also incorporated the Bob Jones Memorial. Carl Stonehewer went on to win an absorbing final, watched by over sixty former Robins and racing friends of Bob Jones. It was a marvellous night of nostalgia and a special celebration was held in the stadium restaurant, which was enjoyed by everyone lucky enough to be present.

## 2000 Onwards

Going into the 2000 season, Swindon made several changes, both on and off the track. Peter Toogood remained as promoter, with Mick Bell becoming promoting manager, while Jed Stone was installed as the new team manager. A new team sponsor was unveiled in the shape of the Swindon Soft Water Centre, whose owner, Brian Cox, had long since been a fan of speedway at Blunsdon. Team changes saw Glenn Cunningham and Steve Masters move into the Elite League, with Peterborough and King's Lynn respectively, while Seemond Stephens joined Exeter, and Krister Marsh went to Reading. Steve Bishop opted for further Conference League racing and linked with the new operation at Somerset. That left just Neil Collins and Oliver Allen from the previous season's septet, and they were joined by the all-action Frank Smart via Newport, and Claus Kristensen from Berwick. It would be fair to say that the Robins management showed great courage with their other three signings, bringing in the vastly experienced duo of Martin Dixon and Paul Fry, while the final team spot went to inexperienced former Coventry mascot Mark Steel.

Things started well, with an away win at Stoke in the Premier Trophy; however, this was quickly offset by a home defeat against the same opponents five nights later. However, that was to be Swindon's only home defeat in a year that saw a remarkable change of fortune to the club's years in the trophy wilderness. Frank Smart and Paul Fry represented Swindon in the Premier League Pairs Championship at Workington on 8 July. However, in a curtailed meeting run in continuous rain, the Robins duo only just failed to reach the semi-final stage in the event that was dominated by the home pairing of Carl Stonehewer and Mick Powell. The Soft Water Robins won the remaining 5 home matches in the Premier Trophy, while collecting a further away success at Reading. That was enough for them to finish on top of the southern section, but despite only losing by only 4 points in the first leg of the semi-final tie at Hull, the Vikings came down to Blunsdon and forced a 45-45 draw, sending Swindon tumbling out of the competition.

In between the Premier Trophy group matches and the semi-final with Hull, the Robins' season had been rocked by the events of 22 June, when the Premier League fixture against Exeter was rained off at Blunsdon. More significantly, as it turned out, six riders, including Frank Smart, were selected at random for a drugs test. Rumours began to do the rounds, until it was revealed on 16 July, that two riders had failed the test. Unfortunately, Frank was one of them, but to his eternal credit, he was quick to admit his guilt and apologized to everyone at Swindon for the embarrassment he had caused. It was subsequently announced that Frank had been handed a 12-month ban from racing, and Swindon ended up using guest replacements for the remainder of the season. Despite the home draw with Hull in the Premier Trophy, Swindon continued to win every one of their league matches at Blunsdon, while serving up some marvellous racing for the public on their wonderful circuit that was so well prepared by Colin Meredith. That was only the fifth time in fifty-two seasons that Swindon had achieved a 100 per cent home

*Swindon 2000. From left to right, back row: Mick Bell (promoting manager), Claus Kristensen, Martin Dixon, Peter Toogood (promoter), Oliver Allen, Jed Stone (team manager), Mark Steel. Front, on bike: Paul Fry.*

record in their league programme. Any reservations that people might have had about the makeup of the side had been dispelled, as Swindon proved to be a very solid outfit, even after the departure of Frank Smart.

The battle for the League Championship saw one of the greatest ever finishes to a speedway season, as five teams fought for supremacy right up to the last match. Swindon were one of the five teams, and on 28 September, it all came to a head as the Robins entertained Newcastle at Blunsdon. The equation was simple – Swindon, having lost 41-49 at Newcastle, needed to win the match and collect the aggregate bonus point, so basically a 50-40 victory would suffice. Things were going along relatively smoothly, as Swindon led 45-33, with just two heats to go. The cruel hand of fate then intervened to scupper Swindon's hopes, as the riders came to the line in heat fourteen. Suddenly, Oliver Allen's clutch disintegrated, and he was excluded for exceeding the two-minute time allowance. When the race got under way, Claus Kristensen held second place, only to suffer a puncture on the last lap and hand the visitors a 5-1 victory. That left Swindon leading 46-38, with one race to go and the scores were tied on aggregate. Newcastle's Danish sensation Bjarne Pedersen took the flag in the final heat, but Paul Fry and Claus Kristensen shared the race to force a run-off for the much sought-after bonus point. It was Pedersen who roared away to take the run-off from Paul Fry and break Swindon's hearts, as Exeter subsequently gained the bonus point at Workington two nights later, which gave them the Championship by the narrowest of margins on race points difference. In fact, in an incredible finish, the top five teams all finished within two points of each other, as follows: (1) Exeter, 44 points; (2) Swindon, 44 points; (3) Hull, 43 points; (4) Sheffield, 42 points; (5) Workington, 42 points.

The amazing Paul Fry remained ever-present throughout Swindon's 26 league fixtures, scoring 272 points for an 8.96 average, in what was his best-ever season since starting way back in 1984. A deserving winner of the Rider of the Year award, 'Fryer' was an undoubted success, for he had arrived via an injury-ravaged year at Stoke and had actually started the season at Swindon with a lowly green-sheet average of only 6.44. The flying 'Fryer' also represented the Soft Water Robins in the Premier League Riders' Championship at Sheffield, where he mustered 8 points with a typical never-say-die effort. The swashbuckling Frank Smart had provided some excellent entertainment while he was around, and this was mirrored in his 8.37 average. Claus Kristensen took a long time to settle down at Swindon, due to a severe dose of glandular fever, but he was popular with the fans and a final average of 7.18 showed great promise of much more to come.

Following his great season in 1999, Neil Collins' average dropped from 8.32 to 7.08, but he still produced plenty of his trademark surges from the back for the supporters to enthuse over. 'Mad Dog' Martin Dixon averaged 6.57, and proved to be the engine-room of the side, with solid scoring both home and away. 'Olly' Allen continued to progress well and finished with an identical figure to that of Martin Dixon. Mark Steel was outstanding, having joined the ranks with limited experience at Conference League level with Buxton, he rode with great maturity throughout the year and finished with a superb 5.40 average, in spite of missing 9 league matches following an alarming track crash at Stoke, in which he lost part of a thumb. Kiwi Nathan Murray stepped in for 7 of Mark's matches and never let the side down, scoring 22 points for a 4.31 average.

In the Knock Out Cup, the Robins enjoyed a very hard-fought first round aggregate victory over rivals of old, Reading. Further success came with an even tougher quarter-final two-point success over Berwick, while in the semi-final, Swindon easily saw off the challenge of Exeter. On 12 October, Swindon proudly staged the first leg of the final against the self-same Hull side that had disposed of them in the Premier Trophy. But the Robins were in no mood for complacency, as they rattled up an outstanding 59-31 victory. Six nights later, they journeyed to Hull for the second leg, and although going down to a 6-point defeat, they had won the trophy – this was their first major silverware in thirty-three barren years – much to the delight of a large travelling contingent.

Swindon also reached the final of the Young Shield, having beaten Edinburgh and Sheffield in the quarter-final and semi-final respectively. They faced League Champions Exeter in the final, but having lost one trophy to the Falcons, the determined Robins gained revenge by winning both legs for an aggregate victory of 112 points to 67. The season was plagued by rain throughout, with 7 home meetings being lost, just one short of the all-time record that was set in 1993 – which, co-incidentally, was the last time that Swindon had maintained a 100 per cent home record in league matches. The year 2000 was definitely a remarkable one for Swindon Speedway.

The highs of the previous season were going to be hard to surpass, but the Swindon management certainly did their utmost to ensure that the Robins remained one of the top sides in the 2001 Premier League. From the successful 2000 side, Paul Fry, Oliver Allen, Martin Dixon, Mark Steel and Claus Kristensen were retained, with Alan Mogridge linking up to add some strength at the top end. The final piece of the jigsaw was then filled by rookie Ritchie Hawkins, who had only previously had limited experience with Sheffield Prowlers in the Conference League. Unfortunately, due to averages and the points limit, Swindon were unable to retain popular stalwart Neil Collins, but even so, everything looked to be in place for the Robins to go one better in 2001 and, hopefully, lift the Premier League Championship.

On track, things started well as the Robins began with home and away victories against Newport to win the M4 Trophy. Everyone rode well, including young Ritchie Hawkins, who certainly impressed the supporters with his all-action style and bubbling enthusiasm. Off track, however, there was a major shock, when it became clear that team manager Jed Stone had quit, even before the first week of the season was over. This meant a quick return to running the side for Mick Bell, who had only moved upstairs at the start of the 2000 campaign, acquiring the role of promoting manager. On 22 March, a joint memorial meeting was staged at Blunsdon, honouring Bob Jones and Ray Morse – two men who had played an important part in the long history of Swindon Speedway. Bob, of course, had been a rider, manager and mechanic during his association with the Robins, while Ray, although lesser known outside Swindon, had been a diligent clerk of the course for many years, as well as being instrumental in setting up the successful Swindon Sprockets junior club. Oxford's super Czech, Ales Dryml, sped to victory in the Bob Jones Memorial, and it was fitting that Ritchie Hawkins produced a breathtaking performance to win the event staged in respect of Ray Morse.

The Premier Trophy began with Swindon taking part in the Southern section, along with six other sides. At Blunsdon, the Robins were dominant, notching successive victories against all their opponents, including huge 68-22 and 60-29 wins against Trelawny and the Isle of Wight respectively. On their travels Swindon also looked good, winning at Newport and Arena-Essex, while going close in the other four matches. The Robins deservedly topped the group and qualified for the semi-final, where they faced Workington. The first leg was staged at the well-appointed Derwent Park Stadium in deepest Cumbria, with Swindon riding superbly to secure a draw. Guarding against complacency, the Robins completed the job with a comfortable 54-36 victory at Blunsdon, and confidently marched into the final to meet Sheffield. The first leg of the final was staged at home on a gloriously sunny Sunday evening, but the Robins completely capitulated against their Yorkshire opponents, suffering an embarrassing 37-53 defeat. What exactly went wrong, nobody knows, but the Swindon side seemed overawed by the occasion, and nothing went right on the day. Needless to say, the second leg at Sheffield was a foregone conclusion, with the rampant Tigers racing to a 65-25 success, and lifting the trophy with a crushing 118-62 aggregate victory.

The first leg of the Premier Trophy final had seen Mark Steel fall while leading heat two, and this was to be the start of a twenty-four-hour roller-coaster ride that would lead to the youngster quitting the sport. Although he eventually managed to glean a paid 7-point return from the match, the lad was clearly troubled. The following night, Swindon were in league action at Exeter, but Mark suffered more problems, starting with another fall in heat two. Later on, he was to suffer two exclusions for exceeding the time allowance, before eventually making an emotional speech over the public address system, citing the difficulties of trying to maintain competitive equipment and hold down a full-time job at the same time. At the time of writing, that proved to be Mark's last appearance in British Speedway, which was a tremendous shame as he possessed undoubted talent and ability.

Swindon's defence of the Knock Out Cup had begun against Glasgow, but although the Robins easily moved through to the next stage, the away match at the brilliant Ashfield home of the Tigers was marred by a serious injury to Oliver Allen.

*Swindon 2001. From left to right, Mick Bell (team manager), Ritchie Hawkins, Alun Rossiter, Paul Fry, Martin Dixon (on bike), Alan Mogridge, Claus Kristensen, Oliver Allen, Peter Toogood (promoter).*

A twice-run heat ten had seen 'Olly' take a couple of nasty looking falls, the second of which had resulted in a hand injury. Despite this, he bravely rode in a second re-run of the race and, although barely able to hold on to his machine, he followed home star Les Collins across the line for 2 points, or so everyone thought. Sensationally, poor 'Olly' was then excluded by the referee for not making a bona fide attempt to race. The youngster was to miss 19 official meetings while he recovered, during which time Swindon operated the rider-replacement facility as cover. Continuing on in the Knock Out Cup, Swindon saw off Workington at the quarter-final stage, securing a tense 6-point aggregate victory. The second leg of the tie with Workington marked the return to the Robins side of Alun Rossiter, who had been released by Elite League Wolverhampton, and he jumped at the chance of re-joining his local team as the replacement for Mark Steel.

Having seen off the challenge of Workington, the Robins moved through to a semi-final encounter against Exeter, with the first leg being staged at Blunsdon. Time and again, the Falcons riders jumped ahead from the tapes and generally made life difficult for a Swindon side, who eventually managed to eke out a 51-39 win. However, it was generally felt that this wouldn't be enough of a lead to take down to the daunting County Ground circuit the following night. And so it proved, when, with one heat remaining, the sides were tied on aggregate at 87 points apiece. There was contact going into the first bend of the final heat, with Alan Mogridge tumbling down as a result. Amid high drama, 'Moggo' was excluded and despite protestations, the referee was adamant that he had seen no contact. The home side gained a 4-2 in the subsequent re-run and Swindon's reign as cup holders was over.

The evening of 19 July was a historic one for Swindon Speedway, for the cameras of Sky Television were in place to beam the league match against Workington, live from the Abbey Stadium. A large crowd was packed in, with a real air of excitement on the terraces as both sides fought out a scintillating draw. That proved to be the Robins' only dropped home point of the league campaign, but on their travels, the rider replacement facility proved to be an unsatisfactory way of covering Oliver Allen's brilliant point-plundering ability. Swindon had to settle for a final league position of fifth, with away wins being gained at Glasgow, Newport and Berwick, while draws were forced at Reading and Exeter. Meanwhile, narrow defeats at Stoke, Edinburgh, Workington and Arena-Essex were to cost the Robins dearly in the final analysis.

'Olly' Allen returned to the saddle late in the season, and showed just what had been missing from the side, rattling up 105 points from 14 matches to top the league averages with an 8.30 figure. A niggling mid-season injury to a knuckle caused Paul Fry to miss several meetings, and he was obviously affected by it upon his return to the track, but even so, he still managed to glean 220 points in the league for an 8.17 average. Claus Kristensen showed flashes of brilliance during the season, but a final average of 7.90 showed only a slight improvement on his 2000 figure of 7.18. Alan Mogridge came into the Robins line-up with a green-sheet average of 8.74, but an end-of-term return of 7.58 reflected something of an inconsistent year for the popular 'Moggo'. Alun Rossiter certainly pepped up the side upon his arrival, and rode extremely well to notch up 136 points for a 7.24 average. Veteran Martin Dixon remained ever-present throughout the year, increasing his average to 6.98, and celebrated twenty-five years in the saddle with a Silver Jubilee Testimonial meeting at Blunsdon on 27 September. Prior to his premature retirement, Mark Steel had again shown glimpses of his terrific riding of the previous year, scoring 38 points for a 5.87 average. Steel's starting partner at reserve, Ritchie Hawkins, certainly took all the plaudits as the season wore on though, riding with great determination to score 110 points for a wonderful 4.54 average in his first full season of racing.

As the season drew to a close, Swindon also lost their grip on the Young Shield they had so brilliantly won in 2000, suffering defeat at the hands of Sheffield in the quarter-final. The Robins put up a much better show than they had in the Premier Trophy final against Sheffield, winning their home leg 49-41, before going down to a 32-58 defeat in the second leg at Owlerton Stadium. Swindon asset Steve Masters became the second rider to stage a Testimonial meeting at Blunsdon in 2001, with a well-organised event which was won in scintillating fashion by Australian ace Ryan Sullivan on 14 October. 'Flyin' Ryan' became the fastest man ever at the Swindon circuit in the opening race, clocking a super-fast 64.65 seconds to eclipse the track record that had been set by Gary Allan in August 1993. There was no better way to bring the curtain down on Swindon's fifty-third consecutive season of racing.